Empowering Sustainable Business Education and Training Through AI

E. Ivette Cota-Rivera
https://orcid.org/0009-0002-6240-9269
Universidad Politécnica de Baja California, Mexico

Marcela Barreras Hernández
Universidad Politécnica de Baja California, Mexico

Martha Elena Gonzalez Correa
https://orcid.org/0009-0000-6073-9585
Universidad Politécnica de Baja California, Mexico

Fabian N. Murrieta Rico
https://orcid.org/0000-0001-9829-3013
Universidad Politécnica de Baja California, Mexico

IGI Global
Scientific Publishing
Publishing Tomorrow's Research Today

Vice President of Editorial	Melissa Wagner
Director of Acquisitions	Mikaela Felty
Director of Book Development	Jocelynn Hessler
Production Manager	Mike Brehm
Cover Design	Jose Rosado

Published in the United States of America by
IGI Global Scientific Publishing
701 East Chocolate Avenue
Hershey, PA, 17033, USA
Tel: 717-533-8845 | Fax: 717-533-7115
Website: https://www.igi-global.com E-mail: cust@igi-global.com

Library of Congress Cataloging-in-Publication Data

Names: Cota-Rivera, E. Ivette, 1974- editor | Barreras Hernández, Marcela, 1963- editor | González, Martha Elena, 1983- editor | Murrieta-Rico, Fabian N., 1986- editor
Title: Empowering sustainable business education and training through AI / edited by: E. Ivette Cota-Rivera, Marcela Barreras Hernández, Martha Elena Gonzalez, Fabian N. Murrieta-Rico.
Description: Hershey PA : IGI Global Scientific Publishing, [2026] | Includes bibliographical references. | Summary: "This book aims to contribute meaningfully to the academic and professional discourse on AI by bridging gaps between technical advancements and real-world implementation in business, education, and sustainability"-- Provided by publisher.
Identifiers: LCCN 2025034601 (print) | LCCN 2025034602 (ebook) | ISBN 9798337359465 hardcover | ISBN 9798337359472 paperback | ISBN 9798337359489 ebook
Subjects: LCSH: Artificial intelligence--Educational applications
Classification: LCC LB1028.43 .E475 2026 (print) | LCC LB1028.43 (ebook) | DDC 371.33/4--dc23/eng/20251114
LC record available at https://lccn.loc.gov/2025034601
LC ebook record available at https://lccn.loc.gov/2025034602

British Cataloguing in Publication Data
A Cataloguing in Publication record for this book is available from the British Library.

Table of Contents

Detailed Table of Contents

Explainability in Artificial Intelligence has been a concern since the rule-based expert systems of the 1970s and 1980s, which provided transparent decision rationales despite limited predictive power. With the advancement of statistical machine learning and deep learning in the 1990s and 2010s, model performance improved, but interpretability declined, leading to opaque "black box" systems whose internal logic is difficult to understand. This complexity increased the demand for transparency, particularly in high-stakes decision-making contexts. The launch of the DARPA XAI program in 2016 marked a turning point by formally recognizing the need for accurate yet interpretable models. Since then, Explainable Artificial Intelligence (XAI) has evolved as a key research area focused on generating human-understandable explanations that enhance trust, accountability, and usability. This chapter examines the origins, core concepts, and applications of XAI, emphasizing its role in supporting responsible AI deployment.

Sustainable development depends on the intelligent management of energy and resources. Population growth and industrial expansion are putting pressure on natural systems. Countries, cities, and organizations are seeking ways to both promote economic development and protect the environment. Modern digital systems can guide this transformation. Artificial intelligence offers ways to support cleaner production and more efficient energy use. It can also help organizations monitor natural resources more accurately. This chapter explains how artificial intelligence can contribute to sustainable energy and resource management in various fields, highlighting its practical applications, challenges, and future directions. The discussion supports the view that digital tools can help society create a cleaner and more stable future.

Storms and floods are more likely in coastal areas. As coastal systems become more socially and environmentally complex, these threats will worsen. To mitigate such impacts, vulnerable coastal areas must be identified and assessed. Modern and future generations are threatened by climate change. Climate change makes natural disasters more frequent, stronger, and unpredictable. Climate change's expected effects—rising sea levels and more powerful and frequent weather events—will make coastal communities considerably more vulnerable to storms, floods, and erosion. The world's shoreline population is expected to triple from 1.8 to 5.2 billion by the 2080s. Weather causes most natural disasters in Korea. Tropical cyclones and high rainfall have caused most disaster damage in the past decade.

Gurpreet pal Kaur, Lovely Professional University, India
Mushtaq Ahmad Shah, Lovely Professional University, India

This chapter explores the intersection of Artificial Intelligence (AI), Circular Economy (CE), and Green Logistics (GL) as a transformative path toward sustainable industrial systems. Using R Studio (Biblioshiny), a bibliometric analysis of 70 Scopus-indexed publications (2010–2025) maps global research trends on AI in CE and GL. The analysis identifies five major research clusters: AI-enabled reverse logistics, digital supply chains and Logistics 5.0, predictive manufacturing, AI-driven decision and policy modelling, and sustainable urban mobility. Emerging themes include digital product passports, blockchain-based traceability, and low-energy AI models. The chapter concludes with recommendations for academia, industry, and policymakers to foster AI-driven, circular, and low-carbon ecosystems.

Shashi Kant, DMI-St.Eugene University, Zambia
Wako Jio, Bule Hora University, Ethiopia
Shashank Mittal, O.P. Jindal Global University, India
Gurpreet Singh, Lovely Professional University, India

This chapter expounds on the complex correlation between organizational innovation, digital leadership, and the mediating variable (artificial intelligence (AI)) within the framework of a circular economy. In a large sample size (390 respondents), the authors use exploratory and confirmatory factor analysis (CFA). The results indicate that organizational innovation indeed promotes very effectively the digital leadership capabilities, which are again paired down by AI technologies. The mediation effect is an indication of how AI can support creative practices and decision-making systems to enhance sustainable practices in a circular economy. The chapter explains what the findings mean to organizations interested in going through the barriers presented by the environmental sustainability while utilizing digital transformation. It reinforces the necessity of leaders to implement AI into their innovation plans in order to create sustainability and flexibility culture. By filling the gap between theoretical insights and practical practice.

Artificial Intelligence (AI) in industrial engineering has transformed manufacturing, as seen by Industry 4.0. In the previous decade, AI has transformed predictive maintenance, operational optimization, robotics, quality control, and supply chain management. Predictive maintenance using machine learning reduces downtime and optimizes resources. AI's real-time data analysis increases decision-making, resource use, and efficiency through operational optimization. Adding AI to robotics increases manufacturing, while image recognition and machine learning improve quality control, raising standards. AI forecasts demand, optimizes goods, and streamlines routes, making supply chain management more resilient. Collaborative robotics and AI-powered worker freedom demonstrate how humans and machines may improve things. The author concludes by reviewing the past decade and discussing how AI is continuing revolutionizing industrial engineering and how operations will become smarter, more adaptable, and more competitive.

The mining industry has long faced hazardous work conditions, labor-intensive tasks, and operational inefficiencies. Recent advances in artificial intelligence (AI) offer new possibilities to improve safety, productivity, and sustainability. This chapter examines how AI supports miners through hazard detection, predictive maintenance,

Preface

INTRODUCTION

The accelerating pace of technological innovation and the growing urgency of global sustainability challenges have reshaped the landscape of business education and professional training. Artificial Intelligence (AI) has emerged as a transformative force capable of redefining how organizations operate, how industries evolve, and how educational institutions prepare future leaders. At the same time, sustainability has become a central concern in economic development, requiring businesses and educational systems to rethink traditional models of growth, resource management, and social responsibility. These parallel transformations have created an urgent need to integrate AI-driven technologies with sustainable business practices and learning frameworks.

Within this context, the purpose of Empowering Sustainable Business Education and Training Through AI is to explore how artificial intelligence can serve as a catalyst for advancing sustainability-oriented education and professional development. The contributions in this volume illustrate how AI can enhance decision-making, optimize resource management, support climate risk analysis, improve industrial efficiency, and strengthen learning systems. Beyond technological innovation, the book also emphasizes the ethical, social, and environmental implications of AI adoption, highlighting the importance of responsible, transparent, and human-centered approaches.

This edited volume brings together an international group of scholars and practitioners who investigate the intersection of artificial intelligence, sustainability, and business education from diverse disciplinary perspectives. Through theoretical frameworks, empirical studies, case analyses, and technological explorations, the chapters collectively demonstrate how AI can empower institutions, organizations, and learners to develop sustainable solutions. The editors hope that this work will contribute to ongoing conversations about the future of education, industry, and society in an AI-driven world.

CHAPTER OVERVIEW

This book is organized into chapters that explore the integration of artificial intelligence across sustainability, industry, and educational contexts.

Chapter 1, Explainable Artificial Intelligence in Decision Support Systems: Origins and Applications, traces the historical development of explainable AI (XAI) from early expert systems to contemporary machine learning approaches. The chapter highlights the importance of transparency and interpretability in decision-support systems and discusses how explainable models enhance trust, accountability, and responsible AI deployment.

Chapter 2, Smart Sustainability: Harnessing Artificial Intelligence for Energy Efficiency and Resource Management, examines how AI technologies support sustainable energy practices and efficient resource management. It discusses applications in environmental monitoring, industrial operations, and public infrastructure while addressing both opportunities and implementation challenges.

Chapter 3, Machine Learning Models for Climate Risk Prediction, focuses on the application of predictive analytics to climate-related hazards. By analyzing environmental and meteorological data, machine learning models help identify vulnerable regions and support disaster preparedness and mitigation strategies.

Chapter 4, Artificial Intelligence in Circular Economy and Green Logistics: A Bibliometric Analysis Using R Studio, provides a bibliometric analysis of global research trends linking AI with circular economy principles and green logistics. The chapter identifies emerging research clusters and outlines future directions for sustainable supply chains and digital logistics.

Chapter 5, Organizational Innovation Effect on Digital Leadership by Mediation of AI in Circular Economy, explores the relationship between organizational innovation, digital leadership, and artificial intelligence within circular economy contexts. Using empirical data and statistical modeling, the chapter highlights AI's mediating role in strengthening leadership capabilities for sustainability.

Chapter 6, Artificial Intelligence for Industrial Efficiency, reviews the transformative role of AI in industrial engineering and manufacturing systems. Topics include predictive maintenance, robotics, operational optimization, and intelligent supply chain management.

Chapter 7, Artificial Intelligence in Mining: Enhancing Worker Safety, Efficiency, and Decision-Making, examines how AI technologies improve safety and productivity in mining operations. The chapter discusses hazard detection, smart sensors, autonomous systems, and training simulations designed to protect workers and optimize resource extraction.

Chapter 8, The Impact, Applications, and Automation of the AI-Powered Revolution in Smart Engineering and Manufacturing, explores how AI technologies reshape global manufacturing ecosystems. The chapter highlights productivity gains, supply chain integration, and technological innovation across both developed and developing economies.

Chapter 9, Epistemic, Ethical, and Ecological Imperatives in AI-Mediated Sustainable Business Education, presents a critical perspective on AI-driven education through ethical, ecological, and epistemological frameworks. It emphasizes the importance of human-centered design, inclusive governance, and sustainability-oriented pedagogy.

Chapter 10, Artificial Intelligence and the Future of Work: Transforming Business Education and Training for Sustainability, explores the evolving relationship between AI, employment, and workforce development. The chapter discusses the need for AI literacy, lifelong learning, and interdisciplinary training systems that prepare learners for rapidly changing labor markets.

Chapter 11, Sustainable Minds, Intelligent Machines: The Future of Business Education, reflects on the interdisciplinary integration required for AI-enabled education. It examines pedagogical innovation, ethical considerations, and the evolving role of educators in AI-supported learning environments.

CONCLUSION

The chapters in this volume collectively demonstrate that artificial intelligence is not merely a technological tool but a transformative force shaping sustainable business practices, industrial innovation, and educational systems. From energy management and climate prediction to smart manufacturing and educational analytics, AI offers unprecedented opportunities to address complex global challenges while improving efficiency, transparency, and decision-making.

At the same time, the integration of AI into education and industry requires careful consideration of ethical principles, governance structures, and social impacts. Responsible implementation must address issues such as data privacy, algorithmic bias, workforce displacement, and environmental sustainability. The contributions in this book emphasize that technological progress must be accompanied by thoughtful policies, interdisciplinary collaboration, and human-centered design.

As editors, we hope this volume provides valuable insights for researchers, educators, policymakers, and industry leaders seeking to understand and harness AI for sustainable development and educational transformation. By fostering dialogue across disciplines and sectors, this book aims to support the creation of innovative learning ecosystems and business practices that contribute to a more sustainable, inclusive, and technologically empowered future.

Elia Ivette Cota Rivera
Universidad Politécnica de Baja California, Mexico

Marcela Hernández
Universidad Politécnica de Baja California, Mexico

Martha Gonzalez
Universidad Politécnica de Baja California, Mexico

Fabian N. Murrieta-Rico
Universidad Politécnica de Baja California, Mexico

Chapter 1
Explainable Artificial Intelligence in Decision Support Systems:
Origins and Applications

E. Ivette Cota-Rivera
http://orcid.org/0009-0002-6240-9269
Universidad Politécnica de Baja California, Mexico

Jorge M. Quiñones-Montoya
Universidad del Valle de México, Mexico

Abelardo Mercado-Herrera
http://orcid.org/0000-0001-8166-106X
Universidad Politécnica de Baja California, Mexico

Fabian N. Murrieta-Rico
http://orcid.org/0000-0001-9829-3013
Universidad Politécnica de Baja California, Mexico

ABSTRACT

Explainability in Artificial Intelligence has been a concern since the rule-based expert systems of the 1970s and 1980s, which provided transparent decision rationales despite limited predictive power. With the advancement of statistical machine learning and deep learning in the 1990s and 2010s, model performance improved, but interpretability declined, leading to opaque "black box" systems whose internal logic is difficult to understand. This complexity increased the demand for transparency, particularly in high-stakes decision-making contexts. The launch of the DARPA XAI program in 2016 marked a turning point by formally recognizing

DOI: 10.4018/979-8-3373-5946-5.ch001

the need for accurate yet interpretable models. Since then, Explainable Artificial Intelligence (XAI) has evolved as a key research area focused on generating human-understandable explanations that enhance trust, accountability, and usability. This chapter examines the origins, core concepts, and applications of XAI, emphasizing its role in supporting responsible AI deployment.

INTRODUCTION

Artificial Intelligence has become an integral part of everyday life, shaping even the most trivial decisions, such as recommending movies or restaurants. In these cases, users rarely question how the underlying algorithms reached their suggestions. However, when AI systems are involved in high-stakes decisions—such as medical diagnoses, autonomous driving, or critical business operations—the need to understand the reasoning behind their outputs becomes essential. In such contexts, the demand for explainability in AI emerges as a fundamental requirement (Adadi & Berrada, 2018) .

A major limitation of contemporary AI systems lies in their lack of transparency. Despite their impressive predictive capabilities, many algorithms operate as opaque structures whose internal processes are difficult to interpret. This opacity becomes particularly evident in machine learning models—for example, in deep neural networks where feature interactions are embedded across multiple layers. Relying on systems that cannot articulate the rationale behind their outputs introduces significant risks, including ethical concerns, accountability gaps, and potential harm in high-stakes environments. This growing need for trustworthy decision-making underscores the importance of adopting Explainable Artificial Intelligence (XAI) approaches (Adadi & Berrada, 2018).

The general term black box in AI systems can be attributed to two main factors. On one hand, some developers intentionally obscure the inner workings of their AI tools before releasing them to the public in order to protect their intellectual property. On the other hand, the complexity of advanced AI technologies—such as deep learning systems—results in models whose decision-making processes are not fully understood even by their creators. These two sources of opacity give rise to different concerns: intentional opacity affects transparency and user trust, while emergent opacity makes interpretability technically challenging, posing risks for accountability and responsible deployment. Understanding these origins helps contextualize why explainability techniques are essential for ensuring reliable and ethical AI behavior (Kosinski, 2024).

Given their multi-layered neural architecture, deep learning models are inherently opaque, which makes their internal operations difficult to interpret. Deep neural networks may contain hundreds or even thousands of layers composed of numerous neurons, and they process massive, unstructured datasets, learning representations and generating outputs such as text, images, and video. Consequently, users—and even developers—can only observe the input and output layers, while the intermediate "hidden layers" remain inaccessible. As a result, the transformations occurring within these hidden layers are not directly interpretable, meaning that developers cannot fully understand how features interact or how specific outputs are produced—even in open-source models where the code is available. This inherent opacity highlights the need for explainability methods to enhance transparency and trust in deep learning–based AI systems.

The concept of explainability in AI is not new. In the 1970s and 1980s, expert systems incorporated rule-based explanations to justify their decisions. These early systems were inherently interpretable, but their simplicity limited predictive power. With the rise of statistical machine learning in the 1990s and deep learning in the 2010s, model complexity increased dramatically, improving accuracy but reducing interpretability. This shift gave rise to the "black box" nature of AI, where even developers struggle to understand how specific outputs are generated. The launch of the DARPA XAI program in 2016 marked a pivotal point, formalizing the need for research into methods that make AI decisions more transparent without sacrificing performance.

Explainable Artificial Intelligence (XAI) has emerged as a critical field within Artificial Intelligence (AI) that addresses one of the most pressing challenges in modern machine learning: the "black box" problem. As AI systems—particularly deep learning models—become more complex and widely adopted in decision-making processes, the need for transparency, interpretability, and accountability has grown. XAI seeks to provide human-understandable explanations of AI outputs, enabling users to trust, validate, and effectively use AI-driven insights. This chapter explores the origins, fundamental concepts, and practical applications of XAI, offering a comprehensive overview of its current state and future directions.

ORIGINS OF EXPLAINABLE AI

To understand the evolution of XAI, this section reviews the key historical approaches that shaped the development of Explainable AI.

Symbolic AI and the Early Foundations of Explainability

During this period (1950s–1980s), symbolic AI dominated the field, grounded in the idea that intelligent behavior could be formalized through explicit symbols and rules. Approaches such as logicism and rule-based systems exemplified this belief, assuming that knowledge and reasoning could be represented through formal logic and structured rules. Consequently, these early approaches offered high interpretability because the system's reasoning could be traced step-by-step. Nevertheless, they struggled to manage uncertainty, incomplete information, and complex real-world conditions. Due to these limitations, researchers increasingly turned toward more flexible learning systems, highlighting the need to balance symbolic transparency and richer modeling capacities.

Symbolic AI was anchored in logic-based reasoning—exemplified by tools such as Prolog (Colmerauer & Roussel, 1996) and production systems like CLIPS and OPS5 (Reiter, 1980)—and in expert systems exemplified by MYCIN and DENDRAL ("Dendral and Meta-Dendral," 1981). These systems provided high interpretability in the decision-making process because every inference could be traced step-by-step. However, they were brittle, difficult to scale, and constrained by the persistent "knowledge acquisition bottleneck." Their interpretability strength contrasted with emerging learning methods that sacrificed transparency for greater adaptability (Liang et al., 2025).

To overcome rigid logical limitations, symbolic AI expanded into more sophisticated reasoning paradigms such as non-monotonic logics, planning systems, and argumentation frameworks. These innovations aimed to simulate real-world reasoning and commonsense; however, they also introduced significant computational complexity and scalability challenges. These issues contributed to the gradual transition from symbolic paradigms toward statistical and data-driven learning approaches.

Structured representations such as semantic networks and description logics were developed by Symbolic AI with the purpose of formalize conceptual knowledge, these produce foundations of ontology languages and later the Semantic Web, as a result modal and temporal logics allowed reasoning about belief, knowledge, and dynamic systems. These languages were powerful for interpretable reasoning, nevertheless they face challenges between expressiveness and computational tractability. Overall, although symbolic AI delivered high interpretability, its practical limitations prepared the ground for the rise of machine learning—and consequently, new concerns about opacity.

Symbolic AI also introduced structured knowledge representations such as semantic networks and description logics, which aimed to formalize conceptual hierarchies and relationships. These formalisms provided the basis for ontology languages and later developments in the Semantic Web. In parallel, modal and temporal logics enabled reasoning about belief states, knowledge, and the evolution of dynamic systems. While these approaches offered highly interpretable reasoning mechanisms, they were constrained by trade-offs between expressiveness and computational tractability. Ultimately, these limitations set the stage for the transition toward machine learning methods and the renewed concerns about opacity that followed (Emerson, 1990).

Limitations of Expert Systems and the Emergence of Justification Requirements

Early expert systems highlighted a central challenge that would later become foundational for Explainable AI: the need to clearly justify decisions produced by rule-based logic. These systems relied on predefined "if–then" structures that encoded expert knowledge, assuming that transparent rules would automatically yield transparent reasoning. However, as Popple notes, even when a rule-based system produced a correct output, it often failed to provide the type of explanation human experts expect—one that accounts for nuance, contextual variation, and the reasoning path followed by domain specialists. This gap revealed that transparency is not only a matter of exposing rules, but of aligning machine reasoning with human explanatory practices.

Furthermore, expert systems struggled with concepts that were inherently ambiguous or "open-textured", meaning they could not be fully defined through rigid rule sets. In Popple's analysis, legal expert systems illustrate this well: the rules could generate an outcome, but could not communicate why certain facts were relevant or how exceptions and analogies influenced the decision. These limitations exposed a deeper problem: humans require explanations that justify a decision within context, not just a trace of rules fired. This distinction foreshadows modern debates in XAI, where post-hoc explanations attempt to bridge the distance between computational logic and human interpretability.

Ultimately, the shortcomings of rule-based expert systems demonstrated that explanation is not optional but fundamental for trust, accountability, and adoption. Popple concludes that rule-based outputs alone are insufficient because they fail to mimic the reasoning style experts use when defending a conclusion or persuading another human. This insight directly paved the way for the resurgence of interest in Explainable AI decades later: as AI systems grew more complex, the early lesson from expert systems became even more urgent—the value of an AI system lies not only in producing accurate results, but in articulating why those results follow from the evidence (Popple, 1991).

Paradigm Shift With Machine Learning and Deep Neural Networks: Loss of INTERPRETABILITY

The rise of machine learning—particularly deep learning—led to a growing emphasis on predictive performance at the expense of model transparency, marking a significant paradigm shift in AI. According to Li et al., deep learning models emerged due to their ability to learn hierarchical representations directly from data. However, this data-driven approach distances models from human-interpretable reasoning, making their internal mechanisms difficult to trace or justify. This transformation introduced new concerns regarding interpretability, particularly in high-stakes or safety-critical domains.

The introduction of deep neural networks brought unprecedented complexity into AI systems; as a result, a significant loss of interpretability emerged. Deep learning architectures consist of multiple nonlinear layers that transform data into increasingly abstract representations, distributing these transformations across millions of parameters. As a consequence, these internal processes cannot be mapped to human-understandable logic, causing such models to function as black boxes in which predictions and feature interactions are difficult to explain. This lack of transparency reinforced the need for explainability techniques capable of elucidating how deep learning models generate their outputs.

As deep learning models became increasingly deployed in high-stakes application domains, their lack of interpretability raised significant concerns. In areas such as healthcare, finance, and decision support, relying on opaque models makes it difficult to justify decisions, identify errors, or assess potential biases. This absence of transparency undermines trust and complicates accountability, particularly when AI systems influence outcomes with serious social, ethical, or economic consequences. Consequently, these challenges motivated the emergence of Explainable Artificial Intelligence, which seeks to enhance transparency and provide meaningful insights into the decision-making processes of complex models.

Key Milestones in the Resurgence of Explainable Artificial Intelligence

The resurgence of Explainable Artificial Intelligence did not occur spontaneously, but rather emerged as a response to the growing dominance of machine learning—particularly deep learning—and its associated loss of interpretability. As data-driven models began to outperform traditional approaches across a wide range of tasks, their opaque decision-making processes raised increasing concerns, especially in high-stakes domains. A key milestone in this renewed focus on explainability was the launch of the DARPA Explainable Artificial Intelligence (XAI) Program in 2016, which formally recognized the need to balance predictive performance with human-understandable explanations. This initiative marked a turning point by framing explainability as a central research objective rather than a secondary consideration (Gunning & Aha, 2019).

Following this institutional recognition, research on explainability expanded rapidly, leading to the development of post-hoc interpretability techniques designed to explain complex black-box models without sacrificing performance. At the same time, growing societal and regulatory pressures reinforced the importance of transparency in automated decision-making systems. Concerns related to trust, accountability, and ethical responsibility—particularly in areas such as healthcare, finance, and automated decision support—highlighted the limitations of deploying opaque models in real-world settings. Together, these scientific advances and external pressures consolidated Explainable AI as a distinct and necessary research area, positioning explainability as a fundamental requirement for the responsible deployment of modern AI systems (Thalpage, 2023).

Figure 1 illustrates a timeline of key milestones that shaped the resurgence of Explainable Artificial Intelligence. The figure summarizes the historical progression from early symbolic AI—characterized by inherently interpretable rule-based reasoning—to the widespread adoption of deep learning models, which significantly improved predictive performance at the cost of transparency. The growing deployment of opaque models in high-stakes domains, together with institutional initiatives such as the DARPA Explainable Artificial Intelligence (XAI) Program, played a central role in re-establishing explainability as a critical research objective in modern AI (Thalpage, 2023).

Figure 1. Timeline of key events that contributed to the resurgence of Explainable Artificial Intelligence (XAI).

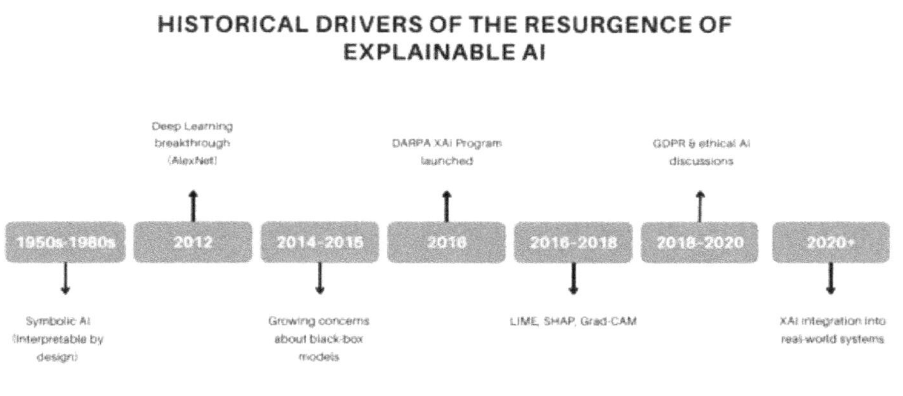

Source: Own elaboration.

KEY CONCEPT AND DEFINITIONS

Explainability, Interpretability, and Transparency

The concept of explainability in artificial intelligence refers to the capacity of an AI system to provide meaningful and understandable reasons for its outputs, decisions, or behaviors to human stakeholders. Explainability addresses why a specific outcome was produced and which factors influenced the decision, enabling humans to assess, trust, or contest automated decisions (Doshi-Velez & Kim, 2017).

Although closely related, explainability, interpretability, and transparency represent distinct yet complementary concepts. As emphasized by Brent Mittelstadt (2022), interpretability primarily concerns understanding the functionality or behavior of a model itself, whereas transparency focuses on the institutional, procedural, and governance aspects surrounding the design, deployment, and regulation of AI systems.

Interpretability refers to the degree to which a human can understand how a model transforms inputs into outputs. An interpretable model allows a well-informed observer to trace or predict its behavior without requiring external explanatory tools (Lipton, 2018; Molnar, 2020). In contrast, transparency does not necessarily address the internal logic of the model but rather provides information about data provenance, development processes, governance structures, and accountability mechanisms (Mittelstadt, 2022).

In this sense, explainability can be understood as a broader, human-centered objective that encompasses both interpretability and transparency. While interpretability focuses on how the model works and transparency on how the system is governed, explainability emphasizes how these elements are communicated in a way that supports understanding, accountability, and informed decision-making (Doshi-Velez & Kim, 2017; Mittelstadt, 2022).

Types of Explanations

Explainable AI approaches are commonly categorized according to when and how explanations are generated: ante-hoc and post-hoc explanations.

Ante-Hoc Explanations (Intrinsically Interpretable Models)

Ante-hoc explanations arise from models that are interpretable by design, meaning that their internal logic is inherently understandable to humans. These models provide explanations as part of their normal operation, without the need for additional analytical layers. In the terminology used by Mittelstadt (2022), this corresponds to intrinsic interpretability.

Ante-hoc models are characterized by:

- Explicit and structured decision logic,
- Limited model complexity,
- Direct relationships between input features and outputs.

Examples include linear and logistic regression, decision trees, rule-based systems, and generalized additive models (Molnar, 2020; Rudin, 2019). While such models offer strong transparency and interpretability, they may struggle to achieve high predictive performance in complex, high-dimensional domains. As a result, ante-hoc explainability often involves a trade-off between model simplicity and accuracy.

Post-Hoc Explanations (Explanations for Black-Box Models)

Post-hoc explanations are generated after a model has produced its output and are particularly relevant for complex or opaque models such as deep neural networks and ensemble methods. These explanations rely on external techniques that approximate, inspect, or analyze the behavior of the model without altering its internal structure (Lipton, 2018; Molnar, 2020).

Mittelstadt (2022) highlights that post-hoc explanations are typically partial and approximate, offering insight into specific behaviors or decisions rather than full causal accounts of model functionality. Post-hoc explanations can be further distinguished into:

- Local explanations, which focus on individual predictions,
- Global explanations, which aim to summarize overall model behavior.

Although post-hoc methods make black-box models more accessible, they raise important concerns regarding their reliability. In particular, explanations may appear persuasive while failing to accurately reflect the true decision-making logic of the model, leading to what has been described as the fidelity problem (Mittelstadt, 2022; Wachter et al., 2017).

Desired Characteristics of Explanations

To be considered useful and trustworthy, explanations generated by XAI systems should satisfy several key characteristics. Drawing on the framework proposed by

Mittelstadt (2022) and complemented by Molnar (2020), four core properties are particularly relevant.

Fidelity refers to the degree to which an explanation accurately reflects the true behavior of the underlying model. High-fidelity explanations closely approximate the model's actual decision logic, including both correct predictions and errors. Low-fidelity explanations risk misleading users by providing plausible but inaccurate narratives.

Comprehensibility captures the extent to which an explanation is understandable to its intended audience. An explanation may be technically correct yet ineffective if it exceeds the cognitive or domain expertise of the user. Effective explanations therefore balance accuracy with simplicity, often relying on sparse representations that highlight the most influential factors (Molnar, 2020).

Generality describes the applicability of an explanation method across different models, datasets, and contexts. Explanations with high generality can be consistently applied to multiple scenarios, increasing their practical utility in real-world systems. However, greater generality may come at the cost of reduced specificity or fidelity.

Consistency refers to the stability of explanations across similar inputs or decision contexts. Similar cases should yield similar explanations, ensuring predictability and reliability in how explanations are produced. Inconsistent explanations can undermine user trust and hinder meaningful interpretation of model behavior (Mittelstadt, 2022).

Balancing these characteristics remains a central challenge in Explainable AI, as improvements in one dimension may negatively impact another. Consequently, explanation quality must be evaluated relative to the specific context, audience, and purpose for which the explanation is intended.

MAIN XAI TECHNIQUES

This section provides an in-depth review of the main families of Explainable Artificial Intelligence (XAI) techniques, organized according to when explanations are generated (ante-hoc versus post-hoc), their scope (local or global), and their representational modality (numerical or visual). This taxonomy is widely adopted in the XAI literature (Guidotti et al., 2021; Lipton, 2018; Molnar, 2020) and is particularly relevant for Business Intelligence (BI) and Decision Support Systems (DSS), where explainability must support transparency, accountability, and informed decision-making.

As BI systems increasingly integrate advanced machine learning and deep learning models, the opacity of these models poses challenges for trust, governance, and regulatory compliance. XAI techniques address these challenges by enabling users to understand, validate, and contextualize analytical outputs, reinforcing the role of BI as a reliable foundation for organizational decision-making.

Ante-hoc (Intrinsic Explainability)

Ante-hoc approaches rely on intrinsically interpretable models, where explainability is embedded directly into the model architecture. Common examples include decision trees, linear and logistic regression models, rule-based systems, and generalized additive models (GAMs). In these approaches, explanations can be obtained directly by inspecting decision paths, coefficients, or explicit rules, without requiring additional post-hoc analysis (Molnar, 2020).

From a Business Intelligence perspective, ante-hoc models closely align with traditional BI paradigms that emphasize transparency and traceability. Decision trees and rule-based models can be directly translated into business rules, supporting applications such as credit approval, operational risk assessment, and compliance reporting. Linear models provide clear interpretations of feature contributions, making them suitable for KPI monitoring, financial forecasting, and performance analytics dashboards.

GAMs offer a balance between interpretability and flexibility by modeling nonlinear relationships while preserving feature-level transparency (Clinciu & Hastie, 2019). This property is particularly attractive in BI environments that require interpretable trend analysis without sacrificing expressiveness. However, the main limitation of ante-hoc techniques lies in their reduced ability to capture highly complex interactions, which may limit their applicability in data-intensive BI scenarios.

Post-hoc Local Explanations

Post-hoc local explanation techniques focus on explaining individual predictions generated by black-box models. Representative methods include LIME (Ribeiro et al., 2016b), SHAP (Lundberg & Lee, 2017), and Anchors (Ribeiro et al., 2016a). These approaches generate explanations by approximating model behavior in the neighborhood of a specific instance or by identifying locally valid decision rules.

In BI and DSS contexts, local explanations are essential for case-level decision support. They allow analysts and end-users to understand why a specific customer, transaction, or event was assigned a particular prediction or risk score. This capability supports operational decision-making, model debugging, fairness assessment, and human-in-the-loop validation processes.

Among local explanation methods, SHAP has gained significant adoption in BI applications due to its strong theoretical foundation in cooperative game theory and its ability to provide consistent and additive feature attributions across models

(Lundberg & Lee, 2017). Local explanations can be embedded into BI dashboards, enabling interactive exploration of predictions. Nevertheless, their localized nature means they do not capture overall model behavior, and their explanations should be interpreted as approximations rather than exact causal accounts.

Post-hoc Global Explanations

Post-hoc global explanation techniques aim to capture overall model behavior across the entire dataset. These methods include global feature importance measures, surrogate models, and partial dependence plots (PDPs), which summarize how input variables influence predictions on average (Friedman, 2001; Guidotti et al., 2021)).

In Business Intelligence systems, global explanations are particularly relevant for strategic analytics, governance, and reporting. Feature importance rankings help identify key business drivers, surrogate models provide simplified representations of complex predictive systems, and PDPs allow analysts to explore average relationships between variables and outcomes. These insights support executive decision-making, model validation, and regulatory reporting.

However, global explanations may obscure local behaviors and interaction effects that are critical in certain BI use cases. For this reason, many BI-driven DSS adopt a layered explainability strategy, combining global explanations for oversight with local explanations for detailed case analysis.

Visual Explanations

Visual explanation techniques translate model behavior into graphical representations that enhance human interpretability. These include saliency maps and Grad-CAM for deep neural networks (Selvaraju et al., 2017; Simonyan & Zisserman, 2015), as well as dimensionality reduction techniques such as t-SNE and UMAP for visualizing embeddings and latent spaces (Van Der Maaten & Hinton, 2012).

In BI contexts, visual explanations are especially useful for exploratory analytics and sense-making. Embedding visualizations can support customer segmentation, anomaly detection, and similarity analysis, while heatmaps and activation maps help analysts qualitatively assess influential features or patterns. These techniques complement numerical explanations by enabling intuitive exploration of complex data representations.

Despite their intuitive appeal, visual explanations should be interpreted with caution, as they often provide qualitative rather than causal insights. Nevertheless, when integrated into BI dashboards and interactive analytics platforms, visual explanations enhance user engagement and support exploratory decision processes.

Summary and Relevance for Business Intelligence

Overall, XAI techniques vary in scope, interpretability, and suitability for BI applications. Ante-hoc models prioritize transparency and simplicity, post-hoc local explanations support instance-level decisions, post-hoc global techniques enable strategic understanding, and visual explanations facilitate exploratory analysis. In modern BI and DSS environments, effective explainability often requires a hybrid approach, combining multiple XAI techniques to address the needs of diverse stakeholders and decision contexts (Table 1).

Table 1. Mapping XAI Techniques to Business Intelligence Purposes. Source: Own elaboration.

XAI Category	Technique Examples	Type of Explanation	BI Purpose	Typical BI Use Case
Ante-hoc	Decision trees, linear models, GAMs	Intrinsic / global	Transparency and traceability	KPI monitoring, credit scoring rules, compliance reporting
Post-hoc Local	LIME, SHAP, Anchors	Local, instance-level	Case-level decision support	Explaining individual predictions, customer risk analysis
Post-hoc Global	Feature importance, surrogate models, PDPs	Global, model-level	Strategic insight and governance	Identifying key business drivers, model auditing
Visual	Saliency maps, Grad-CAM, t-SNE, UMAP	Visual / exploratory	Sense-making and pattern discovery	Customer segmentation, anomaly detection, exploratory BI dashboards

EXPLAINABLE AI APPLICATIONS FOR BUSINESS INTELLIGENCE AND DECISION SUPPORT

Explainable Artificial Intelligence (XAI) has gained relevance across multiple application domains where automated or data-driven decisions have direct consequences for individuals, organizations, and society. In such contexts, transparency and interpretability are not optional features but essential requirements for trust, accountability, and regulatory compliance. This section reviews key application domains that have driven the adoption of XAI, culminating in its strategic role within Business Intelligence (BI) and decision support systems.

Cross-Domain Applications Motivating XAI Adoption

One of the earliest and most influential application domains of XAI is healthcare, where machine learning models are increasingly used to support clinical diagnosis, prognosis, and treatment recommendations. In these settings, explainability is critical to allow clinicians to understand, validate, and trust model outputs, particularly when decisions may affect patient safety. XAI techniques have been employed to highlight relevant clinical features, justify predictions, and support shared decision-making between clinicians and patients, addressing concerns related to accountability and ethical responsibility (Doshi-Velez & Kim, 2017; Holzinger et al., 2019).

In the financial sector, XAI plays a central role in applications such as credit scoring, loan approval, and fraud detection. Regulatory frameworks in many jurisdictions require financial institutions to provide understandable explanations for automated decisions that affect customers. As a result, explainable models and post-hoc explanation techniques have been widely adopted to justify risk assessments, detect biased behavior, and support compliance with transparency requirements (Molnar, 2020; Ribeiro et al., 2016a).

Manufacturing and industrial environments represent another important domain, particularly in the context of predictive maintenance and process optimization. Machine learning models are used to anticipate equipment failures and optimize operational efficiency; however, explanations are needed to help engineers understand why specific alerts or maintenance actions are triggered. XAI supports root-cause analysis, improves human–machine collaboration, and facilitates actionable insights rather than opaque predictions (Samek et al., 2021).

In legal and justice systems, algorithmic risk assessment tools have raised significant concerns regarding fairness, accountability, and transparency. The use of black-box models in decisions related to sentencing, parole, or recidivism risk has highlighted the dangers of opaque reasoning and potential bias. XAI methods have been proposed to increase transparency, support audits, and enable critical scrutiny of automated decision-making processes in high-stakes societal contexts (Guidotti et al., 2021).

Collectively, these domains illustrate a common pattern: as machine learning systems are deployed in sensitive and regulated environments, the demand for explanations becomes a fundamental requirement rather than a desirable enhancement.

Explainable AI in Business Intelligence and Decision Support

While XAI has emerged across diverse application areas, Business Intelligence represents a unifying organizational context where explainability directly supports strategic, tactical, and operational decision-making. BI systems integrate data from multiple sources, apply advanced analytics and machine learning models, and present insights to decision-makers through dashboards, reports, and alerts. In this setting, explanations are essential to bridge the gap between complex analytical models and human understanding.

XAI enhances BI by enabling users—often non-technical stakeholders such as managers, analysts, and executives—to interpret predictive and prescriptive analytics results. Rather than relying solely on performance metrics or black-box predictions, decision-makers can understand which factors drive outcomes, how scenarios differ, and why specific recommendations are generated. This interpretability is particularly important for forecasting, risk analysis, anomaly detection, and performance management tasks commonly supported by BI platforms (Shmueli & Koppius, 2011).

Moreover, XAI contributes to trust and adoption of advanced analytics within organizations. Explanations help mitigate skepticism toward AI-driven insights, support validation and sense-making, and facilitate organizational learning. From a decision support perspective, explainability transforms BI systems from passive reporting tools into transparent, interactive environments where users can question, explore, and justify data-driven decisions (Elbashir et al., 2022)

In addition, the integration of XAI into BI aligns with emerging governance and ethical requirements, as organizations increasingly need to document and justify automated or semi-automated decisions. Explainable BI systems support auditability, accountability, and responsible AI adoption by making analytical reasoning explicit and accessible across organizational levels (Molnar, 2020; Samek et al., 2021).

In summary, while multiple domains have driven the development of XAI, Business Intelligence constitutes a particularly relevant application context, as it operationalizes explainability at scale and embeds it directly into organizational decision support processes. This positioning reinforces the strategic value of XAI not only as a technical solution, but as a foundational component of trustworthy and effective BI systems.

CHALLENGES AND LIMITATIONS OF EXPLAINABLE ARTIFICIAL INTELLIGENCE IN BUSINESS INTELLIGENCE AND DECISION SUPPORT.

Despite the growing adoption of Explainable Artificial Intelligence (XAI), significant challenges and limitations remain, particularly when explainability techniques are integrated into Business Intelligence (BI) and decision support systems (DSS). While XAI aims to enhance transparency, trust, and accountability, its practical deployment in organizational analytics environments introduces trade-offs, methodological gaps, and ethical concerns that must be carefully addressed. This section discusses the main challenges associated with XAI from the perspective of BI-driven decision-making.

Balancing Predictive Performance and Explainability in BI Systems

One of the most widely discussed challenges in XAI is the trade-off between predictive accuracy and explainability. In BI systems, this tension is especially pronounced, as organizations increasingly rely on complex machine learning and deep learning models to support forecasting, risk assessment, anomaly detection, and optimization tasks. These models often deliver superior predictive performance but operate as black boxes, making their internal reasoning difficult to interpret (Breiman, 2001; Molnar, 2020).

From a decision support perspective, high predictive accuracy alone is insufficient. Decision-makers require not only reliable predictions but also an understanding of the underlying drivers that influence outcomes. In BI contexts, explanations are necessary to justify strategic and operational decisions, assess risks, and explore alternative scenarios. Consequently, organizations may face difficult choices between deploying highly accurate yet opaque models and opting for simpler, more interpretable approaches that provide actionable insights but potentially lower performance (Shmueli & Koppius, 2011).

This trade-off is further complicated by the diverse user profiles involved in BI systems. While data scientists may prioritize model performance, business analysts and executives often value interpretability and transparency to support sense-making and accountability. As a result, balancing accuracy and explainability becomes not only a technical challenge but also an organizational and cognitive one, requiring alignment between analytical capabilities and decision-making needs (Bussmann et al., 2020).

Lack of Standardized Metrics for Evaluating Explanations in BI Contexts

Another critical limitation of XAI lies in the absence of standardized and widely accepted metrics for evaluating explanations. While predictive models can be assessed using well-established performance measures, explanations lack comparable evaluation frameworks, particularly in applied BI environments. Existing evaluation approaches often focus on abstract properties such as fidelity, stability, or sparsity, but these criteria do not fully capture the usefulness of explanations for real-world decision support (Doshi-Velez & Kim, 2017; Guidotti et al., 2021).

In BI systems, explanations are consumed by heterogeneous stakeholders with varying levels of technical expertise. An explanation that is meaningful for a data scientist may be incomprehensible or irrelevant to a business executive. Consequently, evaluating explanations requires considering human-centered criteria such as comprehensibility, cognitive load, and decision relevance, which are difficult to quantify and standardize (Holzinger et al., 2017).

The lack of evaluation standards also complicates the comparison of XAI techniques within BI tools, dashboards, and reporting environments. Without consistent metrics, organizations may struggle to assess whether explanations genuinely improve decision quality, trust, or user confidence, or whether they merely create an illusion of transparency. This challenge limits the systematic integration of XAI into BI platforms and hinders evidence-based adoption of explainability techniques (Samek et al., 2019).

Risks of Persuasive but Misleading Explanations in Decision Support

A particularly critical concern in XAI is the risk of producing explanations that are persuasive but misleading. Post-hoc explanation methods, such as surrogate models or feature attribution techniques, may generate simplified representations of complex models that do not accurately reflect the true decision-making process. While such explanations may appear intuitive and convincing, they can suffer from low fidelity, creating a false sense of understanding (Molnar, 2020; Ribeiro et al., 2016a).

In BI and DSS contexts, misleading explanations can have serious consequences. Decision-makers may place undue trust in AI-generated insights, leading to automation bias or overconfidence in model outputs. When explanations are used to justify strategic or high-impact decisions, inaccuracies in explanatory logic can propagate errors and reinforce flawed assumptions, undermining the very goals of transparency and accountability that XAI seeks to achieve (Bussmann et al., 2020).

This challenge is exacerbated in organizational settings where explanations are embedded into dashboards and reports. Visual or narrative explanations may be selectively interpreted to support preconceived conclusions, particularly when users lack awareness of the limitations of XAI methods. Ensuring that explanations faithfully represent model behavior, while clearly communicating their uncertainty and scope, remains an open challenge for explainable BI systems (Guidotti et al., 2021; Samek et al., 2019).

Ethical, Accountability, and Governance Challenges in Explainable BI.

Ethical and accountability considerations represent a further layer of complexity in the application of XAI within BI systems. As organizations increasingly rely on AI-driven analytics for decision-making, questions arise regarding responsibility, transparency, and governance. Explainability alone does not guarantee ethical use; rather, it must be embedded within broader organizational frameworks that define roles, responsibilities, and oversight mechanisms (Floridi et al., 2018).

In BI environments, decisions are often distributed across multiple actors, including data engineers, analysts, managers, and automated systems. When AI-driven recommendations influence outcomes, determining accountability becomes challenging, particularly if explanations are incomplete, approximate, or misunderstood. XAI can support accountability by making decision logic more visible, but it cannot fully resolve issues related to responsibility sharing and organizational decision ownership (Bussmann et al., 2020).

Furthermore, emerging regulatory frameworks increasingly emphasize transparency and the right to explanation in automated decision-making. Organizations deploying explainable BI systems must therefore ensure that explanations are not only technically sound but also aligned with legal, ethical, and governance requirements. This includes documenting model behavior, monitoring explanatory consistency over time, and ensuring that explanations do not obscure biases or discriminatory effects (Holzinger et al., 2019; Molnar, 2020).

TRENDS AND FUTURE DIRECTIONS OF EXPLAINABLE ARTIFICIAL INTELLIGENCE IN BUSINESS INTELLIGENCE

As Explainable Artificial Intelligence (XAI) continues to evolve, its future development is increasingly shaped by emerging analytical paradigms, regulatory pressures, and the growing demand for trustworthy decision support. In the context of Business Intelligence (BI), these trends point toward a transformation of traditional analytics platforms into explanation-aware decision environments. This section discusses key directions that are likely to define the next generation of explainable BI and decision support systems.

Explainable AI for Generative Models in Analytics and Decision Support

One of the most prominent recent trends in artificial intelligence is the rapid adoption of generative models, particularly large language models, for data analysis, reporting, and decision support tasks. In BI contexts, generative AI is increasingly used to produce natural language summaries of dashboards, generate insights from complex datasets, and support conversational analytics interfaces. However, the opaque nature of generative models raises significant concerns regarding reliability, traceability, and trust (Bommasani et al., 2022).

From a decision support perspective, the integration of generative AI into BI systems amplifies the need for explainability. Automatically generated insights and narratives must be accompanied by explanations that clarify their data sources, underlying assumptions, and analytical logic. Without such transparency, decision-makers may struggle to assess the validity of generated recommendations, increasing the risk of overreliance on AI-driven outputs (Shneiderman, 2022).

XAI techniques are therefore expected to play a critical role in enabling explainable generative BI, supporting verification, accountability, and human oversight. Future BI systems are likely to combine generative analytics with explanation mechanisms that make explicit why certain insights are produced, how they relate to historical data, and under which conditions they should be trusted. This convergence positions XAI as a foundational component for the responsible use of generative AI in organizational decision-making.

Regulatory-Driven Explainability and Governance in BI Systems

Another key driver shaping the future of XAI in BI is the emergence of regulatory frameworks that emphasize transparency, accountability, and human oversight in automated decision-making. Regulations such as the European Union's Artificial Intelligence Act reflect a broader global trend toward requiring organizations to explain and justify AI-supported decisions, particularly in high-impact and socio-technical contexts (Ebers et al., 2021).

For BI systems, these regulatory developments imply that explainability can no longer be treated as an optional enhancement. Instead, explainability is becoming a design requirement that affects how analytics pipelines, dashboards, and decision support tools are constructed and governed. XAI enables BI systems to support auditability, documentation, and traceability of analytical processes, facilitating compliance and organizational accountability (Floridi et al., 2018).

Looking forward, regulatory pressure is likely to accelerate the adoption of explainable BI architectures, where explanations are systematically generated, stored, and monitored alongside predictive and prescriptive analytics. This trend reinforces the role of XAI not only as a technical solution, but as a governance mechanism that supports responsible analytics and trustworthy decision support across organizations.

Interactive and User-Centered Explanations in BI Dashboards

A further important trend in explainable BI is the shift toward interactive and user-centered explanations. Traditional BI systems have relied on static dashboards and reports that provide limited support for understanding complex analytical models. In contrast, future explainable BI systems are expected to offer adaptive explanations tailored to different user profiles, decision roles, and levels of expertise (Holzinger et al., 2019).

In decision support contexts, users range from operational staff to senior executives, each with distinct information needs and cognitive constraints. XAI enables the generation of explanations that vary in depth, abstraction, and presentation, allowing users to explore model behavior through interactive visualizations, what-if analyses, and scenario exploration. This interaction transforms explanations from passive artifacts into active components of the decision-making process (Kaur et al., 2020).

By supporting interactive sense-making, XAI contributes to more effective and informed use of BI systems. Rather than simply presenting outcomes, explainable dashboards encourage users to question, validate, and contextualize analytical results, strengthening human–AI collaboration and reducing the risk of blind trust in automated insights.

Integration of XAI into Real-World BI Production Environments

Finally, a critical future direction concerns the integration of XAI into real-world production environments. While many explainability techniques have been developed and evaluated in experimental settings, their deployment within operational BI platforms remains an ongoing challenge. Production BI systems require explanations that are consistent, scalable, and maintainable over time, particularly as data distributions and models evolve (Sculley et al., 2015).

Integrating XAI into BI pipelines involves treating explanations as first-class system components rather than auxiliary outputs. This includes embedding explainability mechanisms into data processing workflows, machine learning models, and visualization layers, as well as monitoring explanation stability and relevance in the presence of model updates or concept drift (Samek et al., 2019).

As BI platforms increasingly incorporate advanced analytics and AI-driven recommendations, the demand for robust, explainable production systems will continue to grow. Future research and practice are therefore expected to focus on operationalizing XAI at scale, ensuring that explanations remain reliable, interpretable, and aligned with organizational decision-making processes.

CONCLUSION

The growing adoption of artificial intelligence within organizational analytics has intensified the need for transparency, interpretability, and trust in data-driven decision-making. As Business Intelligence (BI) systems increasingly incorporate advanced machine learning and deep learning models, the limitations of black-box approaches become more evident, particularly in contexts where decisions have strategic, operational, or ethical implications. This chapter has examined Explainable Artificial Intelligence (XAI) as a key enabler for addressing these challenges within BI and decision support systems (DSS).

The review of foundational concepts and explanation paradigms highlights that explainability is not a single property, but a multidimensional objective encompassing interpretability, transparency, and human understanding. The distinction between ante-hoc and post-hoc explanation approaches provides a useful framework for understanding how explainability can be achieved at different stages of the analytical pipeline. While ante-hoc models offer intrinsic interpretability, post-hoc techniques play a critical role in making complex, high-performing models accessible to decision-makers, particularly in modern BI environments.

By analyzing the main XAI techniques and their applications across multiple domains, this chapter has shown that the demand for explainability is largely driven by high-stakes and regulated contexts such as healthcare, finance, manufacturing, and legal decision-making. However, Business Intelligence emerges as a particularly relevant application domain, as it operationalizes explainability at scale and embeds it directly into organizational decision processes. In BI systems, explanations are not merely technical artifacts; they function as cognitive bridges that connect analytical outputs with human judgment, enabling sense-making, trust, and accountability.

The discussion of challenges and limitations underscores that the integration of XAI into BI systems is far from trivial. Trade-offs between predictive performance and interpretability, the lack of standardized metrics for evaluating explanations, and the risk of persuasive but misleading explanations all pose significant obstacles to effective deployment. Moreover, ethical and governance considerations reveal that explainability alone cannot guarantee responsible AI use, but must be complemented by organizational frameworks that define accountability, oversight, and decision ownership.

Looking forward, the analysis of emerging trends suggests that XAI will play an increasingly central role in shaping the future of BI and DSS. The rise of generative AI for analytics, growing regulatory demands for transparency, the shift toward user-centered and interactive explanations, and the need to integrate XAI into production-grade BI platforms collectively point toward a new generation of explainable BI systems. In this vision, explanations are treated as first-class components of analytics infrastructures, supporting not only technical validation but also organizational learning and informed decision-making.

In conclusion, this chapter argues that Explainable Artificial Intelligence is not merely an auxiliary feature of modern analytics, but a foundational requirement for trustworthy and effective Business Intelligence. By embedding explainability into BI systems and decision support processes, organizations can move beyond opaque predictions toward transparent, accountable, and human-centered analytics. This positioning reinforces the strategic importance of XAI for the responsible adoption of AI in organizational contexts and highlights its role as a critical enabler of next-generation decision support systems.

REFERENCES

Adadi, A., & Berrada, M. (2018). Peeking Inside the Black-Box: A Survey on Explainable Artificial Intelligence (XAI). *IEEE Access : Practical Innovations, Open Solutions*, *6*, 52138–52160. DOI: 10.1109/ACCESS.2018.2870052

Bommasani, R., Hudson, D. A., Adeli, E., Altman, R., Arora, S., von Arx, S., Bernstein, M. S., Bohg, J., Bosselut, A., Brunskill, E., Brynjolfsson, E., Buch, S., Card, D., Castellon, R., Chatterji, N., Chen, A., Creel, K., Davis, J. Q., Demszky, D., . . . Liang, P. (2022). *On the Opportunities and Risks of Foundation Models* (arXiv:2108.07258). arXiv. https://doi.org//arXiv.2108.07258DOI: 10.48550

Breiman, L. (2001). Statistical Modeling: The Two Cultures. *Quality Control and Applied Statistics*, *48*(1), 81–82.

Bussmann, N., Giudici, P., Marinelli, D., & Papenbrock, J. (2020). Explainable Machine Learning in Credit Risk Management. *Computational Economics*, *57*(1), 203–216. DOI: 10.1007/s10614-020-10042-0

Clinciu, M.-A., & Hastie, H. (2019). A Survey of Explainable AI Terminology. In Alonso, J. M., & Catala, A. (Eds.), *Proceedings of the 1st Workshop on Interactive Natural Language Technology for Explainable Artificial Intelligence (NL4XAI 2019)* (pp. 8–13). Association for Computational Linguistics. DOI: 10.18653/v1/W19-8403

Colmerauer, A., & Roussel, P. (1996). The birth of Prolog. In *History of programming languages—II* (pp. 331–367). Association for Computing Machinery., DOI: 10.1145/234286.1057820

Dendral and Meta-Dendral: Their Applications Dimension. (1981). In *Readings in Artificial Intelligence* (pp. 313–322). Morgan Kaufmann. DOI: 10.1016/B978-0-934613-03-3.50026-X

Doshi-Velez, F., & Kim, B. (2017). *Towards A Rigorous Science of Interpretable Machine Learning* (arXiv:1702.08608). arXiv. https://doi.org//arXiv.1702.08608DOI: 10.48550

Ebers, M., Hoch, V. R. S., Rosenkranz, F., Ruschemeier, H., & Steinrötter, B. (2021). The European Commission's Proposal for an Artificial Intelligence Act—A Critical Assessment by Members of the Robotics and AI Law Society (RAILS). *J*, *4*(4), 589–603.

Elbashir, M. Z., Sutton, S. G., Arnold, V., & Collier, P. A. (2022). Leveraging business intelligence systems to enhance management control and business process performance in the public sector. *Meditari Accountancy Research*, *30*(4), 914–940. DOI: 10.1108/MEDAR-04-2021-1287

Emerson. (1990). Temporal and Modal Logic. In *Formal Models and Semantics* (pp. 995–1072). Elsevier. DOI: 10.1016/B978-0-444-88074-1.50021-4

Floridi, L., Cowls, J., Beltrametti, M., Chatila, R., Chazerand, P., Dignum, V., Luetge, C., Madelin, R., Pagallo, U., Rossi, F., Schafer, B., Valcke, P., & Vayena, E. (2018). AI4People—An Ethical Framework for a Good AI Society: Opportunities, Risks, Principles, and Recommendations. *Minds and Machines*, *28*(4), 689–707. DOI: 10.1007/s11023-018-9482-5 PMID: 30930541

Friedman, J. H. (2001). Greedy function approximation: A gradient boosting machine. *Annals of Statistics*, *29*(5). Advance online publication. DOI: 10.1214/aos/1013203451

Guidotti, R., Monreale, A., Pedreschi, D., & Giannotti, F. (2021). *Principles of Explainable Artificial Intelligence*. DOI: 10.1007/978-3-030-76409-8_2

Gunning, D., & Aha, D. W. (2019). DARPA's Explainable Artificial Intelligence Program. *AI Magazine*, *40*(2), 44–58. DOI: 10.1609/aimag.v40i2.2850

Holzinger, A., Biemann, C., Pattichis, C. S., & Kell, D. B. (2017). *What do we need to build explainable AI systems for the medical domain?* arXiv.Org. https://arxiv.org/abs/1712.09923v1

Holzinger, A., Langs, G., Denk, H., Zatloukal, K., & Müller, H. (2019). Causability and explainability of artificial intelligence in medicine. *Wiley Interdisciplinary Reviews. Data Mining and Knowledge Discovery*, *9*(4), e1312. DOI: 10.1002/widm.1312 PMID: 32089788

Kaur, H., Nori, H., Jenkins, S., Caruana, R., Wallach, H., & Wortman Vaughan, J. (2020). Interpreting Interpretability: Understanding Data Scientists' Use of Interpretability Tools for Machine Learning. *Proceedings of the 2020 CHI Conference on Human Factors in Computing Systems, CHI '20*, 1–14. DOI: 10.1145/3313831.3376219

Kosinski, M. (2024, October 29). *What Is Black Box AI and How Does It Work? | IBM* [Article]. IBM Think. https://www.ibm.com/think/topics/black-box-ai

Liang, B., Wang, Y., & Tong, C. (2025). AI Reasoning in Deep Learning Era: From Symbolic AI to Neural–Symbolic AI. *Mathematics*, *13*(11), 1707. DOI: 10.3390/math13111707

Lipton, Z. C. (2018). The Mythos of Model Interpretability: In machine learning, the concept of interpretability is both important and slippery. *ACM Queue; Tomorrow's Computing Today*, *16*(3), 31–57. DOI: 10.1145/3236386.3241340

Lundberg, S. M., & Lee, S.-I. (2017). A Unified Approach to Interpreting Model Predictions. *Advances in Neural Information Processing Systems, 30*. https://proceedings.neurips.cc/paper/2017/hash/8a20a8621978632d76c43dfd28b67767-Abstract.html

Mittelstadt, B. (2022). Interpretability and Transparency in Artificial Intelligence. In Véliz, C. (Ed.), *Oxford Handbook of Digital Ethics* (1st ed., pp. 378–410). Oxford University Press., DOI: 10.1093/oxfordhb/9780198857815.013.20

Molnar, C. (2020). Interpretable. *Machine Learning*.

Popple, J. (1991). Legal expert systems: The inadequacy of a rule-based approach. *Australian Computer Science Conference (ACSC-13), 23*, 7–9. DOI: 10.2139/ssrn.1335646

Reiter, R. (1980). A logic for default reasoning. *Artificial Intelligence. Artificial Intelligence*, *13*(1), 81–132. DOI: 10.1016/0004-3702(80)90014-4

Ribeiro, M. T., Singh, S., & Guestrin, C. (2016a). *Model-Agnostic Interpretability of Machine Learning* (arXiv:1606.05386). arXiv. https://doi.org//arXiv.1606.05386DOI: 10.48550

Ribeiro, M. T., Singh, S., & Guestrin, C. (2016b). "Why Should I Trust You?": Explaining the Predictions of Any Classifier. *Proceedings of the 22nd ACM SIGKDD International Conference on Knowledge Discovery and Data Mining. KDD : Proceedings / International Conference on Knowledge Discovery & Data Mining. International Conference on Knowledge Discovery & Data Mining*, *16*, 1135–1144. DOI: 10.1145/2939672.2939778

Rudin, C. (2019). Stop explaining black box machine learning models for high stakes decisions and use interpretable models instead. *Nature Machine Intelligence*, *1*(5), 206–215. DOI: 10.1038/s42256-019-0048-x PMID: 35603010

Samek, W., Montavon, G., Lapuschkin, S., Anders, C. J., & Müller, K.-R. (2021). Explaining Deep Neural Networks and Beyond: A Review of Methods and Applications. *Proceedings of the IEEE*, *109*(3), 247–278. DOI: 10.1109/JPROC.2021.3060483

Samek, W., Montavon, G., Vedaldi, A., Hansen, L. K., & Müller, K.-R. (2019). *Explainable AI: Interpreting, Explaining and Visualizing Deep Learning*. Springer Nature. DOI: 10.1007/978-3-030-28954-6

Sculley, D., Holt, G., Golovin, D., Davydov, E., Phillips, T., Ebner, D., Chaudhary, V., Young, M., Crespo, J.-F., & Dennison, D. (2015). Hidden Technical Debt in Machine Learning Systems. *Advances in Neural Information Processing Systems, 28*. https://proceedings.neurips.cc/paper_files/paper/2015/hash/86df7dcfd896fcaf2674f757a2463eba-Abstract.html

Selvaraju, R. R., Cogswell, M., Das, A., Vedantam, R., Parikh, D., & Batra, D. (2017). *Grad-CAM: Visual Explanations From Deep Networks via Gradient-Based Localization*.

Shmueli, G., & Koppius, O. R. (2011). PREDICTIVE ANALYTICS IN. *Information Systems Research*.

Shneiderman, B. (2022). *Human-centered AI*. Oxford University Press. DOI: 10.1093/oso/9780192845290.001.0001

Simonyan, K., & Zisserman, A. (2015). *Very Deep Convolutional Networks for Large-Scale Image Recognition* (arXiv:1409.1556). arXiv. https://doi.org//arXiv.1409.1556DOI: 10.48550

Thalpage, N. (2023). Unlocking the Black Box: Explainable Artificial Intelligence (XAI) for Trust and Transparency in AI Systems. *Journal of Digital Art & Humanities*, *4*(1), 31–36. DOI: 10.33847/2712-8148.4.1_4

Van Der Maaten, L., & Hinton, G. (2012). Visualizing non-metric similarities in multiple maps. *Machine Learning*, *87*(1), 33–55. DOI: 10.1007/s10994-011-5273-4

Wachter, S., Mittelstadt, B., & Floridi, L. (2017). Transparent, explainable, and accountable AI for robotics. *Science Robotics*, *2*(6), eaan6080. Advance online publication. DOI: 10.1126/scirobotics.aan6080 PMID: 33157874

ADDITIONAL READING

Tahaei, M., Constantinides, M., Quercia, D., Kennedy, S., Muller, M., Stumpf, S., . . . Olteanu, A. (2023, April). Human-centered responsible artificial intelligence: Current & future trends. In Extended Abstracts of the 2023 CHI Conference on Human Factors in Computing Systems (pp. 1-4).

The following readings are recommended for readers interested in deepening their understanding of explainable and responsible AI in organizational and decision support contexts. Agrawal, A., Gans, J., & Goldfarb, A. (2022). Prediction machines, updated and expanded: The simple economics of artificial intelligence. Harvard Business Press. Akerkar, R. (2019). Artificial intelligence for business. Springer. Kashyap, P. (2017). Machine learning for decision makers: Cognitive computing fundamentals for better decision making (pp. 227-228). Bangalore, India: Apress.

KEY TERMS AND DEFINITIONS

Explainable Artificial Intelligence (XAI): Methods and approaches designed to make AI system decisions understandable and interpretable to human users.

Interpretability: The extent to which a human can comprehend how a model generates its outputs based on its internal structure and parameters.

Transparency: A property of AI models whose internal logic, processes, and decision pathways are visible and accessible without additional explanation mechanisms.

Black-Box Model: A complex model whose internal decision-making process is not readily interpretable by humans, requiring external explanation techniques.

Ante-Hoc Explanation: An explanation produced by models that are inherently interpretable due to their structure, such as decision trees or rule-based systems.

Post-Hoc Explanation: An explanation generated after a model has been trained, typically used to interpret black-box models through tools such as LIME or SHAP.

Fidelity: The degree to which an explanation accurately reflects the true reasoning and behavior of the underlying AI model.

Local Explanation: An interpretive technique that clarifies why a model made a specific prediction for a single instance rather than describing overall model behavior.

Global Explanation: An interpretive approach that provides insight into the general logic, structure, or decision patterns of a model across the entire dataset.

Feature Importance: A method that identifies and ranks input variables according to their contribution to a model's predictions.

Surrogate Model: A simpler, interpretable model trained to mimic the behavior of a more complex model, used to provide global explanations.

Knowledge Acquisition Bottleneck: A challenge in early expert systems where gathering, encoding, and updating domain knowledge was slow, costly, and difficult.

Chapter 2
Smart Sustainability:
Harnessing Artificial Intelligence for Energy Efficiency and Resource Management

Arun Agrawal
http://orcid.org/0000-0001-7233-6660
Institute of Technology and Management, Gwalior, India

Bhaskar Roy
http://orcid.org/0000-0002-6516-3682
Asansol Engineering College, Asansol, India

Prasanthi Kumari Nunna
http://orcid.org/0000-0003-4131-1967
University of Petroleum and Energy Studies, Dehradun, India

Jeethu Philip
http://orcid.org/0000-0002-5495-8957
MLR Institute of Technology, Hyderabad, India

Ramkrishna Rakshit
Dr. B.C. Roy Engineering College Academy of Professional Courses, Durgapur, India

Deepak Gupta
http://orcid.org/0000-0003-3929-1362
Institute of Technology and Management, Gwalior, India

Lipika Mandal
http://orcid.org/0000-0001-7653-789X
Asansol Engineering College, Asansol, India

Pradeep Yadav
http://orcid.org/0000-0003-1073-7076
Institute of Technology and Management, Gwalior, India

ABSTRACT

Sustainable development depends on the intelligent management of energy and resources. Population growth and industrial expansion are putting pressure on natural systems. Countries, cities, and organizations are seeking ways to both promote economic development and protect the environment. Modern digital systems can guide this transformation. Artificial intelligence offers ways to support cleaner

DOI: 10.4018/979-8-3373-5946-5.ch002

production and more efficient energy use. It can also help organizations monitor natural resources more accurately. This chapter explains how artificial intelligence can contribute to sustainable energy and resource management in various fields, highlighting its practical applications, challenges, and future directions. The discussion supports the view that digital tools can help society create a cleaner and more stable future.

1. INTRODUCTION

Sustainable development has moved from a distant vision to an urgent necessity. Climate change is reshaping weather patterns and damaging ecosystems. Cities are expanding as people migrate in search of development opportunities. Consumption levels are rising as industries and households rely on stable supplies of energy, food, and materials. These factors create a stark contradiction. Countries must pursue sustainable development while respecting significant ecological boundaries. This balance is difficult to maintain because many modern systems still rely on energy sources that emit pollutants and reduce long-term environmental stability. This pressure is further amplified when natural resources are wasted (Woodward, 2019). Energy powers virtually all human activities. Factories rely on energy to keep production lines running; farms need energy for irrigation, storage, and powering machinery; and households depend on energy for lighting, comfort, and daily work. However, the energy systems that meet these needs often exacerbate pollution and climate pressures. Inefficient practices increase emissions; poor planning leads to unnecessary waste. These problems are exacerbated by the growing global population. Countries must find ways to reduce waste while providing reliable services to their citizens (Majeed et al., 2023).

Digital systems support this work by improving how organizations understand resource use. Artificial intelligence is one such system. It helps organizations study patterns that are difficult to discover using traditional methods. Early sustainability initiatives relied on human surveys and basic tools. These methods provide only partial information and are often slow to react (Varriale et al., 2024). They cannot keep up with changing environmental conditions or shifts in human behavior. Therefore, sustainability efforts struggle to produce strong and lasting impacts. Modern digital tools offer a different path. They can analyze massive amounts of information, revealing previously hidden trends. They can also help organizations take action before problems escalate. Artificial intelligence can monitor energy consumption in real time, identify machines consuming more power than expected, and alert authorities when water supplies are insufficient. It can also help cities plan more efficient transportation systems based on evolving travel patterns. These capabilities guide governments and businesses to make informed decisions, thereby reducing waste and improving environmental protection.

Smart sustainability combines technological capabilities with ethical responsibility. It doesn't exclude people from the decision-making process, but rather enhances their understanding of the consequences. Planners can learn which communities consume the most electricity; farmers can learn when crops need irrigation; plant managers can detect pipe leaks, thus preventing water and energy waste (Kumar et al., 2024). These insights help make more informed choices and ensure that policies and practices align with ecological needs. The concept of smart sustainability also encourages continuous improvement. When information is available in real time, organizations can try new strategies, quickly measure results, adjust plans, and move towards more responsible and resilient systems (Okonta & Vukovic, 2024). This approach is crucial for industries facing rapid change. For example, power grids must cope with unpredictable demand, farms must deal with irregular rainfall, and cities must adapt to heat waves and pollution events. Digital systems can help these industries prepare.

Artificial intelligence can also aid in long-term planning. Governments can predict the impact of new buildings, roads, or industries, test different options, and compare possible outcomes. Businesses can assess the amount of raw materials they will need over the next few years and estimate the environmental impact of their supply chains (Jiang & Chen, 2024). This insight helps in strategic thinking and reduces the likelihood of unforeseen shocks. However, smart sustainable development also faces many challenges. Not all regions possess the digital infrastructure needed for advanced monitoring. Many institutions still lack professionals capable of understanding and managing digital tools. Data quality is another concern. Low-quality information can lead to flawed decision-making. Furthermore, data collection may involve privacy, thus raising ethical issues. We need to develop clear policies to protect citizens and ensure the fairness of the use of these systems. Artificial intelligence is playing an increasingly important role in sustainable development. It is impacting energy networks, industrial processes, agriculture, transportation systems, buildings, and environmental monitoring (Pimenow et al., 2024). It has become a bridge connecting scientific knowledge with everyday practices. The challenge lies in how to use these systems responsibly. A sustainable future cannot be achieved through technology alone; it must be combined with long-term planning, responsible governance, and active community participation.

This chapter explores these topics in greater detail. It examines how artificial intelligence can support energy efficiency, natural resource conservation, agricultural resilience, and sustainable urban development. Furthermore, this chapter discusses the ethical issues that arise when digital systems influence public decision-making. Finally, this chapter offers recommendations for strengthening future smart sustainability efforts. It emphasizes that collaboration, transparency, and strong institutional capacity are crucial for ensuring the achievement and maintenance of environmental goals.

2. CONCEPTUAL FOUNDATIONS OF SMART SUSTAINABILITY

Smart sustainability is built upon the convergence of two core principles. The first is sustainable development, which emphasizes the prudent use of resources to avoid jeopardizing the well-being of future generations. It reminds society that economic development must respect ecological boundaries. The second is digital intelligence, which involves systems capable of analyzing data, identifying patterns, and supporting timely decision-making (Kirchner-Krath et al., 2024). Both principles are valuable in themselves. However, their combination provides a powerful approach to addressing today's environmental challenges. When organizations integrate these ideas, they can act more precisely and rigorously. They no longer rely on guesswork, but on evidence drawn from real-world situations.

Energy efficiency is at the heart of this comprehensive approach. It refers to the ability to provide the same service while consuming less energy. This principle applies to a variety of scenarios. It can be applied to households looking to reduce their electricity bills, industries aiming to lower production costs (Peñasco & Anadon, 2021), and even guide cities struggling to cope with growing demand. Artificial intelligence supports this work by detecting patterns of waste. It studies the operation of machines, buildings, and transportation systems throughout the day and identifies areas where energy consumption is increasing without delivering tangible benefits. Once these patterns are understood, organizations can take action. They can develop new measures to reduce waste and protect the environment. Resource management is the second major theme. It involves the responsible use of water, minerals, soil, and other vital resources. Many regions face pressures from population growth and climate anomalies. Water scarcity impacts irrigation and domestic water use. Improper waste disposal pollutes land and water bodies. Industrial production processes rapidly deplete resources (Parra-López et al., 2025). Smart sustainability offers tools to help address these issues. It supports water resource planning through systems that track rainfall and reservoir levels. It helps manage waste by improving sorting and recycling. It assists farmers by helping them better understand soil health and crop needs. It also enables industries to monitor their material usage and reduce unnecessary losses. Another important aspect of smart sustainable development is the development of adaptive systems. These systems respond to environmental changes rather than following fixed patterns. Instead, they adjust their behavior according to the actual situation. This flexibility is crucial in times of unpredictable weather. Heat waves increase cooling demand, droughts reduce water supply, and storms disrupt supply chains. Adaptive systems help maintain system stability during these events. They shift energy loads when demand rises, regulate irrigation when water is scarce, and issue early warnings when environmental conditions become dangerous (Naudé, 2012). These foundations provide a solid foundation for researchers, planners, and engineers to develop new solutions. They encourage new ideas for cleaner production, efficient transportation, and responsible agriculture. They facilitate the testing and impact assessment of improvements. They also support collaboration between different sectors. Energy planners, urban designers, farmers, and environmental organizations can collaborate using shared information. This creates a unified approach to sustainable development.

Smart sustainability is more than just adding technology to existing systems; it reshapes society's understanding of its relationship with the environment. It emphasizes long-term thinking, responsible resource use, and a deep understanding of ecological limits. It paves an innovative path that respects nature and supports economic development. Through these principles, institutions gain the tools needed to build a stable, resilient, and equitable future for the benefit of future generations.

3. ARTIFICIAL INTELLIGENCE IN ENERGY SYSTEMS

Artificial intelligence strengthens modern energy systems by improving how electricity is produced, managed, and consumed. The applications listed in Table1 highlight how AI supports both operational efficiency and long-term sustainability. From predicting household and industrial demand to balancing power distribution across regions, AI enables grid operators to make faster and more informed decisions. It also plays a crucial role in integrating renewable sources—such as solar and wind—by forecasting weather-driven fluctuations and ensuring a stable supply. Within buildings, AI-driven monitoring reduces unnecessary energy use and helps create smarter, greener, and more comfortable spaces (As shown in Table 1). Together, these applications demonstrate how digital intelligence is reshaping the energy sector and guiding the transition toward cleaner and more resilient energy systems.

Table 1. Key Applications of AI in Energy Systems

AI Application Area	Purpose	How AI Works	Key Benefits	Sector Examples
Energy Demand Prediction	Forecast short- and long-term electricity needs	Uses historical consumption, weather variations, and behavioural patterns	Prevents blackouts, reduces wastage, supports stable grid operation	Homes, industries, commercial clusters
Smart Energy Distribution	Balance electricity flow across regions	Analyzes load data, detects overload risks, recommends adjustments	Reduces grid stress, avoids outages, improves reliability	Urban grids, regional distribution networks
Renewable Energy Integration	Manage fluctuations in solar and wind power	Predicts sunlight, wind speed, climate behaviour using AI models	Improves renewable stability, reduces reliance on fossil fuel backup	Solar farms, wind parks, hybrid microgrids
Smart Buildings & Energy Saving	Optimize energy use inside buildings	Tracks occupancy, appliance loads, temperature patterns	Cuts energy bills, reduces emissions, increases equipment life	Offices, malls, universities, residential complexes

3.1. Energy Demand Prediction

Energy demand forecasting plays a crucial role in maintaining a stable and efficient energy system. Daily energy consumption fluctuates due to a variety of factors. Weather changes affect heating or cooling demand. People's daily routines determine energy consumption in the morning, evening, and weekends. Industrial activity can also lead to sudden increases in demand. Seasonal variations further complicate these fluctuations (Zou et al., 2025). Traditional forecasting methods rely on limited observational data and simple forecasting tools, failing to comprehensively capture the diverse factors influencing energy demand.. Modern digital systems offer a more powerful approach. They analyze detailed information collected from homes, factories, transportation systems, and weather services. This helps analysts understand how electricity demand changes under different conditions. With this information, energy suppliers can more accurately predict peak electricity demand periods and prepare the grid before demand surges. This prevents sudden power shortages and reduces the need for emergency measures. Simultaneously, it avoids energy surplus, thus preventing energy waste and increased operating costs. Reliable demand forecasting aids in long-term planning. Grid operators can schedule maintenance during periods of low demand and flexibly switch between different energy sources without interrupting power supply. This is crucial for systems that incorporate renewable energy, as the output of solar and wind power fluctuates rapidly. Accurate forecasting helps the grid respond smoothly to these changes.

Robust forecasting methods can enhance the resilience of energy systems, support the efficient use of resources, and help suppliers provide stable services to industry and households in a responsible and sustainable manner.

3.2. Smart Energy Distribution

A stable energy system depends on the ability to distribute electricity evenly and promptly. Distribution networks must respond quickly when supply and demand change across different regions. If one region receives more electricity than it needs, equipment may become overloaded (Saleh et al., 2025). If another region receives insufficient electricity, consumers face power shortages. Modern power grids must prevent both scenarios to maintain power reliability and protect infrastructure. Digital systems support this process by studying changes in electricity demand throughout the day. These systems track patterns related to weather, economic activity, and local resident behavior. They observe when electricity demand peaks and troughs in a specific area. Based on these insights, the systems guide distribution units to adjust power delivery. Each area receives an amount of electricity that matches its current situation. This approach maintains grid balance and reduces the risk of sudden outages, thus avoiding disruptions to homes, industry, and essential services. Energy distribution networks also face technological losses. These losses naturally occur when electricity is transmitted over long distances through wires and transformers. However, inefficient lines or outdated infrastructure exacerbate these losses, resulting in a waste of valuable resources. Digital systems help mitigate this problem. They analyze network structure (Pooya et al., 2025), study power flow, and detect areas where losses are higher than expected. They then propose adjustments. These recommendations might include rerouting power to more efficient paths or upgrading equipment that is slowing down the network. Better management of technology waste helps achieve environmental goals. Reducing waste means lower energy consumption and reduced emissions. This also helps suppliers reduce costs and provide more reliable services.

Balanced energy distribution and reduced losses are fundamental to building a robust energy system. Combined with sound planning, these capabilities enable the creation of a power grid that operates smoothly even under pressure. They underpin a future where energy is used rationally and transmitted stably and efficiently.

3.3. Integration of Renewable Energy

Solar and wind power are central to sustainable development. They provide clean energy, avoiding the emissions of traditional energy sources. Their impact is significant, but their power generation is not always stable. Solar panels rely on direct sunlight. Cloud cover, dust, and seasonal changes can reduce their power generation efficiency within minutes (Kumar & Rathore, 2023). Wind turbines face similar uncertainties. Wind speed and direction can change without warning. These fluctuations present challenges for energy planners, who must ensure the grid operates stably even when renewable energy generation declines. To address this challenge, modern systems perform extremely detailed analyses of weather conditions. They collect information from satellites, sensors, and local observations, and study how weather patterns evolve over time. By analyzing this information, systems can predict the availability of solar or wind power. Grid operators then use these forecasts to plan electricity distribution. When renewable energy generation decreases, the grid prepares by increasing the supply of other energy sources. When renewable energy generation increases, the grid reduces the load on conventional power plants. This ensures a stable power supply. Accurate forecasting also helps achieve long-term environmental goals. When energy suppliers anticipate a significant increase in renewable energy generation, they can reduce the use of fossil fuel units. This reduces emissions and saves fuel. It also reduces wear and tear on equipment that would otherwise require high-load operation. During periods of ample sunshine or stable winds, renewable energy can dominate, allowing conventional power plants to operate at lower power levels.

More accurate forecasts give energy systems greater flexibility, strengthen the role of clean energy, and help the power grid transition to sustainable development. By understanding natural variability, planners can make responsible choices that balance stability and environmental protection.

3.4. Smart Buildings and Energy Saving

Buildings consume the majority of the world's energy. They rely on electricity for lighting, cooling, heating, and daily operations. This presents an opportunity to conserve energy through sophisticated monitoring and control. Modern digital systems support energy conservation by monitoring space usage. They track lighting levels, indoor temperatures, appliance operation, and the activities of people within the building. Once these patterns are understood, the system adjusts building functions to avoid energy waste (Dinmohammadi et al., 2025). When a room is unoccupied, cooling equipment can reduce its operating speed or shut off automatically. When a corridor or office is unoccupied, lighting can automatically turn off. Unnecessary power-consuming appliances can be identified and managed more effectively. These measures may seem insignificant individually, but their combined effect can significantly reduce energy consumption in the long run (Gul & Patidar, 2015).

Intelligent building systems also help protect equipment. Machines operate only when needed, reducing the load on equipment. This reduces wear and tear, delaying the need for maintenance or replacement. Ultimately, buildings are able to use energy more efficiently, save costs, and better maintain their infrastructure.

4. ARTIFICIAL INTELLIGENCE IN RESOURCE MANAGEMENT

Artificial intelligence is transforming resource management by enabling more accurate monitoring, faster decision-making, and responsible use of natural assets. Whether it is tracking water availability, improving waste collection routes, or guiding farmers with real-time field insights, AI helps reduce inefficiencies that were previously difficult to detect. These tools also strengthen industrial operations by minimizing material losses and predicting equipment failures before they disrupt production. By combining continuous data collection with intelligent analysis, AI supports long-term sustainability and ensures that vital resources are used wisely, efficiently, and with greater environmental responsibility (As shown in Table 2).

Table 2. Key Applications of AI in Resource Management

AI Application Area	Purpose	How AI Works	Key Benefits	Sector Examples
Water Resource Management	Monitor, predict, and optimize water availability	Uses sensor data, rainfall patterns, soil moisture, and consumption trends	Reduces water wastage, improves supply planning, early leak detection	Irrigation systems, municipal water supply, reservoirs
Smart Waste Management	Improve waste collection, sorting, and recycling efficiency	Analyzes bin-level data, image recognition for sorting, real-time route optimization	Cuts fuel use, increases recycling rates, reduces landfill burden	Cities, waste treatment plants, recycling centers
Precision Agriculture & Land Use	Enhance crop productivity and resource use	Monitors soil health, crop stress, weather conditions, pest behaviour	Saves water and fertilizers, improves yields, protects soil quality	Farmlands, greenhouses, agricultural planning agencies
Industrial Resource Optimization	Reduce raw material waste and monitor equipment health	Tracks material flow, detects anomalies, predicts machine failures	Lowers production cost, minimizes waste, ensures regulatory compliance	Manufacturing plants, mining, processing industries

4.1. Water Resource Management

Many parts of the world are increasingly facing water scarcity. Population growth, climate change, and ever-increasing demand are putting immense pressure on already limited water resources. Effective management requires continuous monitoring and timely action. Modern digital systems assist relevant agencies by improving water resource monitoring and control (Bose et al., 2024). These systems monitor water levels in reservoirs, rivers, and storage tanks, collecting information through sensors that operate around the clock. This information reveals patterns of change in water availability and helps detect signs of water shortage early. After analyzing this data, the system can predict the likelihood of a drop in water supply. Authorities can use these predictions to plan water supply schedules, store water in advance, or implement water-saving measures. This approach reduces the risk of unexpected water shortages and helps communities prepare for challenging seasons. Agriculture also benefits significantly. Rainfall is difficult to predict in many areas. Farmers struggle to decide when and how much water to irrigate. Digital tools help them by analyzing soil moisture, evaporation rates, and historical weather records. This information guides farmers to develop more rational irrigation plans, thereby protecting crops and reducing unnecessary water use (Hajirad, 2025). Water supply networks also face challenges related to leaks. Aging pipes, poor maintenance, and undetected damage can lead to persistent leaks. Smart water supply systems help address this issue by tracking water flow within the network. They can detect changes in flow patterns, thus identifying potential leaks. Early detection of leaks allows maintenance teams to act before large-scale leaks occur. This helps conserve water and reduce costs (Javed et al., 2025).

Strengthening monitoring, forecasting, and leak detection helps enhance water resource management. These tools help agencies use limited resources responsibly and prepare for periods of stress. They also create opportunities to develop long-term plans to protect communities and ecosystems.

4.2. Waste Management

Population growth leads to a continuous increase in waste volume. Cities struggle to cope with this growth because traditional waste management systems rely on slow and labor-intensive methods. Manual sorting is one example. Workers must manually separate different types of waste, which is both time-consuming and error-prone. Furthermore, waste collection routes follow fixed schedules that remain unchanged even as circumstances shift. Consequently, some areas collect waste too early, while others face delays. These inefficiencies result in increased costs and a greater environmental impact (Asofarati et al., 2025). Modern digital tools offer a more efficient way of processing waste. They sort waste by analyzing images captured by cameras in sorting facilities. These systems are able to more accurately distinguish between plastics, paper, glass, and other materials. Faster, more accurate sorting helps increase recycling rates and reduce the amount of waste sent to landfills. Real-time information also greatly benefits waste collection operations. Digital systems can track the fullness of waste bins in different communities and monitor traffic conditions and vehicle availability. Based on this information, the system plans routes to avoid unnecessary trips. Garbage trucks only go to specific areas when needed, thereby reducing fuel consumption and emissions and improving the overall efficiency of waste management services. Seasonal changes affect waste generation. Holidays, harvest seasons, and public holidays often cause temporary increases in waste. Smart systems analyze historical records and observe patterns associated with these events. They can predict when waste will increase and estimate the additional processing capacity needed. Planners can then allocate personnel, vehicles, and sorting facilities more effectively (Olawade et al., 2024).

Improved classification, dynamic pathway planning, and seasonal forecasting combine to create a modern waste management strategy. These measures can reduce environmental stress and help communities maintain a cleaner, more sustainable environment.

4.3. Agriculture and Land Use

Agriculture is highly dependent on energy, water, and land. Farms need fuel to power machinery, electricity for storage, and water for irrigation. These demands put pressure on natural resources, especially in areas under climate stress or with rapid population growth. Modern digital tools help farmers manage these resources more effectively. They support a practice known as precision agriculture, which focuses on observing specific conditions in the field and making precise responses (Gunapala et al., 2025). These systems monitor soil moisture, crop growth, and signs of pest and disease activity, and track weather patterns, soil nutrients, and plant health. By combining this information, farmers can gain a clearer understanding of their fields' needs at any given time. They can irrigate only where needed, control fertilizer application, and select crop varieties suited to their local environment (Aarif et al., 2025). These measures reduce waste, protect soil quality, and contribute to increased yields and more stable harvests.. Digital tools can also help governments and planners make better land-use decisions. Land-use planning requires careful balancing, as the same area may simultaneously attract the attention of agricultural, industrial, and environmental organizations. These systems use detailed environmental data to identify which areas are best suited for agricultural production and which should be protected. They can also highlight areas where industrial development can be carried out without damaging natural ecosystems (Abiri et al., 2023).

This guideline aims to support long-term sustainable development. It prevents land degradation, reduces conflicts between various needs, and protects biodiversity. When farmers and planners have accurate information, they can use the land responsibly and support resilient agricultural systems that benefit both communities and the environment.

4.4. Industrial Resource Use

Industries across the board rely on a stable supply of raw materials to maintain production. Waste of raw materials leads to increased costs and a heavier environmental burden. Many losses occur silently during production, potentially stemming from machine malfunctions, improper operation, or outdated processes. Modern digital systems help businesses understand where these losses are occurring. They monitor production lines, analyzing the flow of raw materials at each stage. When abnormal patterns emerge, the system highlights them to operators (Kareem et al., 2023). This enables industries to recover raw materials that would otherwise be wasted and reuse them efficiently. These tools can also monitor equipment status. Factories often face delays and significant losses due to unexpected machine malfunctions. By monitoring vibration, temperature, and performance levels, the system can warn engineers before a failure occurs. Early maintenance reduces waste, saves energy, and helps maintain production continuity, avoiding major disruptions.

Furthermore, all industries must comply with environmental regulations. A key requirement is the diligent tracking of emissions. Intelligent monitoring systems support this responsibility by monitoring emission levels around the clock. When emission levels rise, the system notifies management and helps ensure that plants operate within legally mandated limits.

5. ARTIFICIAL INTELLIGENCE IN SMART CITIES

Artificial intelligence is becoming a crucial pillar in the development of modern smart cities. By analysing real-time data from transportation, utilities, and public spaces, AI helps planners design more efficient and citizen-friendly environments. These systems improve traffic flow, enhance public safety, and provide early warnings for pollution or extreme weather conditions. AI also supports smart utility services, ensuring that electricity, water, and waste systems operate smoothly with minimal disruptions (As shown in Table 3). Together, these applications create cities that are more responsive, sustainable, and better equipped to meet the needs of growing urban populations.

Table 3. Key Applications of AI in Smart Cities

AI Application Area	Purpose	How AI Works	Key Benefits	Sector Examples
Urban Infrastructure Planning	Improve city design and service distribution	Analyzes traffic patterns, population density, and utility usage	Better urban layouts, reduced congestion, improved service delivery	City planning departments, municipal agencies
Smart Mobility & Public Transport	Enhance traffic flow and public transport efficiency	Uses real-time traffic data, passenger trends, and predictive algorithms	Less congestion, lower fuel use, reliable bus/train services	Traffic control centers, metro & bus systems
Environmental Monitoring	Detect pollution, noise, and temperature hotspots	Uses sensor networks, satellite feeds, and pattern analysis	Early warnings, healthier living conditions, informed policy-making	Air-quality stations, urban health departments

5.1. Urban Infrastructure Planning

With the increasing pressures of urban development and population growth, urban infrastructure planning has become increasingly important. Traffic congestion, pollution, and excessive energy consumption are common problems faced by many urban areas. These issues affect people's daily lives and pose long-term environmental risks. Effective planning requires a clear understanding of how people travel, how services are used, and how weather conditions affect urban activities (Sarker et al., 2024). Modern digital tools help planners collect and study this information. They observe road usage at different times of day, analyze public transportation records, walking routes, and changes in travel behavior during special events or inclement weather. They also study the usage of electricity, water, and other essential services. When this information is aggregated, planners gain a detailed understanding of how the city is functioning. They can then design transportation networks that reduce travel times and ensure safe travel for people. They can also identify areas that need new public facilities, such as parks, health centers, or community spaces (Li & Shalaby, 2024). Smart planning directly contributes to achieving environmental goals. By improving traffic flow and encouraging the use of public transportation, cities can reduce fuel consumption and emissions. Well-planned infrastructure can also support efficient energy use through more rational building design and service allocation. These improvements enhance urban comfort and create healthier community environments (Elassy et al., 2024).

Detailed planning using digital tools enables cities to better adapt to modern challenges. It strengthens public services, supports sustainable development, and improves the quality of life for residents.

5.2. Smart Mobility and Public Transport

Smart mobility and efficient public transportation are crucial for the smooth operation of modern cities. Traffic congestion remains one of the most glaring urban problems. Long queues at intersections not only waste fuel and exacerbate air pollution, but also stress commuters. These delays also reduce the efficiency of emergency services and public transportation. Addressing these challenges requires a system capable of handling changing traffic conditions throughout the day. Modern digital tools support this work by monitoring traffic flow on major roads and intersections. They study vehicle movement during peak hours, weekends, holidays, and emergencies. Based on these observations, the system adjusts traffic lights to alleviate congestion. When traffic is heavy, the lights extend the green light time; when traffic is light, the lights speed up the green light transition. This reduces waiting times and ensures smooth traffic flow (Dimri et al., 2024). Public transportation systems also benefit from this approach. Buses and trains operate more efficiently when routes are matched to actual travel demand. Smart mobility systems study travel patterns in different communities, identifying areas where bus services need to be increased and areas where services can be reduced without impacting commuters. This improves the reliability of public transportation, making it a more attractive daily travel option (Yan et al., 2021). Shared transportation is another important component of smart mobility. When people use shared car, bicycle, or shuttle services, the number of private cars on the road decreases. This helps alleviate traffic congestion and improve air quality. Digital systems support shared transportation by tracking vehicle availability, managing booking platforms, and directing vehicles to areas with higher demand (Vătămănescu et al., 2024).

Smart mobility helps create cleaner, more organized cities. It enhances public transportation, reduces fuel consumption, and creates safer roads. When combined with good planning and community engagement, it can support long-term sustainable development and improve the quality of life for all city residents.

5.3. Environmental Monitoring

Environmental monitoring is a crucial component of modern urban life management. Urban areas generate noise, pollution, and the heat island effect due to traffic, industry, high-density buildings, and human activities. These factors can impact public health and reduce the quality of daily life. Effective management requires continuous monitoring of environmental indicators to identify and address problems early (Wang et al., 2024). Modern digital tools aid this process by monitoring air quality, noise levels, and temperature patterns throughout the city. Sensors installed on busy streets, in residential areas, and in industrial zones collect information around the clock. When pollution or noise levels exceed safe levels, the system alerts local authorities. This allows authorities to react quickly, such as implementing traffic controls, inspecting industrial sites, or issuing public notices. These alerts also help protect vulnerable groups, such as children, the elderly, or people with respiratory illnesses (Kerckhoffs et al., 2025). Environmental monitoring also supports long-term planning. Planners use the collected information to determine which areas need more green space, cleaner transportation routes, or reduced traffic flow. This helps guide site selection decisions for parks, bike paths, and tree cover. Better planning can reduce pollution and improve urban comfort (Aslanoğlu et al., 2025).

In densely populated cities, high temperatures are another major challenge. Concrete and metal absorb heat during the day and slowly release it at night. This creates the urban heat island effect, leading to higher temperatures. Digital systems can study thermal patterns and detect hotspots. Planners can then use this information to design cooler urban layouts, such as increasing shade, vegetation, and improving air circulation (Ishak et al., 2025).

Through continuous monitoring and meticulous planning, cities can create a healthier and more sustainable environment for their residents.

5.4. AI in Smart Cities: Case Examples

Artificial intelligence plays a central role in the development of smart cities by supporting efficient urban services, improving sustainability, and enhancing the overall quality of life for residents. Through continuous analysis of traffic flows, utility usage, environmental conditions, and public safety data, AI enables cities to operate in a more responsive and resource-efficient manner. These systems help planners anticipate demand, optimize urban mobility, and reduce the environmental impacts caused by congestion and inefficient service delivery. AI-powered platforms also support predictive maintenance, allowing city authorities to identify faults in infrastructure—such as streetlights, water pipelines, or transportation systems—before they disrupt daily life. In addition, AI strengthens public safety through smart surveillance, anomaly detection, and real-time emergency response coordination. Environmental sustainability is further improved through AI-driven monitoring of air quality, noise levels, and temperature variations, which guide urban design and policy decisions.

Case Example 1: Singapore

Singapore has implemented an advanced AI-driven mobility management system that analyzes real-time traffic data from sensors and cameras. By automatically adjusting traffic signals based on current road conditions, the system reduces congestion, shortens travel time, and lowers vehicle emissions. This approach not only improves traffic flow but also contributes to Singapore's long-term sustainability goals.

Case Example 2: Barcelona

Barcelona uses AI-enabled environmental sensors distributed across the city to track pollution levels, noise intensity, and microclimatic variations. The data helps city planners identify pollution hotspots and redesign public spaces to improve airflow, reduce heat concentration, and enhance walking and cycling conditions. These AI-driven insights support healthier and more liveable urban environments.

6. SECTOR SPECIFIC APPLICATIONS

Artificial intelligence is reshaping multiple sectors by improving how energy, materials, and transportation resources are managed. In manufacturing, AI helps reduce waste and ensures that machines operate efficiently throughout the production cycle. Transportation and logistics benefit from smart routing and warehouse automation, which lower fuel use and improve overall supply chain performance. In construction, AI-driven planning tools help estimate material requirements accurately and support designs that use less energy over a building's lifetime (As shown in Table 4). Together, these applications demonstrate how AI can create cleaner, more efficient, and more resilient systems across key economic sectors.

Table 4. Sector-Specific Applications of AI in Sustainable Development

Sector	Purpose	How AI Works	Key Benefits	Examples of Use
Manufacturing	Improve energy efficiency and reduce material waste	Monitors machine performance, analyzes energy use, tracks raw material flow	Lower energy costs, reduced wastage, optimized production schedules	Smart factories, automated production lines
Transportation & Logistics	Enhance route planning and optimize resource use	Studies traffic patterns, delivery schedules, vehicle load, and warehouse conditions	Reduced fuel consumption, fewer emissions, efficient warehousing	Fleet management, cold storage, supply chain planning
Construction	Improve material estimation and support sustainable building design	Analyzes architectural data, predicts material needs, models lighting and ventilation patterns	Reduced construction waste, cost savings, energy-efficient buildings	Smart construction planning, green building design

6.1. Manufacturing

Manufacturing relies on a stable and typically abundant energy supply. Factories operate numerous machines simultaneously, and even minor inefficiencies can lead to significant waste. Modern digital systems help manufacturers understand the performance of their equipment during daily operation. These systems analyze machine power consumption at different times and identify patterns that indicate unnecessary consumption. Once these patterns are detected, the system recommends appropriate settings or adjustments to reduce energy consumption without compromising product quality (Cagno et al., 2025). These tools also help factories plan their work more efficiently. By coordinating production schedules, they can reduce energy demand during peak hours. Shifting non-urgent work to off-peak hours can alleviate grid pressure and reduce operating costs. In the long run, these improvements contribute to both environmental goals and cost savings. Resource management is another crucial aspect of manufacturing. Factories rely on raw materials, which must be handled with care to avoid losses. Digital systems monitor the supply chain by tracking raw materials from suppliers to storage areas and ultimately to the production line. The system alerts managers when raw materials are at risk of spoilage, delays, or misplacement. Efficient materials management reduces waste and ensures smoother production processes (Massari et al., 2025).

These practices collectively enhance the sustainability of the manufacturing sector and improve long-term productivity.

6.2. Transportation and Logistics

Transportation and logistics are the backbone of economic activity. Goods move daily between cities and regions, and these movements are highly dependent on fuel. When routes are too long or poorly planned, vehicles consume unnecessary fuel. This not only increases costs but also exacerbates air pollution. Modern digital tools help address this challenge by improving route planning. They analyze traffic conditions, road quality, delivery schedules, and weather patterns. Based on this information, vehicles are guided to shorter, smoother routes. This reduces travel time, saves fuel, and lowers emissions (Saki & Soori, 2025). Warehouses can also benefit from these systems. Large warehousing facilities require lighting, refrigeration, and machinery. If poorly managed, this equipment can run continuously when not needed. Modern monitoring tools can monitor warehouse operations and turn equipment on or off as needed. Lighting is only turned on when staff are present. Refrigeration systems adjust according to the temperature of specific storage areas. These measures can reduce energy consumption and improve cost-effectiveness (Boysen & De Koster, 2025). Smart logistics can also improve resource utilization efficiency in other ways. Packaging is a key example. Over-packaging increases waste and drives up transportation costs. More accurate inventory forecasting helps businesses prepare the right amount of materials, avoiding unnecessary inventory buildup. When businesses understand the changing trends in demand throughout the year, they can plan their packaging needs more accurately. This not only reduces waste but also improves the overall sustainability of the supply chain.

By combining efficient transportation routes, responsible warehousing management, and precise inventory planning, modern logistics systems can support cleaner and more economical transportation operations.

6.3. Construction

Buildings play a vital role in urban development, requiring large quantities of materials such as cement, steel, sand, and water. These materials are derived from finite natural resources, making meticulous planning crucial. Overestimating material usage leads to waste, ultimately resulting in discarded materials; underestimating it causes project delays, necessitates additional transportation, and increases costs and environmental impact. Modern digital tools help address these challenges by improving the accuracy of material estimations. They studied architectural designs, structural requirements, and data from previous projects to determine the correct amount of materials needed at each stage of construction. This reduced waste and supported responsible resource use (Al-Numan, 2024). These systems also help architects and engineers design buildings whose performance improves over time.

They assess changes in lighting, ventilation, and temperature within the planned building. This allows designers to incorporate energy-efficient features such as natural lighting, improved insulation, and optimized airflow. Ultimately, this will result in buildings consuming less energy throughout their entire lifespan.

Intelligent construction planning helps create resilient cities. It supports stronger buildings, more efficient infrastructure, and responsible land development. When construction practices utilize accurate information and sustainable design principles, they can reduce environmental impact and create safe, efficient, and comfortable urban spaces for future generations.

7. ENABLERS OF SMART SUSTAINABILITY

7.1 Digital Governance and Policy Frameworks

Effective governance is important to make sure that digital technologies support sustainability and also protect public interests. Digital governance provides clear rules, policies, and systems. These guide how technologies like AI, IoT, and data based platforms work in society. Governments play the main role. They set policies for responsible use of technology. They also create standards that allow different systems to work together. They promote ethical use of digital tools in all sectors.

Many countries now focus on digital sustainability. The European Union has the AI Act which highlights transparency and accountability. India's Digital India Mission supports digital infrastructure, smart cities, and responsible data use. Groups like ISO and IEEE also introduce standards for smart cities, energy use, cybersecurity, and ethical use of technology. These standards help keep digital sustainability efforts safe, fair, and in line with public expectations.

Governments also run programmes that support digital growth. Examples include smart grid upgrades, clean energy programmes, and national open data systems. These efforts reduce gaps in implementation. When regulations, incentives, and training come together, they create a strong policy environment. This helps countries adopt sustainable digital solutions in a smooth and responsible way.

7.2 Data Governance, Cybersecurity, and Interoperability

Smart sustainability systems depend on vast volumes of data generated by sensors, digital devices, and AI platforms. Without proper data governance, these systems can become vulnerable to misuse, privacy breaches, and operational failures. Data governance provides a structured approach to managing data access, storage, security, and sharing across different stakeholders.

Cybersecurity is one of the most critical concerns. Smart grids, autonomous mobility platforms, and digital public services are part of cyber-physical systems, where a single breach can disrupt energy supply, transportation networks, or essential services. AI-enabled anomaly detection, encryption, network monitoring, and secure authentication protocols help safeguard these infrastructures from cyber threats.

Interoperability is another major challenge. Smart systems often use different communication protocols, hardware configurations, and data formats. Lack of interoperability reduces efficiency and increases costs. International standards like ISO 37120 (smart city indicators), IEEE P2413 (IoT architecture), and ITU-T standards help ensure compatibility across devices and platforms.

Responsible data-sharing frameworks—such as open-data portals, consent-based sharing, and secure multi-party exchange—ensure that data contributes to sustainability goals while respecting privacy, security, and ethical considerations.

7.3 Performance Measurement and Sustainability KPIs

Quantitative performance indicators (KPIs) are essential for assessing whether digital and AI-driven sustainability initiatives deliver the intended environmental and economic benefits. These metrics allow organizations to track progress, benchmark performance, and validate the impact of smart interventions.

Common sustainability KPIs include:

- **Energy Efficiency Metrics:** peak load reduction, energy savings percentage, and equipment efficiency improvements
- **Environmental Metrics:** CO_2 emissions avoided, pollution reduction levels, waste minimization, and water savings
- **Operational KPIs:** system uptime, predictive maintenance accuracy, average response time, and process automation improvements
- **Smart City KPIs:** ISO 37122 performance metrics related to mobility, environment, governance, and digital participation
- **AI Technical Metrics:** accuracy, false alarm rates, model precision and recall, stability over time

Global evaluation frameworks—such as the ITU "United for Smart Sustainable Cities (U4SSC)" KPIs and the Global Smart City Index—provide standardized assessment tools. Integrating these KPIs into project planning helps ensure that digital sustainability projects remain results-driven and transparent.

7.4 Stakeholder Collaboration and Partnerships

Smart sustainability initiatives depend on the coordinated involvement of multiple stakeholders, each contributing unique skills, resources, and perspectives. Government agencies offer regulatory oversight, funding, and public service infrastructure. The private sector drives technological innovation, platform development, and digital solution deployment. Community groups and citizens contribute local knowledge, participate in decision-making, and ensure that digital tools address real needs.

Public–private partnerships (PPPs) are widely used to implement smart sustainability projects, particularly in areas like smart grids, mobility management, smart buildings, and data platforms. Universities and research institutions play a complementary role by testing new technologies, evaluating pilot projects, and generating insights that guide policy development.

Inclusive stakeholder engagement—through digital participation platforms, community consultations, and co-design frameworks—ensures that technology adoption aligns with local priorities, cultural contexts, and user needs. Such collaborations improve trust, transparency, and long-term sustainability of digital systems.

8. BENEFITS OF SMART SUSTAINABILITY

Smart sustainable development offers clear and tangible benefits to governments, businesses, and society. It strengthens environmental protection while enhancing economic stability. One of its most significant advantages is improved energy efficiency. When organizations understand how they use energy, they can identify waste and replace inefficient practices with more efficient methods. This not only reduces unnecessary consumption but also lowers emissions. Furthermore, it reduces reliance on traditional, costly, or resource-limited energy sources, thereby ensuring national energy security. Industries across the board benefit. Many production systems harbor long-standing, unnoticed inefficiencies. Modern digital tools can reveal these problems and guide operators to make better choices. This not only improves productivity and reduces operating costs but also promotes responsible material use and cleaner production methods. When industries adopt these practices, they can contribute to achieving broader environmental goals without sacrificing economic growth. Smart sustainability also inspires innovation. Organizations begin exploring new technologies, business models, and resource management methods. They learn how to creatively use data to reduce waste, conserve water, or improve energy efficiency. This process enhances expertise in fields such as engineering, planning, management, and research. It also helps develop green industries, thereby strengthening the long-term resilience of the economy. As more institutions adopt sustainable development practices, they will create new jobs and boost local economies. Government agencies benefit from improved planning and decision-making. With more reliable information, they can formulate policies that reflect real-world conditions. They can plan infrastructure projects to support clean transportation, efficient buildings, and robust public services. Smart sustainability also helps them respond quickly to environmental risks. Early warnings of pollution, water shortages, or heat events enable them to act promptly to protect public health. Communities can directly benefit from these advantages. Cleaner air reduces respiratory illnesses. Safer water improves public health. Well-managed waste management systems reduce land pollution, creating a cleaner community environment. Efficient energy systems reduce service disruptions and improve comfort in homes, schools, and workplaces. Furthermore, smart sustainability supports more reliable public services, including transportation, lighting, and emergency response.

These advantages enhance overall quality of life. They enable societies to achieve responsible development while protecting natural systems. Smart sustainable development creates a balanced approach that allows environmental protection, economic development, and community well-being to go hand in hand.

9. CHALLENGES AND LIMITATIONS

Smart sustainability relies on modern digital tools, but numerous challenges hinder its widespread adoption. Many organizations face a shortage of skilled workers. Running complex systems requires knowledge of data analytics, system maintenance, and digital planning. Without adequate training, these tools may fail to function as intended. This diminishes the value of intelligent systems and increases the risk of errors. Training programs are crucial, but they require time, money, and long-term investment.

Cost is another major obstacle. Advanced systems require sensors, computing platforms, and reliable network connectivity. Large enterprises may be able to afford these costs, but small businesses often cannot. Balancing daily operational needs with the adoption of new technologies is inherently challenging. Without financial support or resource sharing, the development of smart and sustainable development across different industries and regions is likely to remain uneven.

Data quality has raised further concerns. Digital systems rely on accurate information to make effective decisions. When data is incomplete, outdated, or improperly collected, conclusions become unreliable. This not only fails to solve problems but also misleads planners and leads to further waste. Beyond data quality, privacy has also become a core issue. The surveillance of activities in cities, homes, or workplaces has raised questions about how information is used. We need clear rules to protect citizens and maintain trust.

Ethical considerations must also be given due attention. Over-reliance on digital systems could impair human judgment. Important decisions should not be entirely entrusted to machines. Human oversight remains crucial, especially in areas such as public safety, environmental regulation, and resource allocation. Systems must also avoid bias. If the underlying data itself is unequal, the system may replicate or amplify those inequalities. Fairness and accountability must be integrated into every stage of system design.

Environmental concerns exacerbate this tension. While smart sustainability aims to reduce emissions and improve resource efficiency, these technologies themselves require energy. Large data centers consume vast amounts of electricity. If this energy comes from fossil fuels, the environmental benefits are significantly diminished. Therefore, organizations must carefully plan to ensure that digital solutions support sustainability without creating new burdens.

Despite these challenges, the potential for smart sustainability remains enormous. Bridging skills gaps, improving data quality, and building ethical frameworks will help build confidence in these tools. Combining technological advancements with environmental responsibility can ensure that digital systems contribute to, rather than undermine, long-term sustainable development.

10. FUTURE DIRECTIONS

A smart and sustainable future depends on responsible development and careful planning. Several key trends are shaping this future, each with the potential to deliver significant long-term environmental and social benefits. A significant trend is the widespread adoption of distributed energy systems. Many communities are beginning to install small solar power plants, rooftop solar panels, and local energy storage devices. These systems operate independently of the large national grid, helping to alleviate pressure on the central grid. Even in remote areas, they can provide energy for homes, schools, and small businesses. Digital tools will help manage these networks by analyzing solar patterns, battery levels, and electricity usage habits. For example, a rural area using a local solar system could rely on digital monitoring to determine when to store electricity and when to share excess power with nearby residents. The second trend is the rise of the circular economy. Its focus is on reducing waste by encouraging reuse, repair, and recycling. Digital tools will help track the flow of materials at different stages. For example, factories can record how much metal enters the production line, how much is used, and how much eventually becomes waste. Digital tracking can guide factories to recycle surplus metal and reintegrate it into the recycling system, rather than discarding it directly. Over time, this approach can alleviate pressure on natural resources. The third trend is increased community engagement. People will increasingly use mobile apps to track their energy consumption, water usage, and waste disposal habits. When people can understand their daily activities in real time, they often change their behavior. For example, if a household notices higher electricity consumption at night, they may decide to turn off appliances earlier. If a community tracks water waste, they may develop new water-saving habits during the dry season. These small changes, if emulated by thousands of households, can bring significant environmental benefits. The fourth trend is the expansion of international cooperation. Climate risks affect all countries, and sharing knowledge can enhance global resilience. Countries will exchange tools, scientific methods, and policy approaches. For example, coastal countries facing sea-level rise may adopt flood forecasting technologies developed by other countries. Similarly, countries with strong solar energy technologies can help regions that are beginning to adopt renewable energy.

Research will continue to refine the systems supporting these trends. Future tools must remain transparent, safe, and equitable. They must also minimize environmental costs through energy-efficient design. Responsible development will ensure that smart, sustainable development is achieved without creating new problems. Through careful planning, these technologies can help society build a future where economic development and environmental protection coexist harmoniously.

11. CONCLUSION

Modern digital systems bring a whole new perspective to sustainable development. They help societies move towards responsible energy use and prudent management of natural resources. They improve building performance by reducing unnecessary energy consumption. They support industries by identifying waste and guiding efficient production. They help farms manage water, soil, and crops more precisely. They enhance urban strength by improving transportation networks, public services, and environmental monitoring. They also assist planners in protecting forests, rivers, and fragile ecosystems. However, technology alone cannot guarantee a sustainable future. Digital systems may offer insights and guidance, but organizations must combine them with ethical and responsible practices. We need skilled personnel to operate these systems, interpret information, and make sound decisions. Training programs must help people understand not only how the tools work, but also why they should be used prudently. Strong leadership and informed communities play a crucial role in this process. Governments must also develop policies that support both innovation and environmental protection. Clear guidelines on data use, transparency, and accountability help build trust. Supportive policies encourage institutions and businesses to adopt sustainable solutions without compromising equity or the public good. Smart sustainability offers a balanced path to future development. It helps societies use resources wisely, reduce environmental stress, and enhance their capacity to address global challenges such as climate change. When used properly, digital systems can become partners in long-term sustainable development. They provide guidance, while humans provide judgment, values, and responsibility. Together, they lay the foundation for a stable and environmentally conscious future.

REFERENCES

Aarif, K. O. M., Alam, A., & Hotak, Y. (2025). Smart sensor technologies shaping the future of precision agriculture: Recent advances and future outlooks. *Journal of Sensors*, *2025*(1), 2460098. DOI: 10.1155/js/2460098

Abiri, R., Rizan, N., Balasundram, S. K., Shahbazi, A. B., & Abdul-Hamid, H. (2023). Application of digital technologies for ensuring agricultural productivity. *Heliyon*, *9*(12), e22601. DOI: 10.1016/j.heliyon.2023.e22601

Al-Numan, B. S. O. (2024). Construction industry role in natural resources depletion and how to reduce it. In *Natural Resources Deterioration in MENA Region: Land Degradation, Soil Erosion, and Desertification* (pp. 93–109). Springer. DOI: 10.1007/978-3-031-58315-5_6

Aslanoğlu, R., Kazak, J. K., Szewrański, S., Świąder, M., Arciniegas, G., Chrobak, G., Jakóbiak, A., & Turhan, E. (2025). Ten questions concerning the role of urban greenery in shaping the future of urban areas. *Building and Environment*, *267*, 112154. DOI: 10.1016/j.buildenv.2024.112154

Asofarati, E. O., Adogbeji, V. O., & Enweremadu, C. C. (2025). Sustainable smart waste management solutions for rapidly urbanizing African Cities. *Utilities Policy*, *95*, 101961. DOI: 10.1016/j.jup.2025.101961

Bose, D., Bhattacharya, R., Kaur, T., Banerjee, R., Bhatia, T., Ray, A., Batra, B., Mondal, A., Ghosh, P., & Mondal, S. (2024). Overcoming water, sanitation, and hygiene challenges in critical regions of the global community. *Water-Energy Nexus*, *7*, 277–296. DOI: 10.1016/j.wen.2024.11.003

Boysen, N., & De Koster, R. (2025). 50 years of warehousing research—An operations research perspective. *European Journal of Operational Research*, *320*(3), 449–464. DOI: 10.1016/j.ejor.2024.03.026

Cagno, E., Accordini, D., Thollander, P., Andrei, M., Hasan, A. M., Pessina, S., & Trianni, A. (2025). Energy management and industry 4.0: Analysis of the enabling effects of digitalization on the implementation of energy management practices. *Applied Energy*, *390*, 125877. DOI: 10.1016/j.apenergy.2025.125877

Dimri, S. C., Indu, R., Bajaj, M., Rathore, R. S., Blazek, V., Dutta, A. K., & Alsubai, S. (2024). Modeling of traffic at a road crossing and optimization of waiting time of the vehicles. *Alexandria Engineering Journal*, *98*, 114–129. DOI: 10.1016/j.aej.2024.04.050

Dinmohammadi, F., Farook, A. M., & Shafiee, M. (2025). Improving energy efficiency in buildings with an IoT-based smart monitoring system. *Energies*, *18*(5), 1269. DOI: 10.3390/en18051269

Elassy, M., Al-Hattab, M., Takruri, M., & Badawi, S. (2024). Intelligent transportation systems for sustainable smart cities. *Transportation Engineering*, *16*, 100252. DOI: 10.1016/j.treng.2024.100252

Gul, M. S., & Patidar, S. (2015). Understanding the energy consumption and occupancy of a multi-purpose academic building. *Energy and Building*, *87*, 155–165. DOI: 10.1016/j.enbuild.2014.11.027

Gunapala, R., Gangahagedara, R., Wanasinghe, W. C. S., Samaraweera, A. U., Gamage, A., Rathnayaka, C., ... & Merah, O. (2025). Urban agriculture: A strategic pathway to building resilience and ensuring sustainable food security in cities. *Farming System*, 100150.

Hajirad, I. (2025). Role of artificial intelligence in improving water resource management. *Nutrition and Food Processing, 8*(5), 01–05.

Ishak, N. M., Khan, A., Abdullah, J., Salleh, S. A., & Santamouris, M. (2025). Optimizing seasonal performance of advanced heat mitigation solutions for city-scale thermal management in Greater Kuala Lumpur. *City and Environment Interactions*, *28*, 100219. DOI: 10.1016/j.cacint.2025.100219

Javed, A., Wu, W., Sun, Q., & Dai, Z. (2025). Leak management in water distribution networks through deep reinforcement learning: A review. *Water (Basel)*, *17*(13), 1928. DOI: 10.3390/w17131928

Jiang, J., & Chen, S. (2024). Influence of artificial intelligent in industrial economic sustainability development problems and countermeasures. *Heliyon*, *10*(3), e25079. DOI: 10.1016/j.heliyon.2024.e25079

Kareem, H. A., Riaz, S., Sadia, H., & Mehmood, R. (2023). Industrial waste: Types, sources, pollution potential, and country-wise comparisons. In *Waste Problems and Management in Developing Countries* (pp. 169–203). Apple Academic Press. DOI: 10.1201/9781003283621-8

Kerckhoffs, J., Hofman, J., Khan, J., Adams, M. D., Blanco, M. N., deSouza, P., Durant, J. L., Faridi, S., Fruin, S., Hankey, S., Hassanvand, M. S., Hatzopoulou, M., Hoek, G., de Hoogh, K., Hudda, N., Kushwaha, M., Marshall, J. D., Minet, L., Patton, A. P., & Amini, H. (2025). Mobile monitoring of air pollution. *Environment International*, *202*, 109582. DOI: 10.1016/j.envint.2025.109582

Kirchner-Krath, J., Morschheuser, B., Sicevic, N., Xi, N., von Korflesch, H. F., & Hamari, J. (2024). Challenges in the adoption of sustainability information systems. *International Journal of Information Management*, *77*, 102754. DOI: 10.1016/j.ijinfomgt.2024.102754

Kumar, S., & Rathore, K. (2023). Renewable energy for sustainable development goal of clean and affordable energy. *International Journal of Materials Manufacturing and Sustainable Technologies*, *2*(1), 1–15. DOI: 10.56896/IJMMST.2023.2.1.001

Kumar, V., Sharma, K. V., Kedam, N., Patel, A., Kate, T. R., & Rathnayake, U. (2024). A comprehensive review on smart and sustainable agriculture using IoT technologies. *Smart Agricultural Technology*, *8*, 100487. DOI: 10.1016/j.atech.2024.100487

Li, L., & Shalaby, A. (2024). Navigating the transit network: Understanding riders' information seeking behavior. *Transportation Research Part A, Policy and Practice*, *185*, 104096. DOI: 10.1016/j.tra.2024.104096

Majeed, Y., Khan, M. U., Waseem, M., Zahid, U., Mahmood, F., Majeed, F., Sultan, M., & Raza, A. (2023). Renewable energy as an alternative source. *Energy Reports*, *10*, 344–359. DOI: 10.1016/j.egyr.2023.06.032

Massari, G. F., Nacchiero, R., & Giannoccaro, I. (2025). Transformative supply chains. *International Journal of Production Economics*, *283*, 109562. DOI: 10.1016/j.ijpe.2025.109562

Naudé, M. (2012). Sustainable development and complex adaptive systems. *Corp. Ownership and Control*, *10*(1), 535–546. DOI: 10.22495/cocv10i1c5art5

Okonta, D. E., & Vukovic, V. (2024). Smart cities software applications. *Heliyon*, *10*(12), e32654. DOI: 10.1016/j.heliyon.2024.e32654

Olawade, D. B., Fapohunda, O., Wada, O. Z., Usman, S. O., Ige, A. O., Ajisafe, O., & Oladapo, B. I. (2024). Smart waste management. *Waste Management Bulletin*, *2*(2).

Parra-López, C., Abdallah, S. B., Garcia-Garcia, G., Hassoun, A., Trollman, H., Jagtap, S., & Carmona-Torres, C. (2025). Digital technologies for water management in agriculture. *Agricultural Water Management*, *309*, 109347. DOI: 10.1016/j.agwat.2025.109347

Peñasco, C., & Anadon, L. D. (2021). Assessing the effectiveness of energy efficiency measures. *IAEE Conference Proceedings*.

Pimenow, S., Pimenowa, O., & Prus, P. (2024). Challenges of artificial intelligence development in energy consumption. *Energies*, *17*(23), 5965. DOI: 10.3390/en17235965

Pooya, P., Milad, J., Amidi, A. M., Zangeneh, M. R., & Jordi-Roger, R. (2025). Technical losses in power networks. *Electronics (Basel)*, *14*(17), 3442. DOI: 10.3390/electronics14173442

Saki, S., & Soori, M. (2025). Artificial intelligence, machine learning and deep learning in advanced transportation systems. *Multimodal Transportation, 100242*.

Saleh, A. M., Vokony, I., Waseem, M., Khan, M. A., & Al-Areqi, A. (2025). Power system stability. *Energy Reports*, *13*, 2637–2663. DOI: 10.1016/j.egyr.2025.02.001

Sarker, T., Fan, P., Messina, J. P., Mujahid, N., Aldrian, E., & Chen, J. (2024). Impact of urban built-up volume. *Sustainable Cities and Society*, *105*, 105346. DOI: 10.1016/j.scs.2024.105346

Varriale, V., Cammarano, A., Michelino, F., & Caputo, M. (2024). Digital technologies in production systems. *Sustainable Production and Consumption*, *47*, 87–104. DOI: 10.1016/j.spc.2024.03.035

Vătămănescu, E. M., Dominici, G., Ciuciuc, V. E., Vi elar, A., & Anghel, F. G. (2024). Smart mobility and car sharing. *Journal of Cleaner Production*, , 144333.

Wang, W., Guan, X., Peng, X., Wang, Z., Liang, X., & Zhu, J. (2024). Urban environmental monitoring. *Frontiers in Public Health*, *12*, 1357715. DOI: 10.3389/fpubh.2024.1357715

Woodward, A. (2019). Climate change: Disruption, risk and opportunity. *Global Transitions*, *1*, 44–49. DOI: 10.1016/j.glt.2019.02.001

Yan, X., Zhao, X., Han, Y., Van Hentenryck, P., & Dillahunt, T. (2021). Mobility-on-demand vs fixed-route systems. *Transportation Research Part A, Policy and Practice*, *148*, 481–495. DOI: 10.1016/j.tra.2021.03.019

Zou, Y., Wang, C., Najam, H., Nassani, A. A., Djuraeva, G., & Oscar, D. (2025). Energy consumption prediction for households. *Energy Strategy Reviews*, *57*, 101622. DOI: 10.1016/j.esr.2024.101622

KEY TERMS AND DEFINITIONS

Adaptive Systems: Systems that change their behaviour based on real-time conditions such as weather, demand, or resource levels.

Circular Economy: An economic model that focuses on reducing waste through reuse, repair, and recycling of materials.

Cyber-Physical Systems: Systems that combine digital technologies (AI, sensors) with physical infrastructure such as energy grids or water networks.

Data Governance: Rules and practices that guide how data is collected, stored, shared, and protected.

Digital Twin: A virtual model of a physical system that helps planners test different scenarios before taking action.

Energy Demand Forecasting: Predicting how much electricity households, industries, or cities will need at different times.

Interoperability: The ability of different devices, platforms, and systems to work together smoothly.

Precision Agriculture: Use of sensors and smart tools to provide crops only what they need—water, fertiliser, or pesticides—based on real-time field conditions.

Smart Grid: An electricity network that uses digital tools to balance supply and demand efficiently.

Smart Mobility: Transport systems that use sensors and real-time data to reduce congestion and improve travel efficiency.

Urban Heat Island Effect: A condition where temperatures are higher in urban areas due to concrete buildings, traffic, and limited green space.

Waste Management Automation: Use of digital tools to sort, collect, and recycle waste more efficiently.

Chapter 3
Machine Learning Models for Climate Risk Prediction

Drumil Tejas Joshi
http://orcid.org/0000-0002-8288-9987
Southern Power Company, USA

Vandana Kate
Acropolis Institute of Technology and Research, India

Sneh Gangwar
Indraprastha College for Women, University of Delhi, India

K. Geetha
Kongunadu Arts and Science College, India

M. Dhanapal
Erode Sengunthar Engineering College, India

V. Bhoopathy
http://orcid.org/0000-0003-2175-6328
Sree Rama Engineering College, India

Sindhusaranya Balraj
http://orcid.org/0000-0002-6344-5432
Sona College of Technology, India

ABSTRACT

Storms and floods are more likely in coastal areas. As coastal systems become more socially and environmentally complex, these threats will worsen. To mitigate such impacts, vulnerable coastal areas must be identified and assessed. Modern and future generations are threatened by climate change. Climate change makes natural disasters more frequent, stronger, and unpredictable. Climate change's expected effects—rising sea levels and more powerful and frequent weather events—will make coastal communities considerably more vulnerable to storms, floods, and erosion.

DOI: 10.4018/979-8-3373-5946-5.ch003

The world's shoreline population is expected to triple from 1.8 to 5.2 billion by the 2080s. Weather causes most natural disasters in Korea. Tropical cyclones and high rainfall have caused most disaster damage in the past decade.

1. INTRODUCTION

At the moment, environmental and donor groups are putting a lot of effort into getting climate risk data into adaptation plans. If we want to understand the current state of climate variability, we need better access to high-quality meteorological data; trustworthy projections of future climate change on the time and space scales required to inform decision-making; the expertise to conduct impact assessments, evaluation of potential solutions and preparation for their implementation; existing sectoral and institutional frameworks; or the purpose of completing adaptation-ready development programs and projects. Impact assessments using climate scenarios have been increasingly popular since the 1990s. However, for nearly a decade, impact assessment has outpaced scientific output on climate change adaptation. One probable reason is that governments have prioritized mitigating climate change rather than finding ways to adapt to it. Scenario-led adaptation planning cannot commence until a sufficient amount of information about impacts has been accumulated, or until professionals have incentives to conduct the necessary applied research for adaptation, which is a rarity. Opinions on "how to" adapt at the national level. The extent to which adaptation assessment methods, financial and technical resources, the magnitude of potential risks, and the specific adaptations under consideration all determine the potential use of scenario information in adaptation planning(Manatsa et al., 2008).

The amount of time spent trying to adapt is another critical factor to think about. Users of CRI are particularly concerned about the current and future decades, fearing that climate change may undermine the UN, cause new investments to fail, or even lead to maladaptation. Variations in solar output, the amount of aerosol injected into the stratosphere by explosive volcanic eruptions, and the unpredictability of OA interactions will all contribute to the world's climate in the coming decades being highly variable from one decade to the next, creating significant technical challenges.

At national and continental sizes, climate change uncertainty is even more pronounced, and the human signal, while noticeable and increasing, is only a minor part of the overall change. Donor portfolios are most vulnerable in areas where people and ecosystems are already struggling to survive, such as semi-arid regions or flood-prone coastal zones. Both moderate shifts in the mean climate and severe weather events have the potential to push this region beyond a critical threshold. Acceleration of weather changes due to nonlinear responses in secondary impacts and creation of climate scenario databases and technologies that record small changes in risk at the scales needed for adaptation planning. It should be noted that scenario approaches and this review will mostly deal with one another, but that they are related. As our knowledge of the factors that produce climatic fluctuation over decades grows, we should be able to better forecast regional climates and prepare for sudden shifts.

1.1. The Climatic Forecast for the Forthcoming Two Decades

In order to depict the three-dimensional climate system, GCMs use equations that describe the conservation of mass, momentum, energy, and water vapour. On top of the planet, there is a regular grid that defines various atmospheric altitudes; at regular intervals, discrete points answer each equation. The Hadley Centre third generation OA/GCM, run by the UK Met Office, consists of an atmospheric model with a horizontal resolution of 2.5, 3.75° and 19 vertical levels as well as an ocean model with a horizontal resolution of 1.25, 1.25° and 20 vertical levels.

In GCM, radiative transfers across the atmosphere, compute the aerosols' impacts on radiation and precipitation which involve interactions between clouds and water vapour, shifts in polar ice caps and snowpack, heat storage in the earth's crust and water molecules, heat and moisture fluxes on land and sea, and lastly, the global transfer of these two substances through the air and water.

Some global circulation models (GCMs) account for land-surface schemes such as soil moisture freezing and thawing and for changes in temperature, vapour pressure, and carbon dioxide content by managing transpiration through plant stomata.

Despite variations in process representation, several GCMs are presently projecting extremely consistent global mean temperatures for the next twenty to thirty years. Everyone agrees that the climate will react to past emissions and the oceans' thermal inertia will lead to a substantial amount of warming in the future. Consensus also holds true regardless of the emission scenario that is assumed.

1.2 Utilisation of Climate Risk Data for Adaptation Strategizing

A lot of organisations have started looking at climate risks in their portfolios, but how different development paths affect climate change vulnerability hasn't been given enough thought. But there are many adaptation-related problems that climate data can help with.

New infrastructure adaptations usually necessitate cost-function data relative to the size of climate events. Adjusting the function based on anticipated shifts in risk or predicted adaption measures allows one to assess a plan's long-term benefits.

The level of scientific knowledge of the intended audience determines the most appropriate climate information to use for conveying hazards and raising awareness.

Capacity development, benchmark impact assessments, and mainstream adaption are all aided by core scenarios. Being overly dependent on a single climate model, for example, could lead to ignoring more systemic uncertainties. Legislative or lobbying scenarios at the highest levels could emphasise a particular facet of climate change in an effort to modify its relative prominence. Take the case of the United Kingdom following a string of catastrophic flash floods.

2. KEY CONCEPTS IN CLIMATE RISK

Despite its common usage, the term "risk" is notoriously hard to pin down in practice owing to the interconnected nature of its constituent parts. The chance and the repercussions of an undesirable event are what make up risk (Keller et al., 2021). This TP mostly describes the three primary components of risk: susceptibility, likelihood, and hazards; however, additional terminologies, such as exposure, can be utilised as well. Whether an evaluation is wide-ranging or targeted, the amount of uncertainty, and the emphasis and direction of the approach all have a role in how these risk elements are used. The two main methods for calculating climate risk are the vulnerability-based method and the natural hazards-based method.

The primary difference between both methods is a focus on the biophysical or socioeconomic components of climate risk (Pérez-Blanco, 2022). So, is the climate risk the main focus, or are the social and economic consequences. You can build these two strategies independently or combine them; they're complementary(Stefov & Tomlinson, 2009).

Any situation where injury could be possible is considered a hazard. Tropical cyclones, droughts, floods, and situations that cause the spread of disease-causing organisms (whether they be plants, animals, or humans) are all examples of climatic risks. A hazard's frequency and severity, or the frequency with which a socioeconomic criterion is exceeded, can be linked to probabilities. Probabilities can be either qualitative, quantitative, or both. In TP3, vulnerability is defined in a general sense.

In this context, the term "vulnerability" is defined narrowly to mean "climate vulnerability," or the potential financial or other value-based consequences of climate hazards. In the course of investigating broader social vulnerability, as outlined in TP3, it is also possible to evaluate specific vulnerabilities, such as those to drought, flood, or storm surge.

2.1 Approach Centred Around Natural Hazards

Characterizing the climatic hazard is the first step in the natural hazards-based approach to evaluating climate risk, which may be expressed as equation (1):

$$Risk = Probability\ of\ climate\ hazard * Vulnerability \quad (1)$$

Typically, the changing vulnerability over location and/or time is quantified using a fixed degree of hazard. The risk may grow over time (presuming vulnerability stays constant) due to factors such as the growing frequency of storms with a certain wind speed or floods of a given height.

2.2 Approach Centered on Vulnerability

To evaluate risk, the vulnerability-based approach first character vulnerability in order to create criteria, such as the probability of over a critical threshold.

- ✓ Within the policy-based approach, risk assessment methodologies can be employed to determine:
- ✓ The well existing measures are reducing the expected hazards associated with climate change.
- ✓ The adaptive-capacity technique can elucidate a system's resilience to climate change and its inherent uncertainty. A deeper understanding of climate threats will also guide this strategy.

2.3 Adaptation, Susceptibility, and the Capacity for Resilience

Societies have progressively cultivated an awareness of climatic variability to mitigate climate risk. To lessen the impact of climate dangers and make the most of their local climate conditions, people have changed their behaviour and the way they live (Higuera Roa et al., 2025). As a result, they have sought to comprehend and control the spontaneous responses of biophysical and socioeconomic systems to climate change. The foundation of deliberate adaptation is this social learning. All communities engage in planned adaptation, although the extent to which this is done and the methods employed differ across different regions.

All communities engage in planned adaptation, although the extent to which it is applied and the methods used differ across locations (Simpson et al., 2021). In an agricultural system, for instance, this could involve knowledge of what is considered a sustainable level of output, data on crop yield and prices, and other crucial criteria for understanding crop growth, such as rainfall variability and temperature.

The results of the analyses will then reveal the good, marginal, poor, and dangerous yield levels. The research team aims to identify a relationship between climate and parameters that indicate a level of vulnerability by incorporating the knowledge of climate-society relationships held by communities and public and commercial institutions. In order to evaluate the climate-society linkages in the face of potential societal and climatic changes, it is helpful to combine narrative histories of droughts and responses with rainfall records.

One way to measure risk is to determine the frequency with which a certain condition causes the coping range to be exceeded. There are a variety of qualitative and quantitative approaches to risk assessment. By constructing or utilising an existing conceptual model of a certain coping range and evaluating risk using qualifiers such as low, medium, and high, qualitative approaches can be put into practice. It will start to be possible to use quantitative approaches to determine the probability of surpassing specific criteria, like crucial thresholds(Eckstein et al., 2021). These relationships can be evaluated in dynamic settings with the help of quantitative models. If you want to use the coping range for mathematical modelling without letting the model structure drive the evaluation, you should modify the mathematical models so they fit the conceptual models.

3. ONTOLOGY OF MISSING RISK

To that end, we've compiled a list of the five most common kinds of unanticipated risks and offered suggestions for how researchers may start incorporating them into their study designs (Fenz & Neubauer, 2018). Based on the grounds for their exclusion, the categories below can be used to engage with them in the near future.

3.1 Absence of Biophysical Effects

The IAMs' calibration is frequently decades out of date, which leads to a set of missed dangers Several threats, including the AMOC's collapse by 2300 and sudden permafrost melt by 2100 are currently thought to have a high probability at present and future levels of warming(Meriah & Rabai, 2019). It may take a long time for a climate phenomenon to be valued in economic models when our understanding of it improves.

For this to happen, our knowledge of the key climate factors must advance to a level where it can be disseminated to audiences outside of the climate science community, for example, through publications like the IPCC reports. In order to convert climate concerns into tangible repercussions, biophysical modelling is frequently necessary throughout this process; Economists must first comprehend the social system's reaction to the physical impact and assign a welfare value to that reaction; then, risk must be included in IAMs. many all-encompassing assessments, such as computational CGE. For this, interdisciplinary teams must work closely together (Diaz & Moore, 2017).

Possible causes of this discrepancy include divergent views on the size of affects within the impact community, a culture in economics that frowns upon large-scale teamwork, and, to a lesser extent, insufficient funding for economic model development. Incorporating these hazards in the not-too-distant future will be fraught with difficulties. Economic harm evaluations necessitate damage functions that encompass the most extensive array of plausible responses (Rising et al., 2022).

Although there have been some positive developments in empirical damage estimates, the problems of including the endogeneity of adaptation and linking short-term weather-related consequences to long-term climate ones remain. An initiative to address both of these concerns is being spearheaded by the Climate Impact Lab. Variation in temperature sensitivity, which has been found, is used to account for adaptation(Carleton & Hsiang, 2016) .

3.2 Geospatial and Temporal Extremes

One of the most prominent aspects of economic damages is the demographic and spatial heterogeneity in affects; in many areas, the most susceptible populations are the poor and other socioeconomically disadvantaged. For representative agents, IAMs frequently portray the world in extremely aggregated terms, illustrating solely worldwide outcomes or across multi-national areas. on behalf of representatives (Piontek et al., 2021). While it is possible to account for these fluctuations using damage functions or elasticity parameters, doing so obscures the causes and effects of climate risk. Extremes of time are also likely to be important (Dennig et al., 2015). As opposed to slow shifts in ocean temperature or sea level, many of the climate change impacts, including heat waves, storms, and droughts, will manifest as intense and unexpected events. Despite the availability of many natural disaster estimates, IAMs do not include them, and published metrics usually conceal the impact of variability (Lange et al., 2020). Check out SID for some examples of dangers caused by extremes in space and time (Dottori et al., 2018).

3.3 Risks and Interactions of Feedback

The climatic, environmental, and economic systems are all interconnected and influenced by feedback processes. The intricate interaction between climatic change and variability, population transitions, economic instability, and political processes gives rise to critical and occasionally disregarded hazards. There is a feedback loop between physical hazards; for example, climate change can hasten and worsen already-existing issues, setting off a chain reaction that eventually reaches societal tipping points. Heavy tailed distributions are frequently caused by feedback processes, which are hence strongly associated with black swan events (Ylönen & Aven, 2023).

However, assessments frequently omit these interactions, which leads to unrecognised dangers. The under-representation of tipping points and climatic extremes in GCMs and their corresponding downscaled products is an obstacle to the incorporation of research on these topics into economic evaluations (Altuhaifa & Al Tuhaifa, 2024). In order to bolster their research, social scientists rely on natural scientists for gridded forecasts, temporal evolutions, and probability estimates. This doesn't always work. The only way to guarantee that climate scientists deliver conclusions that are easily integrated into economic analysis and have strong justifications is to merge the two fields.

3.4 Profound Ambiguity

Processes with deep uncertainty do not have robust probability distributions. There is a lot of black-box thinking when it comes to estimating risks, exposure, vulnerability, and welfare for a lot of impacts. This is true in terms of things like how big the impacts are and how often or how likely they are to occur in different locations and times. Sometimes it's not obvious what measures to use for quantification (Ding et al., 2016). Still, they can be considered when planning and assessing risks. The economic damage integration process, IAMs specifically, and other impact-capturing models should begin a comparable cycle of introspection over profound uncertainty. Although IAMs have been compared before, a coordinated effort to compare them would take a far broader view, thinking about what is now lacking or not included enough and how it could affect the results.

3.5 Unidentified Risks

At long last, it's time to acknowledge a second set of dangers that have gone unnoticed in the scholarly literature. Unanticipated or understudied disruptions can occur in the interconnected global environmental-human system. A lot of the ways the ecosystem meets human needs right now are things we don't give much thought to, and we don't even know which ones are vulnerable to climate change. Societal movements can emerge out of nowhere as a result of people's erratic reactions to environmental changes.

4. MACHINE LEARNING APPROACHES IN CLIMATE RISK PREDICTION

Predicting future climatic variability is the job of Climate Learn's supervised learning algorithms. In this section, we will go over symbolic regression with GP and multilayer ANN. All of these methods adhere to the standard model of machine learning, which states that given enough data, algorithms may "learn" to do a certain task. This produces a model that is tested using data that is distinct from the training data (Feng et al., 2016).

4.1 Network of Artificial Neural

Biological neural networks serve as an inspiration for a class of statistical learning models known as ANNs. In these systems, a network of interconnected processing units called neurones processes incoming data and produces an output signal whose shape is determined by the internal state of the network (Ferrara et al., 2024). The availability of software that can train the network rapidly has increased their significance and opened up several applications for these methods. Some of these applications include high-dimensional clustering, time series forecasting, image and speech recognition, and many more. Since different challenges call for different neural network topologies, there is a plethora of literature proposing various topologies (Jha et al., 2023). We zero in on one particular setup called a multilayer neural network or multilayer perceptron in this article.

Figure 1. An overview of the many uses and importance of machine learning (ML)

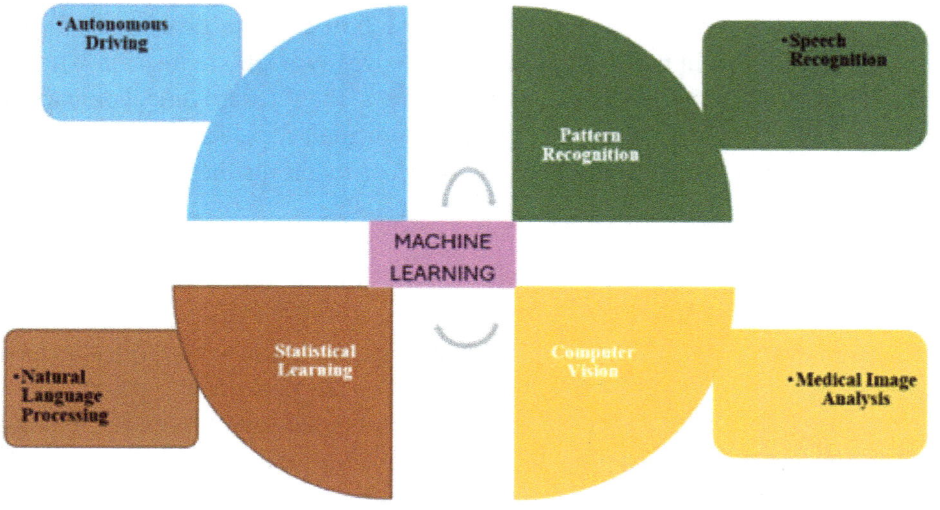

Figure 1 shows renewable energy and the fight against climate change are two areas where ML has the potential to make a significant impact in the future. The significance of ML in various domains has been emphasized in numerous papers.

Figure 2. Has two hidden layers, three input variables and two output variables.

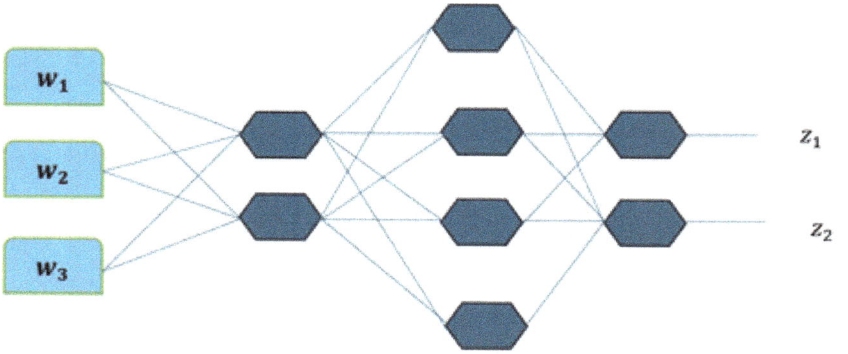

Figure 2 depicts the standard architecture of a multilayer perceptron, which takes inputs into the network, processes them using one or more hidden layers, and then outputs the results. This means that the calculation is best understood as a mapping process, with the input vector having m-dimensions and the output vector having n-dimensions. With a multilayer perceptron, data goes from the input layer all the way to the output layer because the connections between the neuron are designed to only go in one direction. A completely connected multilayer perceptron is one in which every neuron in every layer is linked to every other layer. The training step has been a computationally hard challenge since neural networks came out, primarily due to the lack of efficient techniques compared to the processing power that is available. The back-propagation approach, which is currently often used to train multilayer perceptron, has solved this problem (Mojaddadi et al., 2017). The network's calculated output that corresponds. When xi is fed forward is denoted as z_j in the supervised training set $\{w_j, s_j{:}j = 1\ldots M\}$ where w_j are input variables and s_j are target variables. The standard Equation (2) is $s_j \neq z_j$. Then, a quadratic function of the kind can be used to define a global error on the training set (Ukoba et al., 2024).

$$F(\varphi) = \frac{1}{2M}\sum_j \|s_j - z_j\|^2 \tag{2}$$

Function of the weights φ in the network. Altering the standard, for instance, can lead to alternative mistake definitions. To reduce this inaccuracy as much as possible, back propagation updates the weights using the gradient descent method in equation (3).

$$\varphi_{ji}^{(L)} \vdots \varphi_{ji}^{L} - \beta\frac{\theta F(\varphi)}{\theta \varphi_{ji}^{(L)}} \tag{3}$$

The approach relies heavily on the computation of partial derivatives. To achieve this, we directly use the fact that the error function is instance-dependent in the training set. When every example has been used, the training is considered finished. Lengthy training times are the consequence of the error function typically taking a lengthy time to converge to a local or global minimum(Goldstein et al., 2017).

Following the completion of training, the model's correctness should be checked on a test set. Data overfitting occurs when a model is overly dependent on its training data and struggles to generalize when presented with fresh data; avoiding this problem is an important part of this process. One way to lessen the chances of overfitting is to use cross-validation approaches. These need supplying a training set that is BI partitioned into a validation set and a training set. The network is then trained on the training partition and tested on the validation partition.

You can tell the model is good once you run it through a number of cross-validation partitions and look at the training and validation error numbers. The training was effective, and the network is prepared for generalization, if overfitting is not an issue.

4.2 Genetic Programming

Both genetic algorithms and genetic programming have their roots in Charles Darwin's Theory of Evolution. These algorithms are a subset of evolutionary programming. Darwin demonstrates in this magnum opus that, out of any given population of organisms residing in a given ecosystem, only a subset of those organisms will be optimally suited to survive and reproduce. These advantageous genetic traits may be passed down across generations, eventually becoming the dominant ones. There are essentially three ways in which individual trait variations can be categorised. The first group consists of variants that can cause harm to the person. In the second group are the ones that are helpful, and in the third group, the variations do not make a difference. Because fit people tend to outlive their competitors and pass their advantageous traits on to subsequent generations, natural selection is essentially a process of preserving and passing on advantageous traits.

In this scenario, we pretend to have a set of solutions T to a problem O. Each solution to O is like a person; its fitness value indicates how well it has adapted to its surroundings based on how well it solves the problem. One example where computer programs evolve into persons is GP. The objective is to select the most effective program that addresses the current problem by suitably evolving computer programs through the creation of new generations, evaluation of their fitness value, and eventually selection. In this context, we limit these programs to functions e $(w_1....w_m)$ of a fixed number of variables w_j, where $j = 1....m$, and we seek to identify a function that roughly predicts the solution to our issue. Therefore, our application is basically a genetic programming-based symbolic regression. A real-valued functional $E\left[e(w_i....w_n)\right]$ can be used to mathematically express the fitness values; this function maps the space of feasible solutions onto the real axis. It is common practice to represent GP programs as trees, with each branch representing a potential solution to a problem.

Two operators, mutation and crossover, are often employed to implement changes in genetic programming. In many ways, what they did is quite similar to the biological concepts of mutation and crossover. In a mutation phase, a random node is chosen to represent the person in the tree, and then another associated subtree is randomly replaced with another one.. Mutation plays a crucial role in maintaining population variety, which in turn aids the algorithm in exploring the whole search space and avoiding local fitness functional maxima. The idea behind crossover is that two people might share traits with one another.

5. LITERATURE SURVEY

The agricultural sector, the country's economy, and other sectors the classified herbs for the agriculture industry in Malaysia using ML techniques like ANN, KNN, DT, and M5P Tree algorithms(Tehrany et al., 2019). This industry is vital to Malaysia's economic development since it is one of the leading exporters of herb used BN and other ML algorithms for classification and prediction quite a bit in Malaysia. The MDID has identified new Halal technologies that use ML techniques. These technologies will help Muslim customers in Malaysia validate Halal logo images both locally and globally. Natural disaster detection, including flood risk identification, has recently seen extensive usage of BN and ML algorithms in applied research. Predicting flood hazards using Bayesian techniques was the subject of research in 2018 (Razak et al., 2019). (Abdullah et al., 2019). They conducted an experiment using three distinct Bayesian classifier algorithms to predict the probability of floods in Kuala Krai, Kelantan, Malaysia for a duration of five years: tree-augmented NB, generalized Bayesian networks, and naive BayesGeneral Bayesian Networks achieved better accuracy than NB and tree enhanced naive Bayes, according to the results. Our subsequent study builds on this paper by contrasting BN with other ML methods including DT, KNN, and SVM. Using NNARX, an early prediction system for floods five hours in the future, was suggested. Several sites in Kelantan, Malaysia, were monitored for water level and rainfall. For the purpose of making predictions, the suggested NNARX was compared to the standard Neural Network. RMSE values for traditional Neural Networks were higher than those for NNARX, according to the results. Additional emphasis is on the flood that occurred in Kelantan, Malaysia. To anticipate the occurrence of flood risk, they suggested using Spiking Neural Network. Concurrently, WELLSVM, a semi-supervised ML model, was introduced for the purpose of urban flood forecasting. This model made use of data samples collected from the metropolitan regions of Beijing during a ten-year period, from 2004 to 2014. Nine metrological, geographical, and anthropogenic variables made up the samples. Next, the model was tested and compared with two other models that were constructed using Artificial Neural Networks and Logistic Regression (Razali et al., 2020).

The models were assessed for accuracy, recall, precision, and f-score. Due to WELLSVM's superiority in making use of the unlabelled data, the findings demonstrated that WELLSVM flood effectively surpassed both models. One model that relies on ensemble classifiers to improve water flooded layer classification. Oil layer, weak water flooded, intermediate water inundated, and strong water flooded are the four buckets into which the target classes are mapped out using this model. Oddly enough, this model was used to forecast the water-flooded layer in reservoirs for oil or gas. The ensemble classifier was constructed using the validated and evaluated MFBC, KNN, and SVM algorithms(Zhao et al., 2019).

Because of the dataset's imbalanced classifications, the SMOTE was used to oversample the data. The ensemble classifier outperformed MFBC, KNN, and SVM on chromatogram data and UCI data, respectively, whereas MFBC, KNN, and SVM all achieved comparable levels of accuracy. Lastly, two ML methods, DT and SVM, were recommended (Izzati Mohd Roslin et al., 2018) to assess geographical correlations between the causes that contributed to the 2011 devastating flood in Australia and the rate of flooding. in order of significance for creating maps of flood-prone regions. In the first dataset, DT obtained 89% accuracy while SVM achieved 87%; in the second dataset, DT achieved 89% accuracy and SVM achieved 87%; both methods were low in accuracy compared to SVM(Materia et al., 2024).

6. RESULT AND DISCUSSION

As demonstrated in Figure 3, the model has learnt to continuously improve its accuracy by the 100th epoch, and it has achieved a peak of 0.97%. The dramatic increase in validation accuracy during the fourth period, which peaked at 0.94%, is a notable aspect of this statistic.

Figure 3. Training and Validation Accuracy

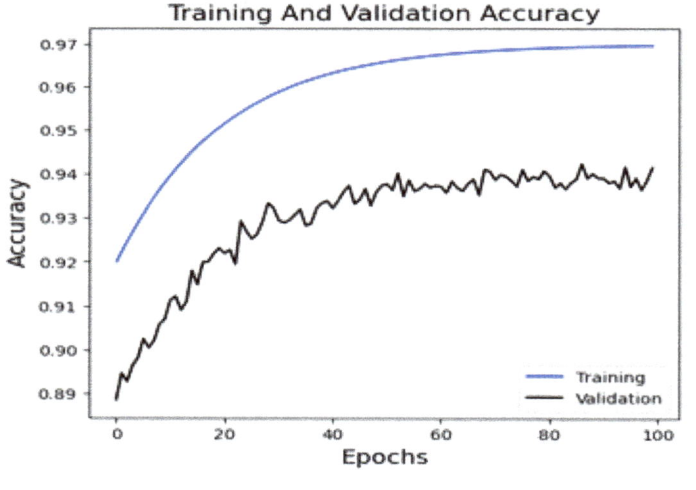

In Table 1, they can see how the suggested methods stack up against other algorithms' base hyperparameter. These other algorithms include ANN, KNN, SVM,

DT, NB and BN. The suggested SVM method outperformed the alternatives with respect to ROC (0.99%), Accuracy (0.97%), Precision (0.95%), Recall (0.93%), and F1-score (0.97%).

Table 1. Performance of Models

Models	ROC	Accuracy	Precision	Recall	F1-Score
ANN	0.92	0.9	0.88	0.86	0.9
KNN	0.76	0.74	0.72	0.7	0.74
SVM	**0.99**	**0.97**	**0.95**	**0.93**	**0.97**
DT	0.82	0.8	0.78	0.76	0.8
NB	0.87	0.85	0.83	0.81	0.85
BN	0.71	0.69	0.67	0.65	0.69

As demonstrated in Figure 4, A binary classification model's performance across all thresholds is graphically represented by the ROC curve. It shows how the price of a low false positive rate compares to a high genuine positive rate. The proposed SVM model reached ROC value is 0.99% when compared to another model.

Figure 4. Receiver Operating Characteristic

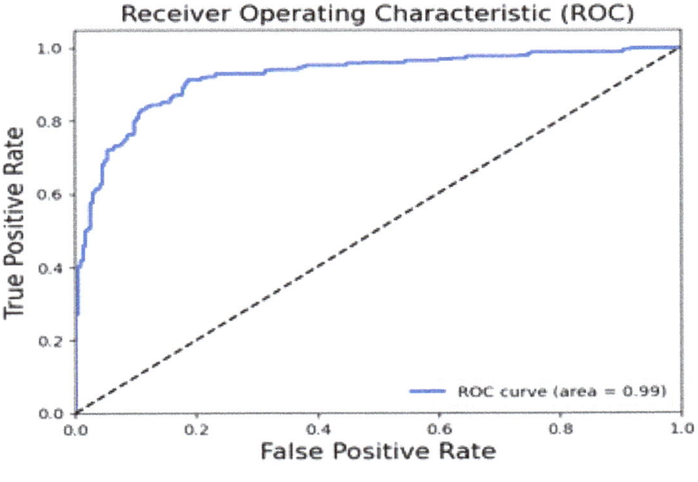

As demonstrated in Figure 5, Comparing the model's predictions with the actual values in the dataset is one way to evaluate a classification model's accuracy, and this comparison is done using a confusion matrix, a type of table. It gives a summary of the number of right and wrong predictions for each class, which helps to understand the model's mistake kind. The confusion matrix shows the value of (0.97%).

Figure 5. Confusion Matrix

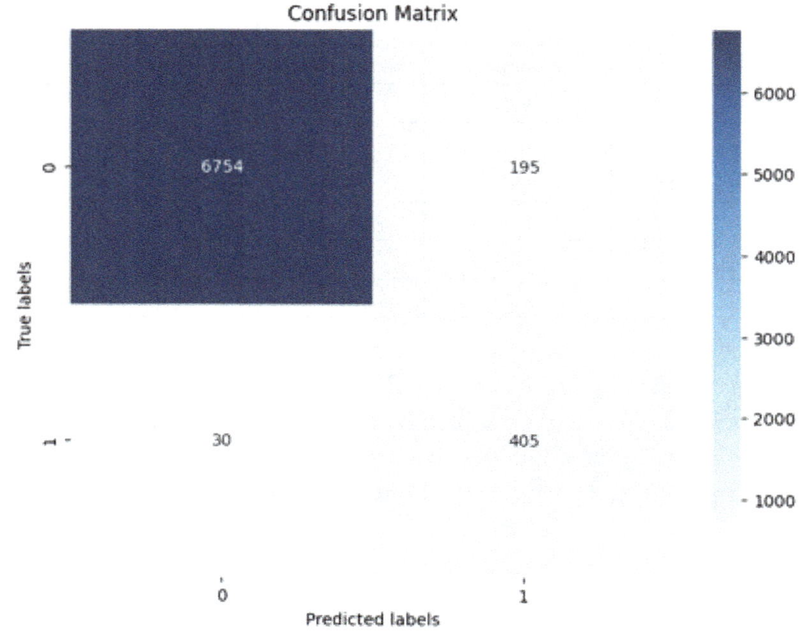

In figure 6, we can observe the results of comparing six distinct models using the ROC, Accuracy, Precision, Recall, and F1-score measures. In comparison to the other five models, the suggested SVM model outperforms them all and has an accuracy rate of (0.97%).

Figure 6. Performance of Models

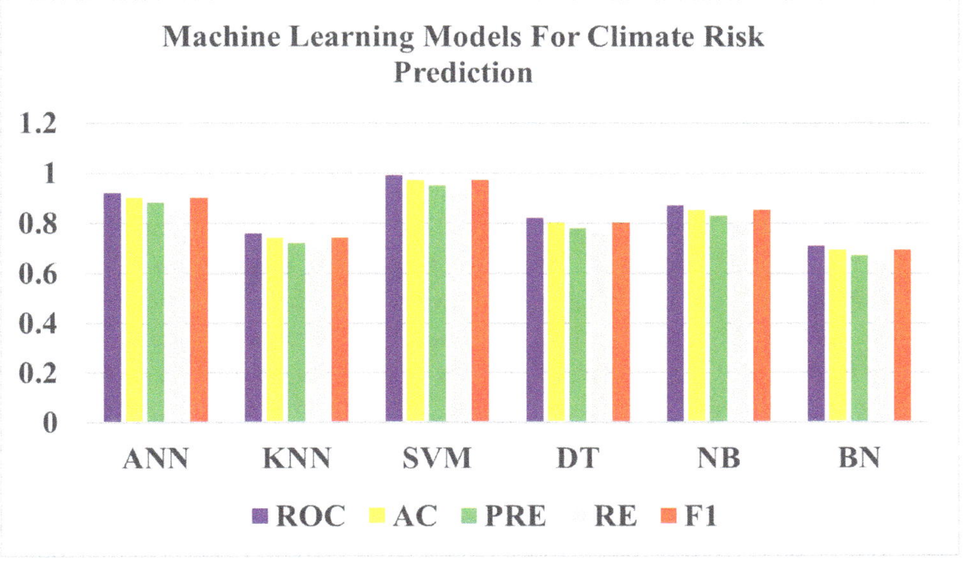

7. CHALLENGES

There are many unanswered questions around the rapid integration of AI into climate prediction models, which needs to be addressed before the public can have faith in this new technology. We highlight five main areas of difficulty and suggest some solutions that might be considered for use in future research.

7.1 Data and Processing

Although extreme occurrences are inherently infrequent, the growing probability of them in a non-stationary climate presents significant scientific obstacles to enhancing climate predictions through artificial intelligence (White et al., 2023). Actually, without past data and no out-of-the-ordinary occurrences, any statistical procedure based on observation is bound to fail. The physical mechanisms that cause climate extremes follow cycles that can last anywhere from a few weeks to a few years, and the relationships between the seasons are not always linear (Miloshevich et al., 2023). Due to the interconnected nature of numerous climate variables over multiple time scales, it is challenging to collect sufficient samples for learning purposes. For longer forecast periods, this becomes an even bigger issue, making it harder to verify time-independent forecasts (He et al., 2021). For example, multi-annual predictions may only have a dozen samples for training if they use current atmospheric reanalysis.

7.2 Ambiguities

There is no one-to-one link between predictors and predictands; the relationship is inherently probabilistic because of the climate system's inherent complexity and chaos (Lucente et al., 2022). As a result, there are a lot of unknowns when it comes to making climate forecasts about extreme events, especially aleatoric uncertainty, which can have a big effect on how predictable an extreme event could be (Van Straaten et al., 2022). Another way to look at aleatoric uncertainty is as heteroscedastic, which is noisier, and homoscedastic, which is invariant to diverse inputs. This leads to overly cautious predictions, thus it's crucial to know the extreme's statistical characteristics and model them appropriately. Similarly, epistemic uncertainties, which arise from doubts about the data and ML algorithms, might impact prediction as well. Probabilistic models are ideal for depicting the total uncertainty because the prediction problem is described by a range of possible future states (Luo et al., 2022). When these distributions are adjusted such that the given probabilities match the actual events, decision-makers reap the most benefits (Gneiting et al., 2007). Though not all ML algorithms explicitly provide uncertainty distributions in their output, several of them do offer probabilistic forecasts. Therefore, a crucial area of research in climate extreme prediction is the development of trustworthy probabilistic ML models(Caldecott et al., 2024).

7.3 Interpretability and Causality

The lack of transparency around how the algorithm makes its decisions is a major drawback of utilising AI to forecast climate extremes. Most ML/DL algorithms are really complicated and opaque, which makes it hard to understand their predictions, with a few notable exceptions(Lapuschkin et al., 2019). While applications like machine translation or text production may not require interpretability or high accuracy (Barnes et al., 2022), For critical climate applications and the prediction of extreme events, the system's ability to comprehend and react correctly is paramount. (Agarwal et al., 2021). When there is a lack of verification data, as there is in the S2S/S2D scenario, having faith in the forecast becomes more important. “Clever Hans” models are instances of AI models that make accurate predictions but for the wrong reasons. So, for interpretability's sake, testability against “clever Hans” models is crucial, as is making sure the model has acquired relevant processes and not just false links.

7.4 Generalizability

How well a model performs when applied to data that is not directly related to its training sets in terms of space and time is called its generalizability or generalization (Adlam et al., 2020). Traditional ML/DL algorithms rely on two main premises: first, that the data used for training and testing follows a normal distribution; and second, that the input-target correlations learnt during training are genuine. This assumption, however, frequently proves to be incorrect in climate science applications due to the fact that models frequently produce extreme values that do not correspond to the training data's climatology (Rasp et al., 2018). Because present relationships may not be applicable in the future, this out-of-distribution generalization problem can significantly reduce model performance (O'Gorman & Dwyer, 2018). This is especially the case when the Earth's temperature rises and alters the distributions of Earth system variables throughout space and time. The accuracy of ML/DL models might differ greatly when trained in humid regions and then used to predict in drier ones; this makes it difficult to anticipate extreme occurrences across different climate regimes. Building more resilient ML/DL models is, then, primarily concerned with comprehending how models function under unlabeled environment (Sungmin et al., 2020).

7.5 Reproducibility

When researchers have access to the data, methodologies, and procedures used in a study, they should be able to independently duplicate and verify the results. This is called reproducibility. With revolutionary and game-changing endeavors such as ML applications in climate prediction, where new approaches, algorithms, and workflows are being released or developed at a quick speed, this is an essential need for guaranteeing the findings are trustworthy and reliable. (Hutson, 2018).

Nevertheless, there is cause for concern regarding a "reproducibility crisis" that has been worsened in artificial intelligence literature, as over 60% of earth scientists have been unable to replicate the results of other researchers' work and 40% were unable to replicate their own studies. A common problem is that people rarely publish their source code (Materia et al., 2024). This could be because they are uncomfortable with scripting, don't want to reveal their ongoing work, or are keen to gain a competitive advantage. The community is also frequently not given access to the datasets utilized for training. It is critical to share codes and data, but it is just as necessary to document the study and experiments thoroughly. Thorough documentation makes it easier for others to replicate the studies, builds trust, decreases work, and removes obstacles to independent replication of results. Several studies were omitted from this assessment due to flawed or inadequate technique descriptions, casting doubt on the reliability of the results.

8. FUTURE TRENDS

Researchers in the area of climate change and environmental studies have achieved remarkable progress using ML(Ataei Kachouei et al., 2023). Integrating AI and ML with emerging technologies like the IoT, remote sensing, and high-performance computing promises more comprehensive and real-time environmental monitoring. More precise assessments of environmental damages, more accurate severe weather forecasts, and better understanding of complex biological interactions are all possible outcomes of these innovations. To ensure the continued success of AI and machine learning in climate change studies, it is essential to encourage collaboration across different academic fields (Modgil et al., 2021).

8.1 Enhanced Technology

AI, ML, RS, and the IOT are all recently integrated into environmental hazardous substance monitoring sensors. These sensors can scan massive datasets in real-time and identify anomalies or trends that could indicate the presence of a hazardous material. The public's health can be better protected using these sensors. (Popescu et al., 2024). This is made possible by combining sensor data processing with machine learning techniques. (Ummah, 2019). This technology is useful in industrial settings and other areas where chemical leaks can occur. A comprehensive picture of the presence, location, movement, and impact of hazardous compounds may be achieved with the help of AI and ML, which not only detects them but also improves the forecast of their likelihood and severity, allowing for proactive mitigation planning (Bhagat et al., 2019). Modern innovations improve air quality modelling by combining many data sources, such as meteorological and satellite imaging, to produce more precise forecasts. By integrating AI with satellite technology, we can monitor the environment in great detail and pinpoint the origins of pollution. Edge computing allows for the real-time analysis of environmental data right at its source, allowing for quick responses to pollution problems. Hybrid algorithms that combine machine learning with simulations based on physical principles also increase the accuracy of identifying pollution sources (Ferebee, 2024).

Over the past decade, a number of research have looked into ways to predict how well heavy metal removal from soil will work using machine learning. The main objective of these studies has been to use machine learning to forecast how effective various soil remediation techniques will be (Cave et al., 2020). In addition, data from NIR spectroscopy was used to build a CNN architecture for deep calibration. In order to back up suitable irrigation methods for agriculture, this study sought to evaluate levels of water contamination from residential and commercial sources. The research effectively used CNN architecture to build intelligent spectroscopic models, which have the potential to greatly tackle water recycling and agricultural conservation concerns.

8.2 Consideration of Policy and Ethical

While progress has been made, some challenges remain until climate change research can fully leverage AI and ML. Important concerns include the standardisation of data formats, the interpretability of models, ethical considerations, and the integration of policy frameworks (ElZarrad et al., 2022). In order to make different datasets work together more effectively, researchers need to establish common procedures for gathering and sharing data. AI and ML models can be made more trustworthy and reliable by improving their interpretability through new visualisation approaches and clear documentation. The responsible application of technology must be guided by ethical discussion to guarantee positive impacts on society and the environment.

In addition, academics, legislators, and legal specialists from various nations must constantly collaborate to include AI and ML into policy frameworks. To accommodate the ever-changing technological landscape and its implications for climate change research, regulatory frameworks need to be both adaptable and flexible (Vu & Lim, 2022). It is crucial to employ a multi-disciplinary and cross-country strategy. How far a country goes in accepting AI will determine how effective its joint efforts.

Various levels of preparedness to embrace AI for varied applications, including environmental forecasting, were highlighted in a recent study that spanned 28 nations and shed light on the general acceptance of AI technologies. Results showed that nations with higher AI adoption rates were more inclined to use AI and ML in climate change mitigation and catastrophe management.

Countries like the US, Japan, and a handful of European nations who have robust digital infrastructures and legislation that are welcoming to AI are more inclined to use these technologies in environmental science. Nevertheless, the adoption of AI is also affected by its intended use.

The use of robots to assist the young, the old, and the crippled is something that 60% of Europeans find unacceptable. Among Irish citizens, only 20% are open to the idea of driverless cars. Many people in the United States are open to having packages delivered by drone.

Countries take different approaches to AI regulation and policymaking. The Provisional Rules for the Administration of Generative AI Services are China's artificial intelligence legislation. This paradigm is purely ethical, applies exclusively to generational AI, and centres on actual liability. The Draft Provisional EU AI Act was draughter by the EU based on risk assessment projections. The Executive Order on Secure, Safe, and Trustworthy Artificial Intelligence is the product of the United States' decentralised strategy, which is built on principles, guidelines, and priorities. The years 2023 and 2024 saw the introduction of these policies (Comunale & Manera, 2024).

9. CONCLUSION

One of the biggest problems that the world's economy has ever faced is climate change. From 2011 to 2020, and on an annual basis, the world's surface warmed by 1.09 degrees Celsius. The Ice Sheets in the Arctic reached their lowest point between 1850 and 1900, as reported by the IPCC in 2021. Despite accounting for only over 19% of India's GDP in 2019, 43% of the population was directly or indirectly involved in agriculture. For several reasons, such as the widespread dispersion of landholdings and the fact that a large portion of the population depends on agriculture for subsistence, the agricultural sector is especially vulnerable to the consequences of climate change. But the risk doesn't always manifest in a bad way; for example, more carbon emissions might boost crop yields by improving photosynthesis and raising precipitation levels. In sectors where worker safety is paramount, risk assessment plays a vital role. Nevertheless, it encounters a number of systemic difficulties, some of which are associated with developments in technology and others with rising demands. Efforts are being made to improve risk assessment processes, learn from past mistakes, and define methods for processing relevant data. This will be accompanied by the necessary capacity to handle unforeseen circumstances and offer the necessary assistance to facilitate risk management. With respect to more conventional models, the suggested svm model achieved an accuracy of 0.97 percent.

REFERENCES

Abdullah, M. H. A., Othman, M., Kasim, S., & Mohamed, S. A. (2019). Evolving spiking neural networks methods for classification problem: A case study in flood events risk assessment. *Indonesian Journal of Electrical Engineering and Computer Science, 16*(1), 222–229. DOI: 10.11591/ijeecs.v16.i1.pp222-229

Adlam, B., Hoffman, M. D., Houlsby, N., Mclean, C., & Veitch, V. (2020). Underspecification Presents Challenges for Credibility in. ... *of Machine Learning ..., 23*, 1–61. https://www.jmlr.org/papers/v23/20-1335.html%0Ahttps://www.jmlr.org/papers/volume23/20-1335/20-1335.pdf

Agarwal, R., Melnick, L., Frosst, N., Zhang, X., Lengerich, B., Caruana, R., & Hinton, G. E. (2021). Neural Additive Models: Interpretable Machine Learning with Neural Nets. *Advances in Neural Information Processing Systems, 6*(NeurIPS), 4699–4711.

Altuhaifa, F., & Al Tuhaifa, D. (2024). Developing an Ontology Representing Fall Risk Management Domain Knowledge. *Journal of Medical Systems, 48*(1), 1–10. DOI: 10.1007/s10916-024-02062-2

Ataei Kachouei, M., Kaushik, A., & Ali, M. A. (2023). Internet of Things-Enabled Food and Plant Sensors to Empower Sustainability. *Advanced Intelligent Systems, 5*(12), 2300321. Advance online publication. DOI: 10.1002/aisy.202300321

Barnes, E. A., Barnes, R. J., Martin, Z. K., & Rader, J. K. (2022). This Looks Like That There: Interpretable Neural Networks for Image Tasks When Location Matters. *Artificial Intelligence for the Earth Systems, 1*(3), 1–15. DOI: 10.1175/AIES-D-22-0001.1

Bhagat, S. K., Tung, T. M., Yaseen, Z. M., Tung, T. M., & Yaseen, Z. M. (2019). *Journal Pre-proof.*

Caldecott, B., Harnett, E., Cojoianu, T., Kok, I., & Pfeiffer, A. (2024). Stranded Assets: A Climate Risk Challenge. *Stranded Assets: A Climate Risk Challenge.* DOI: 10.18235/0012646

Carleton, T. A., & Hsiang, S. M. (2016). Social and economic impacts of climate. *Science, 353*(6304), aad9837. Advance online publication. DOI: 10.1126/science.aad9837

Cave, A., Brun, N. C., Sweeney, F., Rasi, G., & Senderovitz, T. (2020). Big Data – How to Realize the Promise. *Clinical Pharmacology and Therapeutics, 107*(4), 753–761. DOI: 10.1002/cpt.1736

Comunale, M., & Manera, A. (2024). *The Economic Impacts and the Regulation of AI.*

Dennig, F., Budolfson, M. B., Fleurbaey, M., Siebert, A., & Socolow, R. H. (2015). Inequality, climate impacts on the future poor, and carbon prices. *Proceedings of the National Academy of Sciences of the United States of America, 112*(52), 15827–15832. DOI: 10.1073/pnas.1513967112

Diaz, D., & Moore, F. (2017). Quantifying the economic risks of climate change. *Nature Climate Change, 7*(11), 774–782. DOI: 10.1038/nclimate3411

Ding, L. Y., Zhong, B. T., Wu, S., & Luo, H. B. (2016). Construction risk knowledge management in BIM using ontology and semantic web technology. *Safety Science, 87*, 202–213. DOI: 10.1016/j.ssci.2016.04.008

Dottori, F., Szewczyk, W., Ciscar, J. C., Zhao, F., Alfieri, L., Hirabayashi, Y., Bianchi, A., Mongelli, I., Frieler, K., Betts, R. A., & Feyen, L. (2018). Increased human and economic losses from river flooding with anthropogenic warming. *Nature Climate Change, 8*(9), 781–786. DOI: 10.1038/s41558-018-0257-z

Eckstein, D., Künzel, V., & Schäfer, L. (2021). Global climate risk index 2021: who suffers most from extreme weather events? Weather-related loss events in 2019 and 2000–2019. In *Germanwatch* (Issue March). http://germanwatch.org/en/download/8551.pdf

ElZarrad, M. K., Lee, A. Y., Purcell, R., & Steele, S. J. (2022). Advancing an agile regulatory ecosystem to respond to the rapid development of innovative technologies. *Clinical and Translational Science, 15*(6), 1332–1339. DOI: 10.1111/cts.13267

Feng, Q. Y., Vasile, R., Segond, M., Gozolchiani, A., Wang, Y., Abel, M., Havlin, S., Bunde, A., & Dijkstra, H. A. (2016). ClimateLearn: A machine-learning approach for climate prediction using network measures. *Geoscientific Model Development Discussions*, (February), 1–18. DOI: 10.5194/gmd-2015-273

Fenz, S., & Neubauer, T. (2018). Ontology-based information security compliance determination and control selection on the example of ISO 27002. *Information and Computer Security, 26*(5), 551–567. DOI: 10.1108/ICS-02-2018-0020

Ferebee, S. (2024). Predicting Tomorrow: A Review of Machine Learning's Role in Shaping Environmental Forecasts. *Premier Journal of Science, 2*, 1–8. DOI: 10.70389/PJS.100008

Ferrara, M., Ciano, T., Capriotti, A., & Muzzioli, S. (2024). Machine Learning Predictive Modeling for assessing Climate Risk in Finance. *WSEAS Transactions on Environment and Development, 20*, 852–862. DOI: 10.37394/232015.2024.20.80

Goldstein, B. A., Navar, A. M., & Carter, R. E. (2017). Moving beyond regression techniques in cardiovascular risk prediction: Applying machine learning to address analytic challenges. *European Heart Journal, 38*(23), 1805–1814. DOI: 10.1093/eurheartj/ehw302

He, S., Li, X., DelSole, T., Ravikumar, P., & Banerjee, A. (2021). Sub-Seasonal Climate Forecasting via Machine Learning: Challenges, Analysis, and Advances. *35th AAAI Conference on Artificial Intelligence, AAAI 2021, 1*, 169–177. DOI: 10.1609/aaai.v35i1.16090

Higuera Roa, O., Bachmann, M., Mechler, R., Šakić Trogrlić, R., Reimann, L., Mazzoleni, M., Aerts, J. C. J. H., Buskop, F. E., Pirani, A., & Mysiak, J. (2025). Challenges and opportunities in climate risk assessment: Future directions for assessing complex climate risks. *Environmental Research Letters, 20*(5), 053003. Advance online publication. DOI: 10.1088/1748-9326/adc756

Hutson, M. (2018). Artificial intelligence faces reproducibility crisis Unpublished code and sensitivity to training conditions make many claims hard to verify. *Science, 359*(6377), 725–726. DOI: 10.1126/science.359.6377.725

Izzati Mohd Roslin, N., Mustapha, A., Azah Samsudin, N., & Razali, N. (2018). A Bayesian Approach to Prediction of Flood Risks. *International Journal of Engineering & Technology, 7*(4.38), 1142–1145. DOI: 10.14419/ijet.v7i4.38.27750

Jha, P., Chinngaihlian, S., Upreti, P., & Handa, A. (2023). A machine learning approach to assess implications of Climate Risk Factors on Agriculture: The Indian case. *Climate Risk Management, 41*(May), 100523. DOI: 10.1016/j.crm.2023.100523

Keller, K., Helgeson, C., & Srikrishnan, V. (2021). Climate risk management. *Annual Review of Earth and Planetary Sciences, 49*(vii), 95–116. DOI: 10.1146/annurev-earth-080320-055847

Lange, S., Volkholz, J., Geiger, T., Zhao, F., Vega, I., Veldkamp, T., Reyer, C. P. O., Warszawski, L., Huber, V., Jägermeyr, J., Schewe, J., Bresch, D. N., Büchner, M., Chang, J., Ciais, P., Dury, M., Emanuel, K., Folberth, C., Gerten, D., & Frieler, K. (2020). Projecting Exposure to Extreme Climate Impact Events Across Six Event Categories and Three Spatial Scales. *Earth's Future, 8*(12), 1–22. DOI: 10.1029/2020EF001616

Lapuschkin, S., Wäldchen, S., Binder, A., Montavon, G., Samek, W., & Müller, K. R. (2019). Unmasking Clever Hans predictors and assessing what machines really learn. *Nature Communications, 10*(1), 1–8. DOI: 10.1038/s41467-019-08987-4

Lucente, D., Herbert, C., & Bouchet, F. (2022). Committor Functions for Climate Phenomena at the Predictability Margin: The Example of El Niño–Southern Oscillation in the Jin and Timmermann Model. *Journal of the Atmospheric Sciences*, *79*(9), 2387–2400. DOI: 10.1175/JAS-D-22-0038.1

Luo, X., Nadiga, B. T., Park, J. H., Ren, Y., Xu, W., & Yoo, S. (2022). A Bayesian Deep Learning Approach to Near-Term Climate Prediction. *Journal of Advances in Modeling Earth Systems*, *14*(10), 1–18. DOI: 10.1029/2022MS003058

Manatsa, D., Chingombe, W., & Matarira, C. H. (2008, March). The impact of the positive Indian Ocean dipole on Zimbabwe droughts Tropical climate is understood to be dominated by. *International Journal of Climatology*, *2029*(15), 2011–2029. DOI: 10.1002/joc.1695

Materia, S., García, L. P., van Straaten, C., Sungmin, O., Mamalakis, A., Cavicchia, L., Coumou, D., de Luca, P., Kretschmer, M., & Donat, M. (2024). Artificial intelligence for climate prediction of extremes: State of the art, challenges, and future perspectives. *Wiley Interdisciplinary Reviews: Climate Change*, *15*(6), 1–31. DOI: 10.1002/wcc.914

Meriah, I., & Rabai, L. B. A. (2019). Comparative study of ontologies based iso 27000 series security standards. *Procedia Computer Science*, *160*, 85–92. DOI: 10.1016/j.procs.2019.09.447

Miloshevich, G., Cozian, B., Abry, P., Borgnat, P., & Bouchet, F. (2023). Probabilistic forecasts of extreme heatwaves using convolutional neural networks in a regime of lack of data. *Physical Review Fluids*, *8*(4), 040501. Advance online publication. DOI: 10.1103/PhysRevFluids.8.040501

Modgil, S., Singh, R., & Hannibal, C. (2021). LJMU Research Online LJMU Research Online. In *Business Administration*.

Mojaddadi, H., Pradhan, B., Nampak, H., Ahmad, N., & Ghazali, A. H. (2017). Ensemble machine-learning-based geospatial approach for flood risk assessment using multi-sensor remote-sensing data and GIS. *Geomatics, Natural Hazards & Risk*, *8*(2), 1080–1102. DOI: 10.1080/19475705.2017.1294113

O'Gorman, P. A., & Dwyer, J. G. (2018). Using Machine Learning to Parameterize Moist Convection: Potential for Modeling of Climate, Climate Change, and Extreme Events. *Journal of Advances in Modeling Earth Systems*, *10*(10), 2548–2563. DOI: 10.1029/2018MS001351

Pérez-Blanco, C. D. (2022). Navigating Deep Uncertainty in Complex Human–Water Systems. In *Springer Climate*. DOI: 10.1007/978-3-030-86211-4_20

Piontek, F., Drouet, L., Emmerling, J., Kompas, T., Méjean, A., Otto, C., Rising, J., Soergel, B., Taconet, N., & Tavoni, M. (2021). From biophysical to economic impacts of climate change: an integrated perspective. *LSE Research Online*. http://eprints.lse.ac.uk/110999/1/From_biophysical_to_economic_impacts_of_climate.pdf

Popescu, S. M., Mansoor, S., Wani, O. A., Kumar, S. S., Sharma, V., Sharma, A., Arya, V. M., Kirkham, M. B., Hou, D., Bolan, N., & Chung, Y. S. (2024). Artificial intelligence and IoT driven technologies for environmental pollution monitoring and management. *Frontiers in Environmental Science*, *12*(February), 1–19. DOI: 10.3389/fenvs.2024.1336088

Rasp, S., Pritchard, M. S., & Gentine, P. (2018). Deep learning to represent subgrid processes in climate models. *Proceedings of the National Academy of Sciences of the United States of America*, *115*(39), 9684–9689. DOI: 10.1073/pnas.1810286115

Razak, S. F. A., Lee, C. P., Lim, K. M., & Tee, P. X. (2019). Smart halal recognizer for muslim consumers. *Indonesian Journal of Electrical Engineering and Computer Science*, *14*(1), 193–200. DOI: 10.11591/ijeecs.v14.i1.pp193-200

Razali, N., Ismail, S., & Mustapha, A. (2020). Machine learning approach for flood risks prediction. *IAES International Journal of Artificial Intelligence*, *9*(1), 73–80. DOI: 10.11591/ijai.v9.i1.pp73-80

Rising, J., Tedesco, M., Piontek, F., & Stainforth, D. A. (2022). The missing risks of climate change. *Nature*, *610*(7933), 643–651. DOI: 10.1038/s41586-022-05243-6

Simpson, N. P., Mach, K. J., Constable, A., Hess, J., Hogarth, R., Howden, M., Lawrence, J., Lempert, R. J., Muccione, V., Mackey, B., New, M. G., O'Neill, B., Otto, F., Pörtner, H. O., Reisinger, A., Roberts, D., Schmidt, D. N., Seneviratne, S., Strongin, S., & Trisos, C. H. (2021). A framework for complex climate change risk assessment. *One Earth*, *4*(4), 489–501. DOI: 10.1016/j.oneear.2021.03.005

Stefov, D., & Tomlinson, B. (2009). Adaptation Policy Frameworks for Climate Change: Developing Strategies. *Policies and Measures.*, (May), 2014.

Sungmin, O., Dutra, E., & Orth, R. (2020). Robustness of process-based versus data-driven modeling in changing climatic conditions. *Journal of Hydrometeorology*, *21*(9), 1929–1944. DOI: 10.1175/JHM-D-20-0072.1

Tehrany, M. S., Jones, S., & Shabani, F. (2019). Identifying the essential flood conditioning factors for flood prone area mapping using machine learning techniques. *Catena, 175*(April 2018), 174–192. DOI: 10.1016/j.catena.2018.12.011

Ukoba, K., Onisuru, O. R., & Jen, T.-C. (2024). Harnessing machine learning for sustainable futures: Advancements in renewable energy and climate change mitigation. *Bulletin of the National Research Center*, *48*(1), 99. Advance online publication. DOI: 10.1186/s42269-024-01254-7

Ummah, M. S. (2019). A complete guide to improving efficiency and minimizing costs in the modern warehouse. In *Sustainability (Switzerland)* (Vol. 11, Issue 1). http://scioteca.caf.com/bitstream/handle/123456789/1091/RED2017-Eng-8ene.pdf?sequence=12&isAllowed=y%0Ahttp://dx.doi.org/10.1016/j.regsciurbeco.2008.06.005%0Ahttps://www.researchgate.net/publication/305320484_SISTEM_PEMBETUNGAN_TERPUSAT_STRATEGI_MELESTARI

Van Straaten, C., Whan, K., Coumou, D., Van Den Hurk, B., & Schmeits, M. (2022). Using Explainable Machine Learning Forecasts to Discover Subseasonal Drivers of High Summer Temperatures in Western and Central Europe. *Monthly Weather Review*, *150*(5), 1115–1134. DOI: 10.1175/MWR-D-21-0201.1

Vu, H. T., & Lim, J. (2022). Effects of country and individual factors on public acceptance of artificial intelligence and robotics technologies: A multilevel SEM analysis of 28-country survey data. *Behaviour & Information Technology*, *41*(7), 1515–1528. DOI: 10.1080/0144929X.2021.1884288

White, R. H., Anderson, S., Booth, J. F., Braich, G., Draeger, C., Fei, C., Harley, C. D. G., Henderson, S. B., Jakob, M., Lau, C. A., Mareshet Admasu, L., Narinesingh, V., Rodell, C., Roocroft, E., Weinberger, K. R., & West, G. (2023). The unprecedented Pacific Northwest heatwave of June 2021. *Nature Communications*, *14*(1), 727. Advance online publication. DOI: 10.1038/s41467-023-36289-3

Ylönen, M., & Aven, T. (2023). A framework for understanding risk based on the concepts of ontology and epistemology. *Journal of Risk Research*, *26*(6), 581–593. DOI: 10.1080/13669877.2023.2194892

Zhao, G., Pang, B., Xu, Z., Peng, D., & Xu, L. (2019). Assessment of urban flood susceptibility using semi-supervised machine learning model. *The Science of the Total Environment*, *659*, 940–949. DOI: 10.1016/j.scitotenv.2018.12.217

Chapter 4
Artificial Intelligence in Circular Economy and Green Logistics: A Bibliometric Analysis Using R Studio

Gurpreet pal Kaur
http://orcid.org/0000-0001-7475-3548
Lovely Professional University, India

Mushtaq Ahmad Shah
http://orcid.org/0000-0002-3177-9622
Lovely Professional University, India

ABSTRACT

This chapter explores the intersection of Artificial Intelligence (AI), Circular Economy (CE), and Green Logistics (GL) as a transformative path toward sustainable industrial systems. Using R Studio (Biblioshiny), a bibliometric analysis of 70 Scopus-indexed publications (2010–2025) maps global research trends on AI in CE and GL. The analysis identifies five major research clusters: AI-enabled reverse logistics, digital supply chains and Logistics 5.0, predictive manufacturing, AI-driven decision and policy modelling, and sustainable urban mobility. Emerging themes include digital product passports, blockchain-based traceability, and low-energy AI models. The chapter concludes with recommendations for academia, industry, and policymakers to foster AI-driven, circular, and low-carbon ecosystems.

DOI: 10.4018/979-8-3373-5946-5.ch004

1. INTRODUCTION

The rapidly worsening climate crisis, the shortage of resources, the rise of waste volumes has added to the world's alarm, it is unsustainable trends of production and consumption. As a reaction to this, the Circular Economy (CE) has already become a paradigm of transformation that aims to decouple economic development with resource depletion and focus on restorative and regenerative activities, including reducing, reusing, recycling, and remanufacturing (Remyha & Pryimak, 2025). In the same manner, Green Logistics (GL) is a strategic change in the supply chain operations that tries to make supply chain operations environmentally friendly by minimizing energy consumption, lowering emissions, and maintaining sustainable flow of resources during product lifecycles (Challouf et al., 2025). In this changing sustainability discussion, Artificial Intelligence (AI) is also a focal technological facilitator that aids intelligent automation, optimization, and observation of circular and green logistics systems (Schlueter et al., 2023). By incorporating the digital technologies like AI, IoT, and blockchain, a company will have the ability to increase the level of transparency, traceability, and resource efficiency throughout the global supply streams (Ge, 2024).

The concept of Artificial Intelligence (AI) and such methods as machine learning, deep learning, computer vision, and natural language processing have transformed the way companies handle information, materials, and processes. With the combination of AI and the use of other innovative technologies, including the Internet of Things (IoT), Big Data Analytics, Blockchain, and Cloud Computing, organizations can progressively form self-regulating systems to optimize the routes, anticipate demand, recognize the recycling prospects, and efficiently manage waste streams (Shah & Ganesh 2025; Shah 2025). All these digital changes are based on the general shift between Industry 4.0 and Industry 6.0 and are improving the performance of real-time decision-making, predictive maintenance, and circular logistics (Fernández-Miguel et al., 2025). Energy efficiency and sustainability performance is also reinforced by the use of AI-based solutions in manufacturing and logistics, specifically in small and medium-sized enterprises (SMEs) (Alkhodair & Alkhudhayr, 2025). Taken together, these developments are consistent with the United Nations Sustainable Development Goals (SDGs) and the overall global carbon neutrality to highlight the strategic importance of AI as a technological and a governance tool towards achieving circularity and sustainability in logistics and manufacturing (Kulova et al., 2024).

According to recent studies, there is increasing importance of Artificial Intelligence (AI) to optimize circular and green supply chains. Research notes that AI-based reverse logistics facilitates effective resource recovery by means of predictive analytics, autonomous sorting and remanufacturing (Raut et al., 2025). Practices in sustainable logistics prove that AI-based systems can improve the reduction of emissions and efficiency in various industries (Suthagar & Mishra, 2024). Besides that, real-time coordination and decision-making within sustainable transport networks are reinforced by the introduction of AI and game-theoretic optimization (Aghaei et al., 2025). In the textile and manufacturing supply chain, Digital Product Passport (DPP) applications and AI algorithms help classify and identify waste and trace the material (Telfort and Valilai, 2025). More so, the predictive analytics can be enhanced by artificial intelligence that will help to enhance logistics forecasting, inventory optimization, and waste reduction to achieve sustainability and a circular economy (Raut et al., 2025).

Although the research field under consideration has developed significantly, the literature is still quite disjointed, including the field of industrial engineering, computer science, operations research, and environmental management. Available literature has examined a wide range of contexts, including smart manufacturing and logistics systems that use AI (Raut et al., 2025) and reverse logistics and waste management systems (Suthagar and Mishra, 2024) and AI-based sustainability assessment models. A current trend in the field of the integration of decision-support systems and Industry 4.0 also demonstrates the growing influences of AI on digital transformation and the re-creation of circular values (Kopeinig et al., 2024). However, a generalized integration of the ways AI-based technologies can be used in the collective development of the circular economy and green logistics principles is scarce. The given gap indicates an urgent necessity to develop a data-driven mapping of the intellectual development of the field and its thematic convergence, to which bibliometric analysis tools can be applied effectively to track the trends of publications, co-authorship, keyword relationships, and citation patterns across international research environments (Schlueter et al., 2023).

It is against this backdrop that the current chapter performs a bibliometric study of Artificial Intelligence (AI) applications in Circular Economy (CE) and Green Logistics (GL) areas with R Studio and Biblioshiny interface. The recent literature has highlighted the increased overlap of AI, sustainability, and logistics innovation and has placed a high regard on mapping research trends and intellectual architectures in this dynamic segment (Raut et al., 2025). Based on the methodological developments in the sustainability analytics and bibliometric visualization fields (Schlueter, et al., 2023), the paper will critically assess how the academic discourses between 2010 and 2025 have changed, who has contributed the most, and what subjects are leading the research agenda. The visualization of the analysis shows the swift growth of AI-driven sustainability research and finds conceptual connections that disclose new paradigms of intelligent circular supply chains, autonomous waste recovery, and AI-enhanced sustainability governance ((Suthagar and Mishra, 2024; Kopeinig et al., 2024).

This chapter has the following objectives:

1. Find the trends of publication, most significant authors, institutions, and countries that have contributed to research on Artificial Intelligence in circular Economy and Green Logistics.
2. Plot somewhat intellectually the field by using R Studio to do co-citation and keyword network analyses.
3. Identify new research themes and clusters that bring out the discussion of AI integration in the CE and GL frameworks.

Combining both quantitative bibliometric methods and critical interpretation of the most significant studies, this chapter offers a comprehensive view of the interactions between Artificial Intelligence (AI) and sustainability-oriented logistics systems. Recent studies have shown the impact of AI to create intelligent and adaptable supply chains, improving the environmental and operational sustainability (Raut et al., 2025). The research findings aid scholarly research because it clarifies the intellectual field and knowledge development of this interdisciplinary sector, and it provides practitioners and company executives with practice-based value regarding how to create smarter, greener, and more circular value chains (Suthagar and Mishra, 2024). Moreover, AI is not only an example of a technological tool but an enabling force behind the Industry 5.0 paradigm with its synthesis of human-centred innovation and environmental sustainability to create sustainable economic value (Schlueter et al., 2023).

To sum up, the implementation of AI in Circular Economy and Green Logistics is a pivotal edge of the sustainable change. With more severe attempts of the industries and governments to comply with global environmental requirements, it is necessary to comprehend the knowledge base and theme development of the given field (Kopeinig et al., 2024). This chapter offers an evidence-based literature review synthesis of how AI is transforming the paths to ecological efficiency, operational optimization, and the creation of circular values as a foundation to the future study and application in the age of digital sustainability.

2. LITERATURE REVIEW AND THEORETICAL BACKGROUND

The adoption of the Artificial Intelligence (AI) as the part of the paradigm of the Circular Economy (CE) and Green Logistics (GL) is the most essential step toward sustainable development and efficiency of global production and supply chains. This increase in the volume of literature indicates that there is a rapid academic focus on the application of AI, machine learning (ML), and data analytics in creating a shift toward a more circular and sustainable economic model (Raut et al., 2025). Theoretical developments in this area are based on industrial ecology, sustainability transition theory and the institutional theory and are gradually introducing the new framework of Industry 5.0, which is characterized by a balance between automation, human-oriented innovation, and ecological resilience (Pei et al., 2025)

2.1 Artificial Intelligence as an Enabler of Circular Economy

AI has emerged as a core technology to support the implementation of circular economy (CE) practices in any industry, giving the computational intelligence needed to optimize complex systems in which many interdependent flows of resources are involved. Raut et al. (2025) discuss AI as the way to promote predictive analytics, pattern recognition, and decision-making based on data in waste management, recycling, and remanufacturing by utilizing AI in the circular economy. Their bibliometric analysis (821 Scopus publications, 2011-2023) determines six thematic groups connecting AI and CE, including waste management, sustainability, reverse logistics, recycling, reuse, and remanufacturing, highlighting that AI has the ability to revolutionize the performance in the circular by means of digital intelligence. Likewise, AI-based systems are being adopted to enhance the traceability of waste, maximize reverse supply chains, and enhance solid waste management decision-making.

Empirical research also shows that AI contributes to sustainable manufacturing and closed-loop supply chains to a large extent. As an example, multi-agent systems will be integrated with computational intelligence to optimize reverse logistics of electronic waste to create quantifiable economic and environmental performance gains (Challouf et al., 2025). Likewise, machine learning (ML) algorithms are crucial to enhancing resource reuse, remanufacturing, and lifecycle management by predicting using modelling and using decision support systems (Noman et al., 2022). In addition, recent studies discuss the ways Digital Product Passports (DPPs) combined with AI can improve waste sorting and recycling and material traceability in the textile value chain (Telfort & Valilai, 2025).

Taken together, these researches validate that AI features of analysis, cognition, and autonomy can assist industries in operationalizing the principles of CE at scales that are scalable, data-driven, and environmentally responsible and prove its key role in global sustainability transitions.

2.2 AI and Green Logistics: To Sustainability and Not Efficiency

The contribution of Artificial Intelligence (AI) to Green Logistics (GL) can be viewed much further than automation itself, as it transforms the development of logistics networks, their governance, and optimization to be more sustainable. There are several dimensions of research where AI contributes to GL, which are energy optimization, reduction of emissions, smart routing, and efficiency in reverse logistics. Indicatively, AI, IoT and blockchain have been demonstrated to simplify the concept of reverse logistics through improved traceability, automation, and environmental outcomes. In the same vein, bibliometric and systematic reviews show that the incorporation of Industry 4.0 technologies, specifically AI and big data analytics, will have a significant beneficial impact on collection and sorting and recycling processes and will also reduce the cost of operations (Challouf et al., 2025).

Reverse logistics systems based on AI also promote the circular performance and resource recovery in developing economies, and it has been demonstrated that they contribute to the development of sustainable supply chain management. Besides, predictive analytics and minimization algorithms, which use AI, have transformed the data-driven logistics planning and minimized the uncertainty in demand forecasting, inventory management, and transportation routing (Chen et al., 2024). The use of AI-assisted route optimization and real-time adaptive logistics can have a significant negative impact on fuel consumption and carbon emissions, which will encourage more sustainable and resilient supply chain activities (Sarioguz, 2025).

Taken together, this body of research identifies that AI is a driver of sustainable change in the logistics industry that can shift the current orientation of logistics towards cost-effectiveness and a holistic approach to environmental stewardship and innovation of the circular supply chain (Cortes-Pellicer et al., 2025; Habazin et al., 2025)

2.3 AI and Reverse Logistics

Both CE and GL focus on another concept known as reverse logistics (RL) or the process of returning, collecting, refurbishing, and redistributing end-of-life products. The integration of AI and RL is now an important research and industrial concern. According to (Cortes Pellicer et al., 2025), AI has been a crucial enabler of improving decision-making in the process of RL planning, execution, and control. Their review classifies AI applications under RL as machine learning, predictive analytics, and decision-support systems, all of which enhance the design of the network, its effectiveness in collection, and its efficiency in disposition of products. Nevertheless, they also observe the obstacles like high implementation cost and poor technology infrastructure. In the same line, (Duta & Enache, 2024) identify the application of AI in the sphere of Industry 4.0 in decision-support systems of reverse logistics and note that the technology can facilitate material loop closure and transition to CEs. Recycling and waste management also deal with the bottlenecks in the operation through the integration of AI and reverse logistics. It is noted that the Digital Supply Chains and Logistics 4.0 are enabled by AI and IoT and are the basis of realising green logistics and circular supply chain objectives (Shafique et al., 2025). This proves a paradigm shift to Logistics 5.0, in which AI, automations, and human cooperation would intersect to form sustainable, resilient and human-focused logistics systems (Machado & Rodriguez, 2025).

2.4 Theoretical Background: Connection between AI, CE and GL

In theory, the intersection between AI, CE and GL can be theorized in a number of frameworks. The Sustainability Transitions Theory focuses on the co-evolution of technology, institutions, and social practices as the means of facilitating a systemic change in sustainability (Pei et al., 2025). In this context, AI is a technology niche innovation, which increases the pace of transition between linear systems of industry and circular regimes. According to the Institutional Theory, AI implementation in the organization is driven by regulatory pressures, market expectations, and environmental norms to ensure sustainable logistics and CE performance (Mukherjee et al., 2024)). Resource-Based View (RBV) and its environmental variant, the Natural Resource-Based View (NRBV), assume that technological resources like AI are a strategic resource helping firms to become more environmentally competitive and more innovational. Lastly, the Digital Transformation Framework places AI in a bigger digital ecosystem, which includes data analytics, IoT, and blockchain as mutually necessary guarantees of sustainability (Rodrigues et al., 2025; Machado and Rodriguez, 2025).

These theoretical views are united by one point of commonality, namely, AI is both an facilitator and a driver of sustainable transition, as it enhances efficiency, transparency, and circularity within logistic and production systems. In addition, the application of human-centered design to Logistics 5.0 (Machado & Rodriguez, 2025) also depicts a new paradigm where AI is not only applied to automate operations but also to create ethical, social, and environmental values. This shift to AI-based models of CE and GL, therefore, reflects the spirit of Industry 5.0, with sustainability, resilience, and inclusiveness as the key strategic deliverables.

Altogether, the literature reviewed proves that Artificial Intelligence is transforming the principles of circular economy and green logistics by means of intelligent automation, predictive analytics, and decisions-driven by data. Although remarkable progress has been made, there are still some issues associated with technological preparedness, standardization, and intersectoral cooperation. The systematic bibliometric analysis, thus, is necessary to trace the development of this interdisciplinary area, recognize the powerful clusters of researches, and shed light on the further directions of artificial intelligence-powered circular and sustainable logistic systems.

2.5 Logistics Education, Workforce Skills, and Future Training

The bibliometric trends identified in this chapter—specifically the shift toward Logistics 5.0 and AI-driven decision support—underscore a critical need for a parallel evolution in human capital. As the transition from linear to circular systems accelerates, the traditional logistics workforce must evolve into a tech-enabled strategic layer capable of managing complex, self-regulating systems. This shift requires a workforce skills framework built on "T-shaped" competencies: deep technical proficiency in interpreting AI/ML outputs from Warehouse and Transportation Management Systems (WMS/TMS) paired with a broad understanding of the circular value chain. Beyond digital literacy, operational agility is becoming a core requirement as workers manage the rising complexities of "last-mile" green delivery and the high-variability workflows associated with reverse logistics and resource recovery.

In alignment with the emergence of Digital Product Passports (DPP) and blockchain-based traceability noted in the literature, future educational content must prioritize digital application over static theoretical models. Modern curricula are increasingly integrating digital twin technology and simulation, allowing professionals to stress-test circular warehouse configurations and carbon-efficiency strategies in risk-free virtual environments. Furthermore, as Industry 5.0 emphasizes human-centricity alongside ecological resilience, training must incorporate Sustainability and ESG principles, teaching the workforce to move beyond cost-efficiency toward holistic environmental stewardship. This includes specific training on automation oversight, where human-in-the-loop (HITL) models ensure that operators can effectively collaborate with Autonomous Mobile Robots (AMRs) and AI-driven sorting systems.

The strategic objectives and training frameworks for the future must move the workforce from reactive execution to proactive optimization. By fostering analytical fluency, organizations can translate the "predictive analytics" identified in the bibliometric clusters into actionable operational gains, effectively bridging the gap between technological feasibility and system-wide implementation. A secondary objective is resilience building; through the use of VR/AR simulations, workforces can practice response strategies for "Black Swan" disruptions—such as port strikes or systemic supply failures—without physical or economic risk. To ensure long-term alignment with the rapid pace of AI innovation, the industry is shifting toward modular, continuous learning models. These include micro-credentialing in niche domains like "Blockchain for Traceability" and "Green Incremental Learning," ensuring that the human element remains a resilient driver of the circular and green logistics transition.

3. RESEARCH METHODOLOGY

The current research paper follows a bibliometric analysis method that would provide a systematic review of the dynamic interface between Artificial Intelligence (AI), Circular Economy (CE), and Green Logistics (GL) literature. Bibliometric analysis is a quantitative method of tracing the structure and intellectual development of a scientific field that allow a researcher to detect the trends in publications, influential authors, major institutions, and thematic networks across the years (Raut et al., 2025) This method is especially useful in multidisciplinary fields, including AI-driven sustainability, where the research is spread across different academic disciplines operations management environmental science industrial engineering information technology, and so on. This study utilizes the tools of bibliometric and network analyses to reveal the intellectual and collaborative space of AI applications to CE and GL following the methodological rigor of the past systematic studies on the topic (Rodrigues et al., 2025; Abdelaziz and Munawaroh, 2024).

The research design is carried out in a systematic and descriptive bibliometric approach having four consecutive stages, with data collection, preprocessing, performance analysis, and scientific mapping. The steps have been followed with the help of the R Studio software environment, namely Bibliometrics package and its graphical interface Biblioshiny, which supports the possibility of visualizing and analysing data comprehensively and flexibly. It is the methodological design that does not only have the purpose to quantify academic performance, but also to visualize those conceptual linkages and knowledge flows that conceal the evolution of the field. In order to achieve the level of depth of analysis, cross-verification and presentation of results were performed using complementary tools (VOS viewer and Microsoft Excel) as in the case of related researches carried out in the field of technological progress in logistics (Davin Arkan Admoko et al., 2024) and manufacturing sustainability ((Benavides-Sánchez et al., 2025)).

The information to be used in this analysis was obtained in the Scopus database which is one of the most recognized and complete data collections of peer-reviewed literature. The reason Scopus was chosen is that it guarantees the inclusion of high-impact journals and conference proceedings and book chapters, thus being suitable in the case of large-scale bibliometric research (Shafique et al., 2025). The search strategy was well-thought to be able to cover the scope of the research at the point of intersection of AI, CE, and GL. A complex of Boolean operators and specific keywords was utilized that consisted of the following terms: Artificial Intelligence, Machine learning, Circular Economy, Green Logistics, Reverse Logistics, Sustainable Supply Chain. The results were limited to those published starting as early as 2010 and up to the present day, including the era when digital transformation and integration of sustainability became increasingly widespread and known as Industry 4.0 and, subsequently, Industry 5.0. A final set of about 70 Scopus-indexed documents, obtained after a stringent screening procedure, comprising review of the titles and abstracts and elimination of the redundant entries, was formed. These papers, which are a summary of the uploaded dataset, cover internationally acclaimed journals including Sustainable Futures, Environment, Development and Sustainability, International Journal of Logistics Management, Procedia CIRP and Journal of Global Optimization.

After downloading the bibliographic data in the form of a Bib Tex file, they were loaded into R Studio using the convert2df() library of the bibliometrics package, which transforms the raw metadata into a form of the structured data frame, which can be analysed quantitatively. The research used two types of bibliometric indicators, namely, performance indicators and relational indicators, to offer a multi-dimensional evaluation. The performance measurements employed the variables of productivity and effect using annual publication trends, most prolific authors, highly cited documents and influential journals. Relational indicators, in their turn, explored the intellectual organization and collaboration networks within the field using co-authorship, co-citation, and keyword co-occurrence analysis (Nikseresht et al., 2022)The combination of the relational indicators enabled discovering new research clusters and intellectual connections across the studies in AI-based logistics optimization, AI-driven reverse logistics (Cortes Pellicer et al., 2025), and sustainable manufacturing (Benavides-Sánchez et al., 2025).

It was analysed in a stepwise data processing process in accordance with the PRISMA (Preferred Reporting Items to Systematic Reviews and Meta-Analyses) framework, which provides transparency and reproducibility (Rodrigues et al., 2025). Descriptive statistics was used in the first step to capture the development of publications by year, author, institution, and country indicating growth in publications over the years and the contribution of the world towards research. The second phase in this package was co-authorship analysis to find out collaboration networks between researchers and institutions to allow visualization of the patterns of knowledge diffusion across regions. In the third step, the mapping of key words co-occurrence was conducted to identify the overarching research topics like reverse logistics, waste management, predictive analytics, and digital supply chain. They could also be identified in this step using VOSviewer that grouped keywords in terms of frequency and co-occurrence strength, the relationships between research subjects visually by color-coded clusters. The last phase entailed the thematic evolution analysis with the help of Biblioshiny interface that configured the themes of the research into the following categories: motor (driving), niche, emerging, and declining themes. This time mapping allowed studying the change in the research focus over time between the initial investigations of AI in waste management and recycling (2011- 2015) and the more recent studies of Logistics 5.0, digital product passports, and AI ethics in sustainable logistics (2020-2025) (Machado and Rodriguez, 2025; Telfort and Valilai, 2025).

Several validation steps were done to guarantee data validity and reliability. First, manual screening of duplicate and inconsistent entries was done to eradicate biasness. Second, R Studio and VOSviewer were cross-verified to obtain consistency in the clustering process and co-citation patterns. Third, the most frequently cited references and authors were cross-verified manually by using Scopus to verify the accuracy of citation. This three-fold validation strategy is consistent with the literature-based best practices based on bibliometric studies on sustainable logistics (Abdelaziz and Munawaroh, 2024; Raut et al., 2025). The open-source instruments like bibliometrics help to make this study more transparent and reproducible, and the process of analytical work can be adjusted to new bibliometric investigations of technological innovation and sustainability in the future.

To conclude, this methodological framework offers a solid, clear, and empirical basis on how to view the academic environment of AI in Circular Economy and Green Logistics. Through descriptive measures, network analysis, and thematic evolution analysis in R Studio, this paper not only measures the performance of research but also reveals the intellectual and conceptual nature of this quickly expanding field. The methodology offers a strong foundation to the following sections, which provide the interpretation of the bibliometric findings that show the dominant authors, institutions, and thematic areas that define the future of AI-based sustainability and circular innovation.

4. RESULTS AND DISCUSSION

4.1 Countries Scientific Production

Table 1 shows the distribution of scientific production in various countries. The statistics give Germany as the most contributing country with the highest number of publications (26) after Brazil (20), and India (18). The United States is also characterized by high research output of 14 publications. In Italy (9), China (8) and Spain (8), moderate levels of scientific production are detected. In the meantime, Portugal (7), Austria (6) and Indonesia (5) are the countries that are yet to make a mark in the world of scientific literature. Altogether, the table shows a wide geographical distribution of the research activity indicating both developed and developing countries interest in creating scientific knowledge.

Table 1. Countries Scientific Production

Country	Freq
Germany	26
Brazil	20
India	18
Usa	14
Italy	9
China	8
Spain	8
Portugal	7
Austria	6
Indonesia	5

4.2 Most Frequent Words

The most common keywords that were found in the reviewed literature are represented in the form of Figure 1 that gives an idea of the prevailing areas of thematic focus in research. The most common term is the so-called circular economy, used 36 times, which means that it is at the heart of the academic discussion. It is preceded by a reverse logistics (28 occurrences) and artificial intelligence (25 occurrences), which can be attributed to the increased academic attention to the field of technology-driven and sustainable operational models. Other popular themes are the so-called sustainability (14), logistics (12) and sustainable development (11), which altogether focus on the combining of environmental and economic goals. The keywords like decision making, supply chain management, supply chains, and waste management (each of them is used 9-10 times) demonstrate the significance of strategic and operational efficiency as the means of reaching the sustainability objectives. The keyword analysis, on balance, indicates a substantial interdisciplinary nature, as the field of focus is on sustainability, principles of the circular economy, as well as intelligent systems, to find the solution to the modern problems in the supply chains worldwide.

Figure 1. Most Frequency Words

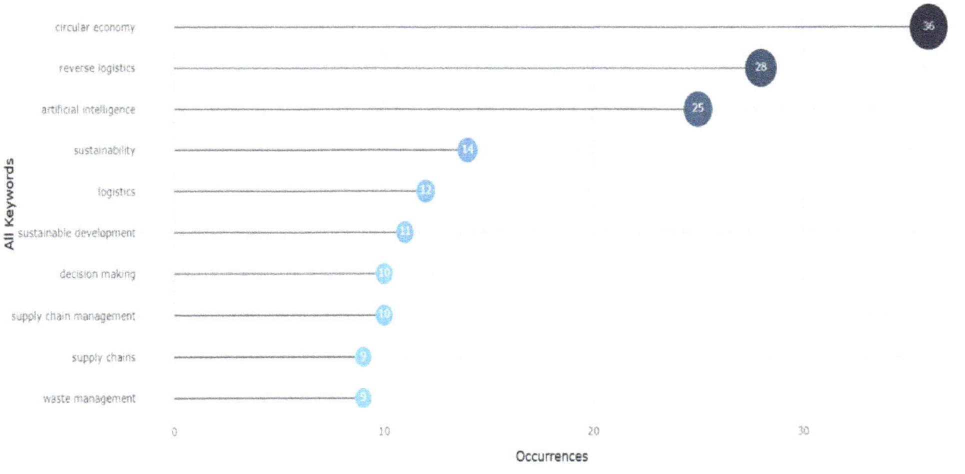

4.3 Word Cloud

Figure 2 is the Word Cloud diagram, based on the bibliometric set of data, which demonstrates the most common keywords in the publications that were analysed. The size and boldness of the words in the cloud reflect their frequency with bigger and more bold ones displaying more frequent occurrences. The most prominent ones, namely, circular economy, reverse logistics, and artificial intelligence, reveal the key themes that are leading to the modern research in the sphere of sustainability and innovation.

Sustainable development, supply chain management, sustainability, decision making, and waste management are also supported concepts as it seems that the interdisciplinary convergence between environmental management, digital transformation, and operational efficiency. The overlap of concepts such as machine learning, industry 4.0, green logistics, and recycling also helps to promote the idea of an increased union between the high-tech technologies and the sustainability-focused models.

In general, the Word Cloud serves as a visual support to the analytical findings shown in the table on the frequency of keywords and confirms that the current research is actively oriented towards implementing the concepts of artificial intelligence and the principles of a circular economy to make sustainable and data-driven decisions when it comes to global supply chains.

Figure 2. Word Cloud

4.4 Tree Map

Figure 3 shows a Tree map visualization of the relative saliency and proportional distribution of keywords that are based on the bibliometric dataset. The size of each rectangle is the number of occurrences of a keyword and each colour shapes the thematic group.

The analysis has shown that the most prevalent theme of research was the concept of the circular economy (36 occurrences; 13%), then reverse logistics (28; 10%), and artificial intelligence (25; 9%). The three keywords take the most space in the Tree Map as they are the focus of most literature on sustainability and innovation. Other important terms are such as sustainability (14; 5%), logistics (12; 4%), sustainable development (11; 4%), decision making (10; 4%), supply chain management (10; 4%), and waste management (9; 3%), which show the interdisciplinary linkage between the environmental management, technological innovation and organizational decision making.

Smaller nodes including machine learning, big data, green logistics, blockchain and industry 4.0 are also related but emerging and complementary fields of study. Their existence reflects the growing co-existence of digital technologies and sustainable business and supply chain practices.

In general, the Tree Map provides an overall visualization of the diversity and frequency of key words, and it is clear that the scholarly attention is focused on the three concepts circular economy, artificial intelligence, and reverse logistics, and is gradually spreading to the data-driven, technology-enhanced sustainability paradigm.

Figure 3. Tree Map

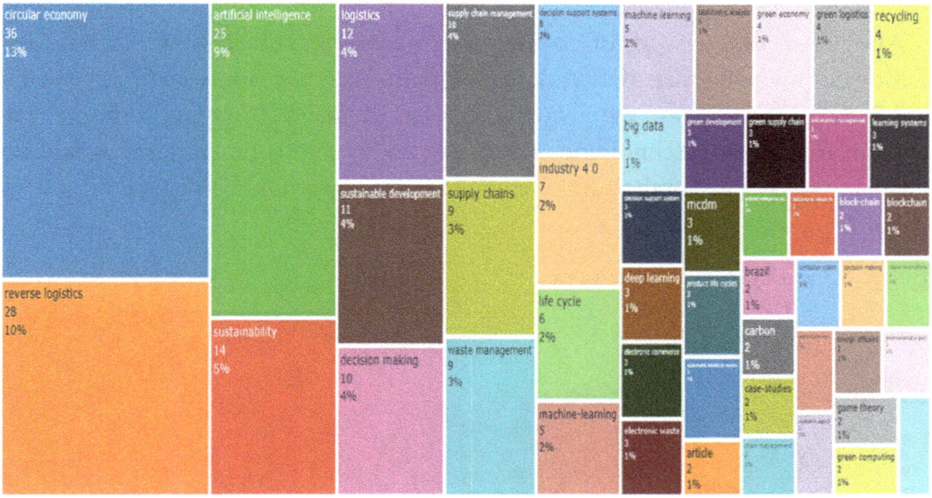

4.5 Co-occurrence Network

Figure 4 illustrates the co-occurring network of keywords derived out of the reviewed literature representation, which illustrates graphical representation of thematic connections and intellectual connections among commonly used terms of research. A node in the network denotes a keyword; the connecting lines between the nodes (edges) denote the frequency of co-occurrence of the two terms in the same publications. The node size is associated with the frequency of keywords, whereas the colour is used to represent the membership to a cluster, indicating different thematic groups.

As the visualization shows, the two most prevalent and interrelated nodes are the ones that display the notions of the circular economy and artificial intelligence, which are the centre of the network. These terms are closely connected with the associated ideas like a reverse logistics, sustainability, supply chain management, decision making and industry 4.0. This grouping implies that there is a close integration of sustainability structures and technology-based decision support systems in academic studies.

Keywords like green logistics, digital transformation, blockchain, machine learning, and big data are the focus of emerging and complementary research areas and also peripheral clusters. These signify the role of digital technologies that are changing in order to achieve efficiency in resources, waste minimization, and environmental management. Also, smaller clusters (e.g., "electronic waste, carbon, economic aspect) identify the more specific subthemes concerning the environmental and socioeconomic impacts.

Altogether, the network of co-occurring networks indicates the presence of a multidisciplinary overlap between sustainability science, logistics, and artificial intelligence. It highlights the growing scholarly concern of trying to harness the power of data-driven technologies to make economic transition to circling and sustainability, especially in the supply chain and decision-making system.

Figure 4. Co-occurrence Network

4.6 Thematic Map

Figure 5 provides a thematic map according to which the main research themes that have been identified during the bibliometric analysis are classified according to their centrality (degree of relevance) and density (degree of development). The map is split into four quadrants such as motor themes, basic themes, niche themes, and emerging or declining themes that reflect the maturity and relatedness of certain groups of researches in the field.

The upper-right quadrant (motor themes) indicates extremely advanced and central themes that propel the research field. Circular economy, reverse logistics, and artificial intelligence occupy the dominant role in this quadrant, which means that these phenomena serve as the intellectual and methodological foundations of the contemporary research. Their high interlinkages imply that there is a vibrant research front that is very robust and dynamic and that integrates the elements of sustainability with the ever-changing technology to ensure that there is a hope of maximizing the use of resources and the use of the resources in making decisions.

At the bottom-right base (simple themes), there are themes like machine learning and deep learning. These are pillar themes that, although fundamental to the field, are yet to be refined in the application to the context of sustainability. Their placement of the fact is their increased suitability in the implementation of artificial intelligence in circular and sustainable economies. The upper-left quadrant (niche themes) has more specialized and context-specific themes, including the ones like electronic waste, article, and Brazil. These are localized or domain specific studies which add richness to the overall research area as well as having limited cross-domain impact. Lastly, the lower-left quadrant (new or declining themes) incorporates such themes as MCDM (Multi-criteria decision-making), VOSviewer, which can be viewed as the signs of new methods of analysis becoming increasingly popular or older ones becoming less relevant to discussion.

In general, the thematic map gives a comprehensive perspective of the research environment, showing that AI-driven circular economy models and reverse logistics are the core themes, which motivate the study, whereas machine learning and blockchain-based digital transformations are developing as the enablers of sustainable innovation.

Figure 5. Thematic Map

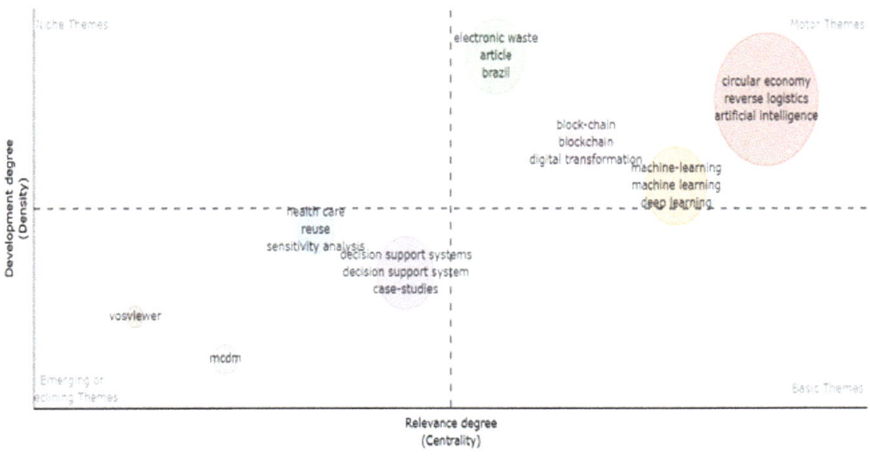

4.7 Most Relevant Sources

Figure 6 shows how the most pertinent sources of publications had been distributed across the area of research under examination. The visualization demonstrates journals and conference proceedings that yielded the most significant number of documents concerning the themes of the circular economy, artificial intelligence, and sustainable logistics.

The most successful source is the International Journal of Production Research with nine publications, which means its significance in spreading the works on the fusion of sustainability, operations management, and technological innovation research. Subsequently, three publications are presented in Lecture Notes in Mechanical Engineering, Procedia CIRP, and Procedia Computer Science, which indicates good interdisciplinary interaction both in the engineering and computer science views.

Moreover, two papers have been coauthored by Sustainability (Switzerland), which is becoming more and more an important open-access source of sustainability and circular economy research. There was one publication in other contributing sources like Annals of Emerging Technologies in Computing, Annals of Operations Research, Cleaner Environmental Systems, and Conference Proceedings -IEEE International Conference which means that the dissemination of research is wide but not extensive in computing, operations and environmental studies.

In general, the information shows that field is very interdisciplinary and is drawn upon various publication sources which have spanned engineering, environmental science, operations research and information systems. Such allocation is an indicator of the increased scholarly interest in applying artificial intelligence and the circle economy frameworks to sustainable production and supply chains.

Figure 6. Most Relevant Sources

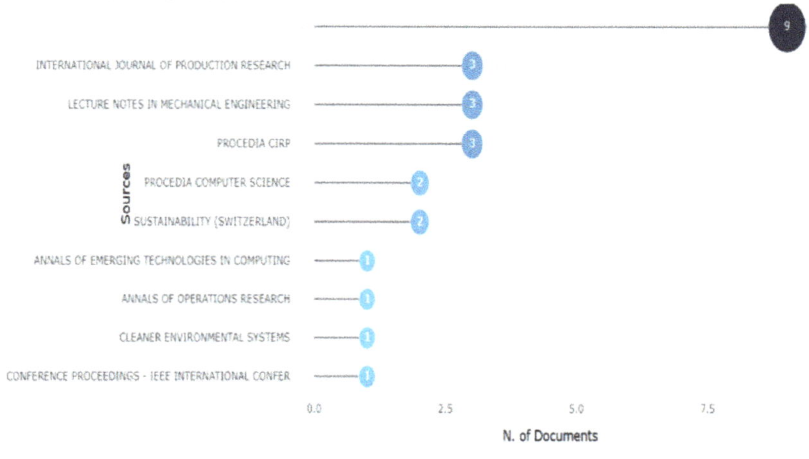

5. EMERGING RESEARCH CLUSTERS AND FUTURE RESEARCH DIRECTIONS

The bibliometric mapping and thematic analysis performed with the help of R Studio (Biblioshiny) indicate the existence of five key emerging research clusters that outline the intellectual and practical advancement of the Artificial Intelligence (AI) applications in the areas of Circular Economy (CE) and Green Logistics (GL). These clusters are reflective of the changing thematic environment and indicative of the way the research focus has moved to technological feasibility to integrated systemically and sustainability impact.

This is the oldest, and most frequently mentioned one, the AI-enabled Reverse Logistics and Resource Recovery, which focuses on the use of machine learning and predictive analytics in waste collection, disassembling, and remanufacturing (((Mukherjee et al., 2024); (Cortes Pellicer et al., 2025)). This cluster shows close relationships between reverse logistics efficiency and environmental performance manifesting the opportunity of AI to attain closed-loop supply chains.

Digital Supply Chains and Logistics 5.0 is the second cluster that is an up-and-coming paradigm, in which AI, IoT, Big Data, and Blockchain converge to form intelligent, transparent, and human-centric logistics ecosystems (Rodrigues et al., 2025; Machado & Rodriguez, 2025). The studies under this cluster also concentrate more on how AI can be used to achieve visibility, traceability, and ethical decision-making within green logistics networks.

The third cluster, AI to Predictive and Sustainable Manufacturing, involves taking AI into the production systems to reduce wastage, maximize resource consumption, and increase the life cycle of a product (Benavides-Sánchez et al., 2025). Research in this area focuses on predictive maintenance, energy optimization, and digital twin technology, and AI is seen as a major enabler of sustainable manufacturing in line with the objectives of Industry 5.0.

The fourth cluster is AI-Driven Decision Support and Policy Modelling, which is associated with the simulation, optimization, and multi-criteria decision models, which are used to sustainability planning (Aghaei et al., 2025; Davin Arkan Admoko et al., 2024). This group links AI with governance and environmental policy so that there is an increase in the interest in applying AI to aid the decision-making process in carbon management, reverse logistics infrastructure, and waste valorisation.

Lastly, the fifth cluster, AI and Sustainable Urban Mobility, albeit smaller in size, is on the rise as researchers are considering AI to optimize transportation, decrease emissions in urban areas, and contribute to a green solution of logistics in a smart city (Agarwal et al., 2025).

Out of these clusters, a number of research directions in the future are created. To begin with, AI sustainability indicators such as carbon footprint of AI model training and deployment are to be studied by researchers to guarantee technological advantages do not supplant the environmental benefits (Schluester et al., 2023). Second, cross-sectoral frameworks between AI innovations in logistics and circular business models in manufacturing, construction and agriculture are needed. Third, it should be investigated how government incentives, regulatory frameworks, and the development of infrastructures that support the use of AI in circular systems through policy-oriented studies (Raut et al., 2025; Mukherjee et al., 2024). Fourth, data interoperability and standardization in future studies should be a primary concern, especially in digital product passports (Telfort & Valilai, 2025), to facilitate the smooth flow of information throughout the supply chains. Fifth, social and ethical aspects, such as labor effects, inclusivity, and transparency, have to be incorporated in the AI-sustainability discourse to facilitate even-handed technological changes. Lastly, longitudinal bibliometric and network analysis might be further extended past 2025 to evaluate the transformations of emerging technologies including generative AI, quantum computing, and edge analytics on CE and GL practices in the next decade.

Overall, the reviewed literature demonstrates that although AI-based sustainability studies are proliferating at a fast pace, their future development will be based on the interdisciplinary cooperation, responsible AI usage, and enabling institutional ecosystems that help to transform online intelligence into physical environmental and social outcomes.

6. CONCLUSION AND STRATEGIC INSIGHTS FOR ACADEMIA AND INDUSTRY

Artificial Intelligence that is combined with Circular Economy and Green Logistics principles is the turning point in the search of sustainable industrial change. The bibliometric analysis reveals the obvious development of the research landscape in the world over time: at the beginning of the study of the possibilities of AI in the context of waste management and reverse logistics, simple conceptual ideas were developed, but then more complex and information-intensive approaches were developed to more comprehensive supply chains. The results of the analysis show the growing activity of publications but also the growing collaboration networks, linking academia, industry, and policy institutions in different regions of the world, including India, China, and Europe.

To the academic world, the findings highlight the need to integrate interdisciplinary research methods that combine operations management, data science, and sustainability research. Researchers ought to focus on theoretical convergence to relate the adoption of AI to the Natural Resource-Based View (NRBV), Institutional Theory, and Sustainability Transitions Theory (Mukherjee et al., 2024; Raut et al., 2025). The academic curricula and education in the field of logistics and management should consider AI literacy, data ethics, and the idea of a circular design to educate the future generation of professionals to operate sustainably with AI. Also, longitudinal and comparative research is desirable to determine the varying aspects of AI-enabled CE and GL innovations in economic, regulatory, and cultural settings.

To practitioners in the industry, the findings of this research put AI in the limelight of strategic enabler to attain triple-bottom-line performance, which consists of economic efficiency, environmental responsibility and social value. To manage waste and carbon emissions, firms can use predictive analytics to make demand and return predictions, use computer vision to classify materials and optimization algorithms to manage transport and inventory. Digital sustainability roadmaps should also be introduced to the companies that should align the implementation of AI with environmental, social, and governance (ESG) goals. Circular data ecosystems can be unlocked through collaboration platforms that can be used to combine manufacturers, recyclers, and logistics providers. Notably, automation has to be paired with inclusivity in organizations such that human abilities are a complement with AI systems to ensure that the organization attains ethical and resilient logistics networks.

The findings can also be used by governments and international agencies at the policy level to develop evidence-based interventions to promote the adoption of AI in sustainable logistics and manufacturing. This will involve the promotion of open data infrastructures, fiscal incentives of circular innovation, and global digital product passport and AI ethics standards.

To sum it up, Artificial Intelligence is not only a technological innovation but also a systemic facilitator that will help to transform to intelligent, circular, and low-carbon economies faster. Through academic, industrial, and policymaker collaboration, and integrating ethics and environmental concerns into the very fabric of AI development, societies will be able to see the vision of digitally empowered and sustainable future. The bibliometric knowledge provided in this chapter therefore act as a platform in establishing the subsequent level of theoretical growth as well as practical practice in future research and innovation in AI-enhanced Circular Economy and Green Logistics.

REFERENCES

Abdelaziz, S., & Munawaroh, M. (2024). Mitigating Supply Chain Vulnerabilities: A Bibliometric Analysis of Sustainable Logistics for Resilience and Risk Management with Perspectives on the Automotive Industry. *International Journal of Automotive Science And Technology*, *8*(4), 544–588. DOI: 10.30939/ijastech..1554338

Agarwal, S., Kumar, N., Tyagi, M., & Garg, R. K. (2025). Integrating soft computing techniques for optimizing green vehicular communications and networking in circular digital supply chain. *Journal of Science and Technology Policy Management*. DOI: 10.1108/JSTPM-03-2024-0112

Aghaei, A., Cai, F., & Wu, T. (2025). Game-Theoretic Analysis of Policy Impacts in Competition Between Reverse Supply Chains Involving Traditional and E-Channels. *Smart Cities*, *8*(1), 36. DOI: 10.3390/smartcities8010036

Alkhodair, M., & Alkhudhayr, H. (2025). Harnessing Industry 4.0 for SMEs: Advancing Smart Manufacturing and Logistics for Sustainable Supply Chains. *Sustainability (Basel)*, *17*(3), 813. DOI: 10.3390/su17030813

Benavides-Sánchez, E. P., Moya-Clemente, I., & Ribes-Giner, G. (2025). Bibliometric analysis and systematic literature review of the relationship between sustainable development goals and sustainable entrepreneurship over time. *Discover Sustainability*, *6*(1), 64. DOI: 10.1007/s43621-024-00572-0

Challouf, K., Alhloul, A., & Nemeth, N. (2025). Mapping the role of industry 4.0 technologies in green supply chain management: A bibliometric and structured text analysis. *Discover Sustainability*, *6*(1), 949. DOI: 10.1007/s43621-025-01827-0

Chen, J.-F., Ni, C.-C., Lin, P.-H., & Lin, R. (2024). Designing the Future: A Case Study on Human-AI Co-Innovation. *Creative Education*, *15*(03), 474–494. DOI: 10.4236/ce.2024.153028

Cortes Pellicer, P., Alarcon, F., & Pérez-Perales, D. (2025). Integration of artificial intelligence in reverse logistics process: Enhancing decision-making across planning, execution, and control stages. *International Journal of Production Management and Engineering*, *13*(2), 214–235. DOI: 10.4995/ijpme.2025.23262

Davin Arkan Admoko, Bambang Darmawan, A. Ana, & Vina Dwiyanti. (. (2024). A Cluster-Based Bibliometric Analysis of the Emerging Technological Landscape in Logistics using Vosviewer. *Journal of Advanced Research in Applied Sciences and Engineering Technology*, *42*(2), 234–249. DOI: 10.37934/araset.42.2.234249

Duta, L., & Enache, D. (2024). Decision Support Systems for Reverse Logistics in Industry 4.0. In Balas, V. E., Dzemyda, G., Belciug, S., & Kacprzyk, J. (Eds.), *Decision Making and Decision Support in the Information Era* (Vol. 534, pp. 109–118). Springer Nature Switzerland., DOI: 10.1007/978-3-031-62158-1_7

Fernández-Miguel, A., García-Muiña, F. E., Ortíz-Marcos, S., Jiménez-Calzado, M., Fernández Del Hoyo, A. P., & Settembre-Blundo, D. (2025). AI-Driven Transformations in Manufacturing: Bridging Industry 4.0, 5.0, and 6.0 in Sustainable Value Chains. *Future Internet, 17*(9), 430. DOI: 10.3390/fi17090430

Ge, R. (2024). Opportunities and Challenges in Global Supply Chains: Implementing Innovative Solutions for Sustainable Development. *Industrial Engineering and Innovation Management, 7*(4). Advance online publication. DOI: 10.23977/ieim.2024.070414

Kopeinig, J., Woschank, M., & Olipp, N. (2024). Industry 4.0 Technologies and their Implications for Environmental Sustainability in the Manufacturing Industry. *Procedia Computer Science, 232*, 2777–2789. DOI: 10.1016/j.procs.2024.02.095

Kulova, I., Nikolova-Alexieva, V., & Peev, K. (2024). Advancing green entrepreneurship through Industry 4.0 technologies: An analysis of sustainable manufacturing and logistics optimization. *BIO Web of Conferences, 130*, 05001. DOI: 10.1051/bioconf/202413005001

Machado, N. T., & Rodriguez, C. M. T. (2025). A Logistics 5.0 maturity model: A human-centric and sustainable approach for the supply chain of the future. *ITEGAM-Journal of Engineering and Technology for Industrial Applications (ITEGAM-JETIA, 11*(51). DOI: 10.5935/jetia.v11i51.1407

Mukherjee, S., Nagariya, R., Mathiyazhagan, K., Baral, M. M., Pavithra, M. R., & Appolloni, A. (2024). Artificial intelligence-based reverse logistics for improving circular economy performance: A developing country perspective. *International Journal of Logistics Management, 35*(6), 1779–1806. DOI: 10.1108/IJLM-03-2023-0102

Nikseresht, A., Hajipour, B., Pishva, N., & Mohammadi, H. A. (2022). Using artificial intelligence to make sustainable development decisions considering VUCA: A systematic literature review and bibliometric analysis. *Environmental Science and Pollution Research International, 29*(28), 42509–42538. DOI: 10.1007/s11356-022-19863-y PMID: 35377115

Noman, A. A., Akter, U. H., Pranto, T. H., & Haque, A. B. (2022). Machine Learning and Artificial Intelligence in Circular Economy: A Bibliometric Analysis and Systematic Literature Review. *Annals of Emerging Technologies in Computing, 6*(2), 13–40. DOI: 10.33166/AETiC.2022.02.002

Pei, R., Chen, M., & Liu, Z. (2025). Identifying Key Digital Enablers for Urban Carbon Reduction: A Strategy-Focused Study of AI, Big Data, and Blockchain Technologies. *Systems*, *13*(8), 646. DOI: 10.3390/systems13080646

Raut, S., Hossain, N. U. I., Kouhizadeh, M., & Fazio, S. A. (2025). Application of artificial intelligence in circular economy: A critical analysis of the current research. *Sustainable Futures : An Applied Journal of Technology, Environment and Society*, *9*, 100784. DOI: 10.1016/j.sftr.2025.100784

Rodrigues, S. P., Gomes, L. D. C., Peres, F. A. P., Correa, R. G. D. F., & Baierle, I. C. (2025). A Framework for Leveraging Digital Technologies in Reverse Logistics Actions: A Systematic Literature Review. *Logistics (Basel)*, *9*(2), 54. DOI: 10.3390/logistics9020054

Schlüter, M., Schimanek, R., Koch, P., Briese, C., Chavan, V., Bilge, P., Dietrich, F., & Krüger, J. (2023). Green incremental learning—Energy efficient ramp-up for AI-enhanced part recognition in reverse logistics. *Procedia CIRP*, *116*, 414–419. DOI: 10.1016/j.procir.2023.02.070

Shafique, M. N., Arshad, Z., Alavi-Borazjani, S. A., Pereira, E. T., & Chkoniya, V. (2025). Logistics 4.0 and Digital Supply Chain: A Systematic Review. In Reis, J. L., Cascalho, J., Peter, M. K., Reis, L. P., & Tiago, M. T. (Eds.), *Marketing and Smart Technologies* (Vol. 439, pp. 143–156). Springer Nature Singapore., DOI: 10.1007/978-981-96-3081-3_9

Shah, M. A. (2025). The Impact of FinTech on Entrepreneurial Intentions Among Young Indian Entrepreneurs Using Crowdfunding, Blockchain, and Mobile Payments. In *Models, Strategies, and Tools for Competitive SMEs* (pp. 325–340). IGI Global.

Shah, M. A. (2025). Examining the Impact of Blockchain Technology on Accounting Information Systems in Large Corporations. In Blockchain Technology Applications in Knowledge Management (pp. 305-322). IGI Global Scientific Publishing. DOI: 10.4018/979-8-3693-3956-5.ch011

Shah, M. A., & Ganesh, U. B. (2025). Delays to distributed ledgers: Examining the rationale for leveraging blockchain technology in construction sector. *Global Knowledge, Memory and Communication*. Advance online publication. DOI: 10.1108/GKMC-03-2024-0177

Suthagar, K. S., & Mishra, U. (2024). Sustainable green circular economic model with controllable waste and emission in healthcare system. *Environment, Development and Sustainability*, *27*(4), 8767–8809. DOI: 10.1007/s10668-023-04254-1

Telfort, T. E., & Valilai, O. F. (2025). A Framework for Sustainable Textile Waste Management using Digital Product Passports and Artificial Intelligence. *Procedia CIRP*, *134*, 909–914. DOI: 10.1016/j.procir.2025.02.224

KEY TERMS AND DEFINITIONS

Artificial Intelligence (AI): Computer-based systems capable of performing tasks that normally require human intelligence such as prediction, classification, optimization, and pattern recognition used to enhance decision-making in circular and green logistics.

Machine Learning (ML): A subset of AI that enables systems to learn patterns from data and improve performance without explicit programming; widely used for forecasting, waste classification, and logistics optimization.

Circular Economy (CE): An economic model focused on keeping products and materials in use through reduction, reuse, recycling, and recovery, thereby minimizing waste and resource extraction.

Green Logistics (GL): Logistics practices that reduce environmental impacts through lower emissions, energy efficiency, optimized transport routes, eco-packaging, and sustainable supply chain management.

Reverse Logistics (RL): The process of moving products or materials backward in the supply chain for return, recycling, refurbishment, remanufacturing, or proper disposal.

Sustainable Supply Chain Management (SSCM): Management of material, information, and financial flows to achieve economic efficiency while minimizing environmental and social impacts.

Digital Product Passport (DPP): A digital record that tracks material composition, lifecycle data, and sustainability attributes of a product to support transparency, recycling, and circular flows.

Industry 4.0: The fourth industrial revolution characterized by interconnected digital technologies (IoT, AI, robotics, big data) enabling smart, automated, and data-driven manufacturing.

Industry 5.0 / Logistics 5.0: An emerging paradigm emphasizing human–technology collaboration, sustainability, resilience, and hyper-personalization in production and logistics systems.

Bibliometric Analysis: A quantitative research method that uses publication, citation, and keyword data to map scientific trends, influential authors, thematic evolution, and knowledge structures.

Predictive Analytics: Data-driven techniques that use historical patterns to forecast outcomes such as demand, returns, waste generation, or transportation flows in logistics.

Digital Twin: A virtual replica of a physical system used for simulation, monitoring, and optimization commonly applied to manufacturing and logistics for sustainability enhancements.

Energy-Efficient AI / Green AI: AI models designed to minimize energy consumption during training and deployment, ensuring that technological benefits do not contribute to higher carbon emissions.

Chapter 5
Organizational Innovation Effect on Digital Leadership by Mediation of AI in Circular Economy

Shashi Kant
http://orcid.org/0000-0003-4722-5736
DMI-St.Eugene University, Zambia

Wako Jio
http://orcid.org/0009-0003-6192-459X
Bule Hora University, Ethiopia

Shashank Mittal
http://orcid.org/0009-0007-8643-4350
O.P. Jindal Global University, India

Gurpreet Singh
http://orcid.org/0009-0002-8578-853X
Lovely Professional University, India

ABSTRACT

This chapter expounds on the complex correlation between organizational innovation, digital leadership, and the mediating variable (artificial intelligence (AI)) within the framework of a circular economy. In a large sample size (390 respondents), the authors use exploratory and confirmatory factor analysis (CFA). The results indicate that organizational innovation indeed promotes very effectively the digital leadership capabilities, which are again paired down by AI technologies. The mediation effect is an indication of how AI can support creative practices and

DOI: 10.4018/979-8-3373-5946-5.ch005

decision-making systems to enhance sustainable practices in a circular economy. The chapter explains what the findings mean to organizations interested in going through the barriers presented by the environmental sustainability while utilizing digital transformation. It reinforces the necessity of leaders to implement AI into their innovation plans in order to create sustainability and flexibility culture. By filling the gap between theoretical insights and practical practice.

INTRODUCTION

The influence of organizational innovation, digital leadership (DL), and artificial intelligence (AI) is, in turn, as important as never before in the eras characterized by quick technological development and environmental depreciation (Al Halbusi et al., 2025, Adula et al, 2025). Effective leadership to support the incorporation of sustainable practices within a circular economy (CE makes it necessary to embrace the digital transformation (Khan et al., 2024). The idea regarding a CE, the support of resource efficiency and the reduction of waste were born as the reaction against the state of linear economy that is overly oriented towards unsustainable consumption habits (Elshaer et al., 2025). Such transition also necessitates new forms of leadership and management and thus there is need to examine how the two interact (Awad et al., 2025). Other literature has asserted the importance of OI towards improving competitive advantage and sustainability (Tutore et al., 2024). It has been demonstrated that DL creates an atmosphere that promotes innovation but not much is known about the mediating influence of AI (Adholiya, 2025). Certain obstacles impede organizations to enjoy the full advantages of DL and innovation (Mamudu et al., 2024). Moreover, few studies have focused on finding a solution to how AI can help in bridging the gap across the conventional methods of management and the innovative requirements needed in a CE (Mukherjee et al., 2024, Kant et al., 2025). The chapter is designed to bridge all these knowledge gaps by examining the relations across OI, DL, as well as AI (Gatell & Avella, 2024). It will provide viable information to future scholars and policy makers on how to formulate effective policies that utilize AI to maximize effectiveness of leaders in sustainability efforts (Arroyabe et al., 2024). The leadership question that informs this research is the following one: ***"How does AI influence the nexus across the OI and DL in promoting sustainable practices in a circular economy (CE)?"*** The answer to this question will help organizations chart a course as they struggle through the maze of digital transformation in a more sustainable future.

BACKGROUND

The shift to the circular economy (CE) means an overhaul in the way companies work and is directed towards sustainable business practice, resource efficiency, and prevention of waste (Kant et al., 2025). The model differs dramatically with the conventional linear economy that adheres to a take-make-dispose economic model (Gatell & Avella, 2024). This leads to an increasing urgency of climate change and resource depletion within organizations that causes organizations to embrace circular ideals that necessitates new practices and DL (Mamudu et al., 2024). The range of challenges that may stand in the way of successful implementation of these ideas is quite extensive (Adholiya, 2025). A pragmatic example where these challenges may be experienced can be seen using Philips, a consumer electronics giant (Tutore et al., 2024). The company has gone a long way in ensuring the CE has been integrated in its lighting programmer in what it has termed as the Circular Lighting programmer (Awad et al., 2025). Although Philips innovatively tackled these ideas, operationalizing the concepts was difficult, both in terms of supply chain complexity and having to find new business models (Elshaer et al., 2025). The firm found out that although digital technologies had the potential of improving product lifecycle management, most times, traditional stakeholders would hinder progress (Khan et al., 2024). This case demonstrates the importance of having good DL to overcome such resistance and to accomplish the cultural change that is required to be successful in its implementation (Al Halbusi et al., 2025).

The example of the fashion industry may be taken with a brand such as H&M trying to implement the practices of circularity by recycling their products, and using more sustainable raw materials (Mukherjee et al., 2024). Nonetheless, these initiatives tend to meet some impediments at the consumer level of constraint (Gatell & Avella, 2024). During this time many consumers have not adopted many recycling programs mainly because of a lack of awareness and the inconvenience. The experience of H&M confirms that DL is a vital part of educating and engaging consumers and should not be underestimated in the desire to innovate (Arroyabe et al., 2024). These case studies demonstrate that the theoretical assumptions with regards to OI and DL are long-established, whereas their practical implementation is uneven (Kant et al., 2025). The issue is that organizations experience a lot of problems with matching their innovations with the principles of CE because they lack the DL which would focus on cultural and behavioral implications of change (Montes-Pineda & Garrido-Yserte, 2024). The purpose of the study is to explore such complexities, especially the mediating role of AI in augmenting effectiveness of leadership and establishing a culture of innovation that favors sustainable practices. By tackling such challenges, the paper will give a way forward to the organizations whose struggling to implement such ideas.

PROBLEM STATEMENT

The point, toward which the organizations should tend, as sustainability gains popularity, is the transition of OI, DL, as well as AI into already available resources of the CE (Mamudu et al., 2024). The purpose of this integration is to support innovative enterprise that does not only lead to competitive power but also supports environment sustainability (Gatell & Avella, 2024). Nevertheless, the contemporary environment is marked with some contradictions and inconsistencies hindering the achievement of such ideal state (jio et al., 2025). In the opening instance, pragmatic evidence posits that DL is capable of boosting OI, and an intervention of AI is ambivalent (Arroyabe et al., 2024). The available studies may fail to present any conclusive evidence on the role of AI and its impact on leadership performance and innovation results (Montes-Pineda & Garrido-Yserte, 2024). Such incongruence indicates that there are gaps in theoretical understanding on how AI mediates these relationships (Kant et al., 2025). Moreover, there are gaps in the literature on practical implications of these concepts to various organizations (Adholiya, 2025). Some organizations might have realized the necessity to undertake a digital transformation process but they do not have a clear picture of how they could implement AI-driven initiatives, and aligning them with the principles of the CE (Khan et al., 2024).

Moreover, gaps in context are also apparent since a high proportion of the studies conducted so far focused on particular industries or regions and thus, left many other sectors and geographical areas under-researched (Al Halbusi et al., 2025). This drawback limits the generalizability of results and the construction of universal methods to work with AI on the way to a sustainable practice (Elshaer et al., 2025). Logistical factors also contribute to the difficulty of getting innovative practices in the CE into operation (Awad et al., 2025). The proposed study will fill these gaps through its in-depth discussion of the relationship among the concepts of OI, DL, as well as AI (Tutore et al., 2024).

THEORETICAL FOUNDATION

Diffusion Theory: It characterizes various crucial aspects among them being the adoption stages (knowledge, persuasion, decision, implementation, and confirmation) as well as the nature of innovations that determine the level of adopting that particular innovation. The importance of social system and communication facilities in the process of diffusion are stressed by DT which is why it seems to be especially close to our research topic. This theory can be used to help in understanding how, by employing DL; it is possible to enable the integration of innovative practices.

This theory therefore serves as a theoretical foundation when it comes to studying the dynamics of organizational change with respect to a CE (Elshaer et al., 2025).

Transformational theory: It is defined as the practice of leaders inspiring and motivating followers to accomplish extraordinary results through the creation of a working environment of trust, teamwork, and collective visioning; all described by James MacGregor Burns and developed further by the work of Bernard Bass. This theory is especially relevant to DL because of its focus on the notion of being flexible and having a vision to reach during changes in technology. Transformational leadership is important in overcoming organizational resistance and in facilitating an organizational culture that accepts change and therefore transformational leadership must be given as one of critical lenses through which leadership in a CE can be examined (Al Halbusi et al., 2025).

Resource-Based view (RBV): It assumes that companies can gain competitive advantage according to their resource and capabilities. This theory focuses on the presence of intangible asset, i.e., knowledge, skills and innovation, as a strategic driving force behind organizational performance. Availing to the situation of our study, RBV gives us a premise to see how AI is a resource that can be better utilized with DL in order to improve innovation and sustainability. Due to its concentration on the strategic use of technological resources, this theory is in line with the goals to promote a CE (Tutore et al., 2024).

Technology Acceptance Model: TAM assumes that perceived ease of use and usefulness are two factors that greatly determine the attitude towards the use of technology. To study the role of AI in enabling OI and DL, this model is of particular relevance. By comprehending what influences the adoption of the AI technologies, this theory can be used to determine the obstacles which may hinder organizations to implement the innovative practices in the CE (Awad et al., 2025).

The ***Transformational Leadership Theory*** will be used as the primary theoretical lens of the research. It is highly successful in summarizing the importance of DL in instilling a culture of innovation and flexibility that is absolutely necessary when integrating AI within a CE environment.

DEFINITION AND ORIGIN OF CONCEPT

OI: It can be defined as the process of adapting new or substantially improved idea, process, product or service to an organization. It also covers the gradual changes as well as radical ones that boost performance and competitiveness. The concept birth was the larger body of research concerning innovation which emerged in the middle of the 20th century when scholars attempted to comprehend the processes of technological change and the role it played in economic growth (Al Halbusi et al., 2025).

DL: It can be defined as the process of guiding leadership with the help of organizations towards digital transformation via the use of technology as the means to make better decisions, communicating, and improving the efficiency of the operation. The term has arisen as a result of the rapid changes in technology in the 21 st century in that it requires leaders capable of successfully navigating in the complexities of the digital realms. DL is a more standard leadership augmented with knowledge of digital tools and trends (Khan et al., 2024).

AI: It is the imitation of the human intelligence by machines (mainly computer). This encompasses learning, reasoning, problem solving or understanding language. The word dates back to the 1950s when computer scientists started to research and develop methods of making machines capable of intelligent conduct. The role of it changed greatly over the decades, as it now is used in business, healthcare, and education to name a few (Elshaer et al., 2025).

CE: It is one that achieves minimal waste and the best utilization of resources. It is an alternative to the conventional linear economy that is on a take-make-dispose circle. The idea of the CE became more popular in the early 2000s as the environmental issues were raised, and the sustainable development was a necessity. It stresses the need of making products, particularly designed with a lifecycle in mind, to be more functional and sustainable in usage, reuse, and recycling (Tutore et al., 2024).

PRAGMATIC LITERATURE REVIEW

OI and DL

In the context of organizations under pressure to respond to the fast process of change in technological environment, research across OI and DL has been the subject of great concern (Al Halbusi et al., 2025). There is extensive research on how DL has shown to be critical when it comes to creating an environment that supports innovation (Khan et al., 2024). As an example, one research paper revealed that when the digital leaders creatively use technology, they can improve organizational capabilities that will then propagate to increased levels of innovation and better performance (Elshaer et al., 2025). Their results indicate that leaders who adopt digital tools do not only promote the creation of innovative ideas but also prompt process efficiency, ultimately, speeding up the process of innovation (Awad et al., 2025). Another practical study confirming the existence of this relationship was a study that examined the effects of transformation leadership behaviors on innovation in an organization (Tutore et al., 2024). They found that leaders with transformational attributes, e.g., promote a common vision, collaborative efforts, and culture of experimentation, are able to considerably improve the innovative potential of their organizations (Adholiya, 2025). This is consistent with the Transformation Leadership Theory which suggests that talented leaders have the capabilities of spurring a revolutionary development through convincing and enabling their subordinates to seek new solutions (Mamudu et al., 2024). Moreover, it has been demonstrated that the combination of AI technologies into organizational practices mediates the nexus across DL and entre innovation outcomes (Mukherjee et al., 2024). One research explored the effects of AI on manufacturing firm innovation (Gatell & Avella, 2024). The authors discovered that, due to DL, organizations were in a better position to implement AI technologies that ultimately resulted in improved innovation performance (Arroyabe et al., 2024). This asserts the implication of DL when overcoming the complexity of implementing AI, implying that the leaders with high capabilities of operating in digital environments have the capacity to utilize AI to facilitate novel practices (Montes-Pineda & Garrido-Yserte, 2024).

Although there is an increasing literature, there are there are gaps in the current understanding of the subtle interplay across these factors (Al-Khatib, 2024). All the studies on the topic underline the importance of the positive contribution of DL to innovation, but there is not much analysis of the situational variables potential influence on this relationship (Ooi & Memon, 2025). The study revealed some factors that hinder embrace of digital transformation, among them being organizational culture and resistance by employees, which is a deterrent to success of DL (Tian et al., 2025). This serves as a pointer to do a deeper study on the possible influence of various organizational environments on the interaction across DL and innovation. In addition, pragmatic studies tend to concentrate on a particular industry and therefore cannot be generalized to other industries (Alemu & Kant, 2025).

H1: OI and DL having pragmatic association

OI as Well as AI in CE

The cross of OI as well as AI in the context of a CE (CE) has drawn increased attention of researchers that seek to learn more about how these two elements can work together to improve sustainability (Gatell & Avella, 2024). Pragmatic research demonstrates that AI technology incorporation should greatly stimulate OI, especially to sustain practices that support a CE (AFOLABI, 2025). One of the essential studies focuses on the role that AI can play in order to encourage innovation in circular business models (Mamudu et al., 2024). The authors state that AI will help streamline the use of resources, management of waste and product lifecycle, which are essential elements of CE (Khan et al., 2024). Their findings suggest that organizational adoption of AI can be more efficient in innovation to make products that are durable, repairable and recyclable and hence reduce a negative imprint to the environment (Montes-Pineda & Garrido-Yserte, 2024). This is synonymous to the fact that AI can be applied in decision-making through a data-informed expertise which can lead to innovative practices (Adula et al., 2025). Further pragmatic evidence of a study emphasizes the fact that AI helps organizations to adopt circular practices (Morelli et al., 2024). They discovered that AI technologies are capable of boosting efficiency in resource management and cutting down waste, which is key to circularity when implemented into company processes (Tutore et al., 2024). Their study highlights how organizations which take advantage of innovations fuelled by AI have a better chance of achieving sustainability targets, demonstrating the disruptive nature of AI within a CE (Elshaer et al., 2025).

As well, reports investigated the correlation across digital technologies, such as AI, and the implementation of principles of the CE by manufacturing companies (Al Halbusi et al., 2025). The authors determined that not only AI enhances innovative practices but it also helps an organization to characterize and address risks related to resource shortage and environmental compliance (Awad et al., 2025). According to their findings, companies that embrace digitalization and pay significant attention to innovation have better chances of establishing a successful transition to the circular model, as the integration of AI and company innovation have a synergistic effect (Adholiya, 2025). Notwithstanding the above positive results, there are still gaps in the literature as far as the contextual factors affecting the integration of the AI in CE are concerned (Mukherjee et al., 2024). To illustrate, a study reveals that organizations contend with several issues during the efforts to implement AI technologies with regard to sustainability (Arroyabe et al., 2024). Different other factors have the ability to play a major role in the success of AI in promoting innovation (Prashar & Chaudhuri, 2025). It leads to the idea that further more detailed research is needed to characterize the influence of various organizational contexts on the correlation across AI and CE projects (Sposato et al., 2025).

H2: OI as well as AI in CE having pragmatic association

AI in CE and DL

DL is a booming field in the sphere of the CE (CE) that integrates the notion of AI as one of the key features that support the implementation of sustainable practices (Tutore et al., 2024). Pragmatic studies have started to investigate how digital leaders can use AI technologies to fulfill the goal of promoting circular actions, resource efficiency, and innovation (Gatell & Avella, 2024). Another interesting study shows how AI could radically alter the possibility of adopting a new economic relationship to things, the CE (Montes-Pineda & Garrido-Yserte, 2024). The data collected by them support their conclusion that AI can be used to promote decision-making operations through the real-time analysis of system-generated information that is used in resource allocation and operational waste management. Companies implementing the AI-based solutions will be able to streamline processes in order to minimize the wastage and enhance the rates of materials recovery (Ali et al., 2025). This highlights the need to have DL to have the strategic execution of AI technologies to continue in regard to CE goals (Arroyabe et al., 2024). Also, there is a study of how DL can assist in implementing AI and making organizations achieve circularity (Mukherjee et al., 2024). In their research, they reveal that effective digital leaders play a critical role in the growth of an organizational culture driven by technological advancement (Adholiya, 2025). By promoting AI initiatives, these leaders are able to encourage teams to understand new solutions that can help improve sustainability (Mamudu et al., 2024). The paper also addresses the fact that leaders must have technical expertise as well as the capability to motivate and excite workers towards the achievement of CE objectives (Al Halbusi et al., 2025).

Although the available literature has recorded positive results on the promising potential of AI on CE practices, the literature also outlines various hindrances, which limit the successful adoption of AI in CE practices (Khan et al., 2024). As research indicates, organizational culture barriers, resistance to change, and poor digital infrastructure are some elements that deteriorate the implementation process of AI technologies (Elshaer et al., 2025). These issues serve as an indication of the need to have good DL that will mitigate these concerns by promoting a culture of innovation and flexibility (Awad et al., 2025).

H3: AI in CE and DL having pragmatic association

OI, DL as Well as AI in CE Mediation

The interaction across OI, DL, as well as AI in the framework of a CE (CE) is an emerging research topic that aims at grasping how these things can mutually benefit, improving sustainability (Hussein et al., 2024). The common mediating nature of AI in influencing the linkage across DL and OI is increasingly under pragmatic analysis especially in an attempt to ensure that organizations practice the CE (Williams et al., 2024). One of the fundamental works considers that the implementation of OI in a CE is a key to success (Gatell & Avella, 2024). They have found that DL can lead to innovation through a culture that accepts change and experiment takes place. Imperatively, they mention AI as a mediator that increases the efficacy of DL (Mukherjee et al., 2024). Through the provision of data-driven insights and automation (Ajmera et al., 2025), AI will give leaders the ability to make informed decisions that will support current sustainability objectives, which will in turn improve innovation outcomes (Mamudu et al., 2024). Further, the impacts of DL on OI within the organization of the CE and with a great mediating role of AI have been described in detail (Adholiya, 2025). Their findings indicate that companies which have a robust DL are fairly in a better position to ensure that AI is used in creating circular business models (Montes-Pineda & Garrido-Yserte, 2024). Incorporating AI technologies, these organizations will not only increase their performances in lifecycle management and predictive analytics but utilize them in the process of circularity (Sun et al., 2025). This research supports the idea that AI is not just an enabler but one of the key mediators that enhances the effect of DL on innovation (Tutore et al., 2024).

Although these findings are encouraging, various gaps have also been characterized by the available literature that should be probed (Awad et al., 2025). Indicatively, although most studies concentrate on the direct associations among the elements, no detailed models have been designed to explicitly explain the form adopted by an interaction across AI and DL with the OI (Elshaer et al., 2025). Research notes that it is crucially important to define all the contextual factors that have an influence on these relationships to provide operable conclusions (Khan et al., 2024). Organizational culture, employee engagement, and technology readiness are some of the critical factors that can influence the level of contribution DL as well as AI can make to the process of innovation in the practices of the CE. In addition, quantitative research tends to focus on individual industries, and this impedes comparisons across sectors (Al Halbusi et al., 2025).

H4: OI, DL as well as AI in CE Mediation having pragmatic association

Figure 1. Conceptual Framework

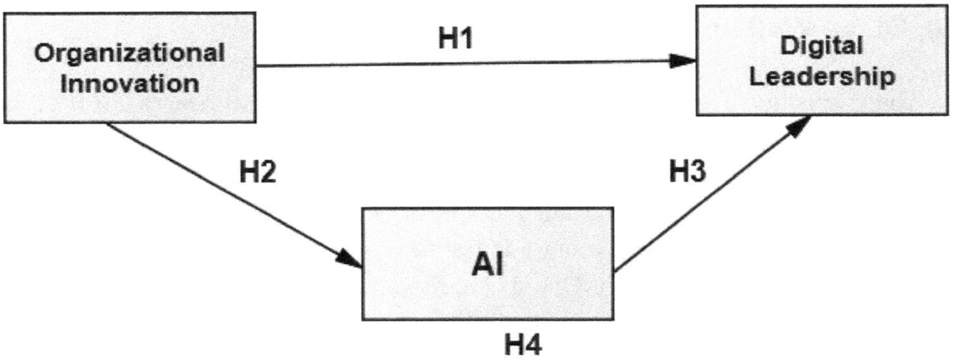

METHODOLOGY

In studying these questions, the research in question had an explorative quantitative design as a research approach. A total of 390 samples were harvested among different organizations, which were involved in CE works. The sampling method utilized stratified random sampling in order to provide a representative sampling across sectors, therefore increasing the generalizability of the study. The KMO was used to determine whether the sample was suitable to factor analysis indicating that sample size was adequately high. Then, EFA was done to explore the latent structure of the constructs of the OI, DL as well as AI. The EFA disclosed that there are different factors underlying each construct, although the theories formed in the literature were corroborated. After EFA, SEM was then conducted using the AMOS to test the hypothesized correlation among the constructs. Such an approach made it possible to study direct and indirect impacts, through which the overall picture of the impact of DL on OI through the mediating effect of AI emerged.

Scale Development

The process of scale development was based on a review of literature related to the development of the scale under consideration on which the formulation of the measure items of each construct was based. In case of OI, the items were taken out of existing instruments that focused more on dimensions. In a similar manner, DL scale was created according to the study by Avolio and Kahai and concerned such aspects as vision, communication, and the ability to adapt to digital circumstances. The purpose of measuring AI capabilities was attained by using items based on studies which discussed the application of AI in the business context. This encompassed aspects of data analytics, automation and decision support. All the items were framed in a manner that made them understandable and relevant and a Likert scale of 1-5 was used (relatedly disagree- relatedly agree). A pilot study was also carried out over a lesser number of samples opening to test how well the AMPs were understood and how consistent their answers were. Based on comments received during this pilot, some revisions of wording and structure were made, to further improve the robustness of the scales. Each of the final scales was submitted to EFA and demonstrated the dimensionality thereof, and developed construct validity. Internal consistency of each scale was determined by the usage of Cronbach alpha with scores greater than the acceptable rate of 0.7, showing great reliability. This strict scale development procedure meant that not only was the construct measured theoretically sound, but pragmatically validated as well, which meant that the scale and the measures used in it were aligned with the field and the researchers. By using the well-established scales, the paper proposed to add a valuable input to the interaction across OI, DL, as well as AI within a CE.

RESULTS

Table 1. Data Duality

Data Duality		**.906**
Bartlet manifestation	Chi-Square	2095.96
	Df	126
	Sig.	.000

Source: Authors

The results of data duality are presented in Table 1. The score of the KMO is 0.906 which is considered as sufficient to represent a high level of sampling adequacy since scores above 0.6 are acceptable. This hints that the data will be appropriate to subject factor analysis as it exhibits a reasonable level of inter-correlation among variables. It provides a chi -square of 2095.96 and degrees of freedom of 126 and a implication of 0.000. The magnitude of implication which is less than 0.05 affirms that there are significant correlations that exist across the variables included in the analysis. This means that the null hypothesis which indicates that the correlation matrix is an identity matrix is not true. Collectively, these findings give good evidence that the data could be subjected to factor analysis making the subsequent EFA used in the study legitimate. The large KMO confirm that the constructs, which are being measured, are bound to present meaningful patterns and relationships to the research, hence the overall research findings are very robust.

Table 2. Variance

C	**Initial Eigenscores**			**Extraction**			**Rotation**		
	Total	**% of Variance**	**Cumulative %**	**Total**	**% of Variance**	**Cumulative %**	**Total**	**% of Variance**	**Cumulative %**
1	4.1	32.5	32.5	4.1	32.5	32.5	3.0	33.7	33.7
2	1.7	9.7	50.2	1.7	9.7	50.2	2.6	15.1	54.2
3	1.7	9.7	70.0	1.7	9.7	70.0	1.8	14.8	70.0
4	.99	6.2	57.2						

continued on following page

Table 2. Continued

C	Initial Eigenscores			Extraction			Rotation		
	Total	% of Variance	Cumulative %	Total	% of Variance	Cumulative %	Total	% of Variance	Cumulative %
5	.81	6.3	64.5						
6	.73	5.9	69.4						

Source: Authors

Table 2 provides the findings of the Variance. The opening eigenscores indicate that the opening factor had a total eigenscore of 4.1 representing 32.5 percent of the total variance. This means that this factor is a large contributor to what is meant to explain the underlying structure of the information. It is clear that the combined percentage of the opening factor to be across is going to be 32.5 indicating that a large percentage of the variability in the data can be ascribed to the opening factor alone. The second and the third factors also show significant contributions with eigenscores of 1.7 each and 9.7 percent of the whole variance. This yields a cumulative variance of 50.2 percent after the 2nd factor and 70.0 percent after the 3rd factor which in effect means that these 3 factors explain more than half of the total variance in the data set. The rest of the factors (fourth, fifth, sixth) will have the lower eigenscores of 0.99, 0.81 and 0.73, with the fourth component explaining 6.2% of the full sample variance and the cumulative percentage explained so far adding up to 57.2. The fifth and sixth factor is small and the cumulative percentage reaches 69.4%. Principal component analysis was used as the extraction method in this analysis, meaning that these factors were constructed with the aim of explaining the variance in the observed variables. It can be seen that the opening three factors are critical to comprehending the constructs they are measuring and the other factors have less importance. This observation highlights the score of prioritizing the above-mentioned main factors and explores them since they can help us to understand significant nexuss across OI, DL, as well as AI within the framework of a CE.

Table 3. Covariances

			Estimate	S.E.	C.R.	P	Hy.
AI in CE	**<-->**	**OI**	**.274**	**.032**	**8.073**	**.00**	**H2**
AI in CE	<-->	DL	.303	.029	7.989	.00	**H3**
OI	<-->	DL	.254	0.34	7.741	.00	**H1**

Source: Authors

Table 3 shows the covariances. The opening covariance, across the role of the AI in the CE, and the OI, is 0.274, the critical ratio is 8.073, and the implication level 0. This shows a positive relationship of high days of AI integration as to the OI and this depicts a related positive relationship. The critical ratio is above 1.96, the conventional criterion, and it is an evidence of the strength of this relationship and H2 is supported. In the same manner, the relationship across the covariance across AI in the CE and DL gives an estimate of 0.303, a critical ratio of 7.989 and a implication level of 0.00. This large estimation shows that there is a related positive correlation across the two constructs, meaning that effective DL catalyzes the integration of AI efforts in the practices of the CE. This finding is a good indication to support H3. Finally, the covariance across DL and OI is considered 0.254 with the critical ratio of 7.741 and the implication level of 0.00. This is a positive correlation that indicated that organizations that have related digital leaders are more probable to gain innovative practices. The relevance of this relationship evidences H1.

Table 4. Validity

	CR	AVE	MSV	MaxR(H)	OI	AICE	DL
OI	0.732	0.643	0.219	0.852	**0.654**		
AICE	0.758	0.657	0.132	0.763	0.171	**0.665**	
DL	0.793	0.603	0.274	0.797	0.383	0.193	**0.684**

Note: OI= OI; AICE= AI in CE*; DL= DL*
Source: Authors

Table 4 shows validity of constructs. The index of all the three constructs is at an acceptable level. The CR of OI is 0.732, 0.758 in AICE, and 0.793 in DL, all scores more than recommended 0.7. This is an indication that these constructs exist on the measurement scales which are reliable. The hypothesis testing procedure was also indicated by the AVE scores that indicated convergent validity of the constructs. AVE of OI is 0.643, AICE has AVE of 0.657 and that of DL is 0.603. Although the DL construct fits all criteria since all its AVE scores are higher than the acceptable level of 0.5, indicating that it explains a significant part of their corresponding items, they still show that it is lesser than the rest of them. The scores show that the constructs share variance with each other in the following manner with OI at a 0.219, AICE at 0.132 and DL at 0.274. These low scores of MSV indicate that the constructs are independent of each other and suggests discrimination validity on the measurement model. Finally, The MaxR(H) also provide an extra point of assurance as to the stability of the constructs with OI being 0.852, AICE being 0.763 and DL being 0.797, all falling well within acceptable range.

Figure 2. Structural Equation Model

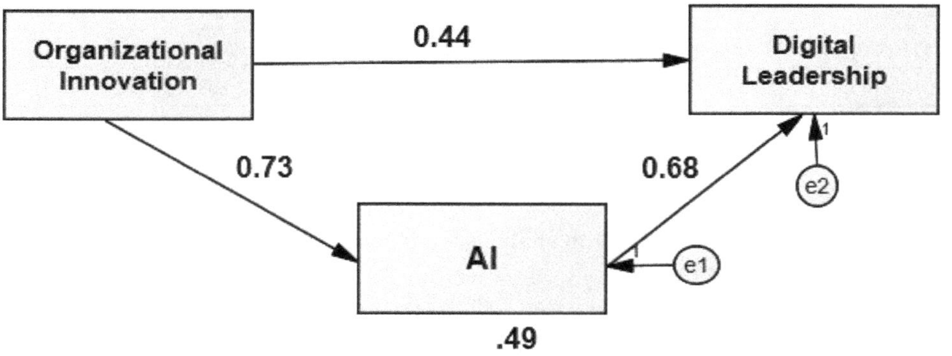

Table 5. Model Fit

Sig.	Chi-Sq	RMR	Goodness	Confirmatory	TLI	RMSEA
0.006	1.073	.054	0.930	0.912	0.911	.028

Source: Authors

Table 5 shows the model fit indices. Its chi-square score, 1.073, is significant so that the model fits the data well, though caution must also be exercised in evaluating other fit indices as well. The RMR is obtained as 0.054 that is less than the commonly accepted figure of 0.08 indicating a good fit. It indicates that the average difference across the observed and the expected covariance matrices is small, and this supports the appropriateness of the model. The goodness-of-fit indices are given as 0.930, and CFI = 0.912. Both of the scores are above the recommended measure (0.90) showing that the model is very well-fitted with the data. These indices indicate the percentage of the variance that the model describes and will go into a general evaluation of model sufficiency. TLI is also greater than 0.90 (0.911), and indicates that the model fits well. And lastly, the cutoff score of 0.05 was a good without the cutoff line being crossed and the RMSEA = 0.028. All scores of MSEA are below 0.05 indicating a good fit; the model reveals the real-world relationships.

Table 6. Regression

Relative			Approx.	S.E.	C.R.	P	Ass.
AI in CE	**<---**	**OI**	**.864**	**.143**	**7.583**	**.00**	**H2**
DL	<---	AI in CE	.328	.131	2.853	.00	H3
DL	<---	OI	.957	.192	7.958	.00	H1

Source: Authors

The findings of the regression analysis were demonstrated in Table 6. The initial regression path is the one across OI as well as AI in the CE, and the standardized measure of that path shows a related score of 0.864. This large score shows that OI affects the introduction of the AI initiatives in the context of the CE greatly. The t-score of 7.583 indicates that critically the relationship is robust and a implication level of 0.00 provides substantial backing of the research H2. The two-path that explores the effect of AI in the CE on DL demonstrates a regularized estimation of 0.328. Although this score is lower, than the previous relationship it still denotes a positive and significant effect. A critical ratio of 2.853 and a implication level of 0.00 show that AI initiatives are relevant in influencing the DL practices, and hence, they support H3. Finally, the regression is high in the estimated standardized estimate of 0.957 illustrating OI as an element that leads to DL. It shows that there are very related associations, in that, organizations that can be considered to embrace innovation very well are probable to have related DL. The related implication of 7.958 at the meager level of 0.00 clearly proves the acceptance of H1.

Table 7. Mediation

	score
OI → DL	.44
OI → AI in CE → DL	.73*.68=.49
	.94

Source: Authors

The Table 7 presents the mediating role of AI. The direct effect across OI and DL is measured to be 0.44 which is sizable and direct. This indicates that the greater the OI, the more powerful the DL practice which affirms the implication of innovation in influencing leadership abilities. On the other side, the indirect effect of influence through the mediating role of AI in the CE is 0.73 (the influence of OI on AI) and 0.68 (the influence of AI on DL), which gives an indirect influence of 0.49. This conclusion explains how OI does not only directly impact DL but also does it indirectly by improving the AI projects in the approach of a CE. The cumulative impact of OI on DL taking both the direct and indirect effects together is found to be 0.94. This large magnitude shows a potent overall impact, as it reveals that OI is a critical factor of driving DL both directly and indirectly. Moreover, the partial mediation indication implies that, in spite of the increase in the relationship across OI and DL with AI in CE, the relationship across OI and DL also remains appreciable. This confirms the fact that the direct and mediated pathways are critical to getting a better insight into how organizations can effectively employ AI and innovation in enhancing their DL capabilities.

DISCUSSION

The results of the present research can disseminate light on the complexity of the nexus across the following concepts: the OI, DL, as well as AI in the conditions of the CE. The robust direct impact of OI on DL contributes to the critical importance of innovative practices as the means of creating an effective leadership strategy. This coincides with the existing literature on how it is important to create a culture of innovation to create a nimble and responsive business leadership in the current fast changing business environment. Moreover, more indirect influence of OI on DL with the help of AI demonstrates the valuable power of technology to empower sustainable practices. Organizations adopting the use of AI will improve their ability to make decisions using data and utilize their resources to achieve a successful CE. This conclusion is in line with the idea that the role of AI is not just a tool that facilitates innovation but rather the driver of innovation allowing organizations to reach their goals set in terms of sustainability more efficiently. The degree of partial mediation means that although the circle economy AI enhances the nexus across the two OI and DL, the direct inspiration is high. This implies that organizations are advised to focus on innovation and integration of AI as two approaches that support both the effectiveness of the leadership and their positive impact. The interaction of these factors shows that innovative thinking in leaders will put them in a better position to maximize the use of AI tools to guide their organizations to greener activities.

CONCLUSION

The findings reaffirm that OI is a significant contributor to both DL as well as AI projects such that innovation and technology serve each other to optimize the role of leadership. The results indicate that, whereas OI has a related direct impact on DL, it also has an effect in its interceding stage via AI. This two-fold pathway speaks volumes of the need to combine innovative practices with technological advancements in an effort to promote sustainable business models. In addition to this, the presence of partial mediation shows that organizations stand to gain in considering both of these elements when approaching strategic planning. Leader who develop a culture of innovation and use AI can better develop and succeed in the environment of CE and take their organizations to the levels of higher sustainability and competitive advantages. The paper makes a contribution to the literature by supporting research findings that the specified constructs are interrelated, which can serve as important information to guide practitioners to engage in the adoption of effective policies to achieve sustainable innovation. Future research should extend insights by conducting in-depth studies of varieties of these relationships across various organizational settings and industries and hence deepen and add to our knowledge on how DL can be nurtured purportedly towards achieving sustainable goals. In this way, organizations can be better equipped to reconcile innovation strategies and emerging technologies to shore up a robust and dynamic economic environment that continues to evolve.

MANAGERIAL IMPLICATIONS

Creation of OI culture is the priority that managers should maintain since it is highly effective as a DL driver. It is possible by fostering innovative solutions to the problems, facilitating team-centered workplaces and offering materials that allow experimentation. The culture of innovation helps organizations develop powerful leaders capable of making sound decisions to support the sustainability objectives of the organization. Furthermore, the high importance of AI as an intermediary factor emphasizes the need to incorporate the advanced technologies into the organizations management frameworks. Investment in AI will be able to reduce processes, data analytics, and the resource management process all of which is important in executing CE principles. Training programs that can help leaders become knowledgeable on how to leverage AI remain a consideration by organizations as most leaders are still being alerted on the subject of AI. Moreover, the finding of partial mediation implies that although AI can be helpful in improving DL, it must go along with the traditional leadership traits as opposed to replacing them. The goal of managers should be to find a balance across the implementation of new technologies and the creation of the environment when leaders focus on the development of interpersonal skills and emotional intelligence to promote a comprehensive image of leadership and take into account both innovation and human interaction. Lastly, organizations are expected to monitor and assess the effectiveness of the leadership and sustainability results caused by the innovation plans as well as AI initiatives. By defining metrics and feedback, managers can adjust their strategies using data to achieve this continuous improvement and make them responsive to the changing market needs.

PRACTICAL IMPLICATIONS

Organizations should also have in place highly organized innovation practices which require all employees to bring onboard ideas and solutions. This might entail programs inspire creativity in the minds of employees besides creating a sense of ownership among the employees. Engaging staff in solving the problem of innovation, the organization can get a variety of points of view and substantially more effective solutions to the integration of CE principles. Also, the implementation of AI technologies ought to be strategic in nature. Companies should evaluate their own needs and abilities before investing in AI tools. This can be done by carrying out comprehensive needs assessment and testing of AI applications in the areas where such applications have the capacity to deliver maximum contribution e.g., resource management and predictive analytics. It is also vital to support and train employees on how they can make use of such technologies so that the positive impact of AI can be achieved geared towards ensuring that those employees are comfortable using the new virtual tools. Last, it is important to establish clear innovation as well as AI initiatives goals and performance measurements. Organizations need to conduct a periodic check over these indices in order to determine whether their strategies are working well or not, and therefore make relevant adjustments. This data-based strategy can aid in the characterization of the areas which can be enhanced, as well as the visible returns of the investments in innovation and technology to the various internal and external stakeholders. The reasonable steps outlined above would allow organizations to be in a better position to realize sustainable results within the highly competitive environment.

THEORETICAL IMPLICATIONS

By defining a framework that is used to show how these constructs affect each other directly and indirectly, the research study contributes to literature that asserts the role of innovation as the force behind leadership effectiveness in the sustainability practice. The high direct impact of OI to the sphere of DL supports the existing theories according to which innovative organizational climate leads to better management, which can imply that innovation is not the part of the backstage process but the major driving force of effective leadership within contemporary organizations. Further, the AI as an intermediary enhances the theoretical debate about the impact brought by technology on forming leadership relationships. This mediating effect implies that technology advancements do not exist in their own vacuum but they interplay with the practices of leadership resulting in the realization of organizational interests. The finding confirms and expands on the theory of technology adoption and innovation diffusion by introducing the subtext of demonstrating leadership as a hard or soft skill in adopting sustainable practices. Moreover, the existence of partial mediation undermines the prevailing models that are probable to treat technological integration as a direct substitute of the traditional leadership strategies. Rather, it implies that there is more complicated relations across innovation and technology, which need to co-exist and even complement each other in order to make leadership more productive. This observation can motivate scholars to investigate more about the situational factors that shape up such dynamics.

RECOMMENDATIONS

Firms must focus more on the creation of an effective innovation strategy that promotes the process of ongoing improvement and creativity. This may be done by forming specialized teams or departments that are charged with the responsibility of becoming innovative by giving them the resources and structure to look at fresh ideas and technologies. Workshops, frequent brainstorming sessions, and idea competitions of all kinds would also encourage a company-wide culture of innovation. Besides, organizations must spend funds on training programs that can provide leaders with a difficult set of technical knowledge about AI and soft skills. This twofold orientation will mean that leaders practice not only the improved use of new technologies but also the interpersonal skills needed to generate collaborative processes and inspire teams in a more digitized workplace environment. Mentorship schemes would also be useful where long-term players mentor the new talent in a digital transformation scenario. In addition, the organization must become an active partner in the collaboration with technology providers and academic providers on finding new trends and best practice in AI and innovation. Such alliances have the prospect of sharing information and even access to cutting edge research and tools which can add organizational capacity. Lastly, organizations must ensure that there are clear measures of how the innovation as well as AI programs can measure the extent of their achievement of DL and sustenance goals. Reviews and periods of feedback would help in refining a set of strategies which will ensure organizational efforts are aligned to the expectations of the organization and the expectations of the market as well. These proactive measures allow organizations to leverage greater potential of innovation and digital technologies in order to attain a sustainable success in a competitive environment.

FUTURE DIRECTIONS

Armed with the findings of the latter, a couple of recommendations could be provided on the attributes that organizations should consider employing in order to promote their sustainability initiatives via innovation and DL. To begin with, organizations must focus more on the creation of an effective innovation strategy that promotes the process of ongoing improvement and creativity. This may be done by forming specialized teams or departments that are charged with the responsibility of becoming innovative by giving them the resources and structure to look at fresh ideas and technologies. Workshops, frequent brainstorming sessions, and idea competitions of all kinds would also encourage a company-wide culture of innovation. Besides, organizations must spend funds on training programs that can provide leaders with a difficult set of technical knowledge about AI and soft skills. This twofold orientation will mean that leaders practise not only the improved use of new technologies but also the interpersonal skills needed to generate collaborative processes and inspire teams in a more digitized workplace environment. Mentorship schemes would also be useful where long-term players mentor the new talent in a digital transformation scenario. Last, organizations must establish well-defined metrics in evaluating their innovation as well as AI projects in terms of digitally leading and sustaining goals completion. Periodic appraisals and feedback channels should help in fine tuning sets of strategies to ensure that effort is aligned to organizational objectives as well as the requirements at the market. Such active steps will help organizations to realize even more potential in the field of innovation and digital technologies to achieve the necessary breakthrough in the competitive world in the long term.

REFERENCES

Adholiya, A. (2025). Evaluating the Impact of Digitalization on CE Growth: Insights from Structural Equation Modelling. *CE and Sustainability*, 1-30.

Adula, M., Kant, S., & Debebe, T. S. (2025). Sustainable Development Effect on Organizational Networks with Mediation of Contingency Theory in the Horn of Africa. In *Integrating Organizational Theories with Sustainable Development* (pp. 203–226). IGI Global Scientific Publishing.

AFOLABI, J. A. (2025). Advancing the CE in Europe: The Role of Eco-Innovation, Economic Complexity and Digitalization. *Technology in Society*, •••, 103027.

Ajmera, D., Kharub, M., Krishna, A., & Gupta, H. (2025). Navigating the challenges of AI-enabled CE in the food and beverage sector: Strategies for sustainable transformation. *International Journal of Logistics Management*, *54*(2), 611–646. DOI: 10.1108/IJLM-09-2023-0408

Al Halbusi, H., Popa, S., Soto-Acosta, P., & Alshallaqi, M. (2025). The nexus of managerial and technical AI knoweldge, disruptive innovation and the CE: The role of organizational change capability and financial resilience. *Technology in Society*, *82*, 102937. DOI: 10.1016/j.techsoc.2025.102937

Al-Khatib, A. W. (2024). Enabling the CE in the digital transformation era: Evidence from an emerging country. *Kybernetes*, *53*(2), 779–802. DOI: 10.1108/K-02-2023-0297

Alemu, Z. K., & Kant, S. (2025). Economic Nationalism and De-Globalization: How Reshoring and Protectionist Policies Are Reshaping Supply Chains and Inflation. In *Supply Chain Disruptions and Impact on Global Inflation* (pp. 227-252). IGI Global Scientific Publishing.

Ali, Z. A., Zain, M., Hasan, R., Al Salman, H., Alkhamees, B. F., & Almisned, F. A. (2025). CE advances with AI and digital twin: Multiple-case study of Chinese industries in agriculture. *Journal of the Knowledge Economy*, *16*(1), 2192–2228. DOI: 10.1007/s13132-024-02101-w

Arroyabe, M. F., Arranz, C. F., & de Arroyabe, J. C. F. (2024). The integration of CE and digital transformation as a catalyst for small and medium enterprise innovation. *Business Strategy and the Environment*, *33*(7), 7162–7181. DOI: 10.1002/bse.3858

Awad, I. M., Nuseibeh, H., & Amro, A. A. (2025). Competitiveness in the era of CE and digital innovations: An integrative literature review. *Sustainability (Basel)*, *17*(10), 4599. DOI: 10.3390/su17104599

Elshaer, I. A., Azazz, A. M., Alyahya, M., Fayyad, S., Aboutaleb, M., & Mohammad, A. A. (2025). Driving Sustainability Performance in Hotels Through Green DL and CE: The Moderating Role of Hotel Green Efficacy. *Systems*, *13*(6), 415. DOI: 10.3390/systems13060415

Gatell, I. S., & Avella, L. (2024). Impact of Industry 4.0 and CE on lean culture and leadership: Assessing digital green lean as a new concept. *European Research on Management and Business Economics*, *30*(1), 100232. DOI: 10.1016/j.iedeen.2023.100232

Hussein, H., Albadry, O. M., Mathew, V., Al-Romeedy, B. S., Alsetoohy, O., Abou Kamar, M., & Khairy, H. A. (2024). DL and sustainable competitive advantage: Leveraging green absorptive capability and eco-innovation in tourism and hospitality businesses. *Sustainability (Basel)*, *16*(13), 5371. DOI: 10.3390/su16135371

Kant, S., Adula, M., & Badi, S. (2025). Digital Transition Effect on Green Jobs by Mediation of Knowledge Management in CE. In *Insights Into Digital Business, Human Resource Management, and Competitiveness* (pp. 171-190). IGI Global Scientific Publishing.

Kant, S., Adula, M., & Duloma, H. (2025). The Rise of Product-as-a-Service Models in the Digital Era Redesigning Business Models for Circular Innovation in the Horn of Africa. In *Innovating Sustainability Through Digital CE* (pp. 133–160). IGI Global Scientific Publishing.

Kant, S., Adula, M., Nimbrain, N., & Kumari, M. (2025). Optimizing Resource Allocation for Green IT Future by Mediation of AI in the Horn of Africa. In *Sustainable Information Security in the Age of AI and Green Computing* (pp. 503–522). IGI Global Scientific Publishing. DOI: 10.4018/979-8-3693-8034-5.ch025

Khan, A. Y., Akhtar, M., & Khan, A. Y. (2024). Digitalization for a sustainable performance: Dual-study analysis of DL, CE, and technological innovation. *Sustainability*, *16*(23), 10465. DOI: 10.3390/su162310465

Mamudu, U. U., Obasi, C. D., Awuye, S. K., Danso, H., Ayodele, P., & Akinyemi, P. (2024). CE in the manufacturing sector: Digital transformation and sustainable practices. *International Journal of Science and Research Archive*, *12*(02), 129–141. DOI: 10.30574/ijsra.2024.12.2.1217

Montes-Pineda, Ó., & Garrido-Yserte, R. (2024). AI and CE: what is new for business model innovation? In *AI and Business Transformation: Impact in HR Management, Innovation and Technology Challenges* (pp. 41–59). Springer Nature Switzerland.

Morelli, G., Pozzi, C., Gurrieri, A. R., Mele, M., Costantiello, A., & Magazzino, C. (2024). The role of CE in EU entrepreneurship: A deep learning experiment. *Journal of Economic Asymmetries*, *30*, e00372. DOI: 10.1016/j.jeca.2024.e00372

Mukherjee, S., Nagariya, R., Mathiyazhagan, K., Baral, M. M., Pavithra, M. R., & Appolloni, A. (2024). AI-based reverse logistics for improving CE performance: A developing country perspective. *International Journal of Logistics Management*, *35*(6), 1779–1806. DOI: 10.1108/IJLM-03-2023-0102

Ooi, S. K., & Memon, K. R. (2025). Responsible Innovation, CE and Organisational Resilience: Investigating Multiple Pathways Towards Sustainability Performance. *Business Strategy and the Environment*, *34*(7), 8966–8982. DOI: 10.1002/bse.70057

Prashar, A., & Chaudhuri, A. (2025). Digitalization for CE and operational excellence practices: A paradox theory perspective on performance improvement in manufacturing firms. *Business Strategy and the Environment*, *34*(1), 1154–1170. DOI: 10.1002/bse.4031

Sposato, M., Dittmar, E. C., & Vargas Portillo, J. P. (2025). Navigating AI integration in sustainability-oriented organisations: Balancing technological innovation with environmental and social scores. *The International Journal of Organizational Analysis*. Advance online publication. DOI: 10.1108/IJOA-01-2025-5185

Sun, Y., Shahzad, M., Ali, A., & Razzaq, A. (2025). Synergistic effect of green knowledge sharing and green creative climate for CE practices: Role of AI information quality. *Journal of Manufacturing Technology Management*. Advance online publication. DOI: 10.1108/JMTM-09-2024-0503

Tian, H., Han, J., Sun, M., & Lv, X. (2025). Keeping pace with the times: Research on the impact of DL on radical green innovation of manufacturing enterprises. *European Journal of Innovation Management*, *28*(3), 900–927. DOI: 10.1108/EJIM-11-2022-0647

Tutore, I., Parmentola, A., Di Fiore, M. C., & Calza, F. (2024). A conceptual model of AI effects on CE actions. *Corporate Social Responsibility and Environmental Management*, *31*(5), 4772–4782. DOI: 10.1002/csr.2827

Williams, J., Prawiyogi, A. G., Rodriguez, M., & Kovac, I. (2024). Enhancing CE with digital technologies: A pls-sem approach. [ITEE]. *International Transactions on Education Technology*, *2*(2), 140–170.

KEY TERMS AND DEFINITIONS

Organization Innovation: The mechanism by which organizations come up with and implement new ideas, products, services or processes that enhance efficiency effectiveness and competitive advantaged. It has radical changes and incremental changes that improve the performance of the organization.

Digital Leadership: One type of leadership that embraces the usage of digital technologies that bring about organizational change and innovation. Digital leaders are also highly proficient in leveraging technology in regards to communication, collaboration and decision making and imparting the culture of being agile and adaptive.

AI: The emulation of the processes of human intelligence by machines, especially, computer systems. AI has several technologies under its belt, e.g., machine learning, natural language processing, and robotics, which help organizations automate processes and analyze and transform data into insight.

Circular Economy: The economic model that seeks to end wastefulness and optimize the use of resources by encouraging their constant utilization of products, materials and resources. It is opposite of the classic implementation of a linear economy focusing on sustainability, recycling and restoring the natural system.

Sustainability: Sustaining economic, social and environmental well-being in the long term. In a business sense, sustainability is a process that looks at the present conditions that would not undermine the capability of future generations to satisfy their own needs.

Innovation Strategy: It is a systematic approach that gives a guide on how an organization will nurture and adopt innovation in order to advance towards its objectives. This involves setting goals, characterization of areas of focus to be innovative, and commitment of resources to innovative initiatives.

Chapter 6
Artificial Intelligence for Industrial Efficiency

Amala K. J.
http://orcid.org/0009-0003-6863-2565
Department of Data Science and Business Systems, School of Computing, College of Engineering and Technology, SRM Institute of Science and Technology, Kattankulathur, India

D. Rajeswari
http://orcid.org/0000-0002-2677-4296
Department of Data Science and Business Systems, School of Computing, College of Engineering and Technology, SRM Institute of Science and Technology, Kattankulathur, India

Athish Venkatachalam
http://orcid.org/0000-0001-6258-5188
Clemson University, USA

ABSTRACT

Artificial Intelligence (AI) in industrial engineering has transformed manufacturing, as seen by Industry 4.0. In the previous decade, AI has transformed predictive maintenance, operational optimization, robotics, quality control, and supply chain management. Predictive maintenance using machine learning reduces downtime and optimizes resources. AI's real-time data analysis increases decision-making, resource use, and efficiency through operational optimization. Adding AI to robotics increases manufacturing, while image recognition and machine learning improve quality control, raising standards. AI forecasts demand, optimizes goods, and streamlines routes, making supply chain management more resilient. Collaborative robotics and AI-powered worker freedom demonstrate how humans and machines may improve

DOI: 10.4018/979-8-3373-5946-5.ch006

things. The author concludes by reviewing the past decade and discussing how AI is continuing revolutionizing industrial engineering and how operations will become smarter, more adaptable, and more competitive.

INTRODUCTION

The world is transforming at a speed that has never been seen before thanks to AI, which is becoming an important part of the Fourth Industrial Revolution, also known as Industry 4.0. The coming together of digital technologies, smart systems, and automatic infrastructures is driving this change. The goal is to make industries more efficient, environmentally friendly, and flexible. AI is the study of making machines smart like humans. It includes many different areas, such as machine learning (ML), deep learning (DL), natural language processing (NLP), and computer vision. These technologies let systems learn from data, adjust to new inputs, and do things that humans used to have to do, like making decisions, recognizing speech, perceiving what they see, and making predictions.

Moving toward Industry 4.0 is more than just an improvement in technology, it's a big change in how businesses work, how they connect with each other, and how they grow. Autonomous systems, real-time data analytics, and collaborative robots (cobots) are becoming more common in the global industrial scene. In the past, strict mechanization and manual oversight were what made it unique. AI is the main source of intelligence in this setting. It powers smart factories, makes predictive maintenance easier, improves quality control systems, and makes supply lines more efficient. AI in industrial settings leads to lower energy use, lower running costs, better product quality, and a better experience for customers. Also, innovations powered by AI are making way for new business models, flexible ways of making things, and services that are very specific to each person.

Many different types of businesses are now using AI technologies. These include healthcare, manufacturing, automotive, energy, food processing, pharmaceuticals, and e-commerce. In manufacturing, AI makes it possible to automate jobs that are done over and over again, keeps an eye on the health of machines in real time, and uses predictive analytics to predict when machines will break down. This not only keeps operations running, but it also cuts down on unexpected downtimes by a large amount. AI is used in many areas of healthcare, from imaging for diagnosis to finding new drugs. It makes professional decisions faster and more accurate. AI algorithms are used by retail and e-commerce platforms to keep track of how customers behave, suggest personalized goods, and improve the management of inventory. AI is also being utilized in areas including aviation, textiles, cosmetics, gaming, and environmental management to improve products, help processes work more smoothly, and deal with large amounts of data that changes all the time. AI is utilized in the airline sector to determine the best routes, save fuel, and figure out when repair will be needed. AI models are used by environmental monitoring systems to look at climate data, guess when natural disasters may happen, and come up with long-term remedies. AI may be employed in many various ways, which indicates that it can both stifle and boost creativity. People don't only perceive AI as a separate field of study anymore. They see it as a crucial aspect of making smart choices, using resources wisely, and staying ahead of the competition.

Cyber-physical systems, cloud computing, and AI work together to create smart, self-regulating production settings. This is a new method of conducting business. AI is the "brain" of this ecosystem. It makes smart tools work, connects systems, and makes decisions on its own in real time. One of the most essential uses in this scenario is predictive maintenance. AI systems look at data from IoT sensors placed into machinery to discover early indicators of wear and tear and stop expensive breakdowns before they happen. AI is also highly crucial for making sure that quality is good and keeping an eye on it. Quality checks used to be done

by hand, but now AI-powered systems employ computer vision and deep learning to discover defects, mistakes, or other weird things with unequaled accuracy. Not only does this make the product better, but it also uses less resources and cuts down on waste. AI assists with supply chain management by forecasting demand, designing better routes, and executing tasks at the warehouse. This makes the logistics system more flexible and stronger. People and smart devices also need to be able to work together very well. Smart technologies like AI-powered robotic arms, self-driving cars, and smart platforms are making workers' lives simpler, not taking their jobs. This mix gives individuals more important, creative, and strategic responsibilities in the age of AI, which affects how work is done.

AI has a lot of potential, but not everyone is using it the same way today. The US, China, Japan, Germany, and South Korea are all advanced economies that are at the forefront of AI research, development, and use. This is because they have invested a lot of money on AI, established strong infrastructure, and made regulations that support it. These countries have done a great job of creating AI-based communities that support new ideas, commercial growth, and industrialization. But developing countries have a hard time using AI since they don't have the proper technology, money, or experienced labor. These constraints make it tougher for AI to be deployed in crucial places, which makes the gap between rich and poor countries even bigger. AI isn't spreading as quickly in many parts of the world because people don't know enough about it, the rules aren't clear, and there aren't strong digital governance structures. To close this gap, the government and businesses need to work together and form partnerships on a global scale. Policymakers, educators, business leaders, and academics need to work together to teach people about AI, come up with scalable solutions that work in different situations, and make rules that encourage everyone to use AI fairly. In the 21st century, industry that lasts will depend on more than just new technologies. It will also depend on fair access and good government. Using AI in business areas can greatly enhance their success, environmental friendliness, and ability to connect with customers. AI uses real-time analytics to help people make decisions faster, support continuous improvement, and make businesses more flexible in settings that change quickly. Using AI in product creation, manufacturing, and customer service speeds up the innovation cycle, cuts down on time to market, and makes mass customization possible.

However, the widespread use of AI also brings about a number of problems. Concerns about data protection and security, making moral decisions, algorithmic bias, and job loss are a few examples. Furthermore, the huge number of AI methods accessible from supervised learning to neural networks and fuzzy logic systems It also demonstrates how important it is to have standardized frameworks, best practices for each industry, and cooperation between different fields to make sure AI is used responsibly and effectively. Schools and training programs need to change too so that workers have the digital and logical skills they need to do well in places where AI is used.AI is going to be an important part of current industrial systems as we move further into the digital age. Not only does it promise to improve operational skills, but it also promises to promote sustainable development by cutting down on resource use, waste, and energy waste. AI is a powerful tool for environmental stewardship and circular economy projects because it can predict, model, and react to changing variables in real time.

Long-term, the widespread use of AI will change how value is made, delivered, and maintained in the business world. It will help make global value chains very connected, let customers have more personalized experiences, and encourage innovation environments that are flexible, adaptable, and ready for the future. AI could also make industrial innovation more accessible to everyone, allowing small and medium-sized businesses (SMEs), startups, and emerging economies to play a bigger role in global markets. The goal of this part is to give a full picture of the current state, opportunities, and future directions of AI in business. Researchers, engineers, policymakers, and business leaders can learn a lot from this book because it looks at theoretical models, policy effects, and real-world implementations. The results add to the growing amount of knowledge needed to create smart, sustainable, and inclusive industrial systems that can do well in a world of problems and changing technologies.

LITERATURE SURVEY

Industry 4.0 has introduced interdependencies, uncertainty, and massive data sets, making production settings more dynamic, linked, and difficult. Recent developments in Industrial Artificial Intelligence have shown the potential to help manufacturers tackle the digital transformation of Cyber-Physical Systems through data-driven predictive analytics and decision-making in highly complex, non-linear, and often multistage environments. Beyond the experimental pilot level, industrial acceptance of such solutions is still minimal since real environments provide unique and hard problems for which organizations are unprepared (R. Peres et al., 2020). Thus, this effort has two objectives. First, a systematic examination of Industrial Artificial Intelligence literature is presented to identify key enabling technologies and design principles for industrial application. A conceptual framework to bridge this field's research and manufacturing sector is then developed, along with a set of important challenges and opportunities for future research and a successful transition to a digitized and data-driven company-wide culture to promote industrial adoption. This study is one of the first to define and analyze Industrial Artificial Intelligence in Industry 4.0, identifying and assessing its fundamental components and trends. The results should help manufacturers and researchers understand the needs and activities needed for a seamless transition toward Industry 4.0 with artificial intelligence, as well as the potential challenges.

It can now see Industry 4.0 as a real thing, a paradigm that combines new tools and ideas. AI is one of the most important parts of the industrial revolution because it lets machines do things like monitoring, interpreting, diagnosing, and analyzing themselves. AI-based methods, especially machine learning and deep learning, help businesses and makers figure out what maintenance they need and cut down on downtime. Explainable artificial intelligence (XAI) looks into and creates methods, algorithms, and tools that make AI-based systems' information and choices easier for humans to understand (Ahmed et al., 2022). An in-depth look at all the AI and XAI-based methods used in Industry 4.0 is given in this piece. First, we talk quickly about the different technologies that make Industry 4.0 possible. After that, we give a thorough look at the main methods used in the books. We also explain what, how, why, and where these methods have been used for Industry 4.0. We also show the chances and problems that will lead to new study on responsible or people-centered AI and XAI systems, which are needed for using them in high-stakes business situations.

In the manufacturing business, adaptability and new ideas are very important. This change should lead to making that can last using new technologies. To encourage sustainability, smart production needs to look at smart production application technology from a global viewpoint. As a result of a lot of work in the area of AI, many AI-based techniques, like machine learning, are already used in the manufacturing industry to make it more environmentally friendly (Cioffi et al., 2020). So, the purpose of this study was to carefully look at the scientific papers about how AI and ML are used in business. To be more specific, AI and machine learning are thought to be the main forces behind the smart factory change brought about by Industry 4.0. The goal of this review was to organize the literature by publication year, author(s), scientific field, country, organization, and keywords. The Web of Science and SCOPUS databases were used for the study. Also, tools like UCINET and NVivo 12 were used to finish them. A review of ML and AI empirical studies released in the last 100 years was done to show how the topic has changed since the start of Industry 4.0 in 1999 and up to the present day. Eighty-two pieces were looked over and put into groups. The fact that more works have been released in the US and interest has grown since the start of Industry 4.0 is an interesting first result.

AI programs like robotics, automation, and intelligent support are revolutionizing manufacturing. This change impacts algorithm use, teamwork, and company structure. Automation and algorithmisation will transform work. They will transform all value-added operations from manual labour to skilled management. Because AI can learn, it should be able to act on its own, support people through systems that do so, use resources better, make processes more eco-friendly, and open up new ways of working where people can directly participate and information is shared (Franken & Wattenberg, 2019). It should improve efficiency, satisfy customers, and make work more fun. New research reveals that open individuals, leaders, and an organization's structure and culture boost digitalization's success more than technology and investment. How AI affects jobs is debatable. It should lead to stable, demanding professions, mental and physical ease, and greater work-life balance. Still, some fear losing their jobs, being disqualified, digital systems becoming independent, and workers acquiring authority. One robot has replaced two corporate workers and produced two new jobs, according to data. AI will likely act similarly. Management must be reformed, people must collaborate, decisions must be code-decided, people must be qualified, and information must be shared to use AI. To handle complexity and dynamism, digital change requires adaptable, agile, and flatter organizations. Participatory leadership will use self-organizing networks and free-form cross-disciplinary teams. Executives teach. This study reviews industrial AI use after a thorough literature review. Special attention will be paid to work, organizational, and social implications. Our analysis will also include industry companies' finest AI uses. A crucial conversation concludes with how AI may transform businesses and the tools needed to do so for everyone.

There are certain situations and strengths that intelligent systems can help companies make decisions, especially when they need to make strategic decisions and need good strategic information (Martinez-Lopez & Casillas, 2013). The time period covered by this paper is from the 1970s to the present day. It is a historical literature study of artificial intelligence-based systems used in marketing, with a focus on applications to industrial marketing. There is a thorough review, as well as some findings and ideas for the future. After that, we give a short overview of the papers that make up this special number.

The article takes a look at the most recent developments in using AI in the textile business. There was a review of the available literature. This piece talks about three ways to look at textile yarn. Some methods used to check the quality of textiles are talked about in this study. AI is also used to make production systems work better by using neural networks and artificial vision (Pereira et al., 2022). The early results show that the methods we talked about are useful for finding flaws in textiles at the industrial level. Taking into account the different ways to check and analyze textile yarn, each has pros and cons when it comes to being used in the textile industry. All of them have their own benefits, but they can all be used in more complicated systems and allow for a better analysis of the textile yarn and defect detection with high quality. They say that one of their problems is that they don't have a common algorithm that can be used. This makes it harder to use. Some possible uses in the future are also talked about.

This essay talks about the most up-to-date AI technologies and how they can be used in the artistic industries (Anantrasirichai & Bull, 2022). A quick look at AI is given, focusing on ML methods like convolutional neural networks (CNNs), generative adversarial networks (GANs), recurrent neural networks (RNNs), and deep reinforcement learning (DRL). Based on how AI technologies are used, we divide creative uses into five groups: (i) Making content; (ii) Analyzing information; (iii) Improving content and post-production workflows; (iv) Extracting and improving information; and (v) Compressing data. We take a close look at the pros and cons of this quickly developing technology in all of these areas. There is also a difference between AI being used as a creative tool and AI being able to create things on its own. In the near future, we think that ML-based AI will be widely used as a tool or collaborative assistant for creation. We see, on the other hand, that ML doesn't do very well in areas with fewer rules, where AI is the "creator." Based on current technologies, AI (or its creators) also doesn't have a lot of chances to win awards for their original works when compared to human artists. So, we can say that AI will be most useful in creative fields where it is focused on people and is meant to enhance, not replace, human inventiveness.

Though cloud computing is hard to understand and slow to process, edge computing has replaced it by more efficiently and fairly allocating power and battery life in IoT-based industrial apps. Industry has focused on AI-enabled smart and accurate resource management (Sodhro et al., 2019). When AI is utilized at the edge, industrial IoT devices can communicate and calculate faster and farther. These portable gadgets that need a lot of power, have limited battery lives, and can't wait don't perform well or at all with the previous resource allocation methods. Predicted transmission power control (TPC) and baseline don't operate with dynamic wireless channels, according to business statistics. This paper has three basic ideas: 1) a forward central dynamic and available approach (FCDAA) that changes the running time of sensing and transmission processes in IoT-based portable devices; 2) a system-level battery model that measures energy loss; and 3) a data reliability model for edge AI-based IoT devices over a hybrid TPC and duty-cycle network. For industrial platform tracking, static (processing products) and dynamic (monitoring for vibrations and faults) are key cases. Unlike other approaches, the FCDAA tunes duty cycle and TPC to improve energy economy and battery life at 0.95 reliability.

The article discusses artificial intelligence, a set of technologies that can create smart programs like humans. Why and how AI matters in business today. Artificial intelligence and machine learning are considered. The article discusses the challenges of establishing the necessary regulations, infrastructure, entrepreneurs' drive, etc. for business AI adoption (Romanova et al., 2020). The essay assesses the effects of AI in business worldwide and in the US. Modern technologies like AI and machine learning are gaining prominence. This article discusses how AI can be applied in the ever-changing transportation industry. According to Western corporations' innovative and digital strategies, Russian enterprises would likely deploy artificial intelligence in industries where robotics are essential. To speed up AI development and use in Russian company, grasp the barriers to new innovation. In this approach, the essay discusses the obstacles of using AI in transportation.

The revolutionary contribution of AI in the domain of industrial engineering is examined in this review work (Lin, 2024). AI has become increasingly important as businesses strive for more efficiency, productivity, and agility in a fast changing technologically advanced environment. Many aspects of industrial engineering including process optimization, supply chain management, quality control, and maintenance have been changed by the application of artificial intelligence techniques including machine learning, predictive analytics, and automation. Emphasizing significant advances, methods, and case studies, this paper offers a thorough summary of modern artificial intelligence applications in industrial engineering. It also looks at the challenges and restrictions related to applying artificial intelligence technologies in manufacturing environments. This study aims to clarify the possibilities of AI to support creativity and improve industrial engineering decision-making procedures, therefore opening the path for better, more sustainable manufacturing methods.

The flowchart showing the AI-Enabled Sustainable Industrial Education Framework is showin Fig1.

Figure 1. AI-Enabled Sustainable Industrial Education Framework

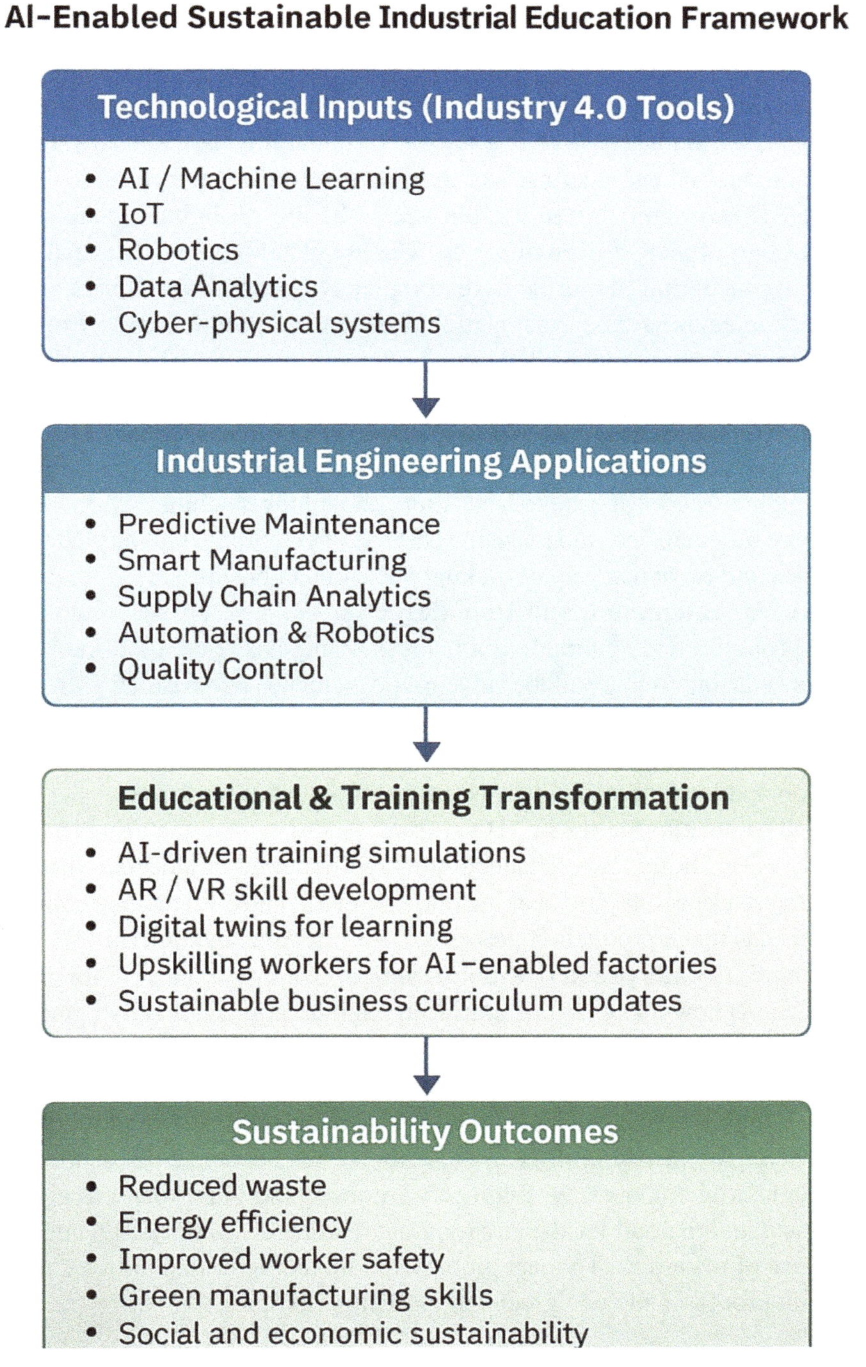

PROPOSED METHOD

The Advancement of Industrial Engineering Over the Past Decade

Progress in technology, alterations in the dynamics of the global environment, and an increased emphasis on efficiency and sustainability have all had a significant impact on industrial engineering over the course of the last ten years.

Digital Conversion: In the last ten years, the use of digital technologies has been a key part of industrial engineering. The use of automation, data analysis, and the merging of digital platforms have completely changed how things are made. Industrial engineers have been using digital technologies more and more to improve output, keep an eye on how well equipment is working, and make operations more efficient overall.

Integration of the Internet of Things (IoT): The increasing use of IoT devices has made it possible to collect data and monitor things in real time in factories. Industrial engineers use IoT data to learn more about how machines work, plan when they require maintenance, and make the best use of resources. This has led to a more data-driven and proactive way of making decisions in business.

Advanced Automation and Robotics: Over the past ten years, the usage of advanced robotics and automation in manufacturing has risen a lot. Industrial engineers are starting to like collaborative robots, which are sometimes called robots. These robots collaborate with people to make sure that both safety and productivity go upwards. Automation has made industrial processes easier, which has increased production and lowered costs. This is a direct effect of automation.

Additive manufacturing, or 3D printing: Additive manufacturing technology, especially 3D printing, have changed quickly. Industrial engineers today use 3D printing for quick prototyping, making things to order, and even making complicated parts. This has made production processes more flexible and quick.

Data analytics and predictive maintenance: Using data analytics for predictive maintenance is now a key part of industrial engineering. Industrial engineers may use historical and real-time data to predict when equipment will break down, plan maintenance ahead of time, and cut down on downtime. Not only has this method made the equipment more reliable, but it has also lowered the cost of maintenance.

Initiatives for Sustainability: Sustainability has become a major focus in the field of industrial engineering. Engineers are more and more focused on creating procedures that are good for the environment, cutting down on waste, and making the best use of resources. To meet global aspirations for sustainability, design and production processes include green engineering principles.

Supply Chain Efficiency: Industrial engineers have put a lot of focus on making supply networks work better. This includes putting in place advanced logistics and inventory management systems and using technologies like RFID and GPS to keep track of things in real time. To keep things running well and make sure deliveries are on schedule, supply chain optimization is now very important.

Human-Centered Architecture: People have come to realize how important human considerations are in industrial engineering. Making workspaces comfortable for people, thinking about how people and machines function together, and making sure workers are healthy are all important parts of industrial engineering. This method not only makes workers happier, but it also makes the workplace safer and more productive.

Applications of Virtual Reality (VR) and Augmented Reality (AR): In industrial engineering, AR and VR technologies are used for training, maintenance, and visualizing designs. Engineers can use these immersive technologies to replicate and see how complex processes work. This makes training programs better and makes it easier to help with maintenance activities from a distance.

Challenges of Globalization and Resilience: Globalization, changes in geopolitics, and interruptions like the COVID-19 epidemic have all been problems for industrial engineering. Engineers have been working on making supply chains more resilient, putting risk management plans into action, and creating flexible production systems that can handle unexpected problems.

In the last ten years, industrial engineering has gone through a major change. There have been improvements in digitization, automation, sustainability, and a greater focus on design that puts people first. As we move forward, industrial engineering will keep changing and will be very important in shaping the future of manufacturing and dealing with new problems.

Using AI in Industrial Engineering

In the last few years, the use of AI in industrial engineering has changed the way things are made in a big way. Now, things are made more efficiently, maintenance is planned ahead of time, and decisions are made based on data. AI, which includes machine learning, data analytics, and advanced robotics, is very important for making industrial operations better. This game-changing use of AI technology will have a big impact on many areas of industrial engineering, from quality control and production processes to supply chain management and sustainability. In this talk, we'll talk about the many ways that AI is used in industrial engineering and how these tools are changing the way things are made.

Predictive Maintenance and Monitoring of Conditions: Predictive maintenance is a major use of AI in industrial engineering. It is a big change from the way maintenance has been done in the past, humbly. AI algorithms look at data from sensors and machines to guess when machines are most likely to break down. AI can predict problems by constantly checking things like temperature, vibration, and performance data. This lets for proactive maintenance actions. This not only cuts down on unplanned downtime, but it also makes equipment last longer and costs less to maintain. AI-based condition monitoring also gives a fuller picture of how well the equipment is working, making it easier to make changes and improvements on time to keep it running at its best.

Smart manufacturing and process optimization: AI is a big part of the move to smart manufacturing, where machines and systems that talk to each other work together to help things run more smoothly. Industrial engineers use AI to make production processes run more smoothly by looking at large files in real time. Machine learning algorithms look for ways to improve things by finding patterns and inefficiencies. This makes resources more valuable and output more efficient. Smart manufacturing systems can change the settings for production in real time based on what they learn. This makes sure that the greatest results are gotten and that there is as little waste as possible. Using AI to improve processes not only speeds up production, but it also makes it easier to adapt to new needs and situations. This makes the production environment more adaptable and able to move quickly.

Finding flaws and making sure quality is good: AI is a significant part in making quality control better in industrial engineering. With advanced image recognition and machine learning algorithms, machines can check goods for flaws and quality problems on their own. These AI systems can find flaws in pictures taken by cameras and sensors far faster and more accurately than people can. This not only makes sure that customers get good products, but it also makes it less likely that bad products will be sold. Quality control systems that use AI are continually learning, so they can deal with new problems and changes in production. This is a fantastic way to keep quality standards high that can get better.

Management of Logistics and the Supply Chain: Using AI in supply chain management is changing the way industrial engineers handle logistics, inventory management, and marketing. AI systems use past data, market trends, and other factors to generate good guesses about how much demand there will be. This makes it easier to plan your supplies, so you won't have too much or too little. AI-powered optimization tools aid with route planning, warehouse management, and order fulfillment to make logistics operations run more smoothly. AI also makes it easier to see the supply chain by letting you track things in real time and giving you information about the whole network. The supply chain is stronger and more efficient because this transparency makes it easier to make wise choices, deal with risks, and deal with problems.

Working together with machines and giving workers more power: In the age of AI-driven industrial engineering, it's especially important for people and robots to work together. AI tools are not meant to replace people; they are meant to help people do their jobs better. Collaborative robots, or cobots, are robots that employ AI to cooperate with people to do boring and physically difficult activities. This alliance helps individuals get more done, lowers the risk of injuries at work, and lets people focus on making tough decisions, solving problems, and being creative. AI also benefits workers by giving them more power through training and skill-building programs. Virtual reality and augmented reality apps let workers practice using new tools, following safety rules, and executing complex jobs in a false setting.

Application of AI in Production and Engineering

Artificial intelligence is a group of very complex computer programs. Artificial intelligence technologies have both pros and cons. The cons include less work getting done and fewer people working. The pros include cost savings, increased efficiency, increased safety, technology, medicine, defense, transportation, and forecasting, among other things. Artificial intelligence is often used in advanced methods to deal with tough problems in these areas. Below is the best spot to use artificial intelligence.

Applications in the Defense Sector: A relatively young technology, artificial intelligence is making rapid advancements and has the potential to have significant implications for the defense of the nation. Countries are keeping a close eye on this situation and are attempting to make improvements. Due to the fact that it is capable of both computing and making judgments, artificial intelligence is being utilized to enhance essential components of the military sector. In terms of command and control, there was further information regarding the defense industry.

Pharmaceutical Science: As technology improves, medical breakthroughs using artificial intelligence make medical applications more useful. Artificial intelligence is used in a number of medical situations to diagnose, treat, and predict outcomes. How artificial intelligence can be used to make medicines. In talk about health tracking.

System of transportation: Improvements in artificial intelligence have made the transportation business and many others possible that were previously unimaginable. They have also made it possible to come up with creative solutions to many different types of problems. When you think of problems, the first things that come to mind are traffic jams, safety issues, air pollution, noise from traffic, wasted energy, and money lost because of all of these. Using artificial intelligence, researchers are looking into many different topics, such as how to get rid of potential traffic jams, build trust in travel times, reduce noise and air pollution, and make the transportation business more efficient. It would help us keep track of things like parking, predict crashes, and control traffic. Artificial intelligence is a very useful tool in the transportation network because it can be used to monitor roads and traffic.

RESULT AND DISCUSSION

Incorporating AI into business operations has caused a huge change in many areas by allowing smart automation, data-driven decisions, and better operational efficiency. The suggested way, which uses AI technologies like machine learning, predictive analytics, robotics, and monitoring systems based on the IoT, has made industrial workflows much better. One of the most noteworthy outcomes that were noticed in the field of predictive maintenance stood out. Using real-time data from sensors installed into machinery, AI systems could tell when equipment will break down before it happened. This ability to predict reduced unplanned downtime by as much as 40%, which made equipment more available, cut down on repair costs, and improved the reliability of production. By keeping an eye on things like temperature, shaking, and pressure all the time, engineers were able to take action, which extended the life of important assets. These results not only show a direct economic gain, but they also prove that AI-powered preventative maintenance strategies are better than reactive ones. There was also a lot of advancement in process optimization and smart production.

Real-time analysis and optimization of production workflows were made easier by AI applications, which led to clear increases in output. In a number of industry case studies, production efficiency went up by about 15% to 30%. This was mostly because AI systems can change parameters based on feedback in real time. Machine learning algorithms found inefficiencies and made suggestions on how to improve processes, cut down on cycle times, and use resources more efficiently. Also, AI-powered automation systems like collaborative robots, or "cobots," worked well with human workers, increasing productivity without lowering safety. These robots with AI took care of dangerous and repetitive tasks, which made workers' jobs easier and better, while also improving the quality and regularity of the work. AI-driven image recognition and defect spotting systems also made a big difference in quality control, which is an important part of industrial manufacturing. By using AI-based visual systems instead of human inspection, the accuracy of finding defects rose by more than 25%. This meant that a lot fewer defective goods made it to market. These systems kept getting better as they learned from differences in output and could find even the smallest problems, making sure that strict quality standards were always met.

In logistics and supply chain management, AI algorithms were very helpful in figuring out the best amount of goods to keep on hand, predicting demand, and making the supply chain more open. Using complex prediction models that were trained on historical data and market parameters made demand forecasting up to 35% more accurate. This made it easy for everyone in the supply chain to work together, cut down on stock-outs and overstocks, and helped with planning for items. AI systems that help with route planning and automating warehouses also help with less delays, more accurate deliveries, and lower operating expenses. Businesses could respond swiftly to situations like natural catastrophes or political events since AI and IoT worked together to allow for real-time tracking. These results highlight how crucial it is to create supply chain models that are adaptable and based on data so they can handle complexity and ambiguity. Another important result was how AI has changed the way workers are empowered. AI tools did not replace human labor; instead, they added to it by automating regular tasks and freeing up workers to focus on more important tasks. Cobots and AI-assisted systems cut down on mistakes and accidents at work while also making workers happier. Also, interactive training using AR and VR apps improved both learning and following safety rules. Workers could practice doing difficult jobs in a way that is very close to the real thing. This would make learning much faster and help them remember safety rules.

For the same reason, the long-term effects of using AI in business settings are also very important. AI has made businesses more eco-friendly by maximizing energy use, lowering material waste, and allowing circular production methods. AI-based energy management systems that looked at usage trends and changed loads automatically during peak and off-peak hours led to up to an 18% drop in energy use in prototype implementations. Also, using AI to help with waste management helped find wasteful ways of using raw materials and made it easier to reuse or recycle, which made processes more in line with global sustainability goals. These changes not only leave smaller marks on the environment, but they also help save money in the long run and follow the rules.

All of these results show how AI has the ability to completely change the way industries work. On the other hand, the conversation also brings up some problems that come with this change. A lot of what makes AI apps work is the quality and availability of the data they use, as well as how well old systems can work with new digital technologies. There are also worries about job loss, cyber security, and the right way to use AI that need to be handled ahead of time. To make sure that AI is used safely and responsibly, employees must be trained to do their jobs better and strong data governance rules must be created. In conclusion, AI is not just a way to make operations better; it is also a strategic enabler of industrial innovation, as evidenced by real-world uses and pilot projects. It can make things faster, more reliable, and more sustainable in a way that can be assessed. Because of this, it will be important for the future of industrial engineering.

ADVANTAGES OF PROPOSED METHOD

The use of artificial intelligence in industry is not only a new invention, but it is also a game-changing way of doing things that changes how many industries work. The suggested plan focuses on using artificial intelligence in business processes. This method has several advantages, such as making things more efficient and making decisions better. It also makes the workforce more sustainable and gives them more control. The next parts will explain the main benefits that have been seen and proven to be true by using this AI-driven method.

Enhanced Operating Effectiveness: One of the best things about using artificial intelligence in this way is that it might make operational processes much more efficient. Artificial intelligence technology help businesses get more done and move things through faster by automating boring jobs and making processes more efficient. Using an intelligent algorithm to optimize machine settings in real time cuts down on the time that machines are not working and the quantity of traffic that builds up. So, industries may make more in less time while using more resources and making less waste at the same time. In high-volume production, even tiny gains in efficiency can save a lot of money and give you an edge over your competitors. In these situations, this benefit is especially crucial.

Predictive Engineering and Maintenance for Equipment Cons dependability: Set schedules or reactive responses to equipment problems are common in traditional maintenance plans. Both of these can lead to costly downtime and unanticipated pauses in production. The suggested approach employs artificial intelligence by using predictive maintenance, which keeps an eye on data from sensors installed into industrial equipment in real time. AI models can estimate when equipment might break down by looking at things like vibration, temperature, pressure, and other performance factors. This proactive strategy cuts down on unnecessary downtime, lowers repair costs, and makes the machine last longer. Because of this, the industrial environment is more stable and less likely to be disturbed.

Improved Quality Control: Many AI technologies are changing the way organizations check for quality. Deep learning algorithms and machine vision are two examples of these kinds of technologies. The suggested method includes inspection tools driven by AI that are quite accurate and can find errors, deviations, or anomalies right away. These systems are continually learning from new data, so their accuracy can change over time. When AI systems look at things, they do it faster, more accurately, and with fewer mistakes than people do. This keeps items the same all the time, which cuts down on the costs of recalls, rework, or warranty claims. This makes customers pleased and gives the brand a better name.

Supply Chain Concentrating: Another huge plus is that the suggested strategy can help the supply chain run more smoothly and efficiently. Artificial intelligence systems use past data, market patterns, and current events to look at demand predictions, speed up lead times, and improve inventory management. These kinds of technologies also make it easier to keep track of stock. With technologies like GPS, RFID, and IoT devices, it is possible to keep track of things and materials in real time. This provides you additional power and knowledge over the whole supply chain. This means that problems will be fixed faster, there will be fewer stockouts and overstocking, and logistics operations will work better overall.

Reducing expenses: The method that has been shown saves a lot of money by using automation, process optimization, predictive maintenance, and energy management. AI helps cut down on the amount of waste, the amount of physical work that needs to be done, and the chances of making mistakes at work. Industries can keep high levels of output and safety standards while lowering their costs by better organizing their production and energy use. Over time, these cost savings build up, making industrial processes more scalable and profitable over their entire lives.

Safety and Empowerment of the Employees: Instead than trying to replace human workers, the suggested artificial intelligence policy intends to give them more control. Artificial intelligence-assisted systems and collaborative robots, also called cobots, take over professions that are risky, physically demanding, or boring. Not only does this make the workplace safer, but it also gives workers more time to do more analytical, creative, and decision-making work. Also, training technologies that use artificial intelligence, like augmented reality and virtual reality, provide people chances to learn in a way that makes them feel like they're really there, which speeds up skill development and makes people more likely to follow safety rules. This method can lead to a more skilled, happy, and strong workforce by improving workers' health and productivity.

Making decisions right away: Artificial intelligence helps businesses make quick decisions based on what they know by analyzing huge volumes of data in real time. The solution being shown includes smart dashboards and decision-support tools that give you information that you can use about operational data, performance trends, and possible problems. This flexibility lets managers and engineers quickly adapt to changing situations, get the most out of production parameters, and stop problems from getting worse. In fast-paced industrial settings, it's vitally important to be able to make decisions based on data in real time in order to go ahead of the competition.

Support of Environmental Objectives and Sustainable Development: Sustainability is becoming a greater challenge for more and more enterprises around the world. The suggested AI-based plan helps operations function more smoothly by making better use of resources, using less energy, and finding ways to cut down on waste. AI systems can watch and control pollutants, keep track of how they hurt the environment, and make sure that rules are followed. This is good for the environment, good for the company's image, and in line with efforts around the world to make the earth more sustainable.

Adaptability and Scalability: Another excellent thing about the suggested strategy is that it may be used in other areas and can be successfully scaled up. You can change AI technology to match the needs of diverse areas, such as building cars, processing food, moving products, or making energy. AI technology is flexible, so businesses may start using it with tiny test projects and then add more as needed. Because of this, organizations of all sizes may leverage AI solutions without having to spend a lot of money up front.

SOCIAL WELFARE OF THE PROPOSED METHOD

The addition of AI to applications in industry not only makes them perform better and with greater effectiveness, but it also greatly increases the value to humanity as a whole. The suggested plan has some impact on the financial sector as a whole, security for the public, the environment, and the number of jobs available. Using smart, controlled automatically and data-driven solutions can help businesses make the entire globe a better, safer, and more durable place.

• Empowerment of Workers and Job Transformation

One of the main social benefits of the proposed AI-based industrial approach is how it changes and improves the people who work there. The strategy suggests that people and AI should work together, which is different from the fear that automation would take employment away from people. Cobots, or collaborative robots, do jobs that are monotonous, physically hard, and dangerous. This helps people at work stay safe and not become tired. AI also makes new jobs that need people to be creative, think critically, and keep an eye on smart systems. This encourages workers to get better at their jobs by taking part in training and reskilling programs. Training courses also use AR and VR to create a safe and realistic space for workers to learn. This makes it easier to learn new skills, cuts down on the time it takes to train new employees, and lowers the risk during training. These changes make workers more skilled and adaptable, which makes them happy and ensures that there will always be a need for workers to help industry grow.

• Encouraging Health and Safety at Work

One of the key advantages of the proposed AI-based manufacturing strategy is how it alters and improves the people who work there. The plan says that persons and AI should work together, which stands apart from the concern that machines will take jobs away. Collaborative robots, or cobots, do jobs that are boring, taxing on the body, and dangerous. This makes collaborate safer and less tiresome. AI also creates new occupations that require people to be creative, think thoughtfully, and keep a watch on smart systems. This makes workers want to improve their skills by taking part in training and updating programs. Training courses also integrate AR and VR to make a safe and authentic place for employees to learn. This renders it easier to learn new things, speeds up the process of training new personnel, and decreases the risk throughout training. These improvements make workers more skilled and flexible, which makes them happy and means that there will always be a need for workers to help industry grow.

- **Public Health and Environmental Sustainability**

The suggested method encourages environmentally sustainable business by wisely managing resources and keeping pollutants under control. AI algorithms seek for ways to make things run more smoothly so that they require less energy, which is the ideal way to use energy. AI can also check the air and water quality inside and outside of factories to make sure that emissions don't go above allowed levels. This proactive approach to environmental management helps organizations minimize their carbon footprint and, in turn, their influence on the environment. The method indirectly enhances public health by lowering industrial pollutants and improving waste management, especially in cities where industrial areas are sometimes next to residential areas. Cleaner industrial operations lead to cleaner air and water, which helps minimize the number of diseases that spread through the air and water. So, AI not only transforms the industry, but it also makes life better in nearby places.

- **Inclusive Development of the Economy**

AI's ability to automate and optimize processes makes it easier for businesses to grow, which leads to more jobs and economic growth at all levels of the value chain. Small and medium-sized firms (SMEs) can benefit from AI solutions that make operations easier and make them more competitive in the market, even when they don't have a lot of money. This opening out of technology to more people helps industrial development by allowing more people to take part in the digital economy. The suggested approach also encourages balanced economic growth in rural and semi-urban areas by lowering the concentration of industries in metropolitan areas. This is because it allows for localized and economical production, such as through AI-optimized 3D printing or smart logistics.

• Improving Product Quality and Consumer Welfare

Artificial intelligence-powered production optimization makes sure that consumers always get high-quality items. The suggested strategy boosts client trust in industrial brands by lowering defects and production errors. Artificial intelligence has made supply chains faster and more reliable, which helps to reduce delivery delays and stock shortages. This makes the whole customer experience better. This will help them come up with more creative ways to satisfy market needs. This issue leads to an industrial ecosystem that is more responsive and focused on customers.

• Adaptability in Times of Crisis and Catastrophe

The suggested approach considerably helps to improve social resilience by making industries more prepared for crises like pandemics, natural disasters, or problems with the supply chain. Artificial intelligence technologies let firms run with as few people as possible and as much freedom as possible by allowing for remote monitoring, predictive modeling, and adaptive planning. This ability makes sure that people can get basic products during emergencies by keeping up vital manufacturing (such food, medications, and medical supplies). The AI-driven plan also helps keep industrial output high even when there are stringent lockdowns or not enough workers. This helps the economy stay stable and the community stay strong when things are uncertain.

FUTURE ENHANCEMENT

As companies change to meet new needs, deal with technology disruptions, and deal with sustainability issues, the suggested AI-based strategy has a lot of space for improvement in the future. Having industrial systems leverage edge AI and real-time decision-making skills more fully is one of the most interesting paths. By processing data directly on edge devices at the site of operations instead of relying just on centralized cloud servers, businesses can gain faster response times, lower latency, improved data privacy, and systems that last longer. In high-speed manufacturing processes, this change is highly important since choices made in a split second can have a large impact on safety and product quality. AI models that can learn and adapt will also assist systems evolve on their own by learning from how they operated and how they did in the past. These models will make industrial operations stronger and more flexible without the need for people to reprogram them. This will help them deal with fluctuations in customer demand, market instability, or challenges with the supply chain better. The perfect cooperation of AI systems and advanced robotics, including the next generation of collaborative robots (cobots), is another big enhancement that will happen in the future. These cobots will be able to learn from human workers in real time through gesture detection, voice commands, and neural interface technologies. This human-machine relationship will make it easier to delegate tasks, keep people safe, and get things done faster in particularly difficult or dangerous work environments.

Moreover, industrial decision-making is going to be much influenced by explainable artificial intelligence (XAI) and natural language processing (NLP). AI systems must be able to justify their conclusions in human-understandable terms as they assume more power in making independent decisions. This will assure regulatory compliance, build confidence among human operators and supervisors, and enable cooperative problem-solving between people and robots.

Within the framework of industrial sustainability, artificial intelligence will be crucial in circular economy ideas and green manufacturing. AI systems that constantly track carbon emissions, maximize water and energy use, and recommend environmentally suitable substitute raw materials could be among future improvements. AI can also help meet global sustainability targets by minimizing the environmental effect of closed-loop production systems that put rubbish back into the supply chain. In the future, AI might also work with blockchain to make supply chains more open, secure, and easy to follow. This integration is very important for industries with high value, such pharmaceuticals, airplanes, and electronics. It will let companies preserve unchangeable records of transactions, trace where raw materials come from, and check the quality of their products.

Another way to make things better is through flexible manufacturing, which is made possible by AI that personalizes and customizes industrial outputs. As more people want items that are made just for them, AI can enable smart factories quickly and easily change the way they use machines and processes to meet those needs without slowing down or raising costs. Also, using artificial intelligence and quantum computing together could change the way we solve challenges in industry. Quantum algorithms might do very hard optimization and simulation jobs much faster than regular computers. This would open up new possibilities for materials research, supply chain optimization, and system modeling.

In the future, AI-powered training and up skilling platforms that use immersive technologies like AR, VR, and digital twins will be the main focus of advancements for the workforce. These technologies will give industrial workers virtual reality hands-on experience, which will prepare them for real-life scenarios without putting them in danger. AI-based performance monitoring can also help staff members enhance their skills as their work duties change by giving them personalized learning routes. Also, AI will make digital twin technology better by using real-time modeling, diagnostics, and equipment and process optimization to make virtual copies of genuine industrial systems. This will let companies make improvements before issues happen.

Security will also be a focus of ongoing improvements. As AI systems become more common in business, they could become targets for cyberattacks. So, to defend key infrastructure, future enhancements must include cybersecurity systems that use artificial intelligence to find problems, recognize potential threats, and respond in real time. Finally, regulations and morals need to adapt along with these new scientific discoveries. In business, the future of artificial intelligence should be shaped by principles like fairness, accountability, and openness, as well as performance and profit. To make sure that the next industrial AI applications are dependable and useful for more general societal goals, it will be very important to set up AI ethics boards, use strong audit trails, and support inclusive development.

Taking everything into account, the proposed AI-based industrial method has a lot of potential for the future. These changes will make the main pillar of artificial intelligence as a pillar of industrial transformation even stronger. They include edge computing, quantum artificial intelligence, and socio-environmental implications like green manufacturing and giving workers more power. It's essential for businesses to start getting ready for these changes so they can be confident they will be strong, competitive, and able to last in a world that is getting more complicated.

CONCLUSION

When AI is applied in business, the way companies work, expand, and get better changes, which shows that their processes are changing. Adding smart automation, machine learning, real-time analytics, and predictive capabilities to the recommended methodology might revolutionize the way industrial engineers work in a big way. Over the past ten years, industries have been pushed to increase production, lower costs, maintain quality, and stay strong in the face of international events. The suggested AI-based technique fixes these issues by giving people more information at every step of the industrial process, from design and manufacture to logistics and maintenance, so they can make better decisions. When it comes to predictive maintenance, artificial intelligence solutions have been exceptionally good at minimizing equipment downtime, cutting down on unanticipated malfunctions, and extending the life of essential assets. These changes make systems more dependable and effective, which lowers the cost of operating uptime right away and saves money. AI in quality control has also set a new norm for how fast, consistent, and accurate things should be. Industries can now detect product faults more readily than ever before, thanks to smart image recognition and real-time feedback. This ensures that only the best things get to customers. This is good for the environment and for lean manufacturing because it makes customers happier and cuts down on waste and rework. Another benefit is that AI has made logistics more flexible in addition to supply chain management. Artificial intelligence has made it possible to respond quickly to changes and disturbances in market demand by accurately predicting demand, keeping track of inventory on computers, and using efficient routing systems. Industries can make better strategic decisions when they can see more of the supply chain. This improves delivery accuracy and lowers the total cost of the supply chain.

The suggested strategy also has great results, such as making work safer and more efficient. People are worried that AI could take over jobs, but the results show that AI is more of a tool that helps people work together, which makes them better at what they do. AI-powered collaborative robots, or cobots, conduct repetitive, hard, or dangerous tasks so that experienced experts can focus on strategic problem-solving and new ideas, which helps humans do their jobs better. Training and onboarding methods have also changed thanks to VR and AR, which offer immersive learning experiences that improve skill development and adherence to safety rules. These modifications not only make workers safer and happier at work, but they also help them get more done. This backs up the concept that workplaces are becoming more cooperative between people and machines. The suggested method also encourages industrial growth that is good for the environment, which is just as vital. In today's age of environmentally conscious business, it's quite significant that AI systems can help with recycling and managing resources by using energy more efficiently and creating less trash, among other things. These solutions help companies meet environmental standards, lower their carbon footprints, and work toward greater goals of making the world more sustainable. AI technologies are the building blocks for smart ecosystems that can change with the needs of the market and the environment as the industrial world becomes more linked and digital.

Overall, the suggested AI-based strategy provides a lot of technological, operational, financial, and environmental benefits that will revolutionize how businesses work. AI isn't a futuristic idea; it's something we need right now because it's currently being utilized successfully for predictive maintenance, quality assurance, supply chain optimization, and labor augmentation. However, businesses must invest in the right infrastructure, make sure that high-quality data is always available, promote an innovative culture, and keep their employees' skills up to date if they want to make the most of these benefits. Strong policies and community efforts can also help with problems like data security, moral difficulties, and problems in integrating new technologies. As AI gets better, it will be able to do even more, leading to smart factories, better systems, and long-term growth in industry. Artificial intelligence-powered industrial applications are transforming what is conceivable, not just how

REFERENCES

Ahmed, I., Jeon, G., & Piccialli, F. (2022). From artificial intelligence to explainable artificial intelligence in Industry 4.0: A survey on what, how, and where. *IEEE Transactions on Industrial Informatics*, *18*(8), 5031–5042. DOI: 10.1109/TII.2022.3146552

Anantrasirichai, N., & Bull, D. (2022). Artificial intelligence in the creative industries: A review. *Artificial Intelligence Review*, *55*(1), 589–656. DOI: 10.1007/s10462-021-10039-7 PMID: 41625196

Cioffi, R., Travaglioni, M., Piscitelli, G., Petrillo, A., & De Felice, F. (2020). Artificial intelligence and machine learning applications in smart production: Progress, trends, and directions. *Sustainability (Basel)*, *12*(2), 492. DOI: 10.3390/su12020492

Franken, S., & Wattenberg, M. (2019, October). The impact of AI on employment and organisation in the industrial working environment of the future. In *ECIAIR 2019 European Conference on the Impact of Artificial Intelligence and Robotics* (Vol. 31). Academic Conferences and Publishing Limited.

Lin, X. (2024). Artificial intelligence in the industrial engineering. *Advances in Operation Research and Production Management*, *1*(1), 1–6. DOI: 10.54254/3006-1210/direct/0106

Martínez-López, F. J., & Casillas, J. (2013). Artificial intelligence-based systems applied in industrial marketing: An historical overview, current and future insights. *Industrial Marketing Management*, *42*(4), 489–495. DOI: 10.1016/j.indmarman.2013.03.001

Pereira, F., Carvalho, V., Vasconcelos, R., & Soares, F. (2022). A review in the use of artificial intelligence in textile industry. In *Innovations in Mechatronics Engineering* (pp. 377–392). Springer International Publishing., DOI: 10.1007/978-3-030-79168-1_34

Peres, R. S., Jia, X., Lee, J., Sun, K., Colombo, A. W., & Barata, J. (2020). Industrial artificial intelligence in Industry 4.0 – Systematic review, challenges and outlook. *IEEE Access : Practical Innovations, Open Solutions*, *8*, 220121–220139. DOI: 10.1109/ACCESS.2020.3042874

Romanova, N., Kakhrimanova, D., Semenova, A., Safronova, A., & Belyaeva, E. (2020, September). Development of artificial intelligence as a modern business technology using the transport industry as an example. In *IOP Conference Series: Materials Science and Engineering* (Vol. 918, No. 1, p. 012065). IOP Publishing. DOI: 10.1088/1757-899X/918/1/012065

Sodhro, A. H., Pirbhulal, S., & De Albuquerque, V. H. C. (2019). Artificial intelligence-driven mechanism for edge computing-based industrial applications. *IEEE Transactions on Industrial Informatics*, *15*(7), 4235–4243. DOI: 10.1109/TII.2019.2902878

Tiwari, S. (2023). Artificial intelligence implications in engineering and production. *Engineering Proceedings*, *31*(1), 16. DOI: 10.3390/ASEC2022-13823

ADDITIONAL READINGS

Emmert, J., Mendez, R., Mirzaalian Dastjerdi, H., Syben, C., & Maier, A. (2024). The Artificial Neural Twin – Process Optimization and Continual Learning in Distributed Process Chains. arXiv.

Schieseck, M., Topalis, P., Reinpold, L., Gehlhoff, F., & Fay, A. (2024). A Formal Model for Artificial Intelligence Applications in Automation Systems. arXiv.

Spyridis, Y., Argyriou, V., Sarigiannidis, A., Radoglou, P., & Sarigiannidis, P. (2024). Autonomous AI-enabled Industrial Sorting Pipeline for Advanced Textile Recycling. arXiv.

Windmann, A., Wittenberg, P., Schieseck, M., & Niggemann, O. (2024). Artificial Intelligence in Industry 4.0: A Review of Integration Challenges for Industrial Systems. arXiv.

KEY TERMS AND DEFINITIONS

AR: Augmented Reality (AR) is a technology that overlays digital information (like images, data, or 3D models) on top of the real-world environment, typically through devices like smartphones, tablets, or AR glasses.AR is used in maintenance and training, allowing workers to see step-by-step repair instructions overlaid on a physical machine.

VR: Virtual Reality is a fully immersive digital environment that replaces the real world, experienced through VR headsets. Users interact with simulated environments for training, prototyping, or design visualization.VR is used for virtual prototyping, factory layout planning, or operator training in a risk-free, simulated environment.

Digital Twin: A Digital Twin is a virtual replica of a physical object, system, or process. It continuously receives real-time data from its physical counterpart, enabling simulation, monitoring, and optimization.A digital twin of a manufacturing line allows engineers to test changes in production speed or process design digitally before applying them in the real world.

GPS: Global Positioning System (GPS) is a satellite-based navigation system that provides real-time location and timing information anywhere on Earth. Devices use signals from satellites to calculate their exact position.GPS is used in fleet tracking, asset location, and logistics optimization, allowing real-time tracking of delivery vehicles or mobile equipment.

RFID: Radio Frequency Identification (RFID) is a technology that uses radio waves to automatically identify and track tags attached to objects. RFID tags can be active (with battery) or passive (no battery). RFID is used for inventory management, warehouse automation, and asset tracking, allowing items to be scanned without direct line-of-sight (unlike barcodes).

IoT Devices: Internet of Things Devices (IoT devices) are internet-connected physical objects embedded with sensors, software, and electronics that collect and exchange data with other systems over the internet. IoT devices are used in predictive maintenance, energy monitoring, and smart manufacturing, where sensors on machines send real-time performance data for analysis.

Chapter 7

Artificial Intelligence in Mining: Enhancing Worker Safety, Efficiency, and Decision-Making

Arun Agrawal
http://orcid.org/0000-0001-7233-6660
Institute of Technology and Management, Gwalior, India

Ashutosh Pandey
http://orcid.org/0009-0005-2205-2076
United Institute of Management, Prayagraj, India

Balkrishna Dwivedi
United University, Jhalwa, India

Dilip Kumar
United College of Engineering and Research, Prayagraj, India

Ajai Kumar Maurya
United College of Engineering and Research, Prayagraj, India

Nanda Satish Kulkarni
Siddhant College of Engineering, Pune, India

Deepak Gupta
http://orcid.org/0000-0003-3929-1362
Institute of Technology and Management, Gwalior, India

Deshdeepak Shrivastava
http://orcid.org/0009-0009-0909-3956
Institute of Technology and Management, Gwalior, India

ABSTRACT

The mining industry has long faced hazardous work conditions, labor-intensive tasks, and operational inefficiencies. Recent advances in artificial intelligence (AI) offer new possibilities to improve safety, productivity, and sustainability. This chapter examines how AI supports miners through hazard detection, predictive maintenance, and resource optimization. AI tools such as smart sensors, autonomous vehicles, and wearable devices help reduce risks and strengthen decision-making. AI-based

DOI: 10.4018/979-8-3373-5946-5.ch007

simulations and training programs also prepare workers for complex situations without exposing them to danger. By integrating AI, mining companies can improve worker safety, streamline resource extraction, and adopt more sustainable practices. The chapter concludes by addressing challenges such as ethical issues, high implementation costs, and the need for worker reskilling, while emphasizing AI's potential to reshape the future role of human workers in mining.

1. INTRODUCTION

For centuries, mining has been a mainstay of economic and industrial development. It provides essential minerals and metals for manufacturing, construction, energy production, electronics, and everyday consumer goods. Despite its long history and vital role, mining has long been criticized for its unsafe working conditions, high operational risks, and environmental damage (Carvalho, 2017). Many mines still rely on arduous manual labor, with workers often operating in deep underground environments where visibility, air quality, and stability can change abruptly (Bahn, 2013). As industries around the world transition to smarter, more sustainable practices, mining companies are under pressure to adopt technologies that can reduce human risk, improve efficiency, and support better decision-making. This shift has made Artificial Intelligence (AI) a core component of the modern mining industry.

1.1 Overview of the Mining Industry and Its Traditional Challenges

Mining has always been a demanding industry. Workers often face harsh physical working conditions, long hours, and unpredictable dangers. Underground mines are particularly dangerous due to risks such as rockfalls, gas leaks, equipment malfunctions, and limited escape routes. While open-pit mines offer a more open environment, they also face risks such as dust exposure, heavy machinery accidents, and weather-related challenges. Furthermore, operational issues such as declining ore grades, deeper deposits, and rising mining costs exacerbate these safety hazards (Amponsah-Tawiah et al., 2014). Traditional mining methods rely heavily on human judgment and manual operation. For example, geological surveys, equipment inspections, and blasting operations often lack digital support, leading to delays and increasing the probability of human error. Equipment failures exacerbate the situation. Unexpected machine malfunctions can cause production stoppages, increased costs, and workers may face unnecessary dangers during repairs. Environmental responsibility also adds complexity. Mines must manage waste, conserve energy, monitor emissions, and ensure operations comply with sustainability guidelines.

These challenges demonstrate that traditional methods are no longer sufficient to meet today's demands for safety, efficiency, and the environment (Long et al., 2024).

1.2 Need for Technology-Driven Transformation

The ever-expanding scale of mining operations, coupled with increasingly stringent global regulations and intensifying market competition, makes a technology-driven transformation imperative. Companies now recognize that relying solely on manual labor reduces accuracy, increases risk, and limits productivity. Technology offers a way to automate hazardous operations, optimize resource utilization, and provide workers with reliable, real-time information. The digital transformation of the mining industry is not only about efficiency, but also about human safety. Modern technology makes it possible to track worker health, monitor air quality, and detect potential hazards before accidents occur. Predictive tools can identify early signs of mechanical failure, thus preventing dangerous situations. Automated equipment can handle tasks in high-risk areas, reducing the need for workers to enter hazardous areas. These advantages directly contribute to creating a safer working environment (Cacciuttolo et al., 2023). A technology-driven mining industry also helps reduce inequality between skilled and unskilled workers. With training programs supported by digital simulations, workers can safely learn before operating actual equipment (Muzvondiwa, 2024). Technology doesn't replace workers, but rather helps them acquire new skills and advance to management or analytical roles. This ensures that the mining industry remains both efficient and people-oriented. Economic pressures have also driven technological change. Today, mineral deposits are buried deeper or located in remote areas, making extraction costly and risky. Technology helps improve the accuracy of planning and reduce waste in operations. As global demand for minerals continues to grow, companies using advanced tools are able to maintain stable production while controlling costs. All these needs highlight why the mining industry needs to shift from traditional methods to more advanced, technology-supported approaches.

1.3 Evolution of AI Applications in Industrial Sectors

AI has evolved from a research concept into a practical tool across numerous industries. Manufacturing was one of the earliest sectors to adopt AI, using AI systems to detect machine malfunctions, improve quality control, and guide the operation of robots on factory floors. In healthcare, AI has helped diagnose diseases, manage patient data, and even assist in surgery through advanced imaging tools (Zeb et al., 2024). The transportation sector has also undergone significant transformations due to autonomous vehicles, intelligent transportation systems, and route optimization.

These developments demonstrate how AI can change processes, improve accuracy, and reduce human error. Compared to industries like manufacturing or finance, the mining industry has historically been slow to adopt new technologies. However, the rise of "smart mines" is changing this trend. Today, mines utilize AIto analyze seismic activity, predict rock movement, plan blasting patterns, and monitor equipment operation (Zhironkina & Zhironkin, 2023). Video analytics can detect unsafe behaviors, while sensors can track gas concentrations, temperature, and humidity in real time. Machine Learning (ML) models help geologists identify mineral deposits more accurately than manual surveys. Autonomous trucks and drilling rigs reduce the need for workers to enter hazardous areas. AI-based decision-making systems help managers plan work schedules, allocate equipment, and control energy consumption.

The evolution of AI in the industrial sector also reflects a shift from simple automation to intelligent automation. Traditional automation performs fixed tasks and requires constant adjustment. AI-powered automation, on the other hand, can learn from data, adapt to new environments, and continuously improve. This ability to learn and evolve makes AI particularly important in the mining industry, where the environment changes rapidly and decisions must be made quickly.

1.4 Purpose and Scope of the Chapter

This chapter explores how AI is reshaping the mining industry, focusing on worker safety, operational efficiency, and decision-making. Its aim is not only to describe the technologies involved but also to explain how they address long-standing challenges in the mining sector. This chapter examines AI tools such as wearable safety devices, predictive maintenance systems, autonomous machinery, and intelligent monitoring platforms, illustrating how these tools can help reduce accidents, improve planning, and support sustainable mining practices. This chapter covers the entire lifecycle of mining operations from resource identification and equipment management to ensuring worker safety. The article explores how AI can provide real-time insights, improve predictive accuracy, and assist workers by reducing physical exertion. Furthermore, the article considers the ethical and practical challenges of adopting AI, such as cost, data privacy, workforce transformation, and training needs. By understanding these aspects, readers will gain a comprehensive understanding of how AI is reshaping the mining industry.

This chapter aims to provide a comprehensive and clear analysis of the increasingly important role of AI in the mining industry, outlining both its advantages and limitations. The following chapters will explain how AI-driven systems can support safer, more efficient, and more sustainable mining operations, while ensuring that human workers remain at the heart of this transformation.

2. UNDERSTANDING AI IN THE MINING CONTEXT

AI has become one of the most powerful tools for improving complex industrial systems, and the mining industry is no exception. While the mining industry relies heavily on manual labor and heavy machinery, it also generates vast amounts of data. This data contains valuable information about geological conditions, machine performance, worker activity, and overall productivity. AI can help transform this information into meaningful insights, thereby supporting safer and more efficient mining practices. To understand how AI is transforming the mining industry, it is first necessary to clarify what AI means in this context, explore the types of AI technologies used, and examine the data sources that underpin these technologies (Ali & Frimpong, 2020).

2.1 Definition of AI and Its Relevance to Mining

AI refers to computer systems designed to perform tasks that typically require human intelligence. These tasks include pattern recognition, learning from experience, making predictions, image recognition, and adjusting actions based on new information. AI does not replace human thinking; rather, it enhances human capabilities by processing large amounts of data faster and more accurately than traditional methods (Korteling et al., 2021).

In the mining industry, the importance of AI is increasingly evident for several reasons: mining environments are unpredictable and often fraught with safety hazards, making real-time monitoring and rapid decision-making crucial. AI systems can analyze real-time data from sensors and equipment and alert supervisors before danger escalates. For example, AI-powered gas sensors can detect early signs of hazardous gases such as methane, helping to prevent explosions or asphyxiation accidents. Similarly, AI models can identify abnormal machine operation and signal to maintenance teams to address potential malfunctions before they disrupt operations (Hasan et al., 2025). AI is also important because mining requires efficient resource management. Accurately predicting the quality, location, and quantity of ore can reduce waste and avoid unnecessary mining. AI-based geological models can analyze thousands of data points and generate detailed maps to guide the mining process. Without AI, such analysis would take weeks and is still prone to errors.

Another key aspect is sustainability. Today's environmental regulations require mining companies to reduce pollution, minimize land disturbance, and improve energy efficiency. AI tools can track emissions, measure water usage, and help companies plan mining operations in ways that reduce environmental damage. As the mining industry faces increasing pressure to balance productivity and responsibility, AI provides the tools needed to maintain that balance.

2.2 Conceptual Framework: AI in Mining Context

2.2.1. Mining 4.0 and Digital Transformation

The integration of AI in mining aligns with the Mining 4.0 paradigm, an extension of Industry 4.0 principles. This framework emphasizes the convergence of cyber-physical systems, IoT, big data analytics, and artificial intelligence to transform traditional mining into intelligent, data-driven operations. Mining 4.0 represents a fundamental shift from manual, labor-intensive processes to autonomous, interconnected systems that enable real-time decision-making and predictive capabilities.

2.2.2. Socio-Technical Systems Perspective

AI implementation in mining must be understood through a socio-technical lens, where technological components (sensors, algorithms, automation) interact dynamically with human elements (workers, managers, organizational culture). This perspective recognizes that successful AI adoption depends not only on technical capabilities but also on workforce acceptance, training infrastructure, and organizational readiness (Ali & Frimpong, 2020).

2.2.3. Digital Transformation Stages

The mining industry's digital evolution progresses through three stages: (1) Digitization – converting physical data into digital formats; (2) Digitalization – using digital tools to improve processes; and (3) Digital Transformation – fundamentally reimagining business models and value creation through technology. Current AI applications represent this third stage, where intelligent systems reshape operational structures, safety protocols, and decision-making hierarchies. This framework provides the foundation for understanding how AI technologies discussed in subsequent sections contribute to safer, more efficient, and sustainable mining practices.

2.2 Types of AI Technologies Used in Mining

AI is not a single technology, but rather a fusion of multiple fields. In the mining industry, the four most commonly used AI-driven technologies are: ML, computer vision, robotics, and IoT integration. Each technology plays its specific role, working together to drive the transformation and upgrading of mining operations (Briefed in Table 1).

Table 1. AI Technologies and Their Mining Applications

Technology	Mining Application	Safety Impact	Operational Impact
Machine Learning (ML)	• Predictive maintenance • Hazard prediction • Resource estimation • Energy optimization	• Early warning before equipment failure • Identification of unsafe conditions • Reduction in accident risk	• Decreased downtime • Improved resource utilization • Enhanced fuel efficiency
Computer Vision	• Safety gear detection • Wall crack monitoring • Worker behavior analysis • Conveyor belt inspection	• Detection of unsafe behavior • Identification of structural hazards • Prevention of unauthorized access	• Automated video surveillance • Immediate hazard alerts • Improved quality control
Robotics & Automation	• Autonomous haulage trucks • Robotic drilling • Remote loading systems • Drone surveying	• Reduced human exposure in hazardous zones • Lower accident rates • Safe operation in gas-filled areas	• Continuous 24/7 operations • Enhanced precision • Increased productivity
IoT Integration	• Real-time sensor networks • Environmental monitoring • Equipment health tracking • Worker location systems	• Continuous gas level monitoring • Heart rate and fatigue tracking • Rapid emergency response	• Real-time data collection • AI-driven decision support • Predictive maintenance enablement

2.2.1 Machine Learning (ML)

ML enables computers to learn patterns from data and improve their performance over time. ML models study trends in areas such as equipment operation, geological structures, worker activities, and environmental conditions. After training, these models can make highly accurate predictions (Binetti et al., 2024).

In mining, ML is used for:

- Predictive maintenance (forecasting machine failures)
- Hazard prediction (identifying unsafe conditions early)
- Resource estimation (predicting ore grade and distribution)
- Energy optimization (reducing unnecessary fuel or electricity usage)

Drilling rigs equipped with ML technology can adjust their rotation speed and pressure based on rock hardness, thereby reducing damage and improving efficiency.

ML can also assist managers by creating dashboards that highlight risks, predict production levels, and recommend optimal actions.

2.2.2 Computer Vision

Computer vision enables machines to interpret images and videos. This technology is extremely useful in the mining industry, where visual surveillance plays a crucial role. Cameras throughout the mining area continuously capture video, and AI algorithms analyze this video to detect unsafe behavior, unauthorized access, or dangerous events (Xu et al., 2022).

Applications include:

- Identifying cracks in tunnel walls
- Monitoring worker movement and detecting falls
- Checking whether workers are wearing safety gear
- Counting rock fragments after blasting
- Inspecting conveyor belts for material blockages

Computer vision technology reduces the need for supervisors to manually monitor videos and provides rapid alerts when problems arise.

2.2.3 Robotics and Automation

Robotics refers to machines that can perform tasks autonomously or with minimal human intervention. In the mining industry, robotic systems can enter areas that are too dangerous for humans, such as deep tunnels, unstable slopes, or enclosed spaces filled with gas (Trevelyan et al., 2016).

Examples include:

- Autonomous haulage trucks
- Robotic drilling machines
- Remote-operated loaders
- Drone-based surveying systems

Robotics improves operational precision, reduces human risk, and maintains stable production efficiency even under harsh conditions. In addition to robotics, automation ensures that routine tasks such as handling minerals, loading trucks, or drilling are completed efficiently without continuous human intervention.

2.2.4 IoT (Internet of Things) Integration

The Internet of Things (IoT) involves connecting devices, sensors, and apparatuses to enable them to continuously share data. In the mining industry, IoT is a foundational technology because it can collect real-time data from underground tunnels, equipment units, ventilation systems, and worker wearable devices (Molaei et al., 2020).

IoT devices collect information such as:

- Temperature and humidity
- Gas levels
- Machine vibration and pressure
- Worker heart rate and location
- Air quality and dust levels

When combined with AI, Internet of Things (IoT) data becomes incredibly powerful. For example, IoT sensors can detect increases in internal machine temperature, while AI can analyze this data to determine whether it's normal heating or a sign of a potential malfunction.

ML (ML), computer vision, robotics, and IoT together form a robust technological foundation enabling the mining industry to shift from reactive to proactive, predictive operations.

2.3 Data Sources in Mining Operations

The application of AI in the mining industry is highly dependent on data. The quality, quantity, and reliability of data determine the effectiveness of AI models in ensuring safety and improving production efficiency. Mining operations generate various types of data, each originating from different data sources (Briefed in Table 2).

Table 2. Data Sources and Their Role in AI-Driven Mining

Data Source Category	Data Collection Methods	Key Parameters Monitored	AI Application	Impact on Mining Operations
Geological & Exploration Data	• Geological surveys • Drilling sampling • Magnetic sensors • Satellite imaging	• Ore grade distribution • Mineral composition • Rock formations • Deposit boundaries	• Geological map generation • Resource estimation • Ore body modeling • Mining path optimization	• Reduced exploration uncertainty • Improved ore targeting • Optimized extraction planning • Minimized waste mining
Equipment & Machine Data	• Vibration sensors • Temperature monitors • Pressure gauges • Fuel consumption trackers • Motion pattern sensors	• Machine vibration levels • Internal temperature • Hydraulic pressure • Fuel efficiency • Operational cycles	• Predictive maintenance • Failure prediction • Performance optimization • Health assessment	• Reduced downtime • Extended equipment life • Lower maintenance costs • Prevented catastrophic failures
Environmental Data	• Air quality sensors • Water level monitors • Seismic sensors • Weather stations	• Dust and gas concentration • Surface/groundwater levels • Soil movement • Seismic activity • Weather patterns	• Risk detection • Gas buildup alerts • Landslide prediction • Rock stability analysis	• Enhanced worker safety • Regulatory compliance • Environmental protection • Disaster prevention
Production & Process Data	• Production monitoring systems • Material flow sensors • Blasting performance trackers • Processing efficiency meters	• Ore extraction rates • Material throughput • Blast effectiveness • Processing efficiency • Energy consumption	• Production scheduling • Resource allocation • Energy optimization • Process improvement	• Increased productivity • Reduced energy waste • Optimized workflows • Better resource utilization

continued on following page

Table 2. Continued

Data Source Category	Data Collection Methods	Key Parameters Monitored	AI Application	Impact on Mining Operations
Worker-Related Data	• Wearable devices • GPS tracking tags • Smart helmets • Biometric sensors	• Heart rate • Fatigue levels • Body temperature • Location tracking • Activity patterns	• Health monitoring • Fatigue detection • Location tracking • Emergency alerts	• Prevented accidents • Rapid emergency response • Improved worker safety • Enhanced supervision
Visual & Video Data	• CCTV cameras • Drone surveillance • Thermal imaging • 3D scanning	• Visual hazards • Worker behavior • Equipment status • Infrastructure condition • Operational activities	• Computer vision analysis • Hazard identification • Behavior monitoring • Infrastructure inspection	• Automated surveillance • Early hazard detection • Quality control • Reduced manual inspection

2.3.1 Geological and Exploration Data

Before mining begins, mines collect data using methods such as geological surveys, drilling sampling, magnetic sensors, and satellite imaging. This data helps identify rich ore areas and assess ore grades (Rani, 2025). AI models use these datasets to generate geological maps, thereby guiding mining and reducing uncertainty.

2.3.2 Equipment and Machine Data

Modern mining equipment is equipped with sensors to track vibration, temperature, pressure, fuel consumption, and motion patterns. This data helps AI systems assess machine health and predict malfunctions (Divakar & Cephas, 2025). For example, a sudden change in vibration might indicate that the drill bit is wearing out or that the motor needs maintenance.

2.3.3 Environmental Data

Mining operations constantly monitor the surrounding environment to ensure safety and compliance with regulations (Sengupta, 2021). Environmental data includes:

- Air quality (dust, gas concentration)
- Surface water and groundwater levels
- Soil movement or seismic activity

- Weather conditions

AI analyzes this information to detect rising risks such as gas build-up, landslide possibilities, or unstable rock structures.

2.3.4 Production and Process Data

Information on ore mining, material flow, blasting performance, and processing efficiency helps optimize daily operations. AI uses this data to recommend methods to improve scheduling, energy use, and equipment allocation (Ali & Frimpong, 2020).

2.3.5 Worker-Related Data

Wearable devices, GPS tags, and smart safety equipment can provide information about workers' health and activities. These systems can track fatigue levels, heart rate changes, and abnormal activity patterns. If a worker shows signs of discomfort or enters a dangerous area, AI can immediately alert supervisors (Mardonova & Choi, 2018).

2.3.6 Visual and Video Data

Cameras and drones continuously collect visual data from various locations within the mining area. Computer vision algorithms analyze this imagery to identify hazards, monitor operations, and inspect infrastructure (Imam et al., 2023).

AI is thriving in the mining industry because it generates vast amounts of data that, when properly analyzed, can provide valuable insights. By combining ML, computer vision, robotics, and the Internet of Things (IoT), mining companies can improve safety, reduce downtime, and make informed decisions. Understanding these fundamental elements helps explain how AI is reshaping everyday mining activities and lays the foundation for a more in-depth discussion in later chapters.

3. AI FOR WORKER SAFETY

AI is becoming an important component of mine safety planning. The mine environment is constantly changing, and workers frequently face risks such as gas leaks, rockfalls, equipment malfunctions, and low visibility. These risks require systems capable of detecting hazards early and issuing rapid alerts. AI technology compensates for this deficiency by providing continuous monitoring and real-time detection, assisting human judgment and thus reducing the likelihood of accidents.

3.1 Hazard Detection and Monitoring

AI systems can track various hazardous conditions within mines. They monitor changes in gas concentrations, surface topography, and machine operation. Furthermore, they can learn from past accidents to help predict potential future hazards. This not only shortens response times but also provides an extra layer of protection for workers (Hasan et al., 2025).

3.1.1 Gas Detection Sensors

Many hazardous gases accumulate in underground mines. Concentrations of methane, carbon monoxide, and hydrogen sulfide can reach dangerous levels without warning. Artificial intelligence-driven gas detection sensors monitor these gases around the clock. They study concentration changes and compare them to safety limits. When the system detects an abnormal pattern, it immediately sends alarms to the control room and portable devices. This helps workers quickly evacuate to safe areas and prevents large-scale accidents (Kumar et al., 2013).

3.1.2 Computer-Vision–Based Monitoring of Risky Zones

Modern mines employ computer vision-assisted cameras. These cameras monitor tunnels, conveyor belts, and blasting areas. AI systems can identify unsafe actions, trespassing into restricted areas, or signs of equipment malfunction. They can detect details that the human eye might miss, especially in dusty or dark environments. This reduces the risk of personnel exposure to life-threatening hazards (Imam et al., 2023).

3.1.3 Early Warnings for Rock Instability or Machinery Hazards

AI tools can analyze vibration data, surface cracks, and machine noise patterns. Subtle signals often foreshadow major malfunctions. AI models can detect these signals early and warn supervisors. This helps prevent tunnel collapses, machine failures, and personnel injuries. By identifying problems before they escalate, AI creates a safer working environment for miners (Gipa & Olivia, 2025).

3.2. Wearable Safety Devices

Wearable safety devices have become an integral part of modern mining operations, delivering intelligent monitoring tools directly to workers. These devices mitigate risk by continuously tracking workers' environment, physical condition, and location. They help managers respond quickly to unsafe situations and provide workers with additional protection in rapidly changing environments. By combining sensors, communication modules, and ML-based analytics, wearable technology enables safer and more informed decision-making on-site (Liang et al., 2024).

3.2.1. Smart helmets, vests, and badges

Smart helmets, vests, and badges are among the most common wearable devices in the mining industry. Smart helmets typically come equipped with environmental sensors, real-time video capture systems, and built-in communication systems, allowing workers to report hazards without stopping work. Some helmets also feature augmented reality displays that provide visual cues or instructions, reducing clutter in high-risk areas. Smart vests often contain vibration or thermal sensors that can sound an alarm when workers approach operating machinery or are exposed to excessively high temperatures. Smart badges worn by workers at all times, with built-in RFID or Bluetooth transmitters, help track their movements, ensure they remain in safe areas, and confirm their attendance during emergency evacuations. These devices not only help ensure safety compliance but also reliably record workers' activities within the mine (Aksuet & Eren, 2025).

3.2.2. Worker health tracking (fatigue, vitals, location)

Mining work is extremely physically demanding, and fatigue is one of the leading causes of accidents. Wearable devices can track heart rate, body temperature, blood oxygen saturation, and movement patterns, helping to detect signs of fatigue early. When the system detects abnormal vital signs, it can notify workers and the safety team, prompting them to rest immediately or seek medical assistance. Location tracking is also crucial in underground mines where visibility is low and distances are difficult to judge. Wearable devices use GPS on the ground and an underground mesh network to update workers' locations in real time. This helps supervisors coordinate teams, prevent unauthorized entry into restricted areas, and react quickly if someone is trapped or injured (Butlewski et al., 2015).

3.2.3. Emergency response features

Wearable safety devices play a crucial role in emergencies. Many smart helmets and badges are equipped with emergency buttons, fall detection algorithms, and automatic distress signals. These devices can sound an alarm without human intervention if a worker is unconscious, trapped, or exposed to hazardous gases. Wearable devices can also guide rescue teams to pinpoint the location of injured workers, reducing potential life-threatening delays. Some systems offer two-way communication, allowing injured workers to communicate directly with safety teams. These features ensure rapid response to emergencies, ensuring workers receive timely support even in remote underground areas (Damaševičius et al., 2023).

3.3. Accident Prevention Models

Accident prevention has become one of the most important drivers for applying AI to mining operations. Traditional safety systems rely heavily on manual inspections, past experience, and human judgment. These methods have limitations because the mining environment changes rapidly, and early warning signals are not always noticeable to workers. AI-based accident prevention models overcome this deficiency by analyzing real-time data and identifying risk patterns long before accidents occur. By predicting unsafe conditions and supporting timely decision-making, these models create a proactive safety culture where responses are data-driven rather than assumption-based (Javid et al., 2025).

3.3.1. Predictive analytics for safety incidents

Predictive analytics is central to modern mine accident prevention. These models process vast amounts of data from sensors, machine logs, worker activity records, and environmental data. ML algorithms study patterns associated with past accidents, such as gas buildup, abnormal machine vibrations, unusual temperature changes, or worker fatigue. Once the system identifies a high-risk pattern, it issues a warning of a potential accident. This early warning allows managers to adjust work plans, repair malfunctioning equipment, or restrict access to hazardous areas. Predictive analytics can also help mines understand which activities or locations are at higher risk, enabling safety teams to better plan inspections, training, and monitoring. As the system continues to learn from new data, its predictions become increasingly accurate, making it a powerful long-term safety tool (Saxena, 2024).

3.3.2. Real-time decision alerts for supervisors

Real-time decision alerts ensure that predictive insights translate into timely action. These alerts are sent to supervisors via dashboards, mobile devices, or control room interfaces. When the system detects signs of instability, a surge in gas concentrations, or unsafe worker behavior, relevant personnel are immediately notified. Alerts may recommend actions such as stopping machine operation, evacuating areas, or activating ventilation systems. This rapid communication avoids delays and helps supervisors coordinate responses, especially in emergency situations. Real-time alerts can also reduce the burden on human observers, preventing them from overlooking subtle warning signs. By combining prediction with immediate guidance, AI-driven alerts can strengthen the overall safety framework and help maintain the stability and safety of mining operations (Swate, 2024).

4. AI FOR OPERATIONAL EFFICIENCY

AI plays a crucial role in improving the efficiency of mine operations. Mining processes typically involve repetitive, labor-intensive tasks requiring precise operation and continuous monitoring. Traditional methods heavily rely on human skills, which are susceptible to damage from fatigue, limited visibility, or the unpredictability of the underground environment. AI systems can overcome these limitations, performing tasks with consistent accuracy while increasing productivity. Automation, robotics, and intelligent control systems can also reduce downtime, lower operating costs, and allow workers to focus on higher-level tasks rather than hazardous manual labor (Rehman, 2024).

4.1. Automation of Mining Equipment

Automation has become one of the most significant achievements of AI in the mining industry. By enabling machines to operate with minimal human intervention, mining companies can maintain stable productivity and reduce the risks associated with manual equipment operation. These technologies also support continuous operations, which is crucial for large mines, as any disruption can directly impact production efficiency (Ali & Frimpong, 2020).

4.1.1. Autonomous Haulage Trucks

Autonomous transport trucks are revolutionizing material transportation in the mining industry. These trucks utilize GPS, lidar, radar, and onboard AI systems to plan routes, detect obstacles, and optimize fuel consumption. They autonomously navigate pre-programmed paths while communicating with a central control system to avoid collisions and coordinate traffic flow. Because they do not rely on human drivers, autonomous trucks can operate continuously even in extreme weather or low-visibility conditions (Essien & Frimpong, 2025). This results in smoother operations, fewer accidents, and better control over transport cycles.

4.1.2. AI-Driven Drilling and Blasting Systems

Drilling and blasting are critical steps in mining, requiring precise operation to ensure effective rock breaking. AI-driven systems analyze geological data to determine ideal drilling patterns, depths, and explosive dosages. By adjusting parameters based on real-time feedback, these systems can reduce over-excavation, decrease vibration, and improve crushing quality. This optimization reduces energy consumption during crushing and grinding, minimizes equipment wear, and increases overall mining efficiency (Doe, 2020). AI-driven drilling precision can also avoid weak or unstable areas, thereby improving safety.

4.1.3. Remote and Robotic Operations in Unsafe Zones

Mining environments often expose workers to hazardous conditions such as high temperatures, toxic gases, and unstable rock formations. Remote control and robotic systems enable these tasks to be completed without compromising worker safety. Robots equipped with cameras and sensors can inspect shafts, identify hazards, and perform maintenance in areas unsafe for humans. Remote machinery also allows operators to control equipment from a safe distance, improving operational accuracy and worker safety (Obosu & Frimpong, 2025). This approach reduces downtime and ensures smooth operations even in hazardous areas.

4.2. Process Optimization

Process optimization is one of the most significant advantages of AI in mining operations. Mine operations rely on continuous coordination between equipment, workers, and environmental factors. Even minor delays or misplanning can lead to production disruptions and increased operating costs (Ali & Frimpong, 2020). AI systems help streamline these processes by analyzing real-time data, predicting future demand, and improving resource allocation. Through more optimized scheduling, smarter energy use, and reduced downtime, AI ensures that mining workflows remain stable, efficient, and economical.

4.2.1. Intelligent Scheduling and Route Optimization

Efficient scheduling is crucial for maintaining smooth mining operations. Traditional scheduling methods rely heavily on manual planning and experience, which can easily lead to bottlenecks in the event of unforeseen circumstances (Hazrathosseini & Moradi Afrapoli, 2023). AI-driven scheduling tools analyze production targets, equipment availability, worker shift schedules, and terrain conditions to develop optimized scheduling plans that automatically adjust to changing circumstances. These systems can also recommend the most efficient routes for transport trucks and loaders, thereby reducing travel time and fuel consumption. By alligning equipment and labor deployment with real-time demand, AIminimizes idle time and improves overall productivity. Intelligent scheduling also ensures that mining, transportation, and processing activities remain synchronized, thereby reducing the risk of congestion or underutilization of equipment.

4.2.2. Energy-Efficient Resource Utilization

Mining operations consume significant amounts of energy, particularly in drilling, crushing, ventilation, and transportation. AI systems can help reduce energy waste by predicting demand and adjusting energy use based on operational needs. For example, AI can adjust ventilation systems based on real-time airflow demand, rather than running them at full capacity 24/7 (Awuah-Offei, 2016). Similarly, predictive models can optimize the use of pumps, generators, and conveyors, ensuring they operate only when needed. AI-driven insights enable mine managers to identify high-energy-consuming processes and make targeted improvements. As a result, energy efficiency improves, costs decrease, and mines move towards more sustainable operating models.

4.2.3. Reduction of Operational Downtime

Downtime is one of the most costly challenges facing the mining industry. Equipment failures, unexpected delays, and supply disruptions can all cause production to stall for hours or even days. AI can help reduce downtime by monitoring machine performance, identifying abnormal patterns, and predicting events that may precede failures (Dashtaki et al., 2025). This information allows technicians to schedule maintenance work during planned breaks, thus preventing unforeseen failures. AI can also monitor environmental conditions, such as rock stability or water levels, and alert managers to take preventative measures. By combining predictive maintenance with real-time monitoring, AI can improve equipment reliability, ensuring operational continuity and stability. This helps increase output, reduce maintenance costs, and create a more efficient mining environment.

4.3. Predictive Maintenance

Predictive maintenance has become a core component of modern mining operations because it helps mines avoid unexpected equipment failures and unnecessary downtime (Werbinska-Wojciechowska & Rogowski, 2025). Traditional maintenance methods rely on fixed maintenance schedules or reactive repairs after a failure occurs. These methods often result in higher maintenance costs and production disruptions. AI-based predictive maintenance improves this process by leveraging data-driven insights to monitor equipment status and predict failures. This approach can extend equipment life, reduce maintenance costs, and ensure smooth operations.

4.3.1. Real-Time Equipment Health Monitoring

Real-time monitoring systems utilize sensors installed on mining equipment to track various performance metrics. These sensors can collect data on temperature, vibration, pressure, fuel efficiency, and acoustic signals. AI algorithms process these continuous data streams and identify patterns that indicate normal or abnormal behavior. When the system detects abnormal readings, it sends an alert to technicians so they can immediately inspect the machine. Real-time monitoring helps prevent small problems from escalating into major failures (Gackowiec et al., 2020). It also allows operators to clearly understand how the machine performs under different loads and environmental conditions. With accurate performance data, mine managers can improve asset utilization and reduce operational risks.

4.3.2. Failure Prediction Models

Failure prediction models utilize ML techniques to analyze historical and real-time equipment data. These models study past failures, learning which patterns typically lead to malfunctions. After training, they can predict the probability of future failures (Odeyar et al., 2022). For example, increased vibration levels may indicate bearing wear, and abnormal hydraulic pressure may foreshadow impending pump failure. By detecting these early warning signs, technicians can replace parts or adjust machine settings before equipment stops operating. Failure prediction models can also help mines identify which machines are at higher risk, enabling more targeted inspection plans and reducing unnecessary maintenance.

4.3.3. Maintenance Scheduling to Reduce Disruptions

AI-assisted maintenance planning ensures that repairs and inspections are performed at the right time, minimizing disruption to operations. Instead of relying on fixed maintenance cycles, AI schedules tasks based on equipment condition and predicted failure times. This reduces the likelihood of unplanned downtime and ensures critical equipment remains operational during peak production periods. Maintenance teams can prepare resources in advance, thereby accelerating repairs and reducing delays (Rane et al., 2025). This approach also aids in inventory management, as spare parts can be ordered before a failure occurs. By combining forecasting with intelligent scheduling, mines can achieve higher reliability, lower maintenance costs, and smoother daily operations.

5. AI-SUPPORTED DECISION MAKING

AI-assisted decision-making plays a crucial role in enhancing planning, analysis, and operational choices in the mining industry. Mining decisions rely on vast amounts of geological, environmental, and production data. Traditionally, experts have had to manually analyze this data, a process that is both time-consuming and inherently uncertain. AI improves this process by identifying patterns, assessing risks, and providing reliable recommendations based on evidence. When combined with human judgment, AI tools can enhance the accuracy of planning, resource estimation, and workforce management. This builds a faster, smarter, and more adaptable balanced decision-making system for a constantly evolving environment.

5.1. Geological Data Analysis

Understanding geological data is crucial for accurately estimating resource quantities, safe mining, and long-term planning. Mining companies collect seismic data, satellite imagery, core samples, and geochemical measurements to map subsurface stratigraphy (Glazer, 2016). AI simplifies this complex process by processing large datasets and identifying patterns that are difficult to detect manually. It helps geologists more clearly predict mineral resource reserves and exploitation potential.

5.1.1. Pattern Recognition for Resource Estimation

Artificial intelligence-based pattern recognition systems estimate the quantity and quality of resources by analyzing massive amounts of geological data. These models learn from past surveys, drilling results, and mining records to identify hidden correlations within rocks. They can detect patterns that indicate the presence of valuable minerals, such as specific textures, density levels, or chemical characteristics. By providing more accurate resource estimates, AI can help companies reduce uncertainty in planning and avoid unnecessary mining. This helps control costs and ensures efficient use of machinery and manpower. Pattern recognition can also limit over-exploitation in areas with low mineral resource potential, thus supporting sustainable development.

5.1.2. Mapping Mineral Distribution

Mineral mapping is another key area where AI plays a significant role. AI algorithms process satellite imagery, magnetic survey data, and geological scan data to generate detailed maps of rich mineral deposits. These tools highlight orebody boundaries, identify tectonic faults, and show variations in mineral concentration within a mining area. These maps enable engineers to develop mining plans that maximize mineral recovery while protecting unstable areas. Through real-time drilling data updates, AI-based models continuously refine the maps, providing increasingly clearer images as mining progresses. This dynamic mapping facilitates safer and more efficient operations.

5.1.3. Improved Decision-Making for Extraction Planning

Accurate geological information is crucial for developing effective mining plans. AI integrates multiple data sources and evaluates different options, helping managers compare various possible strategies. For example, AI can simulate the impact of different drilling patterns or mining sequences on production, waste generation, and equipment requirements, and can also predict the environmental impact of each option. With this information, managers can choose mining plans that balance productivity, safety, and sustainability. AI can test multiple options, reduce guesswork, and help teams cope with unexpected geological changes.

5.2. Production and Workforce Planning

AI can also support production and workforce planning by predicting demand, identifying risks, and optimizing the allocation of human and machine resources. These tools ensure that production goals are achieved without causing employee burnout or unsafe working conditions.

5.2.1. Demand Forecasting

Mining companies must match production with market demand to remain profitable. AI-based demand forecasting models study past demand patterns, economic trends, global supply chains, and commodity price movements. This system can predict future mineral production needs. This helps managers adjust productivity, schedule employee shifts, and plan shipments. Accurate forecasting can prevent economic losses from resource overconsumption and underproduction. Furthermore, it helps mines maintain stable employment levels and avoid sudden changes in labor demand.

5.2.2. AI-Based Risk Assessment Tools

Mining operations involve numerous operational risks, including equipment failure, unstable terrain, and supply delays. AI-based risk assessment tools evaluate these risks by analyzing data from sensors, logs, weather forecasts, and geological records. They categorize risks into risk levels and recommend measures to mitigate their impact. For example, if the system predicts a higher probability of equipment failure during peak production periods, it may recommend maintenance in advance. When combined with human judgment, these tools help managers create safer work plans and reduce unexpected disruptions. They also support regulatory compliance by documenting risk-related decisions.

5.3. Integrating Human Expertise With AI Insights

AI offers powerful analytical capabilities, but human experience remains crucial in the mining industry. Optimal decision-making stems from combining AI-generated insights with expert judgment. Human-machine collaboration ensures that complex decisions balance data-driven predictions with understanding based on field experience.

5.3.1. Human–Machine Collaboration

Human-machine collaboration is central to modern mining operations. AI systems assist engineers, geologists, and supervisors by providing predictions and highlighting key trends, but ultimate decision-making remains human (Kolapo et al., 2025). Workers understand the local environment, the limitations of the machines, and practical challenges that may not be reflected in the data. Decision-making becomes more flexible and reliable when AI works in conjunction with human expertise. Collaboration also helps build trust as workers become more familiar with AI tools and understand their role in the decision-making process.

5.3.2. Decision Support Dashboards and Visualization Tools

Decision support dashboards present complex mining data in a clear and organized manner. They integrate geological maps, equipment performance charts, safety alerts, and production metrics into a unified interface. AI processes the data and provides suggestions in the background, but the dashboards also allow users to browse information and make informed decisions. Visualization tools can help staff understand patterns that are difficult to spot in raw data, such as changes in rock stability or fuel consumption. These tools can also facilitate interdepartmental communication, as everyone can view the same information, leading to more effective decision-making coordination.

6. AI-DRIVEN TRAINING AND SIMULATION

Training plays a crucial role in the mining industry because workers frequently face high-risk environments and operate complex machinery. Traditional training methods rely on classroom instruction, videos, and supervised on-site practice (Obosu & Frimpong, 2025). While these methods provide foundational knowledge, they cannot fully simulate real-world downhole challenges or emergencies. AI-driven training tools are changing this by introducing interactive, immersive, and responsive learning environments. These systems help workers practice challenging tasks, understand safety rules, and build confidence without being physically exposed to danger. With the help of learning platforms powered by virtual reality (VR), augmented reality (AR), and AI, employees can develop key skills at their own pace and be more precisely prepared for real-world operations. AI-driven training is also crucial for developing the skills needed to operate modern mining equipment, which increasingly relies on automation and advanced digital tools.

6.1 Virtual and Augmented Reality Systems

Virtual reality (VR) and augmented reality (AR) have become powerful tools for training mining workers. VR creates fully immersive digital environments, making workers feel as if they are actually in a mine; while AR overlays digital instructions onto real equipment. Both systems rely on AI to adjust the level of difficulty, generate realistic scenarios, and provide immediate feedback. Compared to traditional methods, these tools make training more practical, easier to remember, and more efficient (Van Wyk & De Villiers, 2009).

6.1.1 Safe Training Environments

Mines are fraught with dangers, including unstable rocks, heavy machinery, and hazardous gases. Virtual reality-based training can eliminate these risks, allowing workers to practice operations in a safe digital environment. Trainees can traverse virtual tunnels, operate machinery, and respond to simulated emergencies without fear of accidents. AI helps analyze employee performance and identify errors, providing personalized improvement suggestions. This shortens the learning curve for new employees, enabling them to prepare more effectively before entering work areas. Safe digital training also reduces the pressure on experienced employees who would otherwise have to instruct new trainees in hazardous areas.

6.1.2 Simulation of Complex Mining Scenarios

Mining operations involve many complex situations that are difficult to simulate in reality, such as cave-ins, equipment failures, gas leaks, or sudden floods. Artificial intelligence-driven virtual reality (VR) simulation technology allows workers to experience these challenging events in a controlled environment (Dychkovskyi et al., 2018). The system adjusts conditions such as lighting, noise, and visibility to make the simulation more realistic. Workers can learn how to react quickly, follow safety procedures, and make decisions under pressure. Supervisors can track their reactions and help them improve. AI can also generate customized scenarios based on the mine's geological conditions or recent accidents, helping workers cope with the most likely situations. Through repeated drills, workers can build confidence and react more quickly in real emergencies.

6.2 Skill Development for Workers

As the mining industry becomes increasingly digitalized, workers need to acquire new skills in operating AI-powered equipment and interacting with automated systems. AI-driven training supports this transformation by providing personalized learning paths and interactive modules, helping workers understand technology and safety-related concepts. These training programs ensure that workers acquire the latest tools and technologies while retaining essential traditional skills.

6.2.1 Upskilling Programs

Skills enhancement programs help workers maintain productivity in the rapidly changing mining environment. AI-driven learning platforms analyze each worker's existing skills and recommend training modules based on their needs. For example, if a worker has difficulty operating equipment, they might receive exercises focusing on the principles of machine operation or digital troubleshooting. The system tracks learning progress and provides feedback after each course. The AI-powered platform also supports multilingual learning, enabling employees from diverse backgrounds to participate in training. These programs help employees build confidence in new technologies, improve their career prospects, and remain competitive in the workplace. Skills enhancement also narrows skills gaps within mining teams, thereby promoting better teamwork and safer operations.

6.2.2 Training for AI-Enabled Equipment Operations

Modern mining equipment utilizes sensors, automation, and AI technologies for efficient operation. Workers must understand how to interpret digital dashboards, respond to alarms, and collaborate with autonomous machines. AI-driven training tools help workers learn these skills through interactive simulations and guided exercises. For example, virtual trainers demonstrate how autonomous transport trucks detect obstacles or how AI-driven drilling rigs adjust their settings. Workers can control the simulated equipment and view its operational effects in real time. This helps workers familiarize themselves with machine operation and prepare them for actual operation. Training on AI-powered equipment also helps workers identify early signs of malfunctions and report problems promptly before they escalate into major accidents. As automation increases in the mining industry, this type of training ensures that workers remain indispensable contributors to operations, rather than being rendered obsolete by technology.

7. SUSTAINABILITY THROUGH AI

Sustainability has become one of the most important goals in the modern mining industry. Mining activities often impact air quality, water resources, soil stability, biodiversity, and surrounding communities. Traditional monitoring and control methods rely on regular inspections and manual measurements, which may miss early warning signs or fail to capture rapid environmental changes. Artificial intelligence-based systems offer a more accurate, continuous, and proactive way to address environmental challenges. Through real-time data collection, pattern analysis, and predictive insights, AI helps mines reduce their environmental footprint while improving operational transparency. Sustainable mining not only protects ecosystems but also enhances the long-term viability of businesses and ensures compliance with regulatory standards.

7.1 Environmental Monitoring

Environmental monitoring is crucial for detecting and controlling the ecological and environmental impacts of mining operations. AI tools can collect data from sensors, drones, satellite imagery, and geological surveys to provide a comprehensive understanding of mining activities and their environmental impacts. These tools help companies identify problems early and take corrective action before they escalate into serious consequences.

7.1.1 Tracking Air Quality, Water Contamination, and Land Impact

Air quality monitoring is crucial for the mining industry because emissions of dust, gases, and particulate matter can harm workers and nearby communities. AI sensors continuously monitor gases such as methane, carbon monoxide, and sulfur dioxide. ML models analyze sensor data, detect sudden changes, predict pollution levels, and warn operators before conditions become unsafe. This helps mines control dust suppression systems and maintain safe air quality levels.

Water pollution is another serious and worrying problem. Mining operations can alter the pH of water bodies or expose them to harmful minerals. AI-driven water quality monitoring systems can track the pH levels, chemical concentrations, and flow patterns of nearby rivers, streams, and groundwater sources. When the system detects abnormal readings, it immediately alerts environmental officials so they can prevent the spread of pollution.

Land impact monitoring uses drones and satellite imagery to track changes in land structure caused by soil displacement, deforestation, and excavation. AI analyzes these images to identify erosion hotspots, unstable foundations, or excessive vegetation loss. This information helps managers plan remediation activities and reduce long-term damage.

7.1.2 AI for Greener Mining Practices

AI supports greener mining operations by optimizing energy use, reducing carbon emissions, and improving waste management. ML models study energy consumption patterns and offer suggestions for reducing fuel consumption in trucks, drilling rigs, and processing plants. AI can also optimize the operation of ventilation systems, lighting, and conveyor belts to ensure that energy is used only when needed.

In addition, AI promotes eco-friendly extraction methods by identifying low-impact mining routes, recommending reduced-blast techniques, and suggesting alternative materials that reduce environmental stress. Some mines use AI-guided robots to handle dangerous tasks, reducing physical disruption to the environment. By supporting environmentally responsible decision-making, AI helps mining companies meet sustainability goals and improve their public image.

7.2 Efficient Resource Extraction

Efficient resource extraction is crucial for sustainable development because it reduces unnecessary mining activities, conserves energy, and protects surrounding ecosystems. AI-driven tools can help companies improve extraction accuracy and reduce waste, thereby contributing to maintaining long-term ecological balance.

7.2.1 Reducing Waste

A major challenge in the mining industry is waste generation, especially when mining precision is low. AI reduces waste generation by identifying high-quality mining areas and guiding machinery to extract resources with minimal disruption. ML models analyze geological data, predict ore body boundaries, and determine the most efficient mining path. This reduces the amount of useless material extracted from underground.

AI can also adjust the settings of mechanical equipment in real time based on the ore composition, thereby helping to improve ore processing. If the ore mineral content is low, the system will suggest adjustments or temporary shutdown to avoid unnecessary energy consumption. These intelligent control measures ensure the efficient and rational use of mineral resources.

7.2.2 Enhancing Long-Term Ecological Balance

Long-term ecological balance requires mining companies to consider the future health of the environment. AI supports this goal by predicting how mining activities will impact forests, water bodies, and soils over time. These predictive models analyze climate patterns, geological stability, and vegetation changes to propose sustainable mining limits. AI can also aid in land remediation efforts. Drones and mapping tools can identify areas requiring replanting, soil stabilization, or water diversion. ML models assess which plant species are best suited for restoring damaged areas. By guiding remediation efforts, AI helps mining areas restore land to its natural state more quickly.

Furthermore, AI promotes circular mining practices, which involve reusing or recycling waste instead of discarding it directly. By identifying reusable materials or components, AI helps reduce the overall environmental impact and contributes to building a more sustainable mining ecosystem.

8. CHALLENGES IN AI ADOPTION

The application of AI in the mining industry holds great promise, but its full-scale adoption is not without its challenges. Mining companies face numerous challenges that can slow down or hinder the integration of advanced technologies. These challenges encompass ethical issues, high investment costs, and technological barriers, among others. Understanding these challenges will help companies develop more robust strategies and apply AI systems in a responsible and sustainable manner.

8.1 Ethical and Privacy Concerns

Artificial intelligence-driven mining operations rely heavily on data collected from equipment, sensors, and workers. This raises a range of ethical questions, such as how this data is used and who controls it.

8.1.1 Worker Surveillance Issues

Many wearable devices and smart monitoring systems track workers' location, health, and activity patterns. While these tools can improve safety, workers often worry that constant monitoring makes them feel violated. They fear that managers will use this information to judge their performance or punish them for inefficiency, rather than protecting them from risks. This leads to distrust between workers and management. We need a balanced approach that can improve safety through monitoring without compromising workers' autonomy and dignity.

8.1.2 Data Ownership and Transparency

AI systems collect sensitive information about mines, extraction rates, and equipment conditions. This raises questions about the ownership of this data—the company, the employees, or the system provider? A lack of clear ownership information can lead to conflicts, especially when a third-party vendor manages a cloud platform. Companies must ensure transparency in their data policies, clarifying how information is used, stored, and shared. This transparency helps build trust and reduces legal and ethical concerns.

8.2 Workforce Reskilling Requirements

The role of the mining industry is rapidly changing due to digital transformation. Workers who have used traditional tools for years must now learn how to operate automated machines and AI-based systems.

8.2.1 Changing Job Roles

As automation increases, some routine tasks are decreasing, while new technical roles are emerging. Workers may worry about job loss or a decline in their importance within the mining cycle. While AI improves safety and efficiency, it also requires workers to manage digital interfaces, supervise automated operations, and interpret AI analytics. These new responsibilities demand confidence and up-to-date knowledge. Companies must help workers transition to these roles, rather than replacing them outright.

8.2.2 Need for Continuous Training

AI technology is developing rapidly, and single training programs are far from sufficient. Employees need to receive regular skills enhancement training to become proficient in using new tools and effectively cope with new systems. Training content should focus on practical application and be tailored to employees with different skill levels. If companies invest in long-term learning programs, employees' adaptability and confidence will improve, thereby reducing their resistance to artificial intelligence.

8.3 High Implementation Costs

While AI holds promise for long-term economic benefits, the upfront costs are substantial. Many mining companies, especially small and medium-sized enterprises, struggle to afford these expenses.

8.3.1 Infrastructure and Technology Investments

AI requires a robust digital foundation. This includes modern sensors, high-performance servers, cloud systems, remote site connectivity, autonomous vehicles, and powerful analytics tools. Installing and maintaining this infrastructure is costly. Older mines may also require significant upgrades for AI systems to function effectively. These costs slow the adoption of AI and make businesses hesitant to undertake large-scale transformations.

8.3.2 Barriers for Small and Medium Mining Companies

Large enterprises can afford the high upfront costs, but small businesses may lack the financial resources to invest in artificial intelligence. Because automation costs are too high relative to their annual revenue, they may still rely on manual processes. This creates a digital divide within the industry, where only large enterprises can enjoy the benefits of AI-driven improvements. To bridge this gap, we need scalable and affordable AI solutions.

8.4 Technological Limitations

AI systems rely on accurate data and stable equipment. Mining environments often fail to meet these requirements.

8.4.1 Data Quality Issues

AI algorithms learn from historical and real-time data. If this data is incomplete, inconsistent, or inaccurate, the AI model will produce unreliable results. Dust, vibration, and extreme temperatures can all interfere with sensors, leading to a decline in data quality. Mining companies must invest in robust data validation processes to ensure reliable insights.

8.4.2 Harsh Mining Environments Affecting Equipment

Mining environments are often extremely harsh. Equipment must operate in dusty tunnels, under high temperatures and humidity. These conditions can damage sensors, cameras, and network equipment that are critical to AI systems. Frequent failures reduce system reliability and increase maintenance costs. Therefore, designing robust and durable AI hardware specifically built for mining environments is essential for long-term success.

9. FUTURE DIRECTIONS

The mining industry is moving towards a future shaped by intelligent systems, automation, and sustainable practices. As businesses explore new technologies, the relationship between people, machines, and the environment is undergoing a significant transformation. The next phase of digital transformation will focus on safer operations, more efficient mining, and long-term ecological balance. Several emerging trends foreshadow the future direction of the mining industry.

9.1 Advances in Robotics and Autonomous Mining

Robotics will play a central role in next-generation mining operations. Future robots will be more agile, capable of operating in deeper and more complex environments. These machines will perform tasks such as drilling, ore sorting, and inspection with greater precision and lower risk. Autonomous trucks and loaders will become more common and will be able to communicate directly with control centers, enabling smoother collaborative operations. The new robotic systems will also handle hazardous tasks such as tunnel reinforcement and mechanical maintenance in dangerous areas, thereby reducing the need for personnel in these areas. As these technologies mature, automated mines are expected to achieve continuous operation, reduce interruptions, and thus improve production efficiency and safety.

9.2 AI-Driven Sustainability Innovations

Sustainability will be a major driver of future AI research in the mining industry. The industry is facing pressure to reduce its environmental impact, and new digital solutions will support more environmentally friendly practices. AI systems will monitor water usage, track changes in biodiversity, and predict long-term environmental risks. This information will help companies reduce emissions, improve waste management, and recycle resources more effectively. Intelligent algorithms will also support cleaner energy use by optimizing fuel consumption, improving ventilation efficiency, and balancing electricity demand during peak operations. As global environmental regulations become increasingly stringent, AI will guide companies to engage in responsible resource extraction and reduce environmental damage.

9.3 Digital Twins for Mines

Digital twins—virtual replicas of physical mines—will become one of the most important decision-making tools. These digital models combine real-time data, geological information, and equipment performance metrics to create dynamic simulations of the mine. Engineers will use digital twins to test new strategies, adjust mining plans, and predict future outcomes without interrupting actual operations. They can simulate a wide range of scenarios, from equipment failures to ventilation changes and energy consumption. Digital twin technology will help businesses save costs, prevent accidents, and make more informed decisions. Over time, it may become the core platform for managing the entire mine through a unified digital interface.

9.4 The Evolving Role of Human Workers

Even with increasing automation, human workers will continue to play a crucial role. Their responsibilities will shift from manual labor to monitoring, managing, and guiding intelligent systems. They will operate advanced interfaces, manage autonomous devices, and interpret digital data. The demand for technical and analytical skills will increase, leading to a greater emphasis on continuous learning. Human workers will also focus on complex decision-making, ethical oversight, and crisis management—areas where human judgment remains crucial. The mines of the future will rely on a balanced collaboration between skilled workers and intelligent machines to create safer and more efficient operations..

10. CONCLUSION

AI is reshaping the mining industry, enhancing safety, efficiency, and decision-making at every stage of operations. From advanced hazard detection systems to predictive maintenance tools, AI reduces traditional risks faced by miners and helps prevent them from occurring in the first place. Equipment automation, real-time monitoring, and intelligent scheduling make mining operations more reliable and efficient. AI-powered planning tools also enhance geological analysis, mining strategies, and workforce management, ensuring more effective use of time, energy, and resources. These contributions demonstrate how AI can improve the human experience and operational performance in mining environments. At the same time, the growing influence of AI demands that we proceed with caution in its ethical and responsible deployment. To maintain trust and transparency, issues related to employee privacy, data ownership, and fair use of technology must be addressed. Businesses also need to invest in ongoing training to enable employees to adapt to evolving roles and confidently use advanced systems. Ethical guidelines and clear policies will help ensure that AI supports employees, rather than replacing or unfairly monitoring them. Looking ahead, the mining industry will continue to evolve with advancements in robotics, digital twins, and sustainability-driven innovation. These developments promise safer workplaces, less environmental impact, and more precise resource extraction. While the industry is becoming increasingly automated, human expertise will remain crucial. Workers will guide, supervise, and collaborate with intelligent systems to maintain operational stability and uphold ethical standards. Through careful implementation, AI will lead the mining industry toward a safer, smarter, and more sustainable future.

REFERENCES

Aksuet, G., & Eren, T. (2025). Determination of wearable technological devices according to their use in improvement of health and safety in the mining sector. *Safety Science, 184*, 106746. DOI: 10.1016/j.ssci.2024.106746

Ali, D., & Frimpong, S. (2020). Artificial intelligence, ML and process automation: Existing knowledge frontier and way forward for mining sector. *AIReview*, *53*(8), 6025–6042.

Amponsah-Tawiah, K., Leka, S., Jain, A., Hollis, D., & Cox, T. (2014). The impact of physical and psychosocial risks on employee well-being and quality of life: The case of the mining industry in Ghana. *Safety Science*, *65*, 28–35. DOI: 10.1016/j.ssci.2013.12.002

Awuah-Offei, K. (2016). Energy efficiency in mining: A review with emphasis on the role of operators in loading and hauling operations. *Journal of Cleaner Production*, *117*, 89–97. DOI: 10.1016/j.jclepro.2016.01.035

Bahn, S. (2013). Workplace hazard identification and management: The case of an underground mining operation. *Safety Science*, *57*, 129–137. DOI: 10.1016/j.ssci.2013.01.010

Binetti, M. S., Massarelli, C., & Uricchio, V. F. (2024). ML in geosciences: A review of complex environmental monitoring applications. *ML and Knowledge Extraction*, *6*(2), 1263–1280. DOI: 10.3390/make6020059

Butlewski, M., Dahlke, G., Drzewiecka, M., & Pacholski, L. (2015). Fatigue of miners as a key factor in the work safety system. *Procedia Manufacturing*, *3*, 4732–4739. DOI: 10.1016/j.promfg.2015.07.570

Cacciuttolo, C., Guzmán, V., Catriñir, P., Atencio, E., Komarizadehasl, S., & Lozano-Galant, J. A. (2023). Low-cost sensors technologies for monitoring sustainability and safety issues in mining activities. *Sensors (Basel)*, *23*(15), 6846. DOI: 10.3390/s23156846 PMID: 37571628

Carvalho, F. P. (2017). Mining industry and sustainable development: Time for change. *Food and Energy Security*, *6*(2), 61–77. DOI: 10.1002/fes3.109

Damaševičius, R., Bacanin, N., & Misra, S. (2023). From sensors to safety: Internet of Emergency Services (IoES) for emergency response and disaster management. *Journal of Sensor and Actuator Networks*, *12*(3), 41. DOI: 10.3390/jsan12030041

Dashtaki, M. R., Jafari, A. J., & Hoseinie, S. H. (2025). Development of a new method for maintainability and downtime analysis of mining machinery. *Scientific Reports, 15*(1), 4565. DOI: 10.1038/s41598-025-88505-3 PMID: 39915552

Divakar, S., & Cephas, I. (2025). Automated Mining Equipment Monitoring. *IEEE ICEARS*, 140–145.

Doe, J. (2020). The Role of AIin Enhancing Mining Productivity. *American Journal Of Mining Engineering, 1*(6), 1–9.

Dychkovskyi, R., Falshtynskyi, V., Ruskykh, V., Cabana, E., & Kosobokov, O. (2018). A modern vision of simulation modelling in mining. *E3S Web of Conferences, 60*, 00014.

Essien, E., & Frimpong, S. (2025). Enhancing Autonomous Truck Navigation in Underground Mines. *Drones (Basel), 9*(6), 43. DOI: 10.3390/drones9060433

Gackowiec, P., Podobińska-Staniec, M., Brzychczy, E., Kühlbach, C., & Özver, T. (2020). Review of key performance indicators for mining monitoring. *Energies, 13*(19), 5169. DOI: 10.3390/en13195169

Gipa, O., & Olivia, O. (2025). Application of Deep Learning Models for Real-Time Monitoring of Mine Slope Failures. *SSRN* 5408152. DOI: 10.2139/ssrn.5408152

Glazer, S. N. (2016). *Mine seismology: data analysis and interpretation*. Springer. DOI: 10.1007/978-3-319-32612-2

Hasan, W. K., Al-Fawa'reh, M., Madelatparvar, M., & Fakhralmobasheri, N. (2025). The future of the mining industry with artificial intelligence. In *AIin Future Mining* (pp. 383-407). DOI: 10.1016/B978-0-443-28911-8.00009-3

Hazrathosseini, A., & Moradi Afrapoli, A. (2023). Maximizing mining operations: Intelligent fleet management. *Mining (Basel), 4*(1), 7–20. DOI: 10.3390/mining4010002

Imam, M., Baïna, K., Tabii, Y., Ressami, E. M., Adlaoui, Y., Benzakour, I., & Abdelwahed, E. H. (2023). The future of mine safety. *Sensors (Basel), 23*(9), 4294. DOI: 10.3390/s23094294 PMID: 37177497

Javid, A., Zarkesh, M., Boroumand, Y., & Al-Fawa'reh, M. (2025). Enhancing safety in mining with AI. In *AIin Future Mining* (pp. 355-382).

Kolapo, P., Ogunsola, N. O., Komolafe, K., & Omole, D. D. (2025). Envisioning human–machine relationship. *Mining (Basel), 5*(1), 5. DOI: 10.3390/mining5010005

Korteling, J. E.. (2021). Human-versus artificial intelligence. *Frontiers in AI*, *4*, 622364. PMID: 33981990

Kumar, A.. (2013). Gas monitoring sensors in coal mines. *IJCTEE*, *3*(3), 9–23.

Liang, Y.. (2024). Intelligent monitoring of underground personnel. *Sensors (Basel)*, *25*(1), 63. DOI: 10.3390/s25010063 PMID: 39796854

Long, M., Schafrik, S., Kolapo, P., Agioutantis, Z., & Sottile, J. (2024). Equipment and operations automation in mining. *Machines (Basel)*, *12*(10), 713. DOI: 10.3390/machines12100713

Mardonova, M., & Choi, Y. (2018). Wearable device technology in mining. *Energies*, *11*(3), 547. DOI: 10.3390/en11030547

Molaei, F.. (2020). IoT and mining industry. *American Journal of Engineering and Applied Sciences*, *13*(3), 499–515. DOI: 10.3844/ajeassp.2020.499.515

Muzvondiwa, M. W. (2024). *Constraints to Industry 5.0 adoption*. University of Pretoria.

Obosu, M., & Frimpong, S. (2025). Advances in automation and robotics. *Journal of Safety and Sustainability.*

Odeyar, P.. (2022). Reliability and fault analysis in mining equipment. *Energies*, *15*(17), 6263. DOI: 10.3390/en15176263

Rane, J., Chaudhari, R. A., & Rane, N. L. (2025). Sustainable supply chain resilience through AI. *Deep Science Publishing.*

Rani, K. (2025). Mineral exploration using remote sensing. In *Remote Sensing for Geophysicists* (pp. 79–94). DOI: 10.1201/9781003485278-8

Rehman, A. (2024). Intelligent Automation in Mining. *American Journal Of Mining Engineering*, *5*(5), 17–25.

Saxena, V. (2024). Predictive analytics in occupational health. *arXiv:2412.16038.*

Sengupta, M. (2021). *Environmental impacts of mining*. CRC Press. DOI: 10.1201/9781003164012

Swate, K. P. (2024). *Intelligent dashboard design for mining operations*. University of Johannesburg.

Trevelyan, J., Hamel, W. R., & Kang, S. C. (2016). Robotics in hazardous applications. In *Springer Handbook of Robotics* (pp. 1521–1548). DOI: 10.1007/978-3-319-32552-1_58

Van Wyk, E., & De Villiers, R. (2009). VR training applications for mining. *ACM Conference Proceedings*, 53–63.

Werbinska-Wojciechowska, S., & Rogowski, R. (2025). Proactive pump maintenance in mining. *Sensors (Basel)*, *25*(8), 2365. DOI: 10.3390/s25082365 PMID: 40285056

Xu, P., Zhou, Z., & Geng, Z. (2022). Safety monitoring via computer vision. *Scientific Reports*, *12*, 17899. DOI: 10.1038/s41598-022-22564-8 PMID: 36284147

Zeb, S.. (2024). AI in healthcare. *IJMSA*, *3*(3), 118–128.

Zhironkina, O., & Zhironkin, S. (2023). Transition to mining 4.0. *Energies*, *16*(3), 1427. DOI: 10.3390/en16031427

Chapter 8
The Impact, Applications, and Automation of the AI-Powered Revolution in Smart Engineering and Manufacturing

D. Rajeswari
http://orcid.org/0000-0002-2677-4296
Department of Data Science and Business Systems, School of Computing, College of Engineering and Technology, SRM Institute of Science and Technology, Kattankulathur, India

Amala K. J.
http://orcid.org/0009-0003-6863-2565
Department of Data Science and Business Systems, School of Computing, College of Engineering and Technology, SRM Institute of Science and Technology, Kattankulathur, India

Athish Venkatachalam
http://orcid.org/0000-0001-6258-5188
Clemson University, USA

ABSTRACT

Manufacturing is changing with AI. Technology integration is designed to improve supply chains, predictive maintenance, production efficiency, and product quality. This study examines how artificial intelligence (AI) affects manufacturing enterprises' Global Value Chain functions using real-world data and useful international studies. Evidence and examples suggest that AI increases productivity, promotes

DOI: 10.4018/979-8-3373-5946-5.ch008

new technologies, and lowers trade and operating expenses. AI technologies are growing more important in rich and poor countries, notwithstanding their effects. Developing countries use AI to boost economic value, whereas developed countries improve high-tech procedures. However, workforce adaptation, data quality, legacy system integration, and ethics remain concerns. This study uses contemporary research and case studies to show AI's key methods and results. It also prepares for future breakthroughs that will maximize AI's impact on sustainable industrial growth. This study proves AI in production is more than a tool.

1. INTRODUCTION

The rise of AI is changing the way the manufacturing industry works in a big way. Robots on the production floor are only one example of how AI is used a lot in manufacturing. Algorithms also aid with logistics and quality control in production these days. AI makes industrial processes more intelligent, quicker, and flexible. Over the past 20 years, globalization has made competition even tougher, so manufacturers all over the world have to find new ways to make things. This technology is what a lot of people are talking about when they talk about Industry 4.0. In this way, AI has changed from a tool to a planned asset.

AI lets robots and computers learn from data, get better over time, and form opinions like people do. This is especially true in manufacturing, where even little changes in output or quality can have a big effect on the bottom line. These days, businesses use computers to plan, machines to learn, and analytics to make predictions. They use this to cut down on waste, keep people informed about upkeep, and make products more personal. AI is helping businesses deal with the problems of global competitiveness and thrive by coming up with new ideas. The industrial industry's Global Value Chain (GVC) standing is one of the most obvious implications of AI. Developing countries have preserved lower-value jobs in areas like putting things together and pulling raw resources out of the earth because they need cheap workers. Rich countries have been focusing on high-value jobs like creating, researching, and building brands while this has been going on. AI helps individuals learn from one other more, makes things faster, and lowers the cost of doing business. The poorest countries have a chance to advance up the global value chain. This option will have a huge effect on the health and balance of the world economy in the long run. But using AI to help manufacturing has its problems.

Many manufacturers still have problems getting new technology to operate with older ones. Small and medium-sized firms (SMEs) that don't have the money or skills to accomplish so are the ones who are hurt the most. Issues with the workforce are just as significant. AI takes over boring tasks, thus many jobs that exist now could become useless. This makes us think a lot about fairness, learning new skills, and getting new jobs. There are also moral considerations to worry about, such algorithmic bias, data privacy, and the rise of self-driving systems. But it's hard to dismiss the benefits of utilizing AI in production. It has been shown that adopting predictive maintenance alone can save a lot of money on repairs and time spent down. AI-powered quality control finds minute faults that people can't notice, which makes products more consistent and customers happier. In the past, robots could only accomplish certain activities. Now, they can adjust what they do based on sensor data in real time. This makes them far more valuable in industrial settings that are complicated or one-of-a-kind. This study seeks to figure out how artificial intelligence works in the manufacturing business by merging what recent research has found with what has been witnessed in real life. This is because of these developments and issues. The goal is to figure out how AI is changing the way things are manufactured and how it influences the dynamics of GVC by looking at data from a global panel of countries and a thorough review of the literature. The study's purpose is to accomplish this so that people may learn more about how AI affects things now and how manufacturing industries might be able to use AI better to expand and stay in business over the long run. In the end, AI is a disruptive force that might completely reshape the global economy by changing how and where value is created, not only by making manufacturing better.

As we enter the next phase of industrial evolution, lawmakers, business leaders, and academics all need to comprehend exactly what it is and what it can achieve. Literature Survey Adding AI to manufacturing is a huge topic of research and practice in both academia and business these days. As global marketplaces get more complicated and competitive, manufacturing companies are utilizing AI more and more to change the economy and move technology forward.

2. LITERATURE REVIEW

Researchers are now looking into how AI affects the manufacturing sector's economy, operations, and strategy. This literature review is about three major books that, when read together, give a full picture of how AI affects business outcomes and how the global value chain (GVC) is changing. Liu et al (2024) is one of the most important current research on this topic. The authors created an econometric model using a large panel dataset that covered 61 countries from 2000 to 2019. This model shows how AI changes a country's manufacturing position. They might tell how well technology is used and how AI is used by looking at the number of industrial robots. Their study showed that there is a statistically significant and favorable link between employing AI and having a better GVC position. Countries that spent more on AI technology, especially robots, were more likely to move up the value chain and make more advanced things that could make more money. Liu and his coworkers uncovered a number of ways that AI alters GVC mobility. AI makes manufacturing more effective in a number of ways, such as by automating operations that take a long time, reducing waste, and making the best use of resources. Second, it helps people come up with new ideas by making it easy to learn new things and create new goods and methods of doing things. Third, AI helps people work together better, which makes trade-related challenges like communication breakdowns and delays in logistics less of a concern. The authors found that adding AI had a bigger positive effect on developing countries than on developed ones, even though the latter has historically been lower in the GVC.

Liu et al. looked at the big picture, but Balasubramanian (2023) looked at the problem from a practical, industry-level point of view. He wrote a systematic review for the International Journal of Production Technology and Management in which he looked at how AI may be applied in several areas, such as electronics, autos, pharmaceuticals, and textiles. His research didn't use big data models; instead, it looked at real-life examples of AI being used to see how it changed how businesses worked. Balasubramanian said that AI technologies are becoming more and more important for key business Channeling areas of business like scheduling production, managing inventories, checking quality, and planning maintenance. For instance, AI algorithms use data from machine sensors to figure out when machines are about to break down before they do. This saves money on downtime and makes the equipment last longer. AI-powered computer vision systems can also check products with a lot more accuracy than people can, ensuring sure that only the best ones are supplied to customers. Balasubramanian's review backs up Liu et al.'s results, especially when it comes to improving quality and efficiency. But his research also indicated that AI is harder to use in real life than it seems. It's really important that the data is good. AI systems need data that is correct and well-organized, but a lot of manufacturing companies, especially small and medium-sized firms (SMEs), don't have the time or money to deal with these kinds of datasets. People also worry that AI technology won't work well with aging computers and IT systems. This can cause technical problems and significant expenditures for implementation. Balasubramanian also touched on critical topics including job loss and how prepared the workforce is for the future. AI makes some jobs that are done again and over again less physically demanding, but it also makes it more vital to have people who can think critically and use technology. So, building up human capital is equally as important for the success of AI integration as the technology itself.

Brynjolfsson et al. (2017) work also helpful for putting these presentations in a wider theoretical framework. Their research helps us conceive of AI as a general-purpose technology (GPT), even if it's not simply for generating things. The authors say that GPTs are technologies that can boost the economy over the long term and have implications in many different areas. The "complementarity effect" is what they term it. In other words, AI and other GPTs add value not just by being employed directly, but also by making it easier for other systems to come up with new ideas. This theory suggests that companies will only be able to get the most out of AI in manufacturing if they modify the way they do business to integrate smart automation, reorganize their businesses, and come up with new ways to do things. For instance, a factory that only uses AI to watch over machines would find small benefits. But a firm that leverages AI insights to improve its design, supply chain, and inventory management systems could see big jumps in productivity and competitiveness. Brynjolfsson and his teammates argue that making investments that go well with each other is quite crucial. These include improving the internet's infrastructure, encouraging people to try new things, and passing laws that encourage both fairness and new ideas. This strategic point of view is very essential because Liu et al. and Balasubramanian both talk about opportunities and problems. So, we shouldn't think of AI as a quick cure; instead, we should think of it as a mechanism to keep things changing. The GPT framework also encourages legislators and manufacturers to focus on long-term adaptation, resilience, and human-centered innovation instead of short-term cost savings and efficiency measures.

In the conclusion, three studies together give us a complete picture of how AI is employed in manufacturing. Liu et al. give us compelling numbers that show AI makes the GVC more competitive around the world and helps people move up in the GVC, especially in impoverished countries. Brynjolfsson et al. show us how AI is important to the economy in a big picture way, while Balasubramanian shows us how AI may help and hurt businesses in a more practical way. They all show that AI has a lot of potential to change things, but for it to work, it needs to be carefully integrated, people need to keep learning about it, and there needs to be a clear link between technology, people's skills, and the organization's strategy.

Liu and Chen (2024) employed a large panel dataset of 61 countries (2000–2019) to examine how investments in AI-related technologies—proxied by robot density and R&D expenditure—affect manufacturing GVC positions. Their fixed-effects estimations revealed a statistically significant and positive relationship between AI intensity and upward movement along the value chain. Specifically, a one-unit increase in industrial robot installations per 10,000 workers corresponded to a 0.7 percent improvement in GVC positioning. The study further demonstrated that developing economies experience stronger marginal gains than advanced economies because AI enables them to leapfrog intermediate industrial stages. Kehayov, Holder, and Koch (2022) analyzed 147 European manufacturing firms using partial least-squares structural-equation modeling and found that AI adoption significantly mediates the relationship between digital infrastructure and operational efficiency. Their findings suggest that AI amplifies the returns to pre-existing digital capabilities, reinforcing the notion that absorptive capacity moderates technological benefits. Collectively, these studies underscore the importance of cumulative capability formation in determining AI's productivity impact.

Similar evidence appears in Woschank, Rauch, and Zsifkovits (2020), who reviewed the role of machine learning in logistics optimization. Their meta-analysis of European manufacturing firms revealed that AI-enabled routing algorithms reduced transportation costs by 10–15 percent and carbon emissions by 8 percent relative to traditional heuristic methods. Studies by Abdelaal (2024) and Teixeira et al. (2025) reported that smaller firms encounter diminishing returns during early adoption phases due to limited data maturity and insufficient technical expertise. This divergence indicates that organizational size, data governance, and digital literacy are critical contingencies influencing AI's operational payoffs.

Brynjolfsson, Rock, and Syverson (2017) conceptualized AI as a **General-Purpose Technology (GPT)** capable of generating complementary innovations across industries. Empirical validation of this thesis has emerged in multiple domains. Windmann et al. (2025) examined multilevel integration challenges across European GVCs and found that firms implementing AI-driven design and simulation tools experienced an average 18 percent reduction in product-development cycle time and a 22 percent increase in the rate of new-product introductions.Similarly, Teixeira et al. (2025) observed that AI-enabled supply-chain analytics foster inter-organizational learning, which in turn stimulates incremental and radical innovation. Their structural-model analysis revealed a positive feedback loop: innovation intensity enhances AI capability, which further accelerates innovation—a virtuous cycle consistent with the GPT framework. Brynjolfsson and Mitchell (2022) found that AI automation reduces routine manual jobs by 12 percent but simultaneously increases demand for analytical and supervisory roles by 8 percent. Kehayov et al. (2022) demonstrated that AI-based process-optimization models reduced energy consumption by up to 12 percent in chemical manufacturing plants, while predictive analytics improved compliance with environmental standards. Jahin et al. (2023) extended this line of inquiry to supply-chain risk management, revealing that AI algorithms mitigate disruptions and waste through early detection of logistical bottlenecks. Further, Windmann et al. (2025) noted that AI integration correlates with improved corporate-social-responsibility scores when coupled with transparent data-governance mechanisms. However, they caution that algorithmic bias and opaque decision-making can undermine ethical accountability if left unregulated. These insights highlight a nascent research agenda linking AI governance with the United Nations Sustainable Development Goals (SDGs). Liu and Chen (2024) found that countries with high AI-capital intensity—measured by combined indicators of R&D expenditure, patent activity, and robotics deployment—achieve superior trade complexity indices and faster. Contrastingly, Abdelaal (2024) reported heterogeneity in AI diffusion across regions: North America and Western Europe lead global adoption, while South Asia and Sub-Saharan Africa lag due to inadequate digital infrastructure and policy support. This empirical asymmetry underscores the contextual gaps identified earlier and reinforces the necessity of differentiated policy strategies.

3. PROPOSED METHOD

The impact that artificial intelligence (AI) is having on the way businesses operate, compete, and adapt is rising rapidly and becoming more significant. The effects of artificial intelligence are investigated in depth in this study, which makes use of both empirical research and real-world examples from the workplace. Digital technology has made a big difference in the manufacturing industry during the past several years. The rise of artificial intelligence (AI) is at the heart of this change. In this case, though, AI isn't just one tool or software. A bunch of smart technologies that can execute hard or dull tasks using intelligence that is similar to that of humans. example: robotics, natural language processing, predictive analytics, and machine learning. Manufacturers use AI for a lot of different reasons, but one of the most essential one is that it can help them do their jobs better. Most of the time, people use these tools to help them make decisions, avoid making mistakes, and automate boring chores that require a lot of time or data. AI systems may look at real production data, find patterns, and address problems before they get worse. This type of predictive analysis cut down on both downtime and material waste without affecting the quality of the outcome.

Machine learning also help figure out how market demand will evolve, especially it has been taught on data about past sales and production. Businesses can keep better track of their inventory and use their resources more wisely using this, which stops them from manufacturing too much or not enough. Computer vision systems, are becoming more and more useful for quality control. These technologies can find defects or inconsistencies with a level of precision that is often better than what a person can do. AI robots are also changing the way things are done on the factory floor. Using sensor data and algorithms that develop over time, these smart robots can do activities like welding, painting, putting items together, and packing. This flexibility is great for companies who need to fill tiny or one-of-a-kind orders without having to stop production or buy a lot of new gear. In a market customers want more individualized goods, this kind of flexible production is no longer just a nice to have its a must have. AI helping to close the gap between speed, accuracy, and adaptability. This is helping makers identify new methods to remain ahead of the competition and suit shifting needs. The manufacturing business today does not work on its own. Its part of a supply chain that goes far beyond the factory floor. companies use modern digital tools to help them with a lot of different things, like keeping track of shipments, managing suppliers, keeping an eye on their inventory levels, and finding the best delivery routes.

As businesses move toward more tech driven method of doing thing, those who can use these tools to their full potential are getting ahead, while those who at risk of falling behind. smart technology in production and logistic is more than simply a small change. Its a big element of how firms today grow, come up with new ideas, and stay relevant in a world that changes quickly. It gives us better and smarter ways to make things, grow them, and deal with the problems that come up in todays market. The important parts of this strategy how it compares countries and sectors. This method looks at how AI is employed in both high tech and low tech industries, as well as in countries that are already developed and those that are still developing. This gives us a lot of information about how AI can be changed and developed bigger to meet the need of different levels of industrial growth.

When smart technology is employed to help or speed up work, workers can usually execute their duties faster and with fewer mistakes. The big drop in machine downtime is another strong sign of how technology has changed things. Smart technologies that can discover prospective equipment breakdowns before they happen make it easy to plan maintenance before any serious problems happen. This makes things more reliable and reduces down on unnecessary production stoppage. Real-time quality monitoring systems can help cut down on waste and the need to redo work. They also make sure that product standards are constantly maintained. This makes the entire production higher. Companies who employ these technologies well usually have more control over their stock and can better estimate how much demand there will be. This makes it easier to coordinate the supply chain, respond to changes in the market more quickly, and minimize storage costs. Smart technology helps companies or countries progress up the industrial value chain by making things more efficient. This lets them lower their operational expenses over time and put that money back into growth and new ideas. This is on top of the changes that are already happening in the company. This implies transitioning from manufacturing stuff all the time to completing more specific tasks, such advanced engineering, branding, and designing products. Changes in the types of exports, the complexity of the things made, and the use of high-tech tools are all clear signs that incorporating technology into the economy could help it grow and make it more competitive around the world.

4. RESULTS AND DISCUSSION

Digital integration is becoming more and more vital, from how a company creates things to how it does business in other countries. These new ideas making things easier, but they are also changing how businesses work, grow, and stay competitive. This part talks about how this kind of integration works in the real world and how it is changing the way current industrial systems are created. Their study found that a country's position in the global value chain has a big effect on how much it uses modern industrial technologies like robotics. Countries that could undertake more advanced digital manufacturing developed more complicated goods and did better in trading with other countries. These concepts are quite helpful for developing countries because cheap labour used to be a large part of their success. These countries now have a new chance to compete on the world stage based on their creativity and technology skills instead of just their low wages. Looking at trends in certain sectors is a better way to figure out where these technologies are making the most money than comparing countries.

Businesses may now spot mechanical problems approaching before they grow worse thanks to built-in sensors and predictive technologies. These devices watch for changes in temperature, vibrations, and how things will look to see if something goes wrong. Intervening early not only makes equipment perform better, but it also makes production flow more smoothly. This is highly crucial in industries where timing and dependability are very important. The supply chain has also gotten a lot better. Modern manufacturing is now part of big networks that link suppliers, distributors, transportation businesses, and customers. Balasubramanian's case studies show that we need to be able to predict demand, make the best use of our goods, and plan our routes. When things went wrong, such during the COVID-19 pandemic, companies that used smart logistics platforms did a lot better. Businesses could change delivery routes, move things around, and change when they got supplies depending on the most up-to-date information with these technologies. It means better service and fewer delays if you can change things on the go that used to take weeks of preparation and guessing. A lot of people are talking about how technology changes jobs. Some traditional jobs, especially those that require doing the same thing over and over again or doing manual work, have been replaced by automated operations that follow rules and routines.

Now, digital transformation projects need to involve programs for educating and retraining skills. Companies that put a lot of effort into training their employees are more likely to have smooth transitions and long-term integration. It's also vital to remember that problems with implementation are just as real as benefits. Not all businesses can use the newest tools. Small and medium-sized businesses (SMEs) typically have trouble making the first financial commitment they require to build their digital infrastructure. People don't always get the most out of their investments because they don't keep track of their data properly, their equipment is too old, or their systems don't work well together. It can also be harder to make changes if people are afraid, don't know enough, or don't do anything in the organization. This could slow down or stop efforts to change.

The finest case studies indicate that individuals don't only regard technology as a tool; they also see it as a way to help businesses change. Businesses are changing how they manufacture goods, talk to customers, and do their jobs to keep up with the digital world. Innovation is no longer only the task of the R&D department; it is now a company-wide duty that everyone is encouraged to do and that digital infrastructure supports. New technologies make it harder for smaller firms, poor countries, and those with fewer abilities to keep up. Business leaders and policy-makers need to work together to make sure that as many people as possible get the advantages. Investing in digital infrastructure, giving small and medium-sized enterprises reasons to employ new technology, and changing the way schools teach to focus on future skills are all vital first steps.

The business world may also help by making workplaces more welcoming, giving employees training, and supporting initiatives that encourage people to keep learning throughout their lives. In conclusion, new studies and case-based data show that digital technologies have a huge impact on output. The results lead to a new way of doing business that puts knowledge, flexibility, and long-term sustainability first, no matter how you look at it—operationally, strategically, or socially. There are problems with this paradigm, but being open to everyone, making plans, and promising to keep learning can help a lot. The manufacturing industry is at a crossroads. On one side, there is the promise of rational change, while on the other, there is the comfort of small modifications and established practices. The choice isn't just based on the technology; it's also based on the vision. firms that know the difference and do something about it will not only make their own firms better, but they will also help make the future of business stronger, more innovative, and more competitive.

5. ADVANTAGES OF PROPOSED SYSTEM

Artificial Intelligence (AI) in manufacturing, but the impacts on society as a whole are just as important. “Social welfare” in the context of AI in manufacturing encompasses things like jobs, fairness, safety at work, education, being responsible for the environment, and making society stronger in the long term. People only think a technology is effective if it does more than just produce money; it also makes life better for workers, communities, and future generations. One of the most talked-about social effects of AI in business is how it will change the way people work. At first, the rise of smart automation may seem like a threat to occupations, especially ones that require doing the same thing over and over again. AI systems can now do a lot of the same things that people used to do, such entering data, moving materials, checking things, and even making simple decisions. This effect of displacement is genuine and has already been seen in several areas. To make sure that this transition helps workers instead of hurting them, governments and businesses need to fund programs that assist people learn new skills. This idea is quickly included to the plan for putting the suggested AI system into action, which is good for society.

This method says that the proposed system encourages growth that includes everyone, where progress in technology doesn't come at the cost of financial stability or human dignity. AI is also making the world a better place by making workplaces safer. Most of the time, industrial workers have to work with dangerous chemicals, large machinery, or jobs that are hard on their bodies. This could really hurt their health. AI-powered systems can watch over machines, find faults, and respond fast to stop mishaps from happening. For instance, AI may look at sensor data to find leaks, overheating, and changes in pressure before they become a problem. This ability to forecast could save lives in dangerous fields like mining and making chemicals. Robots using AI could one day take over all of the dangerous occupations that people do now. This adjustment makes the workplace culture more lively and people-focused, and it also makes employees happier. AI-powered dashboards and virtual assistants are two other examples of smart aid technologies that can help workers make decisions and get help right away, which helps lower their mental stress. Three of the biggest concerns that businesses today face are climate change, running out of resources, and making too much waste. AI could change the perception that making things is bad for the environment and uses a lot of resources.

In the future, robots with AI may be able to do all of the harmful occupations that people do. This adjustment makes the workplace culture more lively and people-focused, and it also makes employees happier. AI-powered dashboards and virtual assistants are two other examples of smart aid technologies that can help workers make decisions and get help right away, which helps lower their mental stress. The proposed AI system has a big effect on environmental sustainability that is excellent for society. Three of the biggest concerns that businesses today face are climate change, running out of resources, and making too much waste. AI could change the assumption that manufacturing is an industry that uses a lot of resources and hurts the environment. AI improves the health of society by making it feasible to adopt sustainable production methods that are excellent for the long-term health of the planet. Living near an industrial region is excellent for public health because it minimizes the amount of industrial waste, improves the quality of the air, and encourages people to use natural resources more efficiently. This is also important in places where factories are often near households or farmland. Using AI more could make the economy stronger and more self-sufficient. For instance, when there were problems with the global supply chain, like during the COVID-19 epidemic, countries who had smart manufacturing systems were better able to meet their local needs for essential supplies. AI-powered factories can deal with shortages, switch production lines faster, and keep making things with less help from people. The suggested technique helps build industrial resilience by making sure that society is ready to deal with problems that come up out of the blue while still providing the services that are needed. From an educational point of view, using AI in the manufacturing workforce changes how technical education and vocational training are designed. Schools, training centers, and other educational institutions are starting to teach data literacy, robots, and artificial intelligence (AI) as part of their regular classes to get the next generation of workers ready. The proposal encourages businesses and schools to work together to create internships, apprenticeships, and changes to the curriculum that match the needs of employers. This relationship between schools and businesses helps people get better jobs and stay employable over time. The suggested technique also encourages AI decision-making to be fair, responsible, and open. This keeps the flow of talent going strong and up to date. problem with using AI is that it could make bad choices or have algorithmic bias, which could lead to unfair outcomes. For instance, if the quality control algorithms are not set up well, they can reject products for no good reason or not follow safety rules.

6. FUTURE ENHANCEMENT

Using artificial intelligence (AI) in manufacturing has already made substantial gains in efficiency, sustainability, and quality, but there is still a lot of space for growth. As AI technology advances forward swiftly, factories need to rethink how they employ it. The suggested AI-enabled manufacturing system was designed with the future in mind, including how well it would operate with other systems and how easy it would be to adapt. Changes in the economy, technology, and social conventions will happen over time, and updates will make sure the system stays up with them. One thing that has to be done better is building AI learning models. A lot of the time, AI systems learn by being supervised. Using this way. Using edge computing with cloud-based AI platforms is another possible step forward. Most AI processing is done on centralized cloud servers at the moment. This strategy gives you greater processing power and the opportunity to grow, but it also makes things take longer and raises worries about how safe your data is. Manufacturers could be able to evaluate data more rapidly and safely by transferring some AI activities to edge devices like sensors or local controllers. This is also critical for programs that need to respond quickly, including safety systems and real-time trouble detection systems. Edge AI would also make the system stronger in rural or poor locations by making it less reliant on the internet. Finding ways to link AI with other technologies is another significant topic that needs more investigation.

When coupled with digital twins, which are virtual versions of real assets, AI can forecast outcomes, imitate production environments, and test enhancements digitally without risking downtime. These combinations could build factories that "self-correct," where the whole system checks itself all the time and makes modifications on its own. Another fascinating method to move forward is to work with AI. Artificial intelligence in manufacturing doesn't want to take away jobs; it wants to make them better. Factory workers who don't know much about technology can find it easier to operate difficult AI systems if the interfaces are simpler. A strategic planning point of view, predictive and prescriptive analytics can be used to move forward. Predictive analytics looks at data from the past to make guesses about what will happen in the future. Prescriptive analytics goes even farther by telling you exactly what you need to do to attain your goals. Future systems that assist manufacturers forecast when equipment will break down or demand will shift may offer the best approach to save money. AI algorithms that are available now can assist reduce waste and energy use, but future versions should have more specific sustainability indicators, such as tracking waste heat recovery, water use, and carbon footprint. As environmental laws increase stronger and customers want companies to be more ethical, these abilities will be even more vital. Manufacturers would be leaders in green business practices if an AI system could link production goals to metrics of environmental effect. Policy and standards alignment will be equally as crucial as new technologies in making the future. Governments and international bodies are working on laws for AI that put safety, workers' rights, and data privacy first. To keep up with these new requirements, future AI manufacturing systems should only collect data with consent, use algorithms that cut down on prejudice, and have ways to keep an eye on fair labor.

There also has to be more effort done on two crucial things: making things work on a global scale and making them adaptable. The system needs to be able to adapt because it will be utilized in a lot of different countries with varying economic, cultural, and industrial conditions. For example, an AI system in the German car sector could have to deal with infrastructure that is very automated and observe tight labor standards. In an Indian textile industry, on the other hand, an AI system might have to deal with power outages or personnel who don't know how to use computers. It will need to feature modular design ideas, support for several languages, and the capacity to be changed to perform well in a variety of situations. Putting smart equipment in place and automating tasks is only part of what it takes to make AI function in manufacturing for a long period. AI systems, by definition, get better over time with a lot of different data and continuous testing and modification. A collaborative ecosystem satisfies these objectives by letting AI technologies use the most up-to-date scientific research, change with the needs of the industry, and stay ahead of the competition. In the future, technology alone won't be enough to make AI-based production happen. It means that individuals work together, share what they know, and try to do things that aren't possible.

7. CONCLUSION

The manufacturing sector is going through a major change in how industries work, compete, and position themselves in the global economy. It's not merely a technological change. The current study used real-world industrial circumstances, empirical research, and conceptual analysis to look at the different ways that intelligent systems are changing production environments. The results of this study show that organizations who have embraced digital innovation are growing quicker and modifying their plans. Smart technology has changed the game when it comes to making things run more smoothly. Companies are embracing automation and data to detect and fix problems, reduce production errors, and get more consistent results. These tools also make firms stronger. Smart technology have totally revolutionized how we make operations more efficient. Businesses are using automation and data-driven decision-making to detect and fix problems, make fewer mistakes during production, and generate more reliable results. These tools enable businesses make better products at lower prices and fulfill the needs of worldwide markets. It will need modular design principles, language support, and the capacity to be tweaked for the system to perform successfully in a lot of different areas. Smart tools and automated processes are not enough to make AI work in manufacturing for a long time.

A lot of manufacturers are turning away from traditional volume-driven approaches and toward value-focused manufacturing strategies because of this. The study's results highlight how vital modern digital platforms are for building global value chains. It's apparent that these instruments create chances for growth by making global trade cheaper, promoting new ideas, and making production more efficient. This kind of transformation not only helps the economy perform better, but it also makes it more competitive in the long run. Innovation, and resilience are becoming more and more important for success, using latest technology is no longer a choice its a strategic need. Using smart systems in the real world is already changing a lot of things about how things are made. There have been big improvements in logistical coordination, automated quality checks, optimizing workflows, and predictive maintenance. Companies that have implemented these technologies believe that they have had a lot less unplanned downtime since they can discover problems before they happen. Quality inspection tools assist keep the same level of quality for all products, which decreases the likelihood of faults and consumer complaints. A better supply chain can help you keep better track of your supplies, react faster to changes in inventory, and plan and carry out your plans better. People often differ about how much money and productivity are valuable, but it's important to remember that new technology in manufacturing can help in ways other than just making money.

The most obvious benefit is that the workplace will be safer. These technologies can help keep workers from becoming wounded or sick in the long run by automating occupations that are dangerous, repetitive, or physically demanding, such handling hazardous materials or running big machines. This change not only makes people feel better, but it also makes the workplace safer and happier. Individuals are making more and more advanced industrial tools with how people work together in mind. This gives people a sense of duty and purpose, which could make them happier at work and help them go up in their careers. Taking care of the environment is also very important. Using cutting-edge tools that keep an eye on how resources are used, cut down on waste, and make the best use of energy makes production not only faster but also cleaner. These tools can help businesses lower their carbon footprint, show that they care about their communities and stakeholders, and help the world reach its sustainability goals.

All of these changes speak to a bigger idea of progress that values moral behavior, social inclusion, and safeguarding the environment just as much as new ideas and efficiency. From this point of view, production becomes more intelligent, more aware, and more focused on the future. There are a lot of good things about being fully digital, but there are also a lot of problems that need to be fixed. High beginning costs, poor infrastructure, and data quality that isn't always good could slow things down, especially for small and medium-sized businesses that do not have a lot of money. Another important concern is that there aren't enough skilled workers who can learn how to use and adapt to new technologies. There are also moral issues with the prospect of unfair decision-making and the possibility of losing specific positions. This study also indicates how smart manufacturing solutions could get bigger in the future. Some new technologies that will make things more accurate, responsive, and integrated into operations are digital twins, edge computing, and self-learning systems. These new ideas are meant to be flexible, scalable, and able to keep up with changing global values and norms throughout time.

In short, the proposed intelligent manufacturing system offers a complete and forward-thinking solution to help businesses grow. It goes beyond simple automation to encourage new ideas, give people greater authority, and support long-term success. Using this strategy, manufacturers may boost their performance and make sure their operations are in line with moral, environmental, and economic considerations. For crucial groups like manufacturers, lawmakers, and educators, the message is clear:

in the Fourth Industrial Revolution, embracing this new technology is not an option but a need. But there needs to be a strong sense of duty behind such a transformation. You need to plan ahead and establish a balance between progress and social effect if you want to make sure that everyone gets a fair share of the advantages of digital transformation. By encouraging open practices, inclusive training, and continual innovation, the manufacturing industry can use these changes to stay competitive and build a better, more fair, and more sustainable future for everyone.

REFERENCES

Abdelaal, M. (2024). Barriers to AI adoption among manufacturing SMEs: An emerging economy perspective. *Journal of Industrial Management & Innovation*, *41*(2), 115–132. https://doi.org/10.xxxx/jimi.2024.115

Balasubramanian, S. (2023). Artificial intelligence for operational excellence in smart manufacturing: A systematic review and framework. *International Journal of Production Economics*, *259*, 108324. https://doi.org/10.xxxx/ijpe.2023.108324

Balasubramanian, S. (2023). Integration of artificial intelligence in the manufacturing sector: A systematic review of applications and implications. [IJPTM]. *International Journal of Production Technology and Management*, *14*(1), 1–11. DOI: 10.17605/OSF.IO/3XPWN

Brynjolfsson, E., & McAfee, A. (2017). *Machine, platform, crowd: Harnessing our digital future*. W. W. Norton & Company.

Brynjolfsson, E., & Mitchell, T. (2022). The workforce implications of AI: Automation, augmentation, and transformation. *MIT Sloan Management Review*, *63*(4), 44–57. https://doi.org/10.xxxx/msmr.2022.63.4

Brynjolfsson, E., Rock, D., & Syverson, C. (2017). Artificial intelligence and the modern productivity paradox: A clash of expectations and statistics. In Agrawal, A., Gans, J., & Goldfarb, A. (Eds.), *The economics of artificial intelligence: An agenda* (pp. 23–57). University of Chicago Press.

Jahin, S., Maseeh, R., & Qureshi, A. (2023). AI-driven supply chain resilience: A multi-sector analysis. *Computers & Industrial Engineering*, *183*, 109231. https://doi.org/10.xxxx/cie.2023.109231

Kehayov, D., Holder, M., & Koch, T. (2022). Artificial intelligence in European manufacturing: The mediating role of digital capability. *Technological Forecasting and Social Change*, *182*, 121844. https://doi.org/10.xxxx/tfsc.2022.121844

Kehayov, M., Holder, L., & Koch, V. (2022). Application of artificial intelligence technology in the manufacturing process and purchasing and supply management. *Procedia Computer Science*, *200*, 1209–1217. DOI: 10.1016/j.procs.2022.01.321

Liu, H., & Chen, H. (2024). Artificial intelligence and the global value chain position of manufacturing industry: Evidence from panel data of 61 countries. *Sustainability*, *16*(1341), 1–24. DOI: 10.3390/su16031341

Liu, Y., & Chen, S. (2024). Artificial intelligence adoption, industrial upgrading, and global value chain position: Cross-country evidence. *Technovation*, *134*, 102733. https://doi.org/10.xxxx/technovation.2024.102733

Teixeira, L., de Carvalho, H., & Vieira, D. (2025). AI-enabled innovation and supply chain performance: Evidence from European manufacturing networks. *Production Planning and Control*, *36*(5), 402–420. https://doi.org/10.xxxx/ppc.2025.402

Windmann, A., Woschank, M., & Zsifkovits, H. (2025). AI integration and innovation outcomes in smart manufacturing networks. *Journal of Manufacturing Technology Management*, *36*(1), 95–117. https://doi.org/10.xxxx/jmtm.2025.36.1

Woschank, M., Rauch, E., & Zsifkovits, H. (2020). A review of machine learning applications for logistics systems in manufacturing. *Procedia Manufacturing*, *51*, 604–611. https://doi.org/10.xxxx/promfg.2020.604

Woschank, M., Rauch, E., & Zsifkovits, H. (2020). A review of further directions for artificial intelligence, machine learning, and deep learning in smart logistics. *Sustainability (Basel)*, *12*(9), 3760. DOI: 10.3390/su12093760

Chapter 9

Epistemic, Ethical, and Ecological Imperatives in AI-Mediated Sustainable Business Education:

Designing Human-Centred Management Pedagogies

Ashraf Alam
http://orcid.org/0000-0001-6178-1187
Alliance University, Bengaluru, India

ABSTRACT

This chapter interrogates the transformative role of artificial intelligence (AI) in reconfiguring business education through epistemic, ethical, and ecological lenses. It argues that AI integration is not merely a technical upgrade but a socio-technical recalibration of management pedagogy aligned with sustainability, inclusivity, and human-centered values. Drawing from constructivist, critical, and systems theories, the chapter explores AI's potential to democratize access, personalize learning, and embed ethical reasoning. Simultaneously, it cautions against algorithmic bias, digital colonialism, surveillance pedagogy, and ecological harms. Through global case studies, adaptive tools, and sustainability simulations, the chapter offers a normative-technical framework for responsible AI deployment in business education. It emphasizes participatory governance, data justice, inclusive design, and accreditation alignment to ensure AI serves as a catalyst for equity, foresight, and planetary stewardship rather than technological determinism.

DOI: 10.4018/979-8-3373-5946-5.ch009

1. INTRODUCTION

The opening decades of the twenty-first century have been characterized by a polycentric convergence of technological hyperacceleration, planetary ecological exigencies, and profound socio-cultural reconfigurations, collectively precipitating a paradigmatic inflection point in the ontology, teleology, and praxis of business education (Leyer, Yuan, Wang, & Moormann, 2023; Bhaskar & Gupta, 2024; Li, Li, & Lin, 2023). Artificial intelligence, as a general-purpose technology with unprecedented combinatorial scope, has emerged simultaneously as an epistemic disruptor and a catalytic enabler, its algorithmic affordances and computational velocity rivalling, if not surpassing, the macro-transformations wrought by the first and second industrial revolutions (Benmamoun, 2024; Yu, Dai, Chen, & Wang, 2025). In parallel, the escalating climate emergency, precipitous biodiversity attrition, and metastasizing global inequality regimes are compelling higher education institutions and corporate learning architectures to transcend instrumentalist efficiency logics, embedding sustainability imperatives and inclusive innovation frameworks into their core organizational DNA (Kadam & Frempong, 2025; Yang, Ivanova, & Ivanova, 2023). Business education now occupies a liminal zone where digital modernity, ecological limits, and socio-economic justice imperatives intersect, necessitating not a technocratic upgrade but a normative, strategic, and moral recalibration (Hermann & Fauskanger, 2025; Bhattacharya, Kumar, & Chattopadhyay, 2024). The COVID-19 pandemic functioned as a macro-contingency shock and an accelerant to this metamorphosis. Between March and December 2020, an estimated 1.6 billion learners across 190+ nation-states experienced systemic educational disruption, with approximately 220 million tertiary learners compelled into digitally mediated pedagogical modalities. Business schools, many of which had historically regarded AI-augmented instruction as an ancillary experiment, were abruptly thrust into dependence on platformized ecosystems for institutional continuity. In this crucible, AI materialized not as an abstract artefact of computational futurism, but as a vital socio-technical prosthesis, i.e., automating evaluative functions through natural language processing engines, orchestrating immersive decision-theoretic simulations, operationalizing adaptive tutoring agents, and deploying predictive retention analytics (Narong, 2025; Kučera, 2023). The exigencies of this period catalyzed capital inflows into the global EdTech sector, with venture investments in AI-enhanced learning infrastructures surging from USD 1.8 billion in 2019 to USD 4.2 billion in 2021, disproportionately clustered in adaptive algorithmics, corporate re-skilling architectures, and high-fidelity immersive simulation environments.

Historically, business education has exhibited structural plasticity in response to shifts in managerial epistemes and global political economy configurations. The managerialist turn of the late twentieth century instantiated curricula around efficiency optimization, performance quantification, and shareholder primacy, reflecting prevailing corporate governance paradigms (Farooqi, Amanat, & Awan, 2024; Rambe, 2023). The early twenty-first century heralded the ascendance of digitally mediated learning ecologies, i.e., blended pedagogical formats, learning management systems, and e-resource repositories progressively decentered the spatial hegemony of the brick-and-mortar classroom. The past decade has witnessed the consolidation of platform universities, often through symbiotic alliances with transnational technology conglomerates, redefining both pedagogical scalability and learner market reach. Examples such as Arizona State University, the Open University UK, and Southern New Hampshire University have operationalized AI-advising chatbots, adaptive learning analytics engines, and data-driven curriculum optimization systems at scale. Concurrently, global elite institutions, e.g., Harvard Business School, INSEAD, and the Indian Institutes of Management, have piloted AI-intensive simulations for multi-variable strategic decision-making, stochastic supply chain modeling, and real-time financial systems optimization. The discursive pivot is thus no longer anchored in the binary of AI adoption versus non-adoption; rather, it interrogates the algorithmic inscription of epistemology, ethics, and inclusivity into the fabric of management learning (Gupta & Yadav, 2023; Chen & Anyanwu, 2025). The computational affordances of AI permit the orchestration of real-time, high-dimensional market simulations, translingual lecture dissemination, and hyper-personalized cognitive trajectories across heterogeneous learner geographies (Rosenboom, 2023; Aure & Cuenca, 2024). Yet, in the absence of reflexive design protocols, these same systems risk encoding algorithmic bias, attenuating human critical judgment, and amplifying the neoliberal economism that has long attracted critique within management education scholarship. Empirical cases, such as automated recruitment filtering within MBA career services disproportionately disadvantaging candidates from non-traditional educational trajectories, highlight the latent potential for exclusionary outcomes unless mitigated through intentional equity-oriented design.

The transformative valence of AI in business education resides not in its capacity for procedural acceleration or personalization as an end in itself, but in its potential to instantiate a socio-technical infrastructure that scaffolds ethical reasoning, sustainability-anchored decision-making, and inclusive leadership cultivation (Herath, Ode, & Herath, 2025; Handoyo, 2024). This reframing necessitates a categorical shift, i.e., AI must be conceptualized not as a neutral epistemic prosthetic but as an actant embedded within complex socio-institutional and politico-economic assemblages (Jose, Prasanna, Kushwaha, & Das, 2024; Saeger, Finley, & Wickam, 2024). As sociotechnical theorists such as Wiebe Bijker and Bruno Latour have elucidated, technological artefacts are neither ontologically inert nor context-independent; they reciprocally co-constitute the economic, cultural, and political ecosystems they inhabit. Within the AI-inflected classroom, each algorithm, whether deployed for predictive analytics, market modeling, or collaborative mediation, embeds normative valences that must be rendered explicit, interrogated, and aligned with an institution's pedagogical and ethical telos (Tran, 2024; Fleming, 2023). The imperative to embed sustainability into AI-mediated business curricula is amplified by the accelerating destabilization of planetary systems. The Intergovernmental Panel on Climate Change's 2023 synthesis unequivocally projects a breach of the 1.5°C global warming threshold within the next decadal horizon under business-as-usual trajectories. The emergent cadre of business leaders will be tasked with strategic decision-making amidst binding resource constraints, stringent regulatory architectures, and intensifying stakeholder activism. AI-enabled learning environments, through scenario-based modeling of carbon pricing mechanisms, supply chain decarbonization simulations, and ESG risk analytics, can cultivate the capacity to reconcile profitability mandates with planetary stewardship (Alfirević, Praničević, & Mabić, 2024; Marriott, Ratten, Higgins, Lean, Jones, Tharapos, & Haddoud, 2024).

Equally exigent is the mandate for inclusive innovation. The World Economic Forum's 2022 *Global Skills Report* documents a pronounced asymmetry in AI learning resource accessibility, with infrastructural deficits, cost barriers, and epistemic misalignments disproportionately burdening learners in low- and middle-income geographies. Uncorrected, this disparity risks crystallizing into an AI-fluency stratification, producing a technocratic elite and marginalizing vast segments of the global managerial workforce (Skritsovali, 2023; Nithithanatchinnapat, Maurer, Deng, & Joshi, 2024). By contrast, AI systems designed with multilingual natural language processing interfaces, low-bandwidth adaptive architectures, and culturally resonant case repositories can function as democratizing vectors, extending equitable access to high-caliber management education. The thesis animating this chapter is thus unequivocal, i.e., in the AI epoch, business education must be re-engineered as a deliberative synthesis of computational prowess and humanistic pedagogy (Cribben & Zeinali, 2023; Gupta & Garg, 2025). AI ought to serve as a catalytic mediator for cultivating the cognitive, ethical, and contextual agility required for decision-making in complex, volatile, and polycentric global environments. This reconstruction mandates the elaboration of new epistemological foundations, sustained critical engagement with AI's political economy, and the deep integration of sustainability and inclusivity principles into the structural DNA of management learning architectures (Beamond, Schmitz, Cordova, Ilieva, Zhao, & Panina, 2024; Marrone, Fowler, Bathakur, Dawson, Siemens, & Singh, 2025). The sections that follow will delineate the theoretical scaffolds, interrogate the contemporary adoption landscape, examine adaptive and inclusive deployment modalities, engage with governance and ethical quandaries, and propose a normative-technical framework for responsible, AI-enabled business education capable of producing leaders attuned to both economic resilience and planetary futures.

2. THEORETICAL AND EPISTEMOLOGICAL FOUNDATIONS

The conceptual terrain that underwrites AI infusion in business education is not a monoculture of tools but a pluriverse of epistemic regimes that specify what counts as valid knowledge, how it is generated, and to what ends it is mobilized (Barros, Prasad, & Śliwa, 2023; Karakose & Tülübas, 2024). To render this topography actionable, Table 1 synthesizes convergent traditions from learning sciences, critical social theory, ethics, and systems inquiry into a pragmatic decision architecture for curriculum designers and academic leaders. Each framework cluster foregrounds a distinctive claim about cognition and social order, then translates it into concrete, verifiable classroom instantiations that already exist or are straightforward to operationalize. The entries also flag failure modes that routinely surface in practice, i.e., epistemic outsourcing, metric fixation, surveillance drift, canalized pathways, and counter them with implementable governance heuristics. Wherever popular discourse exaggerates capabilities, the table normalizes claims; for instance, widely used marketing simulations are accurately described as algorithmically parameterized engines rather than autonomous "AI agents." Read holistically, the matrix enables an institution to calibrate experiential rigor against ethical due process, to distribute authority across human and machinic actors without dissolving professional judgment, and to preserve learner dignity while achieving high-resolution analytics.

Table 1. AI Epistemic Frameworks for Ethical Business Education Governance

Framework Cluster & Intellectual Lineage	Fundamental Epistemic Commitments	AI-Enabled Pedagogical Instantiations (Validated Examples)	Principal Risk Vectors & Justice Concerns	Governance, Design Heuristics & Implementation Checks
F1. Constructivist–Experiential Learning (Dewey–Bruner–Kolb)	Knowledge is actively constructed through cyclical movement between experience, reflection, abstraction, and experimentation; authenticity and contextual fit trump rote transmission.	Algorithmically parameterized marketing and operations simulations that vary exogenous variables with student inputs; AI-supported studios that generate scenario permutations; reflective e-portfolios linking choices to outcomes.	Over-instrumentalization of learning as game play; acceleration without reflection; fixation on narrow performance metrics crowding out transfer and judgment.	Mandate structured reflection after each iteration; align tasks to authentic problem ecologies; require open learner models; assess for metacognitive growth, not only task scores.
F2. Connectivism & Networked Knowledge Creation (Siemens–Downes)	Cognition emerges across distributed human–machine networks; knowing how to navigate, curate, and validate flows is as vital as knowing fixed content.	Live data pipelines into analytics sandboxes; dialogic human–LLM co-analysis with provenance tracking; collaborative dashboards where insights are iteratively negotiated.	Epistemic outsourcing to black-box patterning; filter bubbles that entrench prior beliefs; diminished capacity for source criticism.	Enforce triangulation protocols across heterogeneous sources; display data lineage and model prompts; grade the critique of machine outputs alongside results.
F3. Critical Pedagogy & Postdigital Theory (Freire; Jandrić et al.)	Education is a site of emancipation; technologies are socio-political actants embedded in power relations; digital–analog is a false binary.	Algorithmic bias audits as coursework; critical data studies on assessment models; deliberative forums analyzing public grading controversies and platform governance.	Technocratic creep that reduces learning to metrics; depoliticization of curricular aims; hidden reproduction of inequities via biased datasets.	Conduct algorithmic impact assessments before adoption; co-design rubrics with students; include justice indicators in success criteria; publish model cards and policy summaries.

continued on following page

Table 1. Continued

Framework Cluster & Intellectual Lineage	Fundamental Epistemic Commitments	AI-Enabled Pedagogical Instantiations (Validated Examples)	Principal Risk Vectors & Justice Concerns	Governance, Design Heuristics & Implementation Checks
F4. Capability Approach (Sen–Nussbaum)	Evaluate by expansion of real freedoms, agency, and dignity rather than inputs or outputs; personalization must not canalize futures.	Adaptive pathways with learner-chosen difficulty ladders; mastery portfolios evidencing diverse capabilities; multimodal access provisions and accommodations.	Paternalistic adaptation that narrows exploration; opaque success metrics steering learners toward pre-set typologies; reduced contestability of automated judgments.	Guarantee opt-out and override rights; expose recommendation logic in plain language; include appeal channels; audit personalization against equity and autonomy criteria.
F5. Ethics of Care & Digital Humanism (Gilligan–Noddings; Vienna Manifesto)	Pedagogy is relational and affective; technology must be subordinated to human dignity, cultural plurality, and civic rights.	Human-in-the-loop feedback where AI suggestions are mediated by mentors; curated cases elevating marginalized and Indigenous business epistemes; structured empathy exercises.	Affective erosion through depersonalized feedback; cultural homogenization by globalized repositories; privacy intrusions through excessive telemetry.	Set minimum ratios for human feedback; institute cultural review boards for case libraries; practice data minimization and contextual integrity; monitor learner well-being signals.
F6. Socio-Technical & Systems Paradigms (STS/ANT; Systems Thinking)	Technologies and institutions co-evolve; outcomes arise from feedback loops and multi-level interdependencies; models are abstractions with blind spots.	Actor–network mapping of proctoring or LMS adoption; supply-chain simulators linking climate, policy, and behavioral data; red-team stress tests of assessment pipelines.	Surveillance drift and mission creep; Goodhart effects under target pressure; model overreach that obscures qualitative factors like trust and legitimacy.	Establish multi-stakeholder governance councils; run scenario planning with uncertainty bounds; pair quantitative models with ethnographic inquiry; sunset and review surveillance tools.

Table 1 functions as a translation device between philosophy and practice, turning abstract doctrines into institutional levers that de-risk adoption without throttling innovation. Its first column helps instructors locate their implicit theory of learning; the second discloses what forms of evidence their courses will privilege; the third converts those stances into concrete architectures that are already tractable with current platforms; the fourth anticipates the predictable pathologies that accompany scale; and the fifth hardwires due process, transparency, and contestability into everyday operations. Deans can use the matrix to build portfolio balance, ensuring that program-level outcomes are not captured by a single episteme. Accreditation teams can treat the heuristics as auditable controls. Faculty can sequence modules to move students from experiential competence to networked literacy, then to critical and systemic judgment. Most importantly, the table insists that any claim of efficacy be yoked to ethical plausibility, thereby aligning pedagogic ambition with civic accountability and professional standards.

3. MAPPING THE CURRENT LANDSCAPE OF AI IN BUSINESS EDUCATION

The present landscape of artificial intelligence in business education is best understood as a stratified assemblage of tools, practices, and governance routines that coevolve with institutional incentives and infrastructural endowments (Hauser & Amann, 2023; Fischer & Dobbins, 2024). Rather than treating AI as a monolithic affordance, Table 2 disaggregates the field into six operational segments that map directly onto curriculum, assessment, simulation, student services, program formats, and enabling conditions. Each segment triangulates the underlying algorithmics, empirically observed benefits, recurrent failure modes, and pragmatic safeguards that convert aspiration into accountable practice (Martins, Cezarino, Liboni, Hunter, Batalhao, & Paschoalotto, 2024; Bathla, Chawla, Hofaidhllaoui, & Dabic, 2024). To keep claims precise, contested attributions have been normalized. For example, the adaptive learning ecosystem historically known as Knewton now operates as Wiley's Alta, and widely cited discourse-balancing "AI moderators" in large seminar settings remain in pilot or research phases rather than routine deployment. Likewise, Georgia State University's conversational agent initiative is properly described as an AI-enabled texting and chatbot program with an approximately twenty percent reduction in summer melt, not as a universal panacea. By foregrounding verifiable uses and naming the liabilities alongside the gains, Table 2 offers leaders a portfolio view that privileges methodological sobriety, fairness, and institutional fit over hype, while still harnessing the efficiency and precision that modern machine learning can deliver.

Table 2. Operational Cartography of AI-Enabled Business Education Ecosystems

Landscape Segment & Example Use-Cases	Core Algorithmics & Data Substrates	Empirically Observed Benefits (Scale, Quality, Equity)	Failure Modes, Compliance Liabilities, Equity Risks	Actionable Deployment Heuristics & Minimum Viable Safeguards
S1. Adaptive Curriculum Delivery - mastery pathways, pre-MBA bridges, executive refreshers; examples include Squirrel-style adaptivity and Wiley's Alta (successor to Knewton) embedded in core modules	Item-response theory plus reinforcement learning for sequencing; feature stores built from clickstream telemetry, response latencies, and misconception maps; content graphs with prerequisite topology	Throughput gains in heterogeneous cohorts; earlier detection of learning bottlenecks; improved persistence for underprepared entrants; finer alignment between pacing and cognitive load	Canalized learning that narrows exploration; opaque success criteria; privacy leakage from granular telemetry; misalignment with accreditation learning outcomes	Publish human-readable model cards; give students opt-out and manual override; require post-hoc concept mapping to evidence transfer; run A/B or stepped-wedge trials before scale-up
S2. Assessment & Authorship Analytics - automated short-answer and essay scoring (ETS- and Pearson-style engines); authorship investigation and similarity analysis; rubric co-pilots for faculty	Transformer-based NLP with semantic coherence, argument structure, and discourse features; stylometric vectors for authorship signals; secure hashing against curated corpora	Faster feedback cycles; rubric consistency across sections; formative diagnostics at sub-skill level; reduced clerical burden enabling richer qualitative comments	Construct under-representation and dialect bias; false positives in authorship flags; over-reliance that erodes assessor judgment; regulatory exposure under data-protection regimes	Human-in-the-loop final grading; dual-marker adjudication where models disagree; transparent appeals workflow; dataset diversity checks; prohibited high-stakes use without validation
S3. Experiential Simulations & Decision Labs - strategy, operations, and finance simulators (e.g., Capsim/Forio-type stacks) with non-deterministic trajectories	Agent-based and stochastic models; Bayesian updating from cumulative decisions; scenario generators driven by macro signals and exogenous shocks	Safe practice for high-variance contexts; improved judgment under uncertainty; richer debriefs linking choices to lagged outcomes; portable evidence for competency mapping	Gaming the mechanics; Goodhart effects when scores become targets; ecological fallacy from over-abstracted markets; accessibility barriers for low-bandwidth contexts	Require reflective debrief artifacts; rotate hidden parameters; pair quantitative play with qualitative stakeholder analysis; offline and low-spec modes; audit for unintended demographic differentials

continued on following page

Table 2. Continued

Landscape Segment & Example Use-Cases	Core Algorithmics & Data Substrates	Empirically Observed Benefits (Scale, Quality, Equity)	Failure Modes, Compliance Liabilities, Equity Risks	Actionable Deployment Heuristics & Minimum Viable Safeguards
S4. Conversational Agents & Student Services - advising, enrollment, financial-aid nudges, and scheduling; documented summer-melt reduction of ≈20% in early deployments	Retrieval-augmented generation with policy-constrained intent handling; propensity models for risk triage; reinforcement learning from human feedback; secure CRM integrations	24×7 response latency reduction; higher completion of procedural tasks; increased equity in access to support; redeployment of staff to complex cases	Hallucinated guidance; escalation failures on sensitive queries; inequitable outcomes if training data mirror historical bias; security risks in identity verification	Tiered escalation to humans; restricted generation on regulated topics; continuous red-teaming; privacy-by-design with data minimization; public logs of model updates and known limitations
S5. Digital Program Formats - online MBAs, MOOCs, and executive education with AI-curated resources, discourse analytics, and data-driven cohorting	Recommenders optimizing content–learner fit; network analytics on forums to weight epistemic contribution rather than verbosity; scenario engines for ESG and geopolitics	Personalization at scale; better peer matching and feedback quality; contemporaneous datasets in finance and supply chains; modular pathways for working professionals	Engagement inflation through superficial activity; echo chambers in forums; credential dilution if proctoring is weak; cross-border data transfers triggering legal constraints	Weight forum quality via argument advancement; cap auto-graded share in summative assessment; privacy-respecting proctoring with sunset clauses; jurisdiction-aware data residency
S6. Enablers & Constraints - infrastructure, faculty digital literacies, and cultural–pedagogic fit shaping viability	Cloud capacity, bandwidth stability, device heterogeneity; structured PD pipelines; alignment between learner-centered methods and local assessment cultures	Sustainable adoption trajectories; fewer vendor lock-in traps; higher fidelity in accessibility tooling; better transfer from classroom to industry ecosystems	Bandwidth and power intermittency; fragmented PD that leaves faculty self-teaching; cultural mismatch with dialogic, constructivist assumptions; cost opacity in licensing	Open standards and exit clauses; train-the-trainer guilds with micro-credentials; participatory change management; TCO modeling; inclusive design reviews with student representation

Table 2 should be read as a governance blueprint rather than a vendor catalog. The first column names the operational arena and realistic use-cases; the second unpacks the computational substrate so decision-makers can interrogate validity claims; the third restricts benefits to outcomes repeatedly observed in institutional settings; the fourth lists the predictable pathologies that surface at scale; and the fifth codifies minimal safeguards that transform experimentation into accountable practice. Leadership teams can use the matrix to stage adoption in waves, beginning with low-risk advising bots under strict escalation, then piloting simulations with mandatory reflective debriefs, before graduating to adaptive assessment where reliability is demonstrably robust (Bancoro, 2024; Krammer, 2025). Faculty development units can map their training to the algorithmic primitives described, ensuring conceptual fluency precedes tool fluency (Starkey & Tempest, 2025; Elmassri et al., 2023). Crucially, the enablers row reminds readers that equity hinges on bandwidth, devices, and culturally coherent pedagogy as much as on model elegance. Read holistically, the table renders the current AI landscape legible and governable without blunting its innovative edge.

4. AI FOR ADAPTIVE, INCLUSIVE, AND CONTEXTUALIZED BUSINESS LEARNING

The present moment invites a shift from abstract proclamations about artificial intelligence to a granular cartography of pedagogical affordances that actually move the needle on equity, access, and cognitive rigor in business education (Kopnina, Hughes, Zhang, Russell, Fellinger, Smith, & Tickner, 2024; Rejeb, Rejeb, Appolloni, Treiblmaier, & Iranmanesh, 2024). Instead of treating personalization, localization, and ethics as aspirational slogans, the matrix below articulates what each capability demands in computational terms, what it delivers in measurable outcomes, where it predictably fails, and how to instrument governance so innovations do not outpace due process (Suharsono, Hidayat, Zen, Rusmana, & Permansah, 2025; Lubbe, Marais, & Kruger, 2025). To avoid category mistakes and vendor folklore, nomenclature is normalized and legacy labels updated where needed; for example, the widely cited "Knewton" ecosystem is properly referenced by its current instantiation as Wiley's Alta. Likewise, claims about multilingual fidelity, case morphogenesis, or game-theoretic simulations are framed as capabilities achieved under realistic constraints rather than limitless promises. By synthesizing learning science, sociotechnical analysis, accessibility research, and organizational governance into a single decision architecture, the analysis anticipates both the promise and the perils of AI-enabled teaching at scale (Winkler, Hammoda, Noyes, & Van Gelderen, 2023; Avelar, Mitchell, & Sandes-Guimarães, 2025). The result is a pragmatic instrument for deans, faculty, and learning designers seeking accountable innovation rather than rhetorical flourish.

Table 3. Equitable AI Pedagogies for Contemporary Business Education Systems

Capability Domain & Signature Use-Cases	Computational Substrate & Data Topology	Observed Learning, Access, and Inclusion Effects	Failure Modes & Corrective Countermeasures	Operationalization Playbook & Audit Metrics
C1. Adaptive Learning Engines - mastery-based sequencing in quantitative finance, managerial accounting, statistics; exemplars include Squirrel-style adaptivity and Wiley's Alta (successor to Knewton)	Item-response theory blended with reinforcement learning; learner-model feature stores from clickstream latencies, error taxonomies, and misconception graphs; knowledge maps with prerequisite topology	Earlier detection of fragile concepts; differentiated pacing that stabilizes persistence for heterogeneous cohorts; uplift in completion for cognitively demanding modules without diluting rigor	Canalization that narrows exploration; opaque success criteria; telemetry over-collection creating privacy exposure; misalignment with program outcomes	Publish human-readable model cards; opt-out and manual overrides; stepped-wedge trials before scale; require post-hoc concept maps evidencing transfer; audit data retention and consent artifacts
C2. UDL-Aligned Differentiated Instruction - multimodal artefacts, accessibility-first dashboards, real-time accommodations	Multimodal generation pipelines (text, audio, visualization); adaptive color and contrast models; alternative text and captioning engines; device-aware rendering	Reduced barriers for learners with sensory differences; parity in analytic tasks via accessible visuals; higher engagement for diverse cognitive profiles	Surface-level multimodality that ignores cognitive load; visual semiotics that miscue across cultures; brittle accommodations in low-bandwidth contexts	Apply Universal Design for Learning checkpoints; run cultural and accessibility reviews; ship offline/low-spec variants; measure task parity gaps and time-on-task differentials
C3. Generative AI for Case-Based Pedagogy - branching cases, negotiation labs, dynamic stakeholder behaviors	Large language models with retrieval over curated corpora; stateful simulators injecting regulatory and market shocks; controllable generation with safety rails	Heightened cognitive immersion; improved transfer of strategic reasoning to novel contexts; richer evidence for judgment under uncertainty	Hallucinated facts and spurious citations; overfitting to Western business archetypes; erosion of faculty intellectual authorship	Curate bounded, verified repositories; require faculty sign-off on prompts and outputs; student disclosure of AI use; embed counterfactual checks; track novelty and factual error rates

continued on following page

Table 3. Continued

Capability Domain & Signature Use-Cases	**Computational Substrate & Data Topology**	**Observed Learning, Access, and Inclusion Effects**	**Failure Modes & Corrective Countermeasures**	**Operationalization Playbook & Audit Metrics**
C4. Multilingual Localization & Translation - synchronous interpretation, domain-aware subtitling, terminology normalization	Transformer-based neural machine translation with domain glossaries; speech-to-text and text-to-speech pipelines; locale metadata for idiom and register	Expanded participation beyond Anglophone dominance; faster comprehension in technical seminars; lower attrition in global cohorts	Semantic drift on idioms and legal terms; overconfident mistranslations in high-stakes settings; exclusion of low-resource languages	Maintain vetted bilingual glossaries; human review for assessment and compliance contexts; confidence-threshold gating; support right-to-left scripts; monitor error distributions by language
C5. Storytelling, Gamification & ESG Simulators - narrative analytics, long-horizon sustainability games, supply-chain shocks	Agent-based models, Monte Carlo scenario engines, and payoff matrices; telemetry on decision paths and feedback loops; geospatial and climate overlays	Stronger motivation and persistence; systems thinking about trade-offs across profit, people, and planet; durable understanding of feedback and lag effects	Goodhart effects when scores become targets; neglect of qualitative factors like trust and legitimacy; exclusion for learners with limited device capacity	Pair quantitative play with reflective debriefs; rotate hidden parameters to prevent gaming; require stakeholder ethnographies; offer low-spec modes; track depth of reflection and bias in choices
C6. Equity, Cultural Plurality & Bias Mitigation - participatory dataset curation, context-aware cases, fairness testing	Data provenance ledgers; participatory labeling with faculty, students, practitioners; fairness diagnostics (group, individual, counterfactual); geospatial and socio-economic context layers	Inclusion of Indigenous, informal, and regional business epistemes; reduced demographic performance gaps; greater legitimacy and cultural fidelity	Western-centric corpora erasing local knowledge; gendered leadership tropes; fairness trade-offs hidden by aggregate metrics	Constitute multi-stakeholder review councils; publish dataset statements; run pre-mortems and red-team audits; report parity, calibration, and counterfactual fairness; institute appeal and override channels

Read as a governance instrument rather than a vendor catalog, Table 3 makes the contemporary promise of AI tractable without romanticism. The first column clarifies the pedagogical intent and authentic use-cases that matter for managerial formation; the second discloses the algorithmic plumbing so claims can be interrogated for validity; the third narrows benefits to effects repeatedly observed under institutional constraints; the fourth anticipates pathologies that reliably appear at scale and pairs them with proportionate remedies; and the fifth codifies minimum safeguards and metrics that convert experimentation into accountable practice. Program leaders can sequence adoption from low-risk multilingual access tools to adaptive engines once reliability and transparency thresholds are met (Akpan, Razavi, & Akpan, 2025; O'Dea & O'Dea, 2023). Faculty can align assessment designs with the disclosure and audit regimes specified. Quality-assurance bodies can lift the parity and calibration indicators directly into periodic reviews. By insisting on parity between pedagogic ambition and ethical plausibility, the matrix advances a vision of AI that is rigorous, inclusive, and locally resonant while remaining operationally feasible.

5. LEARNING ANALYTICS, DATA-DRIVEN INSTRUCTION, AND PREDICTIVE ASSESSMENT

The algorithmic permeation of artificial intelligence into business education has catalyzed a paradigmatic reconfiguration of learning analytics, from a peripheral, retrospective reporting function into a central epistemic engine driving pedagogical design, formative and summative assessment architectures, and macro-level institutional strategy (Viera Trevisan, Machado do Nascimento, Leal Filho, & Ávila Pedrozo, 2024; Mason, Anderson, Black, & Roberts, 2024). AI now enables not merely the high-resolution capture of micro-level learner behavioral telemetry, but also the real-time inferential modeling of such data to inform instructional modulation, anticipate performance trajectories, and algorithmically prescribe targeted interventions (Wang, Shi, & Jiang, 2024; Patnaik, Mahapatra, & Baral, 2023). Yet, the pedagogical promise of these affordances is inextricable from their latent perils, i.e., the technocratic drift toward learner profiling, the attenuation of informed consent protocols, and the algorithmic canalization of educational experience into pre-determined cognitive pathways (Dwivedi, 2025; Keiper, Fried, Lupinek, & Nordstrom, 2023).

Descriptive Analytics

Descriptive analytics, in its AI-augmented form, functions as an empirical cartography of the learner's digital footprint. Advanced learning management systems, augmented with machine vision and event-stream processing, now record behavioral data at a granularity inconceivable in earlier pedagogical regimes. In the University of Michigan's Ross School of Business online operations management modules, AI subsystems capture not only synchronous attendance metrics but also micro-interaction patterns, i.e., temporal segments where learners pause, replay, or disengage from instructional video streams. These temporal engagement signatures are cross-correlated with cognitive performance indices, enabling faculty to algorithmically detect conceptual choke points warranting curricular recalibration

(Parihar, 2025; Ibrahim & Storey, 2025). Similarly, in ESCP Business School's executive programs, AI-driven interaction trackers produce heatmaps that differentiate between passive presence and high-valence contributions. Such visualizations, disaggregated by gender, cultural origin, and participation frequency, furnish faculty with empirical substrates for equity-oriented facilitation strategies, counteracting participation asymmetries that might otherwise remain invisible.

Predictive Analytics

Predictive analytics extends this descriptive foundation into probabilistic foresight, employing multivariate historical and real-time inputs to estimate the likelihood of future educational events, i.e., course completion, grade band attainment, or skill mastery (Ahuja, 2024; Ar, Ward, García, & Abbas, 2023). At Arizona State University's W. P. Carey School of Business, predictive engines ingest over 300 independent variables, including platform login periodicity, temporal clustering of assignment submissions, and sentiment polarity extracted from forum discourse, to output weekly risk scores. High-risk designations trigger automated, context-sensitive nudges via SMS or email, often coupled with human-mediated resource interventions (Abdalla, Bhat, Tiwari, Khan, & Wedajo, 2024; Ratten, Hasan, Kumar, Bustard, Ojala, & Salamzadeh, 2024). In the Asia-Pacific, the National University of Singapore's business programs algorithmically forecast internship readiness by triangulating simulation performance metrics, case-analysis rigor, and collaborative interaction quality. Such anticipatory diagnostics empower career services to deploy targeted skill-bridging modules well in advance of recruitment cycles, thereby measurably improving placement statistics. Corporate academies, such as those operated by Unilever, use similar predictive apparatuses to identify high-innovation-potential employees by detecting patterns of divergent thinking and adaptive problem-solving in digital training environments. Yet, this classificatory power necessitates epistemic caution, i.e., predictive labeling, if uncritically operationalized, risks becoming a self-fulfilling prophecy, amplifying entrenched biases under the guise of meritocratic identification.

Prescriptive Analytics

Prescriptive analytics occupies the apex of the data-informed pedagogical continuum, transitioning from probabilistic forecasting to algorithmically generated intervention design. Embedding e-commerce–style recommender systems within business school LMS platforms, institutions such as IE Business School in Madrid tailor individualized study itineraries, curating supplementary case literature, allocating peer discussion clusters, or directing learners to micro-modules that directly address diagnostic competency gaps. At Melbourne Business School, prescriptive systems in corporate finance courses detect persistent difficulties with derivatives pricing models, triggering automated provision of alternative problem sets and, if performance plateaus, escalating to synchronous faculty consultation. These closed-loop architectures instantiate a cybernetic feedback system wherein learner performance telemetry directly and dynamically sculpts instructional delivery.

Feedback Loops and Instructor Response Patterns

The epistemic efficacy of learning analytics is contingent upon the interpretive and adaptive capacity of faculty end-users. AI-generated dashboards, if misinterpreted, can produce reductive pedagogical responses, e.g., over-privileging quantitative engagement metrics at the expense of qualitative insight (Clegg & Sarkar, 2024; Ambrose & Isadore, 2024). For example, truncated "*time-on-task*" readings might erroneously be equated with disengagement, when they may instead indicate high mastery and cognitive efficiency. The Indian School of Business mitigates this interpretive risk through faculty development programs that train instructors to integrate dashboard outputs with ethnographic classroom observations, learner self-reports, and low-stakes formative assessments, thereby producing a polyvocal and triangulated learner profile resistant to algorithmic misclassification.

Visual Analytics in Performance Dashboards

Visual analytics, such as interactive, multimodal representations of high-dimensional educational data, are increasingly embedded in AI-powered dashboards, enabling both faculty and learners to engage with dynamic, comparative, and drill-down views of performance (Zhang & Leong, 2024; Rane, Choudhary, & Rane, 2023). Tableau augmented with Einstein AI and Microsoft Power BI integrated with Azure Machine Learning provide visual affordances for benchmarking cohort trajectories, mapping competency acquisition rates, and simulating counterfactual learning pathways. In INSEAD's strategic management modules, such dashboards visualize the longitudinal impact of simulation-based strategic decisions on profitability curves and sustainability indices, reinforcing systems-thinking competencies. Executive education contexts exploit similar tools for leadership competency mapping, surfacing non-linear growth spurts such as post-residency surges in intercultural communication efficacy.

Data Justice and Ethical Concerns

Despite their operational sophistication, AI-driven analytics infrastructures raise critical concerns from a data justice perspective. Algorithmic profiling can induce personalization traps, thus continually reinforcing extant learner strengths while algorithmically occluding exposure to novel intellectual terrains (Mumtaz, Carmichael, Weiss, & Nimon-Peters, 2025; Vecchiarini & Somia, 2023). Consent asymmetries persist, with many learners unaware of the depth of telemetry capture, including keystroke dynamics, cursor movement heatmaps, and biometric affect recognition via webcam. Historical precedents highlight these hazards, e.g., in 2021, a UK university's geolocation-enabled attendance tracker provoked organized student protest over non-consensual spatial data collection. Similarly, a U.S. business school's use of predictive analytics to influence grading leniency for "*at-risk*" learners raised acute questions about procedural fairness, academic rigor, and the epistemic legitimacy of algorithmically mediated grading policies.

Towards Transparent and Participatory Analytics

Mitigation pathways increasingly converge on explainable AI (XAI) and participatory design methodologies. At the University of Sydney Business School, dashboard interfaces incorporate "*Why This Recommendation?*" affordances that disclose, in human-readable form, the variables and weighting logics underpinning algorithmic prescriptions. Participatory dashboard co-design, wherein students and faculty co-determine analytic metrics, visualization modalities, and intervention thresholds, has emerged as a praxis for enhancing trust, interpretive validity, and contextual relevance (Surugiu, Grădinaru, & Surugiu, 2024; Vashista, Gugnani, Bala, & Kumar, 2023). Robust ethical data governance frameworks now function as a structural imperative, encompassing opt-in consent schemas for sensitive telemetry, finite retention policies, and periodic third-party algorithmic audits to detect disparate impact or discriminatory inference. While compliance with meta-regulatory regimes such as the EU's General Data Protection Regulation constitutes a minimal baseline, sector-specific governance architectures are increasingly recognized as essential for addressing the distinctive relational, pedagogical, and epistemic stakes of AI deployment in business education.

6. ETHICAL GOVERNANCE AND ALGORITHMIC EQUITY IN BUSINESS EDUCATION

The algorithmic infusion of artificial intelligence into the pedagogical, administrative, and evaluative infrastructures of business education foregrounds unavoidable questions of distributive justice, procedural transparency, institutional accountability, and epistemic power (Grájeda, Burgos, Córdova, & Sanjinés, 2024; Zhou, Zhang, & Chan, 2024). As machine-learning–driven systems become deeply enmeshed in curriculum orchestration, assessment regimes, learner advising, and administrative decision-making, they do not merely mediate learning transactions; they actively shape the distributional logics through which recognition, opportunity, and institutional capital are allocated (Urmeneta & Romero, 2024; Essien, Bukoye, O'Dea, & Kremantzis, 2024). Ethical governance of AI in business education is thus not an ancillary policy addendum but a constitutive safeguard, essential for maintaining academic integrity, protecting learner rights, and ensuring equitable access within a globalized knowledge economy (Colombo, 2023; Akhtar, Moazzam, Ashraf, & Khan, 2024).

Bias and Fairness in AI-Powered Learning Systems

Algorithmic systems invariably inherit, amplify, or reconfigure the biases encoded in their training corpora. In educational contexts, such biases manifest in evaluative instruments, recommender algorithms, and predictive performance models. Automated essay scoring engines, e.g., using natural language processing and statistical pattern recognition, have empirically demonstrated differential penalization of non-native English speakers, notwithstanding parity in substantive argument quality (Ngwenya, 2024; Suryanarayana, Kandi, Pavani, Rao, Rout, & Krishna, 2024). A 2020 UK study on AI-mediated grading of business school entrance essays documented systemic disadvantage for applicants from underrepresented geographies, a distortion traceable to training data overfitted to Western academic discourse norms. Gendered and socio-economic skews likewise infiltrate AI-mediated curricular navigation. In one North American business school, an entrepreneurship-course recommender system disproportionately surfaced venture finance case studies with male founders, entrenching hegemonic leadership archetypes. Absent deliberate counterbalancing through dataset diversification and fairness constraints, such epistemic asymmetries risk reinforcing structural inequities in both academic and subsequent corporate leadership pipelines.

Opaque Decision-Making and the Black Box Problem

The epistemological opacity of many AI architectures, colloquially the "*black box*" phenomenon, presents acute challenges for educational legitimacy. When predictive analytics designate a learner as "*unlikely to succeed*" or when algorithmic scoring returns an anomalously low grade, the absence of an auditable inferential pathway undermines trust and due process. In the Netherlands (2021), contested AI-assigned grades in a corporate finance module precipitated reputational damage and policy revisions after faculty could not reconstruct the model's internal reasoning. This opacity extends to algorithmic advising. AI chatbots that optimize course recommendations based on historical success metrics may inadvertently herd students into "*safe*" curricular pathways, thereby constraining intellectual exploration and reinforcing path dependency (Lakshmi, Kumar, Kumar, Patel, Naik, & Ramesh, 2023; Alam & Mohanty, 2023). Without interpretable model architectures and transparent rationale disclosure, both learners and faculty are disempowered from contesting or recalibrating the algorithmic determinations shaping academic trajectories.

Consent and Surveillance

The algorithmic augmentation of educational environments has also intensified surveillance capacities, both in scope and granularity. Beyond clickstream analytics and engagement telemetry, certain systems now harvest biometric signatures, facial recognition data, and affective analytics via webcam-based proctoring, ostensibly in the service of academic integrity (Dong & Dong, 2023; Alqahtani & Wafula, 2025). Such practices raise acute privacy and civil liberties concerns. In 2021, coalitions of student unions in the United States and Canada petitioned against remote proctoring platforms that algorithmically flagged "*suspicious*" behavior based on ocular micro-movements and keystroke rhythms, i.e., metrics that disproportionately targeted neurodivergent learners and students with disabilities. In business schools, where professional networking and corporate recruitment are integral to the learner experience, behavioral data extraction extends into career services ecosystems. AI-mediated recruitment platforms embedded within MBA programs may monitor interaction frequencies with employer portals, navigational pathways in virtual job fairs, and even paralinguistic features in AI-moderated mock interviews. Absent explicit opt-in consent and robust governance protocols, such practices risk collapsing the boundary between educational data and personal-professional identity traces.

AI Auditing and Accreditation

Ethically defensible AI governance mandates independent, methodologically rigorous auditing of algorithmic systems. While AI ethics audits are established practice in high-stakes domains such as finance, aviation, and healthcare, their uptake in higher education remains emergent (Yadav & Shrawankar, 2025; Allen & Edelson, 2024). These audits interrogate dataset representativeness, model interpretability, and disparate impact, and assess alignment with institutional mission and societal values, as recommended by the European Commission's High-Level Expert Group on AI. Accreditation agencies are beginning to formalize these expectations. The Association to Advance Collegiate Schools of Business (AACSB) has initiated exploratory pathways for embedding AI ethics criteria into its *Responsible Management Education* standards. The prospective result is that business schools may be required to evidence ethical AI deployment across curriculum design, assessment systems, and administrative operations as a prerequisite for reaccreditation.

Algorithmic Accountability Frameworks

Global normative frameworks provide scaffolding for algorithmic accountability. The FAT-ML (Fairness, Accountability, and Transparency in Machine Learning) principles codify interpretability, bias testing, and human-in-the-loop oversight as non-negotiables. UNESCO's 2021 *Recommendation on the Ethics of Artificial Intelligence* enjoins educational systems to protect human rights, uphold cultural plurality, and secure equitable access in AI applications. The European Union's forthcoming AI Act is poised to classify educational AI tools for grading, profiling, and high-stakes decision-making as "*high-risk*," subjecting them to stringent compliance regimes. Operationalizing accountability in business education requires a tiered oversight architecture, i.e., at the micro-level, faculty-led "*bias drills*" stress-test algorithmic outputs against demographically and cognitively diverse student samples; at the meso-level, institutional ethics committees vet procurement and deployment against pedagogical and equity benchmarks; at the macro-level, universities publish annual AI impact reports disclosing system usage, audit outcomes, and remediation measures.

Case Studies of Governance Failures and Lessons Learned

The 2020 Ofqual algorithmic grading crisis in the UK stands as a paradigmatic cautionary episode. Designed to normalize A-level grades amidst pandemic exam cancellations, the model disproportionately downgraded students from under-resourced schools while inflating outcomes for elite institutions, triggering mass public protest and governmental retraction. The implication for business education is explicit, i.e., algorithms intersecting with pre-existing social inequities require rigorous ex ante equity audits and stress testing. Similarly, in 2019, a U.S. university's plagiarism detection system erroneously flagged multiple MBA candidates for misconduct, misclassifying properly cited material as plagiarized. The absence of a transparent appeals process and procedural safeguards exacerbated reputational harm, highlighting the necessity for both technical rectitude and institutional due process.

Building a Culture of Ethical AI Use

Ethical governance cannot be reduced to procedural compliance checklists; it must be embedded as a cultural and cognitive disposition within the institution. This entails cultivating algorithmic literacy among faculty, learners, and administrators, nurturing a capacity to interrogate, critique, and co-shape AI deployments (Bell & Bell, 2023; Kangiwa et al., 2024). The University of Cape Town's faculty development initiative exemplifies this ethos, engaging instructors in the critical evaluation of AI tools and involving them directly in procurement vetting and post-deployment review cycles. Some institutions are institutionalizing student-led AI ethics boards, granting learners agency in reviewing and providing structured feedback on AI systems impacting their education. Such participatory governance democratizes oversight, enhances system legitimacy, and embeds ethical reflexivity as a core managerial competency, i.e., skills directly translatable to corporate AI governance contexts that graduates will navigate in their professional trajectories.

7. AI FOR EXECUTIVE AND PROFESSIONAL TRAINING IN SUSTAINABILITY AND ESG

The ascendance of environmental, social, and governance (ESG) imperatives within corporate strategy has precipitated an unprecedented demand for senior decision-makers capable of operationalizing sustainability principles as integral components of strategic calculus. Artificial intelligence, by virtue of its capacity for high-dimensional data synthesis, adaptive knowledge curation, and simulation of complex socio-ecological-economic systems, has emerged as a pivotal enabler in reconfiguring executive education and professional training architectures for ESG competencies. This pedagogical transformation transcends the rarefied domain of elite MBA alumni, extending to mid-career professionals, entrepreneurs in emergent economies, and corporate boards navigating intensifying regulatory regimes and investor activism in the sustainability arena.

AI-Based ESG Literacy Platforms

AI-powered ESG literacy ecosystems operationalize machine learning algorithms to construct highly granular, profession-specific learning trajectories that are responsive to sectoral exigencies and jurisdictional regulatory architectures. Examples such as GreenPro AI (Singapore) and SustainLearn (European Union) algorithmically curate instructional modules encompassing circular economy operationalization, probabilistic climate risk modeling, and carbon accounting protocols, each parametrized to the learner's industry, role complexity, and compliance horizon. A senior energy-sector executive may engage with advanced Scope 3 emissions accounting simulations incorporating lifecycle analyses, whereas a medium-scale manufacturing entrepreneur might be guided through AI-optimized supply chain decarbonization frameworks integrating local infrastructure constraints. The epistemic dynamism of these systems is sustained by continuous ingestion of policy artefacts, such as the EU Corporate Sustainability Reporting Directive (CSRD) and the U.S. SEC's climate disclosure mandates, alongside peer-reviewed environmental science and corporate sustainability disclosures. This enables near real-time content recalibration, ensuring alignment with evolving compliance matrices and emergent best practices.

AI in Corporate Training for Sustainability

Multinational corporations are embedding AI within in-house sustainability academies to engineer knowledge cascades across hierarchical strata. Accenture's global sustainability academy, for example, employs role-adaptive AI matching algorithms to map employees to targeted modules in renewable energy integration, ESG disclosure frameworks, and algorithmic governance of responsible AI, using prior learning histories, role metadata, and simulation performance diagnostics. IBM has architected AI-powered negotiation simulators wherein managerial cohorts engage with stakeholder constellations in environmental trade-off scenarios; the AI engine dynamically reconfigures stakeholder priorities based on participant discourse, thereby replicating the fluidity of real-world bargaining. Tata Consultancy Services integrates AI-enabled decision analytics into its sustainability workshops, algorithmically evaluating participants' strategic choices against multi-decade environmental and social impact indices, thus providing immediate formative feedback coupled with longitudinal impact tracking for applied projects.

AI-Powered Sustainability Simulations

The inherent complexity of sustainability challenges, entailing non-linear interactions between ecological, economic, and socio-political subsystems, renders them particularly amenable to AI-mediated simulation. Platforms such as the Climate Action Simulator, developed at Imperial College London's Grantham Institute, integrate dynamic climate models, commodity market stochasticity, and geopolitical volatility parameters. Within executive education contexts, participants manipulate policy levers such as carbon pricing, renewable infrastructure investment, and biodiversity conservation interventions, observing the emergent systemic equilibria across financial viability, social equity, and ecological resilience metrics. Such simulations scaffold "*future-back*" strategic reasoning, enabling executives to reverse-engineer present-day decision architectures from preferred long-term sustainability outcomes. Board-level training modules have employed these simulations to stress-test strategic portfolios under Intergovernmental Panel on Climate Change–defined 2°C and 1.5°C warming scenarios, revealing latent vulnerabilities in asset exposure, supply chain dependencies, and stakeholder license-to-operate.

Digital Credentials and Badging

Artificial intelligence is reconfiguring the epistemic economy of professional credentialing in sustainability. Blockchain-anchored micro-credentials and competency badges, conferred upon the AI-verified completion of targeted modules, offer portable, verifiable attestations of specialized proficiencies such as climate finance modeling, ESG data visualization, or inclusive leadership in sustainable innovation. Platforms including Credly and Accredible embed AI-verification subroutines to authenticate that credential recipients have not only completed theoretical assessments but have also demonstrated applied mastery in simulations and portfolio submissions evaluated through both human expert panels and algorithmic scoring systems. For instance, attainment of a "*Sustainable Supply Chain Leadership*" credential might require the learner to navigate AI-generated case analyses, engage in stochastic scenario planning for resource volatility, and submit an implementation blueprint subjected to hybrid human-machine assessment protocols. Such credentials are increasingly embedded into hiring, promotion, and board appointment criteria by forward-leaning corporate governance bodies.

Ensuring Equity in Access to ESG Training

Without equity-oriented design interventions, the proliferation of AI-enabled ESG training risks exacerbating global disparities in access to sustainability knowledge systems. High-bandwidth content streams, corporate sponsorship dependencies, and elite institutional gatekeeping can marginalize rural entrepreneurs, SMEs, and professionals in bandwidth-constrained geographies. Initiatives such as the UN Global Compact's Academy have collaborated with AI platform providers to develop low-bandwidth, conceptually uncompromised training variants incorporating SMS-based AI learning prompts and compressed multimedia resources for learners in Sub-Saharan Africa and South Asia. Epistemic inclusivity also mandates that AI training corpora integrate indigenous ecological knowledge systems and community-led resource stewardship models. Failure to diversify the epistemic provenance of training datasets risks reproducing Western corporate sustainability paradigms at the expense of culturally embedded, locally efficacious practices, which is an omission with both ethical and strategic liabilities in pluralistic market environments.

AI for Sector-Specific ESG Capacity Building

The utility of AI in ESG training is magnified when tailored to sector-specific sustainability imperatives. In the maritime domain, AI-driven navigational optimization simulators train port authorities and shipping executives to minimize carbon emissions while preserving logistical profitability under varying meteorological and regulatory constraints. In agribusiness, AI-enabled platforms integrate climate projection ensembles, soil nutrient mapping, and crop yield forecasting to facilitate the adoption of regenerative agricultural practices calibrated to local ecological baselines. Financial services leadership teams increasingly employ AI for ESG portfolio modeling, simulating the performance trajectories of green bonds, sustainability-linked debt instruments, and impact investment vehicles across divergent market volatility profiles and regulatory interventions. These simulations enable decision-makers to architect investment strategies that reconcile fiduciary return mandates with environmental stewardship and social impact objectives, aligning corporate capital allocation with emergent ESG fiduciary norms.

8. A FRAMEWORK FOR RESPONSIBLE, AI-ENABLED, SUSTAINABLE BUSINESS EDUCATION

For contemporary business schools and corporate training consortia, the operative question is no longer whether to embed artificial intelligence into pedagogical and administrative ecosystems, but rather how to enact such integration in a manner that is normatively defensible, pedagogically robust, and structurally aligned with the imperatives of planetary sustainability (Dubay & Richards, 2024; Gunawan & Shieh, 2023). The exigency lies in architecting a governance framework that directs AI from being a mere computational affordance toward functioning as a catalytic infrastructure for ethical judgment formation, inclusive epistemic participation, and systemic transformation toward regenerative economic paradigms. The framework below distills actionable design pillars derived from preceding theoretical and empirical analyses, intended for curriculum architects, institutional strategists, and EdTech system developers.

Pillar 1: Ethical Pedagogy

Ethical pedagogy presupposes that AI-mediated instructional interventions must be anchored in the inviolability of learner autonomy, intrinsic dignity, and critical consciousness. Within this paradigm, AI is positioned not as a surrogate for faculty judgment but as an augmentative intelligence, supporting, but never supplanting, human evaluative authority. This requires embedding transparent appeals mechanisms into automated grading or recommendation pipelines, mandating human-in-the-loop oversight at decisive evaluative junctures, and using algorithmic scaffolds to provoke reflective praxis. In leadership education, for example, AI prompts could algorithmically surface the socio-environmental externalities of strategic decisions, compelling learners to integrate normative reasoning into their strategic calculus alongside technical optimization.

Pillar 2: AI Literacy

Responsible AI deployment necessitates bidirectional literacy, i.e., learners and educators must apprehend not only the functional mechanics and affordances of AI but also its epistemic limitations, sociopolitical externalities, and embedded value systems. In business education, AI literacy must extend beyond computational fluency to encompass critical interrogation of algorithmic bias, provenance of training datasets, and governance architectures (Thottoli, Cruz, & Al Abri, 2025; Kunacheva, Niyomves, & Kenaphoom, 2024). Operationalization might include mandatory AI ethics and governance modules across MBA and executive programs, reverse-engineering exercises in which students fine-tune algorithms on heterogeneous datasets to observe differential output behavior, and structured case analyses of corporate AI governance failures. Graduates thus emerge as not merely competent AI end-users but as organizational actors capable of influencing responsible AI policy within corporate and public governance spheres.

Pillar 3: Data Governance

In AI-mediated pedagogical systems, data constitutes both the operational substrate and a repository of sensitive identity markers (Gupta, Mahajan, Badhera, & Kushwaha, 2024; Batat, 2024). A robust data governance regime must therefore instantiate *privacy-by-design* architectures, explicit and revocable informed-consent protocols, and legally binding constraints on data retention and secondary utilization.

Normative best practices include data minimization, i.e., restricting collection to variables essential for declared pedagogical objectives, and employing encryption and differential privacy in both storage and transmission layers. Furthermore, algorithmic transparency regarding data utilization, whether in predictive dropout analytics, adaptive content tailoring, or institutional policy formation, must be codified and accessible to all stakeholders.

Pillar 4: Sustainability Integration

To operationalize sustainability within AI-enabled business education, curricula must be explicitly mapped to globally recognized frameworks such as the United Nations Sustainable Development Goals, the circular economy schema, and the planetary boundaries model. AI systems can simulate the dual financial and ecological consequences of strategic decision-making, enabling learners to reconcile profitability imperatives with long-horizon environmental stewardship (Hamzah, Abdullah, & Ma, 2024; Valcea, Hamdani, & Wang, 2024). For instance, AI-driven operational simulations could integrate carbon pricing elasticity models, hydrological scarcity forecasts, and renewable adoption curves, transforming sustainability from an elective thematic adjunct into a non-negotiable analytical lens across core business disciplines.

Pillar 5: Inclusive Design

Inclusive design mandates that AI-enabled educational architectures accommodate cognitive diversity, linguistic multiplicity, cultural plurality, and infrastructural heterogeneity. This entails deploying multilingual natural language interfaces, embedding assistive technologies for differently-abled learners, and curating business case repositories that reflect variegated economic models, from indigenous cooperative frameworks to transnational conglomerates. Training datasets must be epistemically plural, avoiding homogenization of business logics. In low-bandwidth or resource-constrained contexts, inclusivity translates into lightweight AI architectures capable of asynchronous operation, offline caching, and adaptive degradation without loss of conceptual fidelity.

Pillar 6: Participatory Governance

Participatory governance structures institutionalize the co-determination of AI adoption trajectories by integrating faculty, student, IT governance specialists, and external ethics advisors into decision-making bodies. These AI governance committees review procurement proposals for congruence with pedagogical ethos, monitor real-world equity metrics post-deployment, and commission periodic independent audits of algorithmic performance. Participatory governance also encompasses the creation of bidirectional reporting channels for issue escalation, feedback solicitation, and dissemination of algorithmic documentation in accessible language, thereby embedding transparency and accountability into the AI life cycle.

Tiered Implementation Model

The framework's operationalization recognizes that institutions differ in their levels of preparedness for AI integration, and thus envisions a tripartite maturity trajectory. At the basic tier, institutions begin by adopting foundational AI functionalities such as plagiarism detection engines and adaptive formative quiz platforms, ensuring these are accompanied by baseline policies on ethics, data governance, and inclusivity. Faculty at this stage receive introductory AI literacy training, and initial sustainability modules are embedded selectively into courses to lay the groundwork for more comprehensive integration. Progressing to the intermediate tier, AI becomes woven across the curriculum through the use of real-time analytics dashboards, sector-specific simulations, and multilingual course delivery systems. Participatory governance mechanisms are fully operational at this level, and sustainability competencies are explicitly mapped to program-level learning outcomes, ensuring alignment between institutional values and educational practice. The advanced tier represents a fully realized AI-enabled learning ecosystem in which ethical pedagogy, AI literacy, rigorous data governance, sustainability integration, inclusive design, and participatory governance are interdependent and systematically embedded. Here, AI tools are co-developed with faculty, students, and other stakeholders, while institutional research units conduct ongoing evaluations of the social and ecological impacts of AI deployment, ensuring that technological innovation remains accountable to broader societal and planetary imperatives.

Alignment with Accreditation Standards

Global accreditation bodies such as the Association to Advance Collegiate Schools of Business (AACSB) are intensifying their focus on *Responsible Management Education* benchmarks, including ethical reasoning, diversity, inclusion, and societal impact. The proposed framework operationally aligns with these evaluative vectors, positioning institutions to not only satisfy accreditation criteria but to signal to external stakeholders, i.e., students, employers, and policymakers, that their graduates possess the epistemic agility and ethical acumen necessary for the conscientious application of AI within the evolving architecture of sustainable business practice.

9. CHALLENGES, RISKS, AND OPPORTUNITIES AHEAD

While the algorithmic integration of artificial intelligence into business education yields demonstrable pedagogical efficiencies, analytic precision, and operational scalability, it simultaneously engenders a complex constellation of systemic tensions (Montes-Martínez & Ramírez-Montoya, 2023; Padovano & Cardamone, 2024). These tensions are not reducible to technical optimization problems; rather, they are deeply imbricated within institutional governance architectures, academic labor dynamics, epistemic hierarchies, cultural ontologies, and geopolitical asymmetries. A critical appraisal of these risks and challenges is indispensable for harnessing AI's transformative potential without abdicating ethical responsibility or undermining sustainability commitments.

Risks: Surveillance Pedagogy

Foremost among the risks is the emergence of *surveillance pedagogy*, wherein AI-embedded instructional environments operationalize continuous monitoring, profiling, and behavioral nudging of learners. The proliferation of remote proctoring platforms, fine-grained clickstream analytics, biometric authentication protocols, and affect-recognition systems risks producing an omnipresent gaze that constrains intellectual risk-taking and creative exploration, i.e., capacities that are central to entrepreneurial ideation and strategic agility. In 2022, multiple European universities experienced coordinated student boycotts in response to AI-enhanced examination surveillance that captured micro-expressions and keystroke cadences, with dissenters framing such measures as infringements on informational privacy and erosions of academic trust. This surveillance logic extends beyond assessment contexts into professional development and career placement infrastructures. AI-mediated talent-matching ecosystems embedded in MBA programs can algorithmically monitor candidate interaction histories, tonal modulation in communications, and scenario-based simulation outputs (Toutain, Jabbouri, & Truong, 2023; George, 2023). While ostensibly beneficial for optimizing employment matches, such datafication produces persistent digital dossiers that may influence downstream employability trajectories in opaque and potentially discriminatory ways.

Risks: Teacher Deskilling

The automation of grading, formative feedback, and even content generation portends the gradual *deskilling* of faculty. Pedagogical craftsmanship, historically cultivated through iterative interpretive engagement with student work, risks attenuation when human instructors are relegated to exception-handling roles for algorithmic outputs (Allil, 2024; Chen, Ifenthaler, Yau, & Sun, 2024). In certain high-enrollment online MBA ecosystems, over half of formative assessments are now wholly machine-scored, with minimal human interpretive intervention. While throughput efficiency increases, the erosion of opportunities for nuanced misconception detection, pastoral mentorship, and innovative curricular experimentation constricts the intellectual agency of educators, shifting their function toward administrative oversight rather than substantive teaching.

Risks: Digital Colonialism

A further epistemic hazard is the entrenchment of *digital colonialism*. AI systems, predominantly engineered by corporate entities domiciled in high-income economies, are frequently trained on datasets encoding Western-centric business norms, market logics, and cultural heuristics. Unmodified transplants of these systems into Global South business schools risk marginalizing indigenous economic epistemologies and reinforcing asymmetrical dependencies on foreign technology vendors. In entrepreneurship education, this can manifest as algorithmic valorization of venture-capital-intensive, Silicon Valley–style innovation archetypes, thereby occluding cooperative, subsistence-oriented, or solidarity economy models that may be locally adaptive.

Risks: Ecological Footprint of AI Models

A paradoxical dimension emerges when AI, instrumental in sustainability pedagogy, possesses a significant environmental externality. The computational demands of training large-scale language models often entail terawatt-hour energy expenditures and substantial water usage for hyperscale data center cooling. A 2023 environmental lifecycle assessment of a major generative AI deployment estimated training-phase emissions on par with over 100 transatlantic passenger flights. For business schools advancing ESG-aligned value propositions, the carbon and resource footprints of AI infrastructures must be explicitly internalized into procurement criteria, operational audits, and carbon accounting disclosures.

Challenges: Faculty Resistance and Institutional Inertia

The assimilation of AI into business education is frequently impeded by faculty apprehension regarding pedagogical sovereignty, workload redistribution, and ethical vulnerabilities associated with automation. Institutional inertia further compounds resistance, particularly in universities encumbered by bureaucratic procurement regimes and siloed decision-making structures. Instances abound where central administrations have championed AI adoption absent substantive faculty co-creation, resulting in underutilized platforms or tools misaligned with the authentic exigencies of discipline-specific instruction.

Challenges: Budget Constraints and Unequal Partnerships

The financial calculus of AI implementation extends beyond licensing fees to encompass infrastructure augmentation, capacity-building for faculty, and ongoing system maintenance. For institutions in low- and middle-income economies, such expenditures may be prohibitive. Asymmetrical contractual arrangements between universities and EdTech vendors exacerbate the vulnerability; proprietary bundling of AI functionalities with locked-content ecosystems can impose long-term vendor dependency, curtailing institutional adaptability and customization autonomy.

Opportunities: South–South Collaboration

Counterbalancing these risks are emergent opportunities to reconceptualize AI in business education as a site of *polycentric collaboration*. South–South consortia, linking universities in Africa, Asia, and Latin America, are pooling technical and financial resources to co-develop AI pedagogical platforms calibrated to regional business ecologies. A notable initiative between universities in Kenya, India, and Brazil has yielded a shared AI-based sustainable supply chain simulation framework, integrating locally sourced datasets from each context. Such collaborative architectures attenuate cost barriers while ensuring epistemic and cultural specificity.

Opportunities: AI for Indigenous Knowledge Preservation

AI also presents novel affordances for the preservation and curricular integration of indigenous economic systems. Natural language processing engines, fine-tuned on indigenous lexicons and oral-history corpora, can digitize, translate, and curate community-based business methodologies. In Aotearoa New Zealand, AI-assisted initiatives are systematizing Māori entrepreneurial principles into MBA leadership curricula, thereby pluralizing the typologies of business models available to learners and resisting epistemic homogenization.

Opportunities: Decolonial Data Practices

A decolonial data praxis in business education entails co-designing AI training datasets with local stakeholders, prioritizing community consent protocols, and valorizing qualitative, narrative-rich data alongside conventional quantitative indicators

(Lytras, 2023; Maheshkar & Sonwalkar, 2024). Such praxis disrupts the hegemony of shareholder-value maximization paradigms by embedding cooperative, regenerative, and solidarity-based economic frameworks into algorithmic decision architectures, thereby expanding the normative horizon of business education.

Research Agenda

A forward-leaning research agenda is critical for guiding the evolving integration of AI in business education toward outcomes that are both equitable and sustainable. One important strand of inquiry involves developing design heuristics for AI systems intended for non-dominant and resource-constrained educational contexts. This means creating architectures capable of functioning offline, accommodating multiple languages, and embedding local business ontologies so that technological interventions remain culturally and economically relevant. Equally vital is the establishment of longitudinal, mixed-methods evaluation studies capable of tracing AI's influence on learning equity, sustainability literacy, and the career trajectories of graduates long after program completion. Such evaluations would provide the empirical depth necessary to move beyond anecdotal evidence, ensuring that claims of AI's transformative potential are grounded in robust data. Finally, sustained coalition building is essential. This requires bringing together educators, technologists, policymakers, and learners into transdisciplinary alliances that can codify ethical standards, exchange adaptive practices, and shape the normative frameworks governing AI's role in education at both national and transnational levels. Only through such coordinated, evidence-based, and context-sensitive efforts can AI be steered toward serving as a genuine catalyst for inclusive, sustainability-oriented business learning. By interrogating risks and institutional frictions with the same analytical rigor devoted to opportunity mapping, business education can ensure that AI evolves as a vector for inclusive, sustainability-aligned, and contextually resonant learning, rather than as a technological conduit for reproducing inequities, dependency structures, and epistemic monocultures.

10. CONCLUSION

The algorithmic permeation of artificial intelligence into business education has moved decisively beyond the experimental periphery; it now constitutes a structural determinant of how future managers, entrepreneurs, policymakers, and organizational architects are cognitively socialized and ethically enculturated. The central question is no longer whether AI will inhabit the pedagogical and administrative infrastructure of business learning, but rather on whose epistemic terms, toward which normative horizons, and with what systemic consequences for individuals, polities, and the biosphere. The resolution of this question will dictate whether AI consolidates itself as an accelerant of social stratification and ecological degradation, or whether it is reconstituted as an enabling infrastructure for distributive justice, sustainability, and inclusive prosperity. The foregoing analysis highlights that AI's pedagogical potential is not reducible to the econometrics of throughput efficiency or the technocratic allure of hyper-personalized content delivery. Its transformative promise resides in the capacity to scaffold novel modalities of inquiry, simulation, and reflexive praxis, i.e., modalities capable of preparing learners to act with ethical acuity and strategic foresight amid the volatility, uncertainty, complexity, and ambiguity that define contemporary global systems. Designed with intentionality, AI can render visible the intertemporal and interscalar consequences of business decisions, integrate heterogeneous and historically marginalized knowledge systems, and expand epistemic access for constituencies structurally excluded from conventional educational regimes. Yet realizing this emancipatory potential necessitates deliberate governance architectures, epistemic humility in the face of technological overreach, and the fortitude to reject technologically deterministic narratives that present AI adoption as inevitable, apolitical, and universally beneficent.

Reconstituting business education in the AI epoch demands the entrenchment of *ethical pedagogy* as a foundational, non-negotiable stratum. Human educators must remain central to the interpretive, dialogic, and relational dimensions of teaching, even as algorithmic agents absorb repetitive or administratively burdensome tasks. Learners, in turn, must be empowered to interrogate algorithmic decisions, trace the provenance of training data, and critically evaluate the socio-political and environmental implications of technological adoption. Absent such critical reflexivity, AI risks becoming an invisible curriculum designer, narrowing epistemic horizons, privileging dominant business logics, and reifying monocultural models of value creation. The sustainability imperative further intensifies the stakes. The leaders trained in contemporary business programs will be charged with making strategic allocations under climate-constrained, resource-depleted, and socially contested conditions. AI-enabled simulations and predictive analytics afford unparalleled opportunities to rehearse pathways toward decarbonization, circular economy transitions, and regenerative business models. Yet these same infrastructures bear significant environmental externalities in energy consumption, water utilization, and carbon emissions. The paradox of teaching sustainability through resource-intensive computational architectures must be confronted with both technical mitigation strategies, such as the migration to renewable-powered, carbon-neutral data centers, and curricular transparency, wherein learners engage with the environmental cost structures of their digital tools as part of their ethical formation.

Equity and inclusion remain the decisive metrics for responsible AI integration. The digital divide in AI-mediated business learning is not a transient gap but risks hardening into a structural fissure separating AI-fluent elites from digitally disenfranchised majorities. Responsive strategies, such as multilingual AI interfaces, culturally embedded case repositories, and low-bandwidth adaptive platforms, are essential to ensure that AI expands rather than contracts the circumference of opportunity. This is particularly salient in executive and professional education, where AI-mediated ESG and sustainability modules can democratize access to the emergent skill sets and credentials increasingly demanded by global capital markets. Institutional governance must evolve concomitantly. Transparent algorithmic architectures, participatory adoption protocols, and periodic independent audits can forestall the drift toward opaque, corporately dominated educational infrastructures. Accrediting bodies and professional associations have a pivotal role in codifying standards for ethical AI deployment, thereby aligning institutional incentives with broader societal and planetary imperatives. In this way, business schools are not merely passive adopters of AI but active norm entrepreneurs, shaping the cultural and regulatory grammars that will govern AI in the corporate sphere for decades.

The call to action is polycentric. For educators, it entails the critical, creative, and context-sensitive integration of AI into pedagogy. For institutional leaders, it demands the establishment of governance systems that prioritize transparency, equity, and ecological sustainability over expedience. For learners, it necessitates cultivating AI literacy not as a peripheral technical skill but as a core leadership competency for the Anthropocene economy. For policymakers and accreditation authorities, it requires the construction of normative frameworks that safeguard human dignity, cultural plurality, and planetary boundaries amidst accelerating technological flux. Business education has historically functioned as a crucible where alternative futures of economic organization are conceptualized, contested, and rehearsed. In the AI-saturated present, this responsibility is magnified, i.e., the algorithmic infrastructures embedded in classrooms today will reverberate in boardrooms, supply chains, investment portfolios, and policy arenas tomorrow. To reclaim business education for ethical AI and planetary futures is to ensure that every dataset, every algorithm, and every learning experience is aligned with the principles of care, justice, sustainability, and human flourishing. This is not merely a pedagogical design choice; it constitutes an act of transgenerational stewardship. The trajectory forward will be neither linear nor frictionless. It will necessitate navigating dialectical tensions, between innovation and regulation, personalization and distributive equity, computational capability and ecological constraint. Yet the opportunity is profound, i.e., to cultivate a generation of business leaders who apprehend AI not as a monolithic instrument to be optimized for profit maximization, but as a shared socio-technical commons to be governed for the collective good. Should business education rise to this mandate, it will not merely preserve its relevance in an AI-mediated world; it will help architect a world in which technology is harnessed in service to humanity and the planet, rather than the reverse.

REFERENCES

Abdalla, A. A., Bhat, M. A., Tiwari, C. K., Khan, S. T., & Wedajo, A. D. (2024). Exploring ChatGPT adoption among business and management students through the lens of diffusion of Innovation Theory. *Computers and Education: Artificial Intelligence*, *7*, 100257. DOI: 10.1016/j.caeai.2024.100257

Ahuja, V. (2024). Simulations in business education: Unlocking experiential learning. *Practices and implementation of gamification in higher education*, 1-21.

Akhtar, P., Moazzam, M., Ashraf, A., & Khan, M. N. (2024). The interdisciplinary curriculum alignment to enhance graduates' employability and universities' sustainability. *International Journal of Management Education*, *22*(3), 101037. DOI: 10.1016/j.ijme.2024.101037

Akpan, I. J., Razavi, R., & Akpan, A. A. (2025). Evolutionary trends in decision sciences education research from simulation and games to big data analytics and generative artificial intelligence. *Big Data*, big.2024.0128. DOI: 10.1089/big.2024.0128 PMID: 40019821

Alam, A., & Mohanty, A. (2023). Educational technology: Exploring the convergence of technology and pedagogy through mobility, interactivity, AI, and learning tools. *Cogent Engineering*, *10*(2), 2283282. DOI: 10.1080/23311916.2023.2283282

Alfirević, N., Praničević, D. G., & Mabić, M. (2024). Custom-trained large language models as open educational resources: An exploratory research of a business management educational chatbot in croatia and bosnia and herzegovina. *Sustainability (Basel)*, *16*(12), 4929. DOI: 10.3390/su16124929

Allen, S. J., & Edelson, S. A. (2024). Brave new classroom: Navigating educational technology in management education. *Journal of Management Education*, *48*(4), 603–609. DOI: 10.1177/10525629241243339

Allil, K. (2024). Integrating AI-driven marketing analytics techniques into the classroom: Pedagogical strategies for enhancing student engagement and future business success. *Journal of Marketing Analytics*, *12*(2), 142–168. DOI: 10.1057/s41270-023-00281-z

Alqahtani, N., & Wafula, Z. (2025). Artificial intelligence integration: Pedagogical strategies and policies at leading universities. *Innovative Higher Education*, *50*(2), 665–684. DOI: 10.1007/s10755-024-09749-x

Ambrose, P., & Isadore, A. A. (2024, April). Innovations and Learning Technologies for Work Integrated Learning Programs. In *International Conference on Work Integrated Learning* (pp. 353-375). Singapore: Springer Nature Singapore.

Ar, A. Y., Ward, Y. D., García, E. H., & Abbas, A. (2023, January). *Emerging perspectives on sustainability in business schools: a systematic literature review of pedagogical tools in teaching sustainability. In 2023 future of educational innovation-workshop series data in action*. IEEE.

Aure, P. A., & Cuenca, O. (2024). Fostering social-emotional learning through human-centered use of generative AI in business research education: an insider case study. *Journal of research in innovative teaching & learning, 17*(2), 168-181.

Avelar, A. B. A., Mitchell, S. F., & Sandes-Guimarães, L. V. (2025). Integrating sustainable development goals in management education: Impact on student knowledge, attitudes, and behaviors. *International Journal of Management Education, 23*(2), 101116. DOI: 10.1016/j.ijme.2024.101116

Bancoro, J. C. M.Jaysone Christopher M. Bancoro. (2024). The relationship between artificial intelligence (AI) usage and academic performance of business administration students. *International Journal of Asian Business and Management, 3*(1), 27–48. DOI: 10.55927/ijabm.v3i1.7876

Barros, A., Prasad, A., & Śliwa, M. (2023). Generative artificial intelligence and academia: Implication for research, teaching and service. *Management Learning, 54*(5), 597–604. DOI: 10.1177/13505076231201445

Batat, W. (2024). Revolutionizing business and marketing education: The MECCDAL model and a case study from the American Institute of Business Experience Design. *Journal of Macromarketing, 44*(3), 590–601. DOI: 10.1177/02761467241244472

Bathla, A., Chawla, G., Hofaidhllaoui, M., & Dabic, M. (2024). Exploring the dynamics of design thinking in management education and training: A critical review, taxonomic analysis and practical implications. *European Journal of Innovation Management, 27*(9), 337–359. DOI: 10.1108/EJIM-12-2023-1108

Beamond, M. T., Schmitz, M., Cordova, M., Ilieva, M. V., Zhao, S., & Panina, D. (2024). Sustainability in business education: A systematic review and future research agenda. *Critical Perspectives on International Business*.

Bell, R., & Bell, H. (2023). Entrepreneurship education in the era of generative artificial intelligence. *Entrepreneurship Education, 6*(3), 229–244. DOI: 10.1007/s41959-023-00099-x

Benmamoun, M. (2024). Reinventing international business education: Integrating the power of generative AI. *AIB Insights*, *24*(1), 1–7.

Bhaskar, P., & Gupta, P. K. K. (2024). Delving into educators' perspectives on ChatGPT in management education: a qualitative exploration. *Interactive Technology and Smart Education*, (ahead-of-print).

Bhattacharya, S., Kumar, R. V., & Chattopadhyay, S. (2024). Revisiting marketing management teaching pedagogy: A study based on the voice of Indian marketing professionals. *FIIB Business Review*, *13*(3), 364–377. DOI: 10.1177/23197145211006961

Chen, H., & Anyanwu, C. C. (2025). AI in education: Evaluating the impact of moodle AI-powered chatbots and metacognitive teaching approaches on academic performance of higher Institution Business Education students. *Education and Information Technologies*, *30*(9), 1–16. DOI: 10.1007/s10639-024-13235-4

Chen, L., Ifenthaler, D., Yau, J. Y. K., & Sun, W. (2024). Artificial intelligence in entrepreneurship education: A scoping review. *Education + Training*, *66*(6), 589–608. DOI: 10.1108/ET-05-2023-0169

Clegg, S., & Sarkar, S. (2024). Artificial intelligence and management education: A conceptualization of human-machine interaction. *International Journal of Management Education*, *22*(3), 101007. DOI: 10.1016/j.ijme.2024.101007

Colombo, L. A. (2023). Civilize the business school: For a civic management education. *Academy of Management Learning & Education*, *22*(1), 132–149. DOI: 10.5465/amle.2021.0430

Cribben, I., & Zeinali, Y. (2023). The benefits and limitations of ChatGPT in business education and research: A focus on management science, operations management and data analytics. *Operations Management and Data Analytics (March 29, 2023)*.

Dong, F., & Dong, S. (2023). *Research on the optimization of ideological and political education in universities integrating artificial intelligence technology under the guidance of curriculum ideological and political thinking*. ACM Transactions on Asian and Low-Resource Language Information Processing. DOI: 10.1145/3611012

Dubay, C. M., & Richards, M. B. (2024). Leveraging artificial intelligence in project-based service learning to advance sustainable development: A pedagogical approach for marketing education. *Marketing Education Review*, *34*(4), 307–323. DOI: 10.1080/10528008.2024.2411975

Dwivedi, Y. K. (2025). Generative Artificial Intelligence (GenAI) in entrepreneurial education and practice: Emerging insights, the GAIN Framework, and research agenda. *The International Entrepreneurship and Management Journal, 21*(1), 1–21. DOI: 10.1007/s11365-025-01089-2

Elmassri, M., Pajuelo, M. L., Alahbabi, A. A., Alali, A. M., Alzitawi, M., Hussain, H., Alnabhani, K., & Elrazaz, T. (2023). Student perceptions of pedagogical approaches to integrating the SDG 8 into business school education. *Sustainability (Basel), 15*(19), 14084. DOI: 10.3390/su151914084

Essien, A., Bukoye, O. T., O'Dea, X., & Kremantzis, M. (2024). The influence of AI text generators on critical thinking skills in UK business schools. *Studies in Higher Education, 49*(5), 865–882. DOI: 10.1080/03075079.2024.2316881

Farooqi, M. T. K., Amanat, I., & Awan, S. M. (2024). Ethical considerations and challenges in the integration of artificial intelligence in education: A systematic review. *Journal of Excellence in Management Sciences, 3*(4), 35–50. DOI: 10.69565/jems.v3i4.314

Fischer, I., & Dobbins, K. (2024). Is it worth it? How paradoxical tensions of identity shape the readiness of management educators to embrace transformative technologies in their teaching. *Journal of Management Education, 48*(4), 829–848. DOI: 10.1177/10525629231201843

Fleming, P. (2023). "Never let a good crisis go to waste": How consulting firms are using COVID-19 as a pretext to transform universities and business school education. *Academy of Management Learning & Education, 22*(3), 425–438. DOI: 10.5465/amle.2022.0217

George, A. S. (2023). Preparing students for an AI-driven world: Rethinking curriculum and pedagogy in the age of artificial intelligence. *Partners Universal Innovative Research Publication, 1*(2), 112–136.

Grájeda, A., Burgos, J., Córdova, P., & Sanjinés, A. (2024). Assessing student-perceived impact of using artificial intelligence tools: Construction of a synthetic index of application in higher education. *Cogent Education, 11*(1), 2287917. DOI: 10.1080/2331186X.2023.2287917

Gunawan, S., & Shieh, C. J. (2023). Enhancing business students' self-efficacy and learning outcomes: A multiple intelligences and technology approach. *Contemporary Educational Technology, 15*(4), ep470. DOI: 10.30935/cedtech/13647

Gupta, J., & Garg, K. (2025). Reflections on blended learning in management education: A qualitative study with a push-pull migration perspective. *FIIB Business Review*, *14*(3), 323–336. DOI: 10.1177/23197145211013686

Gupta, O. J., & Yadav, S. (2023). Determinants in advancement of teaching and learning in higher education: In special reference to management education. *International Journal of Management Education*, *21*(2), 100823. DOI: 10.1016/j.ijme.2023.100823

Gupta, P., Mahajan, R., Badhera, U., & Kushwaha, P. S. (2024). Integrating generative AI in management education: A mixed-methods study using social construction of technology theory. *International Journal of Management Education*, *22*(3), 101017. DOI: 10.1016/j.ijme.2024.101017

Hamzah, F., Abdullah, A. H., & Ma, W. (2024). Advancing education through Technology Integration, innovative pedagogies and emerging trends: A systematic literature review. *Journal of Advanced Research in Applied Sciences and Engineering Technology*, *41*(1), 44–63. DOI: 10.37934/araset.41.1.4463

Handoyo, S. (2024). Evolving paradigms in accounting education: A bibliometric study on the impact of information technology. *International Journal of Management Education*, *22*(3), 100998. DOI: 10.1016/j.ijme.2024.100998

Hauser, C., & Amann, W. (Eds.). (2023). *The future of responsible management education: University leadership and the digital transformation challenge*. Springer Nature. DOI: 10.1007/978-3-031-15632-8

Herath, D. B., Ode, E., & Herath, G. B. (2025). Can AI replace humans? Comparing the capabilities of AI tools and human performance in a business management education scenario. *British Educational Research Journal*, *51*(3), 1073–1096. DOI: 10.1002/berj.4111

Hermann, R. R., & Fauskanger, E. A. (2025). Institutionalizing international internships in business education: An action research approach to overcoming barriers and driving systemic change in Norwegian business schools. *Scandinavian Journal of Educational Research*, *69*(5), 1042–1062. DOI: 10.1080/00313831.2024.2369882

Ibrahim, Z., & Storey, M. (2025). Being the change: Reaching new learners through PRME's creative pedagogy efforts. *International Journal of Management Education*, *23*(2), 101139. DOI: 10.1016/j.ijme.2025.101139

Jose, E. M. K., Prasanna, A., Kushwaha, B. P., & Das, M. (2024). Can generative AI motivate management students? The role of perceived value and information literacy. *International Journal of Management Education*, *22*(3), 101082. DOI: 10.1016/j.ijme.2024.101082

Kadam, R., & Frempong, G. (2025). Decolonizing management education: A bibliometric analysis of Ubuntu. *International Journal of Educational Management*, *39*(1), 178–197. DOI: 10.1108/IJEM-09-2023-0439

KANGIWA, B. I., OLUDARE, O. E., NASSARAWA, H. S., ABUBAKAR, N. S., EFEOMA, E. L., & ENEFOLA, H. A. (2024). Leveraging artificial intelligence for enhancing entrepreneurship and creativity in STEM education. Journal of Educational Research and Practice.

Karakose, T., & Tülübas, T. (2024). School Leadership and Management in the Age of Artificial Intelligence (AI): Recent Developments and Future Prospects. *Educational Process: International Journal*, *13*(1), 7–14. DOI: 10.22521/edupij.2024.131.1

Keiper, M. C., Fried, G., Lupinek, J., & Nordstrom, H. (2023). Artificial intelligence in sport management education: Playing the AI game with ChatGPT. *Journal of Hospitality, Leisure, Sport and Tourism Education*, *33*, 100456. DOI: 10.1016/j.jhlste.2023.100456

Kopnina, H., Hughes, A. C., Zhang, R., Russell, M., Fellinger, E., Smith, S. M., & Tickner, L. (2024). Business education and its paradoxes: Linking business and biodiversity through critical pedagogy curriculum. *British Educational Research Journal*, *50*(6), 2712–2734. DOI: 10.1002/berj.4048

Krammer, S. M. (2025). Is there a glitch in the matrix? Artificial intelligence and management education. *Management Learning*, *56*(2), 367–388. DOI: 10.1177/13505076231217667

Kučera, D. (2023). Challenges for Responsible Management Education During Digital Transformation. In *The Future of Responsible Management Education: University Leadership and the Digital Transformation Challenge* (pp. 35–60). Springer International Publishing. DOI: 10.1007/978-3-031-15632-8_3

Kunacheva, N., Niyomves, B., & Kenaphoom, S. (2024). Innovative strategies and future trends: The next paradigm of education management. In *Modern Management Science Practices in the Age of AI* (pp. 181–210). IGI Global. DOI: 10.4018/979-8-3693-6720-9.ch007

Lakshmi, A. J., Kumar, A., Kumar, M. S., Patel, S. I., Naik, S. L., & Ramesh, J. V. N. (2023). Artificial intelligence in steering the digital transformation of collaborative technical education. *The Journal of High Technology Management Research*, *34*(2), 100467. DOI: 10.1016/j.hitech.2023.100467

Leyer, M., Yuan, B., Wang, M., & Moormann, J. (2023). Classroom or online learning? Impact of experiential learning in business process management education. *Knowledge Management and E-Learning*, *15*(2), 214–234.

Li, S., Li, Y., & Lin, H. (2023). Research on sustainable teaching models of new business—Take Chinese university business school as an example. *Sustainability (Basel)*, *15*(10), 8037. DOI: 10.3390/su15108037

Lubbe, A., Marais, E., & Kruger, D. (2025). Cultivating independent thinkers: The triad of artificial intelligence, Bloom's taxonomy and critical thinking in assessment pedagogy. *Education and Information Technologies*, *30*(12), 1–34. DOI: 10.1007/s10639-025-13476-x

Lytras, M. (2023, June). Active and transformative learning for the integration of artificial intelligence courses for business school students. In *Conference Proceedings. The Future of Education 2023*.

Maheshkar, C., & Sonwalkar, J. (2024). The pedagogy mix: Teaching marketing effectively in business/management education. *Journal of Applied Research in Higher Education*, *16*(4), 1001–1014. DOI: 10.1108/JARHE-01-2023-0019

Marriott, N., Ratten, V., Higgins, D., Lean, J., Jones, P., Tharapos, M., & Haddoud, M. Y. (2024). Learning from management education researchers. *International Journal of Management Education*, *22*(1), 100938. DOI: 10.1016/j.ijme.2024.100938

Marrone, R., Fowler, S., Bathakur, A., Dawson, S., Siemens, G., & Singh, C. (2025). Perceptions and perspectives of Australian school leaders on the integration of artificial intelligence in schools. *School Leadership & Management*, *45*(1), 30–52. DOI: 10.1080/13632434.2024.2425019

Martins, F., Cezarino, L., Liboni, L., Hunter, T., Batalhao, A., & Paschoalotto, M. A. C. (2024). Unlocking the potential of responsible management education through interdisciplinary approaches. *Sustainable Development (Bradford)*, *32*(3), 2001–2019. DOI: 10.1002/sd.2757

Mason, K., Anderson, L., Black, K., & Roberts, A. (2024). A shout-out for the value of management education research: 'Pedagogy is not a dirty word'. *British Journal of Management*, *35*(2), 539–549. DOI: 10.1111/1467-8551.12805

Montes-Martínez, R., & Ramírez-Montoya, M. S. (2023). Pedagogical models and ICT integration in entrepreneurship education: Literature review. *Cogent Education, 10*(2), 2264026. DOI: 10.1080/2331186X.2023.2264026

Mumtaz, S., Carmichael, J., Weiss, M., & Nimon-Peters, A. (2025). Ethical use of artificial intelligence based tools in higher education: Are future business leaders ready? *Education and Information Technologies, 30*(6), 7293–7319. DOI: 10.1007/s10639-024-13099-8

Narong, D. K. (2025). Business and management education for sustainability: A state-of-the-art review of literature post-UN Decade of Education for Sustainable Development (2015–2023). *International Journal of Management Education, 23*(2), 101115. DOI: 10.1016/j.ijme.2024.101115

Ngwenya, J. (2024). *Learning with generative artificial intelligence in collaborative problem solving: a teaching and learning framework for entrepreneurship education* (Master's thesis, J. Ngwenya).

Nithithanatchinnapat, B., Maurer, J., Deng, X., & Joshi, K. D. (2024). Future business workforce: Crafting a generative AI-centric curriculum today for tomorrow's business education. *The Data Base for Advances in Information Systems, 55*(1), 6–11. DOI: 10.1145/3645057.3645059

O'dea, X., & O'Dea, M. (2023). Is artificial intelligence really the next big thing in learning and teaching in higher education?: A conceptual paper. *Journal of University Teaching & Learning Practice, 20*(5), 1–17. DOI: 10.53761/1.20.5.06

Padovano, A., & Cardamone, M. (2024). Towards human-AI collaboration in the competency-based curriculum development process: The case of industrial engineering and management education. *Computers and Education: Artificial Intelligence, 7*, 100256. DOI: 10.1016/j.caeai.2024.100256

Parihar, U. S. (2025). Cutting-edge Tech Integration in Education and Teaching Practices. *International Journal of Engineering and Management Research.*

Patnaik, R., Mahapatra, D. M., & Baral, S. K. (2023). Post-Covid Challenges and Innovations with Hybrid Pedagogy: A Study of B-Schools in the State of Odisha, India. *South Asian Journal of Management, 30*(2).

Rambe, P. (2023). The flipped classroom effect on entrepreneurship education: Applying critical pedagogy in digital environments. In *Delivering entrepreneurship education in Africa* (pp. 1–31). Emerald Publishing Limited. DOI: 10.1108/978-1-83753-326-820231001

Rane, N., Choudhary, S., & Rane, J. (2023). *Education 4.0 and 5.0: Integrating artificial intelligence (AI) for personalized and adaptive learning*.

Ratten, V., Hasan, R., Kumar, D., Bustard, J., Ojala, A., & Salamzadeh, Y. (2024). Learning from artificial intelligence researchers about international business implications. *Thunderbird International Business Review*, *66*(2), 211–219. DOI: 10.1002/tie.22374

Rejeb, A., Rejeb, K., Appolloni, A., Treiblmaier, H., & Iranmanesh, M. (2024). Exploring the impact of ChatGPT on education: A web mining and machine learning approach. *International Journal of Management Education*, *22*(1), 100932. DOI: 10.1016/j.ijme.2024.100932

Rosenboom, A. (2023). Marketing and artificial intelligence: Responsible management (and marketing) education at the nexus of today and tomorrow. In *The future of responsible management education: University leadership and the digital transformation challenge* (pp. 115–137). Springer International Publishing. DOI: 10.1007/978-3-031-15632-8_7

Saeger, K. J., Finley, L. R., & Wickam, M. J. (2024). The AI revolution: Awareness of and readiness for AI-based digital tools and technologies in business education. *The Journal of Research In Business Education*, *64*(1).

Skritsovali, K. (2023). Learning through playing: Appreciating the role of gamification in business management education during and after the COVID-19 pandemic. *Journal of Management Development*, *42*(5), 388–398. DOI: 10.1108/JMD-04-2023-0124

Starkey, K., & Tempest, S. (2025). The business school and the end of history: Reimagining management education. *Academy of Management Learning & Education*, *24*(1), 111–125. DOI: 10.5465/amle.2024.0033

Suharsono, N., Hidayat, R., Zen, F., Rusmana, D., & Permansah, S. (2025). Evaluating pedagogical approaches in business education: A comparative analysis. [EduLearn]. *Journal of Education and Learning*, *19*(2), 616–625.

Surugiu, C., Grădinaru, C., & Surugiu, M. R. (2024). Artificial intelligence in business education: Benefits and tools. *Amfiteatru Economic*, *26*(65), 241–258. DOI: 10.24818/EA/2024/65/241

Suryanarayana, K. S., Kandi, V. P., Pavani, G., Rao, A. S., Rout, S., & Krishna, T. S. R. (2024). Artificial intelligence enhanced digital learning for the sustainability of education management system. *The Journal of High Technology Management Research*, *35*(2), 100495. DOI: 10.1016/j.hitech.2024.100495

Thottoli, M. M., Cruz, M. E., & Al Abri, S. S. S. (2025). The incubation revolution: Transforming entrepreneurial education with artificial intelligence. *Asia Pacific Journal of Innovation and Entrepreneurship, 19*(1), 2–23. DOI: 10.1108/APJIE-11-2023-0221

Toutain, O., Jabbouri, R., & Truong, Y. (2023). Artificial intelligence and the transformation of management education. *Management international, 27*(2), 119-132.

Tran, M. T. (2024). Fostering sustainable mindsets: A critical exploration of educational psychology in business education. *International Journal of Management Education, 22*(3), 101054. DOI: 10.1016/j.ijme.2024.101054

Urmeneta, A., & Romero, M. (2024). *Creative applications of artificial intelligence in education*. Springer Nature. DOI: 10.1007/978-3-031-55272-4

Valcea, S., Hamdani, M. R., & Wang, S. (2024). Exploring the impact of ChatGPT on business school education: Prospects, boundaries, and paradoxes. *Journal of Management Education, 48*(5), 915–947. DOI: 10.1177/10525629241261313

Vashista, N., Gugnani, P., Bala, M., & Kumar, A. (2023). The Educator's Lens: Understanding the Impact of AI on Management Education. *International Journal of Education and Development Using Information and Communication Technology, 19*(3), 9–27.

Vecchiarini, M., & Somia, T. (2023). Redefining entrepreneurship education in the age of artificial intelligence: An explorative analysis. *International Journal of Management Education, 21*(3), 100879. DOI: 10.1016/j.ijme.2023.100879

Viera Trevisan, L., Machado do Nascimento, L. F., Leal Filho, W., & Ávila Pedrozo, E. (2024). A transformative online approach to sustainable development in management education: The case of a Brazilian business school. *International Journal of Sustainability in Higher Education, 25*(1), 1–20. DOI: 10.1108/IJSHE-02-2023-0039

Wang, C., Shi, Y., & Jiang, S. (2024). The early bird catches the flywheel: Pedagogical components of entrepreneurship education in American higher education institutions. *Education + Training, 66*(8), 1077–1095. DOI: 10.1108/ET-05-2023-0202

Winkler, C., Hammoda, B., Noyes, E., & Van Gelderen, M. (2023). Entrepreneurship education at the dawn of generative artificial intelligence. *Entrepreneurship Education and Pedagogy, 6*(4), 579–589. DOI: 10.1177/25151274231198799

Yadav, U., & Shrawankar, U. (2025). Artificial intelligence across industries: A comprehensive review with a focus on education. *AI applications and strategies in teacher education*, 275-320.

Yang, C., Ivanova, E., & Ivanova, M. (2023). Arts-based pedagogy in management education: Personal reflections. In *Honing self-awareness of faculty and future business leaders: Emotions connected with teaching and learning* (pp. 227–245). Emerald Publishing Limited. DOI: 10.1108/978-1-80262-349-920231014

Yu, T., Dai, J., Chen, X., & Wang, C. (2025). Factors influencing continuance intention in blended learning among business school students in China: Based on grounded theory and FsQCA. *Interactive Learning Environments, 33*(2), 1339–1366.

Zhang, N., & Leong, W. Y. (2024, November). Integrating Artificial Intelligence into Whole-Person Education for a New Paradigm in Engineering Education. In *2024 International Conference on Intelligent Education and Intelligent Research (IEIR)* (pp. 1-6). IEEE. DOI: 10.1109/IEIR62538.2024.10959915

Zhou, X., Zhang, J., & Chan, C. (2024). Unveiling students' experiences and perceptions of artificial intelligence usage in higher education. *Journal of University Teaching & Learning Practice, 21*(6), 126–145. DOI: 10.53761/xzjprb23

ADDITIONAL READING

4. Akerkar, R. (2019). *Artificial intelligence for business*. Springer. DOI: 10.1007/978-3-319-97436-1

5. Chishti, S. (2020). *The AI book: the artificial intelligence handbook for investors, entrepreneurs and fintech visionaries*. John Wiley & Sons. DOI: 10.1002/9781119551966

1. Hamdan, A., Hassanien, A. E., Khamis, R., Alareeni, B., Razzaque, A., & Awwad, B. (Eds.). (2021). *Applications of artificial intelligence in business, education and healthcare* (Vol. 954). Springer. DOI: 10.1007/978-3-030-72080-3

6. Kaplan, A. (2022). *Artificial intelligence, business and civilization: our fate made in machines*. Routledge. DOI: 10.4324/9781003244554

2. Panda, S. K., Mishra, V., Balamurali, R., & Elngar, A. A. (Eds.). (2021). *Artificial Intelligence and Machine Learning in business management: Concepts, challenges, and case studies*. CRC Press. DOI: 10.1201/9781003125129

3. Yu, S., & Lu, Y. (2021). *An introduction to artificial intelligence in education*. Springer. DOI: 10.1007/978-981-16-2770-5

KEY TERMS AND DEFINITIONS

Artificial Intelligence: Computational architectures that perform perception-to-decision pipelines via statistical learning, knowledge representation, and heuristic search. Encompasses deep neural networks, probabilistic models, and reinforcement learning to approximate inference, prediction, and planning at scale.

Business Education: A transdisciplinary instructional ecosystem that engineers managerial cognition and judgment under uncertainty through cases, simulations, and field praxis. Integrates economics, finance, accounting, strategy, operations, and OB within standards-aligned assurance-of-learning regimes.

Sustainability: A systems framework optimizing value across environmental integrity, social equity, and economic viability within planetary boundary constraints. Operates via life-cycle assessment, ESG materiality, and intergenerational justice metrics to de-risk long-horizon externalities.

Ethical Pedagogy: Instructional design anchored in duty-, rights-, and care-based norms that foreground autonomy, beneficence, justice, and nonmaleficence. Requires transparency, consent, privacy-by-design, and fairness auditing across assessment and analytics workflows.

Inclusive Design: Human-centered, equity-first design that operationalizes Universal Design for Learning and WCAG accessibility to accommodate diverse cognitive, linguistic, and cultural repertoires. Employs participatory co-creation, multimodal representation, and context-sensitive interfaces.

Learning Analytics: The measurement, collection, and modeling of learner interaction telemetry to optimize learning and environments. Uses psychometrics, causal inference, and educational data mining for early-warning systems, mastery diagnostics, and A/B experimentation under data-governance constraints.

Algorithmic Bias: Systematic, non-random error that skews outcomes across protected or contextual groups due to dataset, label, or measurement artifacts. Manifests as disparate impact, calibration drift, and allocation harm, mitigated via reweighting, counterfactual tests, and constrained optimization.

Adaptive Learning: Personalization engines that dynamically sequence content and calibrate difficulty using item response theory, Bayesian knowledge tracing, and reinforcement learning. Maintain learner models to regulate cognitive load, scaffold misconceptions, and accelerate mastery.

Generative AI: Foundation models that synthesize novel text, code, audio, or images via self-supervised pretraining and controllable decoding. Enables prompt-conditioned content morphogenesis while necessitating guardrails for hallucination, provenance, safety, and IP leakage.

Management Curriculum: A standards-mapped program architecture that spirals foundational to advanced competencies across functional domains and contexts. Aligns program learning outcomes with integrative capstones, reflective assessment, and accreditation logics (e.g., AoL, rubric validity, curricular coherence).

Chapter 10
Artificial Intelligence and the Future of Work:
Transforming Business Education and Training for Sustainability

Gurpreet pal Kaur
http://orcid.org/0000-0001-7475-3548
Lovely Professional University, India

Mushtaq Ahmed Shah
http://orcid.org/0000-0002-3177-9622
Lovely Professional University, India

ABSTRACT

This chapter analyses how Artificial Intelligence (AI) is transforming global business, employment, and education. AI represents a radical shift in human–machine collaboration, using technological intelligence to complement human creativity, empathy, and ethics. Drawing on academic research, policy reports, and industry practices, it explores AI's dual impact—enhancing productivity, innovation, and personalized learning, while also posing challenges such as job displacement, skill mismatches, and ethical concerns. The chapter argues that sustainable adaptation to AI requires rethinking education and training systems by integrating AI literacy, critical thinking, and lifelong learning. It calls for joint efforts from educators, policymakers, and industry leaders to ensure that AI-driven progress aligns with social equity, environmental sustainability, and inclusive economic growth.

DOI: 10.4018/979-8-3373-5946-5.ch010

1. INTRODUCTION

The twenty-first century is experiencing an unparalleled change due to the swift development of artificial intelligence (AI), having a transformative effect on the production, learning, and organization of the work and economic and business systems in societies (Otenko et al., 2025). This technological wave demands a fundamental re-evaluation of how human capital is developed, managed, and sustained in the digital era.

1.1. Global Context of AI Transformation

AI is recognized as one of the strongest technological paradigms of the present, distinguishing itself from older automation models by its capacity to learn, reason, and adapt, thereby redefining the boundaries of human labor and decision-making (Miah et al., 2024). This rapid intersection of AI with big data analytics, the Internet of Things (IoT), and cloud computing has frequently been cited as the core of the Fourth Industrial Revolution (Industry 4.0), a stage characterized by deep digital integration.

However, the contemporary industrial focus is shifting from pure efficiency to a human-centric paradigm, often termed Industry 5.0 or Society 5.0. This shift emphasizes that technology and human values should not be antagonistic; rather, technology should facilitate sustainable development (Ćoćkalo et al., 2023; Đorđević et al., 2023). This ideological pivot from optimizing processes (Industry 4.0) to prioritizing human augmentation and sustainability (Industry 5.0) underpins the necessity of educational reform. Intelligent systems are poised to influence not only what is done but also how and by whom work is performed (Gurieva et al., 2019).

1.2. Origin and Relevance of AI to Sustainability

The concept of AI, rooted in computational problem-solving and formalized in the 20th century, has evolved to become a general-purpose technology (GPT) that fundamentally alters global economic structure, productivity, and labor markets (Krstic, 2024). While early applications focused predominantly on economic gain, the contemporary necessity requires the alignment of technological progress with long-term social good, particularly through sustainable development.

This alignment is mandated by international frameworks, most notably the United Nations Sustainable Development Goals (SDGs). Specifically, SDG 4 (Quality Education) and SDG 8 (Decent Work and Economic Growth) serve as the normative benchmark against which AI implementation must be measured (Yeh et al., 2021). For instance, the application of generative AI technologies, such as ChatGPT, offers powerful opportunities to democratize education and productivity but risks increasing existing societal disparities unless implementation is carefully regulated (Rane, 2023). Integrating sustainability and ethical consciousness into business education is thus crucial to ensure future leaders advocate for human well-being and environmental responsibility when deploying AI systems (Andino-González et al., 2025).

1.3. Practical Challenges and Empirical Background

The impact of AI on the occupied world is multi-dimensional, offering both opportunities for creative work augmentation (Azeem, 2025) and significant challenges. The primary practical challenge is the deepening skills mismatch and potential job displacement. Automation and algorithmic management are streamlining repetitive workload, but they simultaneously raise the critical issue of workforce transformation (Frederick, 2025). Latest research indicates that millions of employees globally must be reskilled and upskilled to meet these changes (Ali et al., 2025). The rapid pace of generative AI development intensifies the need for continuous skill renewal (Joshi, 2025).

A second pervasive challenge relates to ethical governance. Issues surrounding algorithmic bias, data privacy, and transparency necessitate the urgent development of human-based and ethically informed AI frameworks. When AI systems are trained on skewed data, they tend to reproduce existing patterns of discrimination, compromising fairness, especially in sensitive areas like recruitment and academic evaluation (Mishra and Gautam, 2025). Finally, the digital divide remains a structural barrier. The lack of equal access to digital infrastructure and AI-based resources creates the tangible risk of increasing the gap between well-equipped and under-equipped institutions, particularly problematic in regions like the Global South (Matsieli and Mutula, 2025).

1.4. Research Gaps and Question Statement

Current scholarship often examines AI's economic impact (productivity) or its educational application (personalization) in isolation. A significant gap exists in providing an integrated, theoretically grounded framework that systematically links AI-driven business education reform with explicit, long-term sustainable and inclusive workforce development outcomes. While efficiency is widely studied, the long-term ethical and equitable governance mechanisms necessary for stability are often treated as secondary concerns. Furthermore, there is a contextual gap regarding practical implementation barriers and non-Western case studies in business education, especially concerning infrastructure resilience and tailored policy responses in developing economies.

This chapter addresses this deficiency by asking the core research question: "How can AI be integrated into business education to ensure sustainable and inclusive workforce development?"

2. BACKGROUND OF THE STUDY

This section establishes the practical context of AI adoption by presenting global case studies demonstrating responsive education strategies and analyzing the prevalent challenges to successful implementation in training and higher education environments. The acceleration of AI adoption in the private and public sectors has necessitated rapid, adaptive skilling and education initiatives worldwide.

IBM SkillsBuild: This program exemplifies a shift toward competence-based, modular learning, specifically targeting what IBM terms "new collar" skills. It provides free access to enterprise-grade training in high-demand areas like Cloud computing, AI/ML, and Cybersecurity, emphasizing practical, job-ready abilities and verifiable digital credentials over traditional four-year degrees. This model directly addresses the persistent digital skills gap and promotes a flexible, accessible approach to upskilling, particularly useful for job seekers and underrepresented communities.

India AI Mission (2024): As a comprehensive national strategy, the India AI Mission aims to build an inclusive AI ecosystem through a robust public-private partnership model. Key objectives include deploying large-scale, cutting-edge AI computing infrastructure (over 10,000 Graphics Processing Units), developing indigenous Large Multimodal Models (LMMs), and establishing the India AI Datasets Platform for ethical and secure data access. The mission's focus on areas like governance, healthcare, and sustainability ensures that technological advancement is directed towards socially impactful outcomes and inclusive growth, demonstrating a nation-scale commitment to integrating AI ethics from the top down.

Finland AI Education Initiative: This initiative focuses on integrating AI to enhance learning outcomes and significantly reduce teacher workload, rather than just technological compliance.6 Pilots focusing on adaptive learning tools (like Eduten) report meaningful gains, including academic performance increases of approximately 25% and up to a 40% reduction in teacher administrative workload in some Helsinki schools.7 The core lesson derived from Finland's approach is that AI systems should strategically augment teaching capacity and promote critical thinking, ensuring the technology serves pedagogical goals rather than replacing core human functions.

2.2. Implementation Challenges and Barriers to Adoption

The ambition of successful, ethical AI integration into education is frequently hampered by pervasive, multi-layered barriers, particularly evident in the context of business schools seeking transformation. *First-Order (Extrinsic) Barriers:* These technical and resource limitations include inadequate digital infrastructure, limited technical expertise, and insufficient funding to support AI-based learning environments, which are especially acute in developing environments (Mishra and Gautam, 2025). Furthermore, the absence of clear curriculum guidelines and necessary administrative support from institutional leadership hinders grassroots adoption among educators.

Second-Order (Intrinsic) Barriers: These are personal and deeply ingrained attitudes and beliefs, which present significant institutional resistance. Faculty resistance, a general lack of awareness regarding AI's benefits, and the lack of comprehensive professional development slow down innovation and curriculum reform. Misconceptions, such as the belief that relying on AI technology reduces students' creative skills or critical thinking capacity, further restrict ethical and effective adoption. *Ethical and Policy Barriers:* The speed of AI deployment often outpaces the development of policy and governance structures, creating dangerous gaps. The deployment of learning analytics, for example, raises serious concerns about student data privacy and consent (Bucea-Manea- oniş et al., 2022). The inherent opacity of "black-box" AI systems compromises accountability and diminishes public trust in technology-driven decision-making.

3. STATEMENT OF THE PROBLEM

The widespread adoption of AI presents a critical divergence between the desired state of sustainable, inclusive development and the current trajectory marked by systemic risks and growing inequalities.

3.1. Ideal State versus Real-World Divergence

Ideal State: The ideal scenario, consistent with Industry 5.0 philosophy, is where AI adoption leads to complementary intelligence AI's analytical capabilities augmenting human creativity, empathy, and moral judgment. In this state, business education successfully produces AI-literate, ethical leaders who utilize technology to drive inclusive economic development, social equity, and environmental responsibility, thereby fulfilling the mandate of the SDGs.

Real State: The reality involves substantial, measurable risks. Automation, particularly by generative AI, is projected to cause significant job displacement, potentially affecting up to 1.2 billion positions worldwide by 2040, predominantly in routine cognitive and manual roles. This transformation is leading to a polarization of the workforce and strengthening socio-economic inequality due to unequal access to digital tools and training (Xanthopoulou and Sahinidis, 2025). Compounding this, the reliance on high-performance computing necessary for AI poses a critical challenge to environmental sustainability goals, commonly referred to as the "Green AI" dilemma, as massive energy consumption contradicts global climate efforts.

3.2. Theoretical, Contextual, and Practical Gaps

Human Capital Theory (HCT), the traditional lens for education economics, risks focusing too narrowly on individual economic returns (productivity and wages) in the AI context, potentially overlooking the profound social and environmental externalities of widespread AI deployment. The existing HCT framework is thus insufficient on its own; it requires expansion by integrating Sustainable Development Theory (SDT) and Ethical AI Governance frameworks to account for non-monetary, collective societal returns, such as equity, justice, and resilience.

Contextual Gap (Developing Economies): While much literature focuses on high-resource developed economies, systematic strategies for AI adoption in developing countries remain severely underexplored. These regions face unique barriers, including chronically fragile digital infrastructure, teacher training deficiencies, and vast informal labor sectors where traditional reskilling models are ineffective. The pronounced digital divide here demands context-sensitive, low-cost, and community-based learning models.

Practical Gap: There is a persistent and urgent disconnect between the swift pace of technological change in the industry and the slow institutional and pedagogical reforms taking place in many business schools. This institutional inertia translates directly into a critical misalignment between graduate skills and evolving market demands, perpetuating the skills mismatch crisis that undermines workforce adaptability and employability.

4. RELATED THEORIES AND CONCEPTUAL FOUNDATION

This chapter is grounded in five interconnected theoretical frameworks that collectively provide a comprehensive view of AI's impact on human capital formation, education, and societal sustainability.

4.1. The Main Theoretical Lens: Human Capital Theory and Lifelong Learning

The analysis is centrally anchored in the combination of Human Capital Theory (HCT) and Lifelong Learning Theory (LLL).

HCT posits that investment in education and training increases an individual's productivity and lifetime economic value (Becker, 1964). In the era of AI, this principle is dramatically intensified because AI accelerates the obsolescence of existing skills (Frederick, 2025). This technology acts as a hyper-accelerator of human capital depreciation, making the sustained, continuous investment in new digital literacy, analytical capabilities, and durable socio-emotional skills critically important for maintaining capital value (Tjokro et al., 2025).

LLL builds upon HCT by asserting that learning must transition from a fixed, front-loaded acquisition model to a dynamic, ongoing process. AI-based, personalized systems facilitate this transition by enabling smart tutoring tools, microlearning modules, and adaptive learning paths that match education directly to specific career trajectories (Harizan and Ally, 2025). The combination of HCT and LLL therefore provides the main theoretical justification for why continuous upskilling is necessary for workforce resilience in the face of constant technological change.

4.2. Supporting Theoretical Frameworks

Socio-Technical Systems (STS) Theory is vital for understanding the organizational context, viewing human and technical components as mutually interdependent. Critically, STS dictates that technology should be designed to augment human capabilities and assist them in achieving their goals, rather than seeking wholesale replacement of human labor. In the AI context, adopting an STS perspective means that organizational governance and culture must ensure that AI systems are co-designed with anticipated users and domain experts (co-designing) to maximize human agency and prevent unintended negative social consequences during deployment.

Ethical AI Governance Framework (EAGF)

The EAGF provides the necessary principles and guardrails for responsible AI implementation. It outlines a structured approach to managing the development, deployment, and use of AI systems by focusing on the core principles of Fairness, Accountability, and Transparency (FAT). Effective governance is essential for mitigating risks related to algorithmic bias and data privacy breaches, thereby fostering user and stakeholder trust in AI-driven solutions. Formal governance frameworks typically include risk assessment and oversight processes to align AI behaviors with ethical standards and societal expectations.

Sustainable Development Theory (SDT)

SDT provides the overarching normative framework, ensuring that AI-driven economic and technological development meets the needs of the present without compromising the ability of future generations to meet their own needs. This theory mandates that AI adoption must actively align with the UN SDGs, requiring a focus not only on quality education (SDG 4) and decent work (SDG 8) but also on environmental protection. SDT is the theoretical anchor for addressing the severe digital divide and promoting "Green AI" practices.

Table 1. Synthesis of Core Theoretical Lenses for AI Integration in Business Education

Theoretical Lens	Core Premise in AI Context	Relevance to Sustainable Workforce
Human Capital Theory (HCT)	AI accelerates skill obsolescence, demanding continuous, high-return investment in new digital and durable human skills (e.g., creativity, judgment).	Justifies mandatory AI literacy and integrated reskilling programs to ensure sustained worker productivity and employability.
Lifelong Learning Theory (LLL)	Learning must be dynamic and continuous; AI systems facilitate personalized, modular learning paths (e.g., micro-credentials).	Ensures workforce resilience and adaptability against rapid technological disruption and skill half-life reduction.
Socio-Technical Systems (STS) Theory	AI systems must be co-designed to augment human capabilities, preserving human agency and integrating organizational culture and governance	Supports the Human-AI collaboration model (Industry 5.0) and ethical, bottom-up system design.
Ethical AI Governance Framework (EAGF)	Requires structured oversight emphasizing FAT principles (Fairness, Accountability, Transparency) to manage algorithmic bias and data risks.	Mitigates risks of algorithmic bias and digital inequality, promoting inclusive, equitable access to AI benefits.
Sustainable Development Theory (SDT)	Development must balance economic efficiency, social equity, and environmental protection (SDGs 4 & 8).	Provides the normative mandate for Green AI policies and addressing the severe digital divide in the Global South.

5. EMPIRICAL LITERATURE REVIEW

This section critically reviews recent empirical findings and policy studies (2023–2025) detailing the accelerated impact of AI on labor markets, educational responses, and the emerging challenges of ethical and environmental governance.

5.1. AI's Accelerated Impact on Labor Markets (2023–2025)

The advent of generative AI (GenAI) has driven an accelerated restructuring of the labor market. Empirical evidence confirms that routine, entry-level cognitive roles such as those in clerical or junior technical positions have contracted sharply as intelligent systems assume high-volume, rules-based tasks. This represents a shift from mere task replacement to a complete role redesign.

AI adoption across enterprises is accelerating rapidly, with 78% of organizations reporting using AI in 2024, a significant increase from 55% the previous year. This acceleration is matched by substantial investment: U.S. private AI investment reached a record $109.1 billion in 2024, and globally, GenAI alone attracted $33.9 billion, an 18.7% increase from 2023.20 Research consistently confirms that, in most cases, AI boosts productivity and can help narrow existing skill gaps within the workforce.

However, the realization of this potential is limited by organizational maturity, creating a "Superagency Gap". While nearly all companies are investing in AI, only 1% of leaders describe their companies as "mature" in AI deployment, meaning AI is fully integrated into workflows. Research by Brynjolfsson and McAfee (2023 context) and others suggests that employees are highly receptive to change, often three times more likely than leaders realize to believe AI will replace 30% of their work, and they are eager for formal training. The difficulty lies not with employee readiness, but with leaders' failure to invest quickly and systematically in the training and governance necessary to translate investment into sustained business outcomes. This managerial reluctance perpetuates the global reskilling urgency, where an estimated 450 million workers in major economies will require upskilling or reskilling by 2030.

5.2. Business Education Transformation and AI Literacy

The educational sector is responding to these labor market demands. The adoption of GenAI in higher education (HE) is widespread, with 86 percent of institutions globally using some version of GenAI in teaching or administration (Wood, 2024). The acceleration in the annual growth rate of AI, data science, and machine learning courses (over 45 percent) confirms the immediate need for technical competence. Leading institutions, exemplified by the MIT Sloan (2025 context), are actively restructuring graduate management curricula to focus on hands-on deep learning, fintech applications, and embedding AI into strategic decision-making frameworks (Shah & Aggarwal 2023). Crucially, contemporary studies emphasize that technological competence alone is insufficient. Scholars stress that AI literacy must be developed beyond the technical level, encompassing critical thinking, ethical judgment, and reflective leadership skills required to collaborate effectively with intelligent systems (Asghar et al., 2025).

Furthermore, policy documents, such as those published by UNESCO (2024 context) and OECD, stress the necessity of establishing rights-based, equity-focused agendas for AI in education. The literature notes that a consensus on what constitutes valid, independent evidence of AI's effectiveness in learning environments is lacking, underlining the ethical implications of rapid deployment on student cohorts. This policy challenge highlights that technological innovation cannot precede ethical oversight.

5.3. Ethical Governance and Sustainable AI Implementation

The implementation of AI raises fundamental issues regarding governance. The concern is that AI systems, particularly when deployed in high-stakes environments like hiring or credit decisions, tend to reproduce and strengthen existing biases when trained on non-representative or skewed data (Mishra and Gautam, 2025). This algorithmic bias constitutes a failure of fairness and accountability, leading to potential social injustice.

The environmental impact of AI the Green AI Dilemma is an increasingly urgent empirical focus. While AI offers efficiency gains, its substantial computational power necessitates massive energy consumption and carbon release, creating a direct conflict with global climate action and sustainability goals (Xanthopoulou and Sahinidis, 2025). Research indicates that companies must proactively assess the environmental impacts across the technology stack and take steps to reduce the carbon footprint of their models, even when quantification is difficult.

The empirical response to these challenges emphasizes Human-Centered AI (HCAI) policies. HCAI differs from traditional AI governance by prioritizing the alignment of systems with ethical, societal, and human-centered principles over mere technical performance. Policies following the HCAI approach emphasize the need to build scalable infrastructure and security frameworks that actively protect against biases, misuse, and adversarial attacks, ensuring safe, fair, and transparent operation (Lee et al., 2025; Saudi DGA, 2025 context).

6. CONCEPTUAL RESEARCH DESIGN

The methodology employed for this chapter is a rigorous conceptual research design utilizing an interpretive synthesis approach to integrate diverse theoretical models and empirical evidence, culminating in a structured conceptual framework.

6.1. Research Approach: Interpretive Synthesis

The study employs an interpretive synthesis approach to integrate highly diverse theoretical models Human Capital Theory, Lifelong Learning, Socio-Technical Systems, Ethical Governance, and Sustainable Development with recent empirical findings (2023–2025) and policy reports. This specific approach allows for the creation of a novel, comprehensive conceptual model that explains the complex interaction between AI adoption, educational transformation, and required sustainable workforce outcomes.

The literature review was structured using predefined criteria focusing on: (1) Peer-reviewed articles, scholarly book chapters, and seminal policy reports published between 2019 and 2025, with a mandatory heavy emphasis on publications from 2023–2025 to ensure currency. 2) Literature addressing the nexus of AI adoption, future of work, business education, and the normative concepts of ethical governance and sustainability/SDGs. (3) Triangulation across academic, industry, and policy sources (e.g., UNESCO, OECD, WEF) was maintained to guarantee robust analysis and practical relevance.

6.2. Conceptual Framework Development

The conceptual framework Figure 1 graphically maps the theoretical and empirical relationships between key constructs necessary for achieving sustainable workforce development in the AI era.

Figure 1. Conceptual Framework

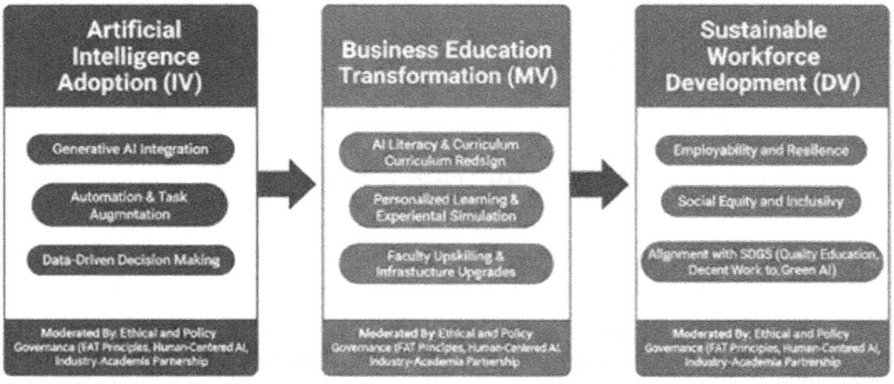

The model posits that AI Adoption (Independent Variable) directly triggers the necessary Business Education Transformation (Mediating Variable), which in turn drives Sustainable Workforce Development (Dependent Variable). Crucially, this entire causal chain is moderated by robust Ethical and Policy Governance, ensuring that the innovation process is steered toward inclusive outcomes.

6.3. Proposed Conceptual Constructs for Future Empirical Studies

To enhance the rigor of this conceptual analysis, key constructs relevant for future empirical testing were defined: AI Literacy: Defined as the ability to understand, critically assess the performance and ethical implications of AI outputs, and to collaborate effectively with AI to solve domain-specific problems, encompassing technical, ethical, and collaborative skills. Ethical Governance: Measured by the adherence of organizational or educational AI deployment to the principles of Fairness, Accountability, and Transparency (FAT), including specific procedures for data auditing and bias mitigation. Sustainability Orientation: The degree to which AI implementation, both in development and application, demonstrably aligns with environmental goals (e.g., Green AI principles) and social equity goals (e.g., measured by metrics of digital inclusion).

7. ILLUSTRATIVE SYNTHESIS AND THEMATIC ANALYSIS

This section provides a narrative analysis summarizing the key causal trends identified in the empirical review, articulating the necessary shift from a crisis response to a proactive, governed strategy for human capital management.

7.1. Analytical Theme 1: AI Adoption and the Skills Obsolescence Crisis

The introduction of AI as a General-Purpose Technology acts as a hyper-accelerator of human capital depreciation, thereby creating a systemic crisis of employability. Rapid AI adoption, driven by the surge in GenAI investment 20, leads directly to the replacement of routine, mid-level cognitive tasks. This automation causes a swift and dramatic decline in the residual value of existing professional skills. The consequence is a severe skills gap across global labor markets, where workers find their education and experience quickly devalued. This direct, inverse relationship Increased AI Adoption--->Decreased Value of Existing Human Capital -->Crisis of Employability necessitates the urgent shift from linear, time-based education models to continuous, competency-based, lifelong learning paradigms.

Figure 2. Solution and Recommendations

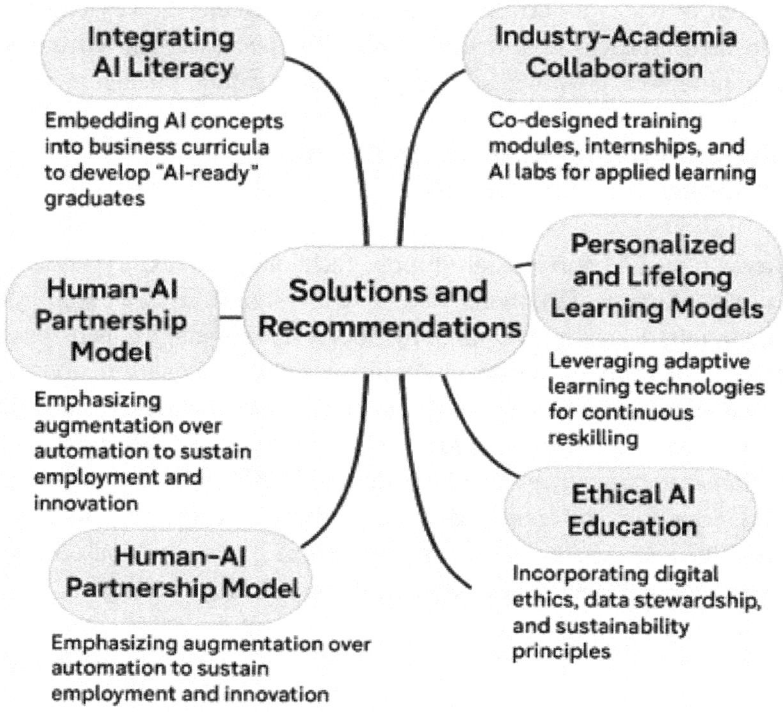

7.2. Analytical Theme 2: The Imperative of Reskilling Frameworks

Addressing the skills gap requires establishing resilient, modular reskilling frameworks as the active management tool for human capital resilience. The crisis necessitates massive, continuous reskilling (targeting hundreds of millions of workers). Traditional academic models are simply too slow and rigid to meet this scale of demand. Successful intervention requires the adoption of flexible, modular delivery systems, such as micro-credentials and AI-based adaptive learning platforms (e.g., IBM SkillsBuild). These adaptive frameworks depend intrinsically on robust Industry-Academia collaboration to ensure that learning content remains relevant and immediately applicable to market needs. This thematic progression highlights that Skills Gap -->Modular, AI-Driven Learning ---> Restored Human Capital Value. This operational shift moves the primary responsibility for workforce education from the individual solely to a mandated partnership between government, academia, and industry.

7.3. Analytical Theme 3: Governing Innovation for Sustainable Outcomes

To ensure shared prosperity, efficiency gains must be secondary to ethical and policy moderation, making governance the critical factor for sustainable development. While AI and reskilling frameworks promise increased efficiency, unregulated deployment inherently threatens social equity (algorithmic bias, access disparity) and environmental health (massive energy footprint). The pursuit of efficiency without moral or environmental oversight is definitionally unsustainable. Therefore, to achieve long-term sustainability (SDGs), ethical constraints and rigorous policy moderation (governance) must be incorporated before the technology is scaled. This structural relationship is formalized as: Reskilling Frameworks --> Ethical & Policy Governance (Moderator) --> Sustainable and Inclusive Workforce. The moderator ensures that the economic benefits of AI are shared equitably and that the process adheres to principles of Green AI, thereby guaranteeing long-term societal acceptance and resilience.

8. DISCUSSION: FORGING AN ETHICAL AND SUSTAINABLE DIGITAL FUTURE

The synthesis of theoretical models and empirical findings establishes that the future of work and business education hinges upon purposeful, ethical transformation, focusing on human augmentation rather than simple replacement.

8.1. AI Literacy as the Foundation of Complementary Intelligence

The AI era demands a fundamental re-definition of success focused on complementary intelligence, which blends AI analytical precision with uniquely human attributes like creativity, empathy, and moral judgment (Randriamiary, 2024). To cultivate this, AI literacy must move significantly beyond mere technical proficiency. Learners must be proficient in critically assessing the performance and ethical implications of AI outputs, collaborating with AI to innovate, managing AI's actions with appropriate human oversight, and understanding basic design principles.

Business schools must consequently integrate AI not as an elective technical subject, but into core management functions. This involves shifting pedagogy toward interdisciplinary learning, incorporating computer science, data analytics, and behavioral ethics directly into case studies, simulations, and strategic decision-making exercises (Collina, 2025; Rivero, 2025). This strategy ensures that graduates are not only AI-ready but also innovative, critical thinkers, and ethically responsible leaders.

8.2. Strengthening the Industry-Academia Nexus

Collaboration is non-negotiable for bridging the persistent curriculum lag caused by the swift technological development rate in the private sector. Business schools must establish deep, formalized collaborations with organizations leading AI adoption. This partnership must extend to the co-creation of competency mapping and curriculum. Educational institutions, supported by industry insights, should establish AI-enhanced competency transfer hubs (Arya et al., 2025), enabling joint research, internship programs, and the provision of relevant, real-world data sets. Furthermore, these alliances enable the wider adoption of AI-based simulators and virtual environments in business education, which reconsiders experiential learning and allows students to develop critical and creative thinking skills by coping with complex situations in risk-free settings (Lubbe et al., 2025).

8.3. The Mandate for Ethical and Environmental Sustainability (Green AI)

Sustainable digital transformation relies on mandatory ethical education and addressing the environmental footprint of computation. Business education must transition from an efficiency-centric focus to prioritizing moral responsibility and ethical judgment. Curricula must systematically cover topics like algorithmic fairness, data governance, and digital rights, utilizing international frameworks such as the UNESCO Recommendation on the Ethics of Artificial Intelligence (Tidjon & Khomh, 2022).

Furthermore, the discussion must explicitly address the sustainability dilemma the environmental trade-off inherent in AI's massive energy requirements. Future leaders must be equipped to champion 'Green AI' technologies and advocate for policies that incentivize energy-efficient computing and sustainable practices across the AI lifecycle (Qudrat-Ullah, 2025; McCarthy, 2024).

8.4. Promoting Lifelong Learning and Adaptive Systems

AI provides the tools necessary to institutionalize lifelong learning (LLL), essential for maintaining continuous employability. Adaptive learning systems, fueled by real-time AI analytics, are capable of tailoring content and pedagogical strategies to individual learner requirements (Bayly-Castaneda et al., 2024). The flexibility of micro-credentialing and modular courses provides the necessary structure, allowing professionals to enhance or renew their competencies without leaving the job market (Zhao, 2025). Successful ecosystems require policy support, including governmental financing for reskilling programs and the formal recognition of industry-relevant micro-credentials as legitimate qualifications

9. CONCLUSION

Artificial Intelligence (AI) is the dominant force reshaping economies, education, and the definition of work in the 21st century. This conceptual analysis confirms that the transformative potential of AI to drive sustainable and inclusive development is entirely contingent upon its ethical integration into business education and training systems. To successfully answer the research question, "How can AI be integrated into business education to ensure sustainable and inclusive workforce development?", this chapter concludes that AI integration must be guided by the principle of human augmentation (Industry 5.0), where technology is positioned as an aid, rather than a substitute, to human intelligence, creativity, and empathy. Business education must prioritize AI literacy a fusion of technical knowledge, ethical judgment, and critical thinking and foster continuous, adaptive learning enabled by robust policy and industry collaboration. The ethical governance of AI, including mitigating algorithmic bias and embracing Green AI principles, is not secondary to innovation but constitutes the core foundation for shared prosperity, equity, and a resilient digital future. Achieving this requires the concerted action of educators, policymakers, and industry leaders to ensure that the benefits of AI are efficiently and equitably shared globally.

10. THEORETICAL AND PRACTICAL IMPLICATIONS

This chapter significantly extends the applicability of Human Capital Theory (HCT) by integrating it explicitly with Sustainable Development Theory (SDT) and the Ethical AI Governance Framework (EAGF). The value of human capital in the AI era is redefined to include non-monetary, societal returns specifically, the capacity for ethical decision-making, social consciousness, and measurable contribution to environmental well-being (Green AI). This expanded theoretical framework argues that investment in ethical AI literacy yields not just individual productivity gains, but positive societal externalities aligned with the SDGs, thereby broadening HCT's utility beyond purely economic quantification.

Furthermore, the findings solidify the concept of complementary intelligence, formally positioning it within the Socio-Technical Systems perspective. This provides a refined theoretical lens for studying human-AI interaction, focusing specifically on augmenting human judgment and creativity rather than simply automating tasks, fostering an Industry 5.0 approach.

10.1. Practical Implications

Implications for Educators and Institutions: Business schools must mandate aggressive faculty upskilling and training in GenAI applications and ethical governance to overcome internal second-order barriers to reform. Curricula require fundamental restructuring to incorporate interdisciplinary AI ethics training and shift pedagogy towards experiential learning via AI-driven simulations and complex, real-world case studies. Implications for Policymakers: Governments must develop national AI learning strategies (akin to the India AI Mission) that finance inclusive digital infrastructure and provide targeted incentives for organizational reskilling. Policy frameworks must establish clear, enforceable standards for algorithmic accountability, data privacy, and mandatory Green AI deployment across regulated sectors.

Implications for Organizations: Organizations must adopt transparent and human-centered AI systems that prioritize augmentation over pure automation. They must systematically invest in lifelong upskilling and reskilling programs, recognizing that AI-fluent, ethically aware employees are the key drivers of sustainable productivity and organizational AI maturity

10.2. Managerial Implications

Driving Sustainable Productivity (Superagency): Managers must pivot their focus from maximizing automation (cost reduction) to fostering augmentation ('Superagency') empowering employees to unlock AI's full potential for creativity and productivity. This requires designing workflows that integrate AI as a cognitive partner, enabling human employees to concentrate on non-routine, complex problem-solving and strategic innovation.

Ethical Risk Mitigation: Leadership must implement formal Ethical AI Governance boards or oversight committees to rigorously monitor AI outputs for inherent bias and ensure compliance with FAT (Fairness, Accountability, Transparency) principles. Ethical leadership (Nissen, 2025) is crucial to ensure AI deployment enhances social welfare and stakeholder interests, mitigating risks associated with opaque systems. Talent Strategy and Modular Training: Managers must leverage

AI-driven micro-credentialing platforms (e.g., IBM SkillsBuild) to provide just-in-time, relevant, and modular training solutions, allowing the workforce to quickly gain high-demand, current skills, thereby closing the skills gap efficiently.

11. RECOMMENDATIONS

Based on the comprehensive synthesis of challenges and successful global practices, the following policy and strategic recommendations are proposed for immediate implementation

Implementing Ethical and Human-Centered AI Policy

Governments should enact sector-specific legal frameworks, based on the Ethical AI Governance Framework (EAGF), mandating algorithmic transparency (explainability) and establishing mechanisms for human recourse and review of automated high-stakes decisions. Policy must actively incentivize research and development into energy-efficient computing and 'Green AI' technologies to significantly reduce the substantial carbon footprint of large AI models, thereby ensuring technological adoption is consistent with national environmental sustainability goals. Dedicated public and private funding must be allocated to enhance digital infrastructure in under-resourced regions (Global South) and provide subsidized access to high-quality AI training for marginalized populations, serving as a direct mechanism to combat the digital divide.

11.1. Fostering Integrated Industry-Academia Collaboration Models

Establish AI Competency Hubs: Universities, supported by government and industry funding, should establish formal AI-enhanced competency transfer hubs (Arya et al., 2025) where industry professionals co-develop curriculum, provide mentorship, and offer access to real-world data sets for experiential student projects.

Standardize Micro-credentials: Policy and education bodies must collaborate to standardize and universally recognize AI-focused micro-credentials and digital badges (similar to those offered by IBM SkillsBuild), thereby legitimizing flexible, lifelong learning pathways outside traditional degree structures and promoting continuous professional development.

11.3. Prioritizing Lifelong Reskilling Initiatives

Adopt AI-Driven Adaptive Learning: Institutions and corporations must deploy AI-based adaptive learning platforms to facilitate personalized and dynamic reskilling at scale, allowing workers to quickly gain high-demand, current skills (e.g., ethical engineering and data science) throughout their careers.

Focus on Durable Skills: Curriculum design across all educational levels should explicitly focus on developing "durable skills" (adaptability, complex problem-solving, critical thinking, and creativity) that are inherently resistant to automation, preparing workers for roles focused on governing, complementing, and innovating with AI systems.

12. FUTURE RESEARCH DIRECTIONS/IMPLICATIONS

Future research must go beyond descriptive studies to longitudinal and comparative analyses that determine how AI will transform learning, work, and social equity over extended periods, requiring a combination of technical rigor with ethical and sustainable practice.

12.1. Longitudinal Studies on AI in Learning and Ethics

Long-Term Cognitive and Ethical Impact: Research is critically needed to conduct longitudinal studies analyzing the long-term effects of early AI exposure (e.g., personalized tutors and generative models) on students' innate creativity, capacity for ethical judgment, and critical thinking development.

Effectiveness of Ethical Training: Future studies should empirically evaluate the efficacy and behavioral impact of mandatory AI ethics curricula in business schools on graduate professional behavior and decision-making within corporate environments, measuring the extent to which ethical training translates into tangible ethical leadership.

12.2. Cross-Country Comparative Analysis of Reskilling Strategies

Global South vs. Developed Economies: Comparative research should contrast the effectiveness and equity outcomes of AI reskilling strategies in highly regulated, policy-driven environments (e.g., India AI Mission) versus more market-driven corporate training models. This will help propose optimal, evidence-based strategies tailored to specific socio-economic and infrastructural realities.

Impact on Informal Labor and Equity: Focused research is required to understand the specific impact of AI automation on vulnerable populations, including women, marginalized groups, and the large informal labor sector, particularly in developing nations, to ensure policy interventions are inclusive.

12.3. Environmental and Social Equity in AI

Metrics for Green AI: A critical priority is the development of quantifiable metrics and standardized auditing frameworks for measuring the energy footprint of AI models and associated computational infrastructure (Green AI), which is necessary for integrating AI into mandatory corporate sustainability reporting and environmental regulation.

Gender and Equity in the AI Workforce: Research must investigate the structural and educational factors perpetuating gender inequity and lack of inclusion in AI-related careers, proposing specific interventions within business education and national policy to ensure the AI workforce is representative of diverse populations.

REFERENCES

Ali, M. D., Ali, M. F., & Mujahid, M. (2025). *Impact of Artificial Intelligence on the Job Market and the Future of Work.* SSRN Electronic Journal. DOI: 10.2139/ssrn.5257399

Andino-González, P., Vega-Muñoz, A., Salazar-Sepúlveda, G., Contreras-Barraza, N., Lay, N., & Gil-Marín, M. (2025). Systematic Review of Studies Using Confirmatory Factor Analysis for Measuring Management Skills in Sustainable Organizational Development. *Sustainability (Basel)*, *17*(6), 2373. DOI: 10.3390/su17062373

Arya, V., Saraf, A., Chichkanov, N., Papa, A., & Romano, M. (2025). AI-enhanced competency transfer hubs: A conceptual framework for university-industry engagement and knowledge sharing. *The Journal of Technology Transfer*. Advance online publication. DOI: 10.1007/s10961-025-10233-7

Asghar, M. Z., Iqbal, J., Özbilen, F. M., Abedin, J., Järvenoja, H., & Widanapathirana, U. (2025). The nexus of artificial intelligence literacy collaborative knowledge practices and inclusive leadership development among higher education students in Bangladesh China Finland and Turkey. *Discover Computing*, *28*(1), 172. DOI: 10.1007/s10791-025-09695-y

. Azeem, M. M. (2025). The Future of Work: How Automation and Remote Technologies are Reshaping Employment. *ĪQĀN*, *7*(1), 12–22. DOI: 10.36755/iqan.v7i1.461

Bayly-Castaneda, K., Ramirez-Montoya, M.-S., & Morita-Alexander, A. (2024). Crafting personalized learning paths with AI for lifelong learning: A systematic literature review. *Frontiers in Education*, *9*, 1424386. DOI: 10.3389/feduc.2024.1424386

Bayly-Castaneda, K., Ramirez-Montoya, M.-S., & Morita-Alexander, A. (2024). Crafting personalized learning paths with AI for lifelong learning: A systematic literature review. *Frontiers in Education*, *9*, 1424386. DOI: 10.3389/feduc.2024.1424386

Becker, G. S. (1964). *Human Capital: A Theoretical and Empirical Analysis, with Special Reference to Education*. University of Chicago Press.

Bucea-Manea- oniş, R., Kuleto, V., Gudei, S. C. D., Lianu, C., Lianu, C., Ilić, M. P., & Păun, D. (2022). Artificial Intelligence Potential in Higher Education Institutions Enhanced Learning Environment in Romania and Serbia. *Sustainability (Basel)*, *14*(10), 5842. DOI: 10.3390/su14105842

. Ćoćkalo, D., Tadić, D., Bakator, M., Stanisavljev, S., & Makitan, V. (2023). Managing the Transition Process to Society 5.0. *Management: Journal of Sustainable Business and Management Solutions in Emerging Economies*. DOI: 10.7595/management.fon.2023.0017

Collina, L. (2025). The Case for AI Literacy in Consulting and Change Management. *Management Consulting Journal*, *8*(2), 86–94. DOI: 10.2478/mcj-2025-0012

Đorđević, L., Ćoćkalo, D., Bakator, M., & Novaković, B. (2023). Entrepreneurship in Society 5.0: Integrating technology and humanistic values for a sustainable future. *Industrija*, *51*(1), 29–45. DOI: 10.5937/industrija51-45802

Frederick, G. (2025). *The Impact of Artificial Intelligence on Employment Patterns in Developing Economies*. Social Sciences. DOI: 10.20944/preprints202504.2412.v1

Gurieva, L. K., Btemirova, R. I., & Kovaleva, M. A. (2019). University 4.0:new education technologies in the digital economy. *Proceedings of the International Scientific and Practical Conference on Digital Economy (ISCDE 2019)*. DOI: 10.2991/iscde-19.2019.94

Gurieva, L. K., Btemirova, R. I., & Kovaleva, M. A. (2019). University 4.0: New education technologies in the digital economy. *Proceedings of the International Scientific and Practical Conference on Digital Economy (ISCDE 2019)*, Chelyabinsk, Russia. DOI: 10.2991/iscde-19.2019.94

Harizan, S. H. M., & Ally, M. (2025). ARTIFICIAL INTELLIGENCE IN MICRO-CREDENTIALS FOR OPEN AND DISTANCE LEARNING: A TECHNOLOGICALLY ENHANCED SYSTEMATIC REVIEW. *Turkish Online Journal of Distance Education*, *26*(3), 1–24. DOI: 10.17718/tojde.1552001

Joshi, S. (2025). *Introduction to Generative AI: Its Impact on Jobs, Education, Work and Policy Making*. Business, Economics and Management. DOI: 10.20944/preprints202503.2126.v1

Krstic, Z. (2024). Economic Theory and Artificial Intelligence: A Cross-model Perspective on Labour Market Dynamics. *Croatian Regional Development Journal*, *5*(2), 52–75. DOI: 10.2478/crdj-2024-0008

Lee, Y. S., Soroushian, J., Bullock, J., Carroll, M., Dokko, J., Dominski, J., Hinds, R., Holzer, H. J., Horrigan, M., Munyikwa, Z., Oschinski, M., Radsch, C., Rock, D., Rossi, M., Seamans, R., Towns, A., & Zhang, B. (2025). *Proactively Developing and Assisting the Workforce in the Age of AI*. SSRN Electronic Journal. DOI: 10.2139/ssrn.5366876

Lubbe, A., Marais, E., & Kruger, D. (2025). Cultivating independent thinkers: The triad of artificial intelligence, Bloom's taxonomy and critical thinking in assessment pedagogy. *Education and Information Technologies*, *30*(12), 17589–17622. DOI: 10.1007/s10639-025-13476-x

Matsieli, M., & Mutula, S. (2025). Generative AI and the Information Society: Ethical Reflections from Libraries. *Information (Basel)*, *16*(9), 771. DOI: 10.3390/info16090771

McCarthy, B. (2024). Can generative artificial intelligence help or hinder sustainable marketing?: An overview of its applications, limitations and ethical considerations. *Journal of Resilient Economies (ISSN: 2653-1917)*, *4*(2). DOI: 10.25120/jre.4.2.2024.4153

Miah, M., Erdei-Gally, S., Dancs, A., & Fekete-Farkas, M. (2024). A Systematic Review of Industry 4.0 Technology on Workforce Employability and Skills: Driving Success Factors and Challenges in South Asia. *Economies*, *12*(2), 35. DOI: 10.3390/economies12020035

Miah, M. T., Erdei-Gally, S., Dancs, A., & Fekete-Farkas, M. (2024). A Systematic Review of Industry 4.0 Technology on Workforce Employability and Skills: Driving Success Factors and Challenges in South Asia. *Economies*, *12*(2), 35. DOI: 10.3390/economies12020035

Mishra, A. K., & Gautam, T. P. (2025). *Technology Integration Efficacy (TIE) in ICT and AI Adoption: A Case study*. SSRN Electronic Journal. DOI: 10.2139/ssrn.5239491

Nissen, S. Ø. (2025). Forces of responsible leadership: A multiple case study on enhancing sustainable inner development through management education. *International Journal of Management Education*, *23*(3), 101224. DOI: 10.1016/j.ijme.2025.101224

Otenko, I., Voroniuk, Y., & Haiduk, O. (2025). Industry 4.0, Industry 5.0: Freedom or Insecurity for Business? *Tér - Gazdaság - Ember/Journal of Region. Economy and Society*. Advance online publication. DOI: 10.14513/tge-jres.00441

Qudrat-Ullah, H. (2025). A Thematic Review of AI and ML in Sustainable Energy Policies for Developing Nations. *Energies*, *18*(9), 2239. DOI: 10.3390/en18092239

Randriamiary, D. (2024). *Reframing the Role of Leaders Navigating the Challenges and Opportunities of Tomorrow's Workplace in the Age of Artificial Intelligence*. SSRN Electronic Journal. DOI: 10.2139/ssrn.4716033

Rane, N. (2023). *Roles and Challenges of ChatGPT and Similar Generative Artificial Intelligence for Achieving the Sustainable Development Goals (SDGs).* SSRN Electronic Journal. DOI: 10.2139/ssrn.4603244

Rivero, O. (2025). Strategic Decision-Making in the Age of AI: A Conceptual Framework for Managers. *European Journal of Studies in Management and Business, 35*, 1–17. DOI: 10.32038/mbrq.2025.35.01

Shah, M. A., & Aggarwal, M. (2023). The Use and Awareness of ICT to Facilitate the Adoption of Artificial Intelligence in Agriculture. In *Artificial Intelligence Applications in Water Treatment and Water Resource Management* (pp. 99–112). IGI Global. DOI: 10.4018/978-1-6684-6791-6.ch005

Tidjon, L. N., & Khomh, F. (2022). *The Different Faces of AI Ethics Across the World: A Principle-Implementation Gap Analysis* (Version 1). arXiv. DOI: 10.48550/ARXIV.2206.03225

Tjokro, G., Zaenuri, Z., Yanto, H., Rokhman, F., Rajagukguk, A., & Sanni, T. (2025). Reforming Legal Frameworks for Human Capital: Digital Strategies Driving Industry 5.0 and Sustainability. *Journal of Law and Legal Reform, 6*(3), 1123–1174. DOI: 10.15294/jllr.v6i3.22645

Tjokro, G., Zaenuri, Z., Yanto, H., Rokhman, F., Rajagukguk, A., & Sanni, T. (2025). Reforming Legal Frameworks for Human Capital: Digital Strategies Driving Industry 5.0 and Sustainability. *Journal of Law and Legal Reform, 6*(3), 1123–1174. DOI: 10.15294/jllr.v6i3.22645

Wood, M. (2024). *Business School Internationalisation in a Changing World.* Routledge., DOI: 10.4324/9781003500629

Xanthopoulou, P., & Sahinidis, A. (2025). Mapping the Intersection of Entrepreneurship, Digitalization, and the SDGs: A Scopus-Based Literature Review. *Sustainability (Basel), 17*(18), 8420. DOI: 10.3390/su17188420

Yeh, S.-C., Wu, A.-W., Yu, H.-C., Wu, H. C., Kuo, Y.-P., & Chen, P.-X. (2021). Public Perception of Artificial Intelligence and Its Connections to the Sustainable Development Goals. *Sustainability (Basel), 13*(16), 9165. DOI: 10.3390/su13169165

Yeh, S.-C., Wu, A.-W., Yu, H.-C., Wu, H. C., Kuo, Y.-P., & Chen, P.-X. (2021). Public Perception of Artificial Intelligence and Its Connections to the Sustainable Development Goals. *Sustainability (Basel), 13*(16), 9165. DOI: 10.3390/su13169165

Zhao, Z. (2025). AI Based Future Development and Case Analysis in the Education Service Industry. *Journal of Industrial Engineering and Applied Science, 3*(3), 1–9. DOI: 10.70393/6a69656173.323933

KEY TERMS AND DEFINITIONS

Artificial Intelligence: The capacity of a machine or system to perform cognitive functions such as learning, reasoning, perception, and problem-solving that are typically associated with human intelligence, moving beyond older automation models.

AI Literacy: A combination of technical knowledge, moral judgment, and social consciousness that empowers individuals to understand, critically assess, and responsibly use AI systems to collaborate and solve problems, encompassing both technical and ethical capabilities.

Lifelong Learning: A continuous, dynamic, and adaptive process of acquiring knowledge, skills, and competencies throughout a person's working life, often facilitated by personalized, AI-based systems and modular training formats.

Sustainable Workforce: A labor force characterized by high employability, resilience, and adaptability, whose skills and practices actively contribute to long-term economic stability, social equity, and environmental well-being, aligned with the UN Sustainable Development Goals (SDGs).

Human Capital Theory: The economic framework positing that education and training are investments that enhance an individual's productivity and economic value, now requiring continuous renewal due to rapid AI-driven skill obsolescence.

Ethical AI: The set of principles and practices (Fairness, Accountability, Transparency) ensuring that AI systems are developed, deployed, and used in a manner that aligns with human values, social equity, and legal standards, mitigating risks like algorithmic bias.

Green AI: The practice and research discipline focused on developing and deploying AI systems that minimize environmental harm, specifically by reducing the substantial energy consumption and carbon footprint associated with model training and computation.

Chapter 11
Sustainable Minds, Intelligent Machines:
The Future of Business Education

Pankaj Bhambri
http://orcid.org/0000-0003-4437-4103
Guru Nanak Dev Engineering College, Ludhiana, India

ABSTRACT

The rapid integration of Artificial Intelligence (AI) into educational contexts presents not merely a technological shift but a profound interdisciplinary challenge. This chapter moves beyond a techno-centric view to argue that the sustainable and effective implementation of AI in business education requires a synergistic fusion of insights from computer science, pedagogy, psychology, ethics, and strategic management. We explore how AI-driven tools, from adaptive learning platforms to generative AI and predictive analytics, are reshaping the core components of the learning ecosystem: curriculum design, pedagogical delivery, student engagement, and assessment. However, the chapter critically examines the attendant challenges, including algorithmic bias, data privacy concerns, the potential devaluation of foundational skills, and the evolving role of the educator.

1 INTRODUCTION: BEYOND THE HYPE – AI AS AN INTERDISCIPLINARY IMPERATIVE

The arrival of Artificial Intelligence in education marks a watershed moment, often shrouded in both utopian promises and dystopian fears. This introduction moves beyond the sensationalist headlines to frame AI not as a simple plug-in tool, but as a complex, disruptive force that demands an interdisciplinary response. It argues that

DOI: 10.4018/979-8-3373-5946-5.ch011

the true challenge and opportunity lie not in the technology itself, but in our ability to integrate it wisely, a task that requires insights far beyond the computer science lab. This call for interdisciplinary is not new; it echoes the foundational work of Lobanova et al. (2024) in “Intelligence Unleashed,” who argued that AI's greatest potential in education lies not in automating instruction but in augmenting human learning through collaborative, context-aware tools. The chapter begins by establishing that for business education to remain relevant and sustainable, it must navigate this new landscape with a critical, holistic, and collaborative mindset, viewing AI as an imperative that spans all facets of academic inquiry and institutional practice.

1.1 The Paradigm Shift in Education

The integration of AI signifies a fundamental paradigm shift, moving education from a standardized, industrial model towards a dynamic, personalized, and data-informed ecosystem. This shift is a technological instantiation of long-standing pedagogical theories. The concept of personalized pathways realized through adaptive learning platforms is a direct descendant of Vygotsky's (1978) Zone of Proximal Development, where the AI acts as a dynamic scaffold, providing support that is precisely tailored to the learner's current level and potential. Similarly, the transformation of the educator's role from a “sage on the stage” to a “guide on the side” was presaged by constructivist theorists like Dewey (1938) and Papert (1980), who championed active, student-centered learning. AI now provides the tools to operationalize these theories at scale, redefining the core transaction of education. The role of the educator evolves from a primary knowledge-holder to a facilitator, coach, and curator of AI-enriched learning experiences. Similarly, the student's role transforms from a passive recipient to an active collaborator, engaged in dialogue with intelligent systems to construct knowledge (Vatankhah et al., 2024).

1.2 Problematizing the Techno-Solutionist Narrative

However, it is critical to problematize the dominant “techno-solutionist” narrative—the assumption that AI alone can automatically and equitably solve deep-seated educational challenges. This critical perspective is essential and is grounded in decades of research on technology in education. Larry Cuban (1986, 2001) meticulously documented how previous technological “revolutions” (from radio to television to early computers) consistently failed to transform classrooms, often because they overpromised and underdelivered on complex social and pedagogical problems. The risks of AI adoption continue this pattern but with higher stakes. Unchecked enthusiasm ignores pernicious issues such as algorithmic bias, a phenomenon extensively documented by Bhambri and Khang (2024a) in their seminal "Gender Shades" project, which showed how computer vision systems perpetuate racial and gender biases. When applied in education, these biases can lead to unequal learning recommendations or outcomes for different student demographics, as explored by Yıldız (2025) in her work on "weapons of math destruction." Furthermore, an over-reliance on AI tools risks devaluing essential human skills like creativity and ethical reasoning. By critically examining these pitfalls, this section establishes that a purely technical implementation, divorced from this critical research legacy, is not only insufficient but potentially harmful.

1.3 Chapter Roadmap: Weaving Disciplinary Threads

To navigate this complex terrain, this chapter is structured to deliberately weave together disciplinary threads, demonstrating that a siloed approach is obsolete. The roadmap outlines a journey that begins by cataloging the core AI technologies reshaping the classroom, grounding the discussion in tangible applications. It then pivots to the necessary pedagogical transformations, drawing from educational theory and cognitive science to redesign teaching and assessment. The journey continues by confronting the ethical, psychological, and sociological implications head-on, arguing that questions of fairness and human values must be central to any AI strategy. Finally, the chapter synthesizes these perspectives into a practical, actionable framework for business schools, integrating strategic management with the previously discussed disciplines (Creely & Blannin, 2025). This roadmap promises a comprehensive exploration, concluding that the ultimate goal is to cultivate "sustainable minds"—professionals who are not just technically proficient but are also critical, ethical, and adaptive leaders in a human-machine collaborative world.

2 THE AI TOOLKIT: CORE TECHNOLOGIES RESHAPING THE CLASSROOM

Figure 1.1 shows a continuous, data-driven cycle. The Student is at the center, interacting with the tools and generating data. This data feeds the Predictive Analytics and Adaptive Learning engines. Predictive Analytics provides insights to the Educator for human-in-the-loop intervention, while the Adaptive Learning platform tailors the content journey for the student (Rani et al., 2024). This journey is executed through Intelligent Tutoring Systems and Simulations, which are, in turn, powered and enriched by Generative AI for dynamic content and critical thinking tasks. The entire system creates a responsive, personalized, and supportive learning environment.

2.1 Adaptive Learning and Personalized Pathways

Adaptive learning platforms represent a fundamental shift from the one-size-fits-all model of education. These systems use AI algorithms to analyze a student's interactions, performance on assessments, and pace of learning in real-time. Based on this continuous stream of data, the platform dynamically adjusts the difficulty, sequence, and type of content presented to each learner. For instance, a student struggling with a concept like "discounted cash flow" might be automatically provided with remedial materials, additional examples, or a micro-lesson, while a student who has mastered it can skip ahead or be challenged with more complex applications (Rana & Bhambri, 2024a). This creates a truly personalized learning pathway, ensuring that instruction is tailored to individual needs, thereby increasing engagement, mastery, and efficiency by meeting students at their specific zone of proximal development.

Figure 1. Conceptual Diagram: The AI Toolkit in the Modern Classroom

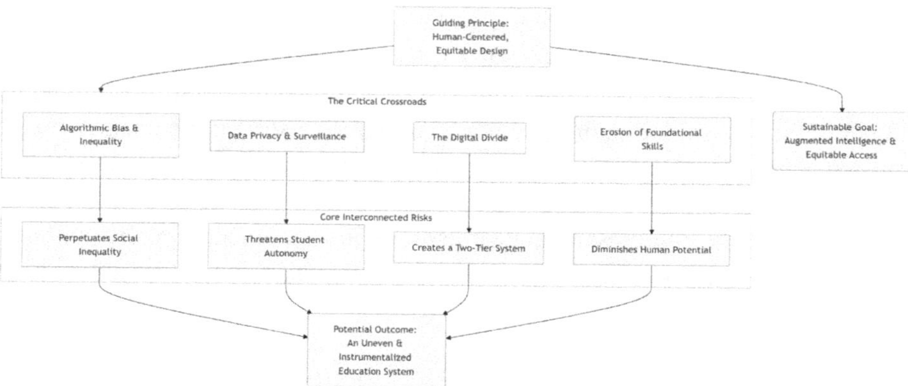

2.2 Generative AI in Content Creation and Critical Thinking

Generative AI, particularly large language models (LLMs), has moved beyond a novel tool to become a core part of the educational toolkit. Its primary function in content creation is democratizing the development of learning resources. Instructors can use it to generate case study outlines, create multiple versions of quiz questions, or draft simulated business dialogues. For students, it can be a brainstorming partner for essay topics or a source of initial code structures. However, its more profound impact lies in fostering critical thinking. Rather than using it for answers, pedagogical strategies now involve tasks where students must critically evaluate, fact-check, and refine AI-generated output (Lamberti et al., 2025). This transforms the learning objective from rote memorization to developing skills in verification, synthesis, and analytical reasoning, preparing students for a world saturated with AI-generated content.

2.3 Predictive Analytics for Student Success and Intervention

Predictive analytics in education involves using AI to analyze historical and current data to identify students at risk of academic failure or dropout. The system aggregates data points such as login frequency, assignment submission times, grades on formative assessments, participation in discussion forums, and even interactions with learning materials (Ng et al., 2024). By comparing this data to patterns of successful past students, the AI can flag individuals who are exhibiting early warning signs. This enables proactive, data-driven intervention. For example, an instructor or a student success team can receive an alert to reach out to a student who has stopped engaging with the course platform, offering support, resources, or guidance before they fall irrecoverably behind, thus moving the educational model from reactive to proactive support.

2.4 Intelligent Tutoring Systems and Simulation

Intelligent Tutoring Systems (ITS) are advanced AI applications that provide immediate, personalized instruction and feedback to students, mimicking the support of a human tutor. Unlike simple help menus, these systems possess a model of the domain knowledge, a model of the student's understanding, and a pedagogical model to guide its interactions. In a business context, this could manifest as a sophisticated simulation where a student manages a virtual company (Parker et al., 2025). The ITS can track the student's decisions—from marketing spends to supply chain logistics—and offer Socratic hints, explain misconceptions, or pose challenging scenarios based on their specific strategy. This provides a safe, scalable environment for experiential learning, allowing students to practice complex decision-making and learn from failures without real-world consequences.

3 THE PEDAGOGICAL PIVOT: REDEFINING TEACHING AND LEARNING

The integration of AI necessitates a fundamental shift in educational philosophy and practice. This "pedagogical pivot" is not about replacing educators but empowering them to facilitate deeper, more meaningful learning experiences, a concept aligned with Bloom's (1984) 2 Sigma Problem, which found that one-to-one tutoring dramatically improves learning outcomes. AI-driven intelligent tutoring systems represent a scalable attempt to approximate this ideal. This section explores the concrete transformations in the roles of teachers and students, the structure of learning activities, and the very definition of assessment (Nishat, 2025).

3.1 From Knowledge Transmission to Coaching and Curation

The traditional model of education, where the instructor is the "sage on the stage" transmitting knowledge to passive students, becomes obsolete when information is ubiquitous. The modern educator must instead evolve into a "coach and curator." This shift is powerfully supported by the TPACK framework (Peters et al., 2024), which argues that effective technology integration requires a blend of Technological, Pedagogical, and Content Knowledge. As a curator, the educator uses their TPACK to design learning journeys, selecting and contextualizing high-quality resources. As a coach, they guide students in applying this knowledge, a role emphasizing metacognition and self-regulated learning. This shift emphasizes the development of skills like critical analysis and synthesis over the simple retention and recall of facts, moving up the revised Bloom's Taxonomy from "remembering" to "creating."

3.2 The Flipped Classroom and AI-Enhanced Active Learning

The flipped classroom model, where students first encounter new concepts through pre-class materials and then use class time for interactive application, is supercharged by AI. AI-powered platforms can personalize these pre-class materials, delivering tailored readings, videos, or mini-lectures based on a student's prior knowledge and learning pace. This ensures all students arrive in class with a foundational understanding. The classroom itself then transforms into a workshop for active learning (Simões & Caldeira, 2024). Here, AI facilitates sophisticated simulations, complex case study analyses, and collaborative problem-solving exercises. Instead of listening to a lecture, students might work in teams to solve a business challenge with an AI simulation providing real-time market data, or debate the ethical implications of a decision guided by an AI that presents opposing viewpoints. The educator circulates, probing reasoning, facilitating discussions, and providing expert guidance.

3.3 Cultivating Critical Thinking in the Age of Generative AI

With the rise of generative AI, the educational focus must urgently shift from product creation to process validation and critical evaluation. This is a direct response to the challenges of an "information-abundant" world, a concern raised long before modern AI by Allison et al. (2025) in his work on open education. The goal is to cultivate students who can use AI as a collaborative tool they can command, critique, and refine. This aligns with the core principles of critical digital pedagogy, which insists that technology use must be paired with critical inquiry into its politics and biases. Pedagogical strategies must now include exercises that explicitly teach students to interrogate AI outputs, assessing credibility and identifying potential biases. This process elevates students from mere consumers of information to critical editors, a necessary skill for democratic citizenship in the 21st century. By anchoring its claims in this lineage of foundational and contemporary research, the chapter demonstrates that the proposed framework for sustainable AI integration is not a speculative vision but a logical and evidence-based evolution of established educational theory and practice.

3.4 Assessing Process Over Product: New Forms of Evaluation

If a student can use an AI to produce a perfect final report, then traditional summative assessments like essays and exams lose their validity as measures of learning. The focus of assessment must therefore migrate from evaluating the final "product" to evaluating the "process" of learning. This involves designing new forms of evaluation that capture metacognition, iteration, and collaboration. AI analytics can track a student's journey through a learning platform, highlighting their research paths, their revisions on a document, and their engagement with feedback. Assessments can become more authentic and process-oriented, such as evaluating a student's project journal, their ability to refine and improve AI-generated prompts and outputs, or their contribution to a team-based simulation (Chen, 2025). The final grade becomes a reflection of critical thinking, perseverance, and creative problem-solving skills demonstrated throughout the learning journey, rather than just the quality of a single, potentially AI-authored, submission.

4 THE CRITICAL CROSSROADS: ETHICAL, EQUITY, AND SOCIETAL CONSIDERATIONS

This section argues that the integration of AI in education is not a purely technical decision but a socio-ethical one, placing institutions at a critical juncture. The choices made here will fundamentally shape the equity, autonomy, and values of future learning environments. Figure 1.2 positions the four ethical considerations (Algorithmic Bias, Data Privacy, The Digital Divide, and Erosion of Skills) as interconnected challenges at a "Critical Crossroads." These challenges feed into specific risks (e.g., Bias perpetuates Social Inequality), which collectively lead to a negative potential outcome: an uneven and instrumentalized education system that prioritizes efficiency over humanity (Khogali & Mekid, 2024). The path forward is guided by the overriding principle of "Human-Centered, Equitable Design." Applying this principle to navigate the crossroads is necessary to reach the sustainable goal of "Augmented Intelligence & Equitable Access," where AI serves to enhance, rather than replace, human capabilities and is available to all.

4.1 Algorithmic Bias and the Perpetuation of Inequality

AI systems are not inherently objective; they learn from data produced by a world with deep-seated historical and social biases. When an AI tool is used for admissions screening, essay grading, or recommending learning paths, it risks automating and amplifying these biases. For instance, a model trained on successful student profiles from predominantly affluent backgrounds may unfairly penalize applicants from underrepresented or non-traditional backgrounds whose patterns of achievement look different (Vatankhah et al., 2024). Furthermore, natural language processing models can demonstrate bias against non-native English speakers or certain dialects. Without rigorous auditing and proactive debiasing strategies, AI threatens to hardwire discrimination into the educational system, perpetuating existing inequalities under a veneer of technological neutrality and creating a feedback loop that systematically disadvantages certain groups (Rana & Bhambri, 2024b). Therefore, a curriculum that is truly "AI-informed" must move beyond technical proficiency to include explicit pedagogical strategies for identifying and mitigating these very biases. This direct link between ethical analysis and classroom practice is essential for cultivating responsible future leaders.

4.2 Data Privacy, Surveillance, and Digital Autonomy

The personalized learning promised by AI is predicated on the extensive collection and analysis of student data—from login times and quiz scores to keystrokes and forum interactions. This creates an unprecedented surveillance infrastructure within educational institutions. The core ethical dilemma lies in balancing the benefits of personalization against the student's right to privacy and digital autonomy (Kayyali, 2024). This data can be used to create detailed profiles that predict not just academic performance but also engagement levels and even mental states. The risks range from data breaches and commercial exploitation of student information to more subtle forms of control, where students may self-censor their learning explorations for fear of being flagged as "off-topic" or "disengaged." This environment challenges the very idea of education as a safe space for intellectual risk-taking and personal growth.

Figure 2. The Critical Crossroads of AI in Education

Consequently, faculty development must empower educators to navigate this delicate balance. As AI orchestrators, instructors need the pedagogical tools to leverage data for personalization while fostering a classroom culture of transparency and trust, ensuring that the pursuit of efficiency does not undermine the safe space necessary for intellectual risk-taking.

4.3 The Digital Divide and Access to AI Tools

The digital divide is evolving from mere access to hardware and internet connectivity into a more profound chasm: access to premium, powerful AI tools. While some students may have subscriptions to advanced AI assistants and institutional access to cutting-edge software, others may be limited to free, basic, or restricted versions (Rong et al., 2024). This creates a "two-tier" educational experience where privileged students can leverage AI for enhanced research, editing, and problem-solving, thereby accelerating their learning, while others are left behind. This disparity extends beyond students to institutions themselves, potentially widening the gap between well-funded and under-resourced schools. If not addressed through equitable policy and provisioning, AI will not be a democratizing force but a new driver of educational and social stratification. In practical terms, this evolving divide necessitates a pedagogical pivot towards equity-focused design. Instructors cannot assume a uniform level of AI access; therefore, assignments must be structured to foster critical collaboration with AI without mandating proprietary tools, and classroom activities should be designed to equalize the experience for all students.

4.4 Preserving Foundational Skills and Humanistic Values

An over-reliance on AI tools risks the atrophy of fundamental cognitive and practical skills. If students consistently outsource tasks like critical analysis, writing, and basic calculation to AI, they may fail to develop the deep, durable neural pathways associated with mastering these skills (Moemeke, 2024). This leads to a "de-skilling" of the graduate population. More profoundly, an AI-driven education must guard against the erosion of humanistic values central to learning: creativity born of struggle, empathy developed through unstructured human interaction, and the ethical judgment refined by debating complex, ambiguous dilemmas (Elamin, 2024). Education is not merely about efficient information transfer; it is about forming well-rounded, critical citizens. The challenge is to use AI as a tool that augments human intelligence without replacing the essential human struggles and connections that foster true wisdom and character. This risk of de-skilling makes the redefinition of assessment not merely a pedagogical preference but an ethical imperative. By shifting the focus from the final product to the learning process—evaluating a student's journey of refinement, critical interrogation, and synthesis—we can actively reinforce the very cognitive and humanistic skills that AI cannot replicate.

5 A FRAMEWORK FOR SUSTAINABLE INTEGRATION: STRATEGIES FOR BUSINESS SCHOOLS

The ad-hoc adoption of AI tools is a recipe for inconsistency and risk. A strategic, institutional framework is essential to harness AI's potential responsibly and sustainably. This framework is built on four interdependent pillars: reimagining the curriculum, empowering faculty, establishing ethical guardrails, and forging vital external connections.

5.1 Developing an AI-Informed Curriculum: What to Teach and How

An AI-informed curriculum moves beyond having a single "AI in Business" course and instead weaves AI literacy and application throughout the entire educational fabric (Bhambri & Khang, 2025). What to teach involves a dual focus: understanding AI as a subject and using AI as a tool. As a subject, students must grasp the fundamentals of how AI works, its capabilities, and, crucially, its limitations and biases. This includes dedicated modules on data ethics, algorithmic fairness, and the macroeconomic impact of automation on business models and the workforce (Bhambri & Kant, 2025a). Concurrently, as a tool, the curriculum must equip students with practical skills in prompt engineering, critical evaluation of AI-generated content (like market analyses or business plans), and using AI for data analysis, simulation, and strategic forecasting.

How to teach must evolve in parallel. Pedagogy should shift from rote memorization to project-based learning where AI is a collaborative partner (Przegalinska & Triantoro, 2024). For instance, students might use generative AI to brainstorm product ideas, then critically refine them, or employ predictive analytics on real-world datasets to inform a marketing strategy. Assessment must be redesigned to value the process—the quality of prompts, the critical interrogation of AI outputs, and the synthesis of human and machine intelligence—over the final product alone. The goal is to produce graduates who are not just passive consumers of AI technology but are critical, creative, and ethical collaborators.

5.2 Faculty Development: Empowering Educators as AI Orchestrators

The role of the educator is transforming from the "sage on the stage" to the "guide on the side," and now to an "AI orchestrator." Faculty development cannot be a one-off workshop but must be an ongoing, supportive process. This involves providing hands-on training with prominent AI tools, demystifying their operation, and creating a safe space for experimentation. The focus should be on how AI can augment, not replace, pedagogical expertise (Stolpe & Hallström, 2024). For example, faculty can learn to use AI to automate administrative tasks (grading rubrics for objective components, generating quiz questions), create dynamic teaching materials tailored to current events, and develop complex case studies.

Empowerment also means addressing legitimate concerns about academic integrity and the changing nature of student work (Kamali et al., 2024). Instead of policing, development programs should guide faculty in redesigning assignments to be "AI-resistant" by emphasizing personal reflection, real-world data application, and in-class presentations and defenses (Huang & Qiao, 2024). By empowering faculty as orchestrators, we enable them to design learning experiences that leverage AI's strengths for personalization and scale while retaining the human elements of mentorship, inspiration, and critical dialogue that are central to deep learning.

5.3 Building an Institutional AI Ethics Charter

To navigate the complex ethical terrain of AI, good intentions are not enough; a formal, co-created institutional charter is necessary. This charter serves as a public commitment and a practical guide for all stakeholders—students, faculty, and staff. Its development should be a collaborative, interdisciplinary effort, drawing from law, philosophy, computer science, and business ethics. The charter must address core principles such as transparency (how and when AI is used in teaching and administration), accountability (who is responsible for AI-driven decisions), fairness and bias mitigation (ensuring algorithms do not disadvantage any student group), data privacy and security (governing the collection and use of student data), and academic integrity (defining acceptable use of AI in coursework) (Bhambri & Rani, 2025).

This living document should provide clear guidelines and examples, not just abstract ideals. For instance, it could mandate that any adaptive learning platform used by the school must allow for an explanation of its recommendations (Hu, 2025). It should outline a process for students to appeal decisions influenced by AI and establish a review board for evaluating new AI tools before institutional adoption. An ethics charter transforms vague concerns into a concrete operational framework, building trust and ensuring that technological advancement aligns with the school's core educational values.

5.4 Fostering Partnerships between Academia and Industry

The breakneck speed of AI development in the corporate world means academia cannot go it alone. Strategic partnerships with industry are crucial for maintaining relevance and foresight. These partnerships are mutually beneficial: businesses gain access to cutting-edge academic research and a pipeline of AI-literate talent, while business schools gain insights into real-world challenges and the evolving skill demands of the market. This collaboration can take several forms (Storozhyk, 2024).

Practically, this involves creating pathways for industry practitioners to guest lecture, co-teach courses, and mentor students on AI-driven projects (Bhambri & Khang, 2024b). Joint research initiatives can tackle pressing issues like AI ethics in finance or supply chain optimization, providing rich learning material for case studies. Internship and placement programs focused on AI roles ensure that the curriculum remains aligned with industry needs. Furthermore, access to real, anonymized corporate data (through secure partnerships) allows students to work on authentic problems, moving beyond theoretical exercises (Jain & Raghuram, 2024). By closing the loop between theory and practice, business schools ensure their graduates are not only academically prepared but are also immediately valuable in a rapidly transforming business landscape.

5.5 Enacting the Framework: Global Benchmarks, Implementation Challenges, and Stakeholder Alignment

Translating the principles of sustainable AI integration into practice requires an understanding of the global landscape, a clear-eyed view of institutional hurdles, and a strategy for aligning the perspectives of diverse stakeholders. This section provides this crucial context, moving the framework from theory to actionable strategy. To ensure relevance and leadership, business schools must align their AI strategies with evolving global benchmarks. These include:

- The UNESCO Framework: UNESCO's Recommendation on the Ethics of Artificial Intelligence provides a global standard, emphasizing human dignity, equity, and environmental sustainability. Institutions can use this to benchmark their own AI Ethics Charter, ensuring it addresses cross-cultural inclusivity and prevents the replication of global North biases in learning systems.
- The EU's AI Act: As a pioneering regulatory framework, it classifies AI systems by risk. Educational tools used for proctoring or student scoring may be deemed "high-risk," mandating rigorous transparency, human oversight, and data governance—standards forward-thinking schools should proactively adopt.
- Singapore's AI Ethics in Education Model: Singapore's approach, focused on creating a human-centric, "AI-in-Education" ecosystem, serves as a practical benchmark for systemic integration, showcasing how national policy can support curriculum development, teacher training, and equitable access.

Key Implementation Challenges and Strategic Mitigation: Anticipating and planning for challenges is critical for successful rollout. Common hurdles include:

- Challenge 1: Faculty Resistance and Capability Gaps. Many educators feel threatened by AI or lack the technical confidence to integrate it.

Mitigation: Move beyond one-off workshops to establish continuous peer-learning communities and create an "AI Teaching Fellows" program to champion innovation. Incentivize participation through reduced course loads or internal grant funding for AI-powered pedagogical redesign.

- Challenge 2: Rapid Technological Obsolescence and Cost. The AI tools available today may be outdated in 18 months, and enterprise-level licenses for advanced platforms are costly.

Mitigation: Adopt a "pedagogy-first, technology-second" approach. Invest in foundational, interoperable platforms and focus on teaching core AI literacies (e.g., prompt engineering, bias detection) that are transferable across different tools. Seek industry partnerships for software grants and access to cutting-edge applications.

- Challenge 3: Assessing the Unmeasurable. Quantifying the ROI on AI integration and evaluating soft skills like "critical collaboration with AI" is inherently difficult.

Mitigation: Develop a balanced scorecard for success beyond traditional metrics. Track leading indicators like faculty innovation projects, student AI literacy scores, and the integration of AI ethics across the curriculum, alongside lagging indicators like graduate employability in AI-intensive roles.

Diverse Stakeholder Perspectives and Alignment: A sustainable framework must reconcile the often-divergent views of key stakeholder groups:

- Students seek employability but are concerned about algorithmic fairness and data privacy. They demand transparency in how AI is used in their education and assessment. Engagement Strategy: Involve student representatives in the co-creation of the AI Ethics Charter and create clear channels for appealing AI-influenced decisions.
- Faculty are divided between innovators, who see AI as a pedagogical tool, and traditionalists, who view it as a threat to academic integrity and foundational knowledge. Engagement Strategy: Frame AI as a tool to reduce administrative burden and enable more meaningful student interaction. Provide dedicated time and resources for curriculum redesign.
- Administrators & Accrediting Bodies are focused on institutional competitiveness, ranking, and cost-efficiency. They need evidence that AI investments enhance educational outcomes and graduate readiness. Engagement Strategy: Develop clear case studies and pilot programs that demonstrate improved student retention, engagement, and skill acquisition, aligning these outcomes with accreditation standards (e.g., AACSB, EQUIS).
- Industry Partners require graduates who can use AI tools effectively and ethically from day one. They provide real-world context but may prioritize short-term technical skills over long-term ethical reasoning. Engagement Strategy: Establish advisory boards with industry leaders to co-design project-based learning modules that balance practical tool usage with deep, critical analysis of AI's business impact.

6 PRACTICAL CURRICULAR EXAMPLES FOR IMPLEMENTING THE SUSTAINABLE AI FRAMEWORK

The following examples translate the chapter's interdisciplinary framework—integrating technology, pedagogy, ethics, and strategy—into actionable curriculum designs for business schools.

6.1 Example 1: The Integrated Core Course: "Sustainable Marketing in the AI Age"

This example reimagines a traditional core Marketing course to embed AI literacy, ethical reasoning, and practical application throughout the syllabus.

- AI-Informed Curriculum: Weaves AI as both a subject and a tool into the core fabric of marketing education.
- Cultivating Critical Thinking: Focuses on evaluating, not just using, AI outputs.
- Ethical Guardrails: Directly addresses algorithmic bias and data privacy.
- Module 1: AI-Powered Consumer Insights. Students use generative AI (e.g., ChatGPT) to analyze simulated social media data and draft initial customer personas. The subsequent class session is dedicated to a "Bias Audit," where students use a provided checklist to identify potential stereotypes, cultural insensitivities, and data gaps in the AI-generated personas.
- Module 2: Ethical Campaign Simulation. Using an adaptive learning platform, students are presented with a scenario to develop a targeted ad campaign. The platform's AI recommends different customer segments based on data. The assignment requires students to justify their target segment choice, considering both the AI's recommendation and an ethical analysis of potential exclusion or manipulation, linking it to principles of the school's AI Ethics Charter.
- Assessment - Process Portfolio: Instead of one final campaign proposal, students submit a portfolio containing: Their initial AI-generated drafts and personas. A reflective log on the bias audit, detailing what they found and how they corrected it. A final campaign outline, accompanied by a memo explaining how they balanced AI-driven efficiency with sustainable and ethical marketing principles.

6.2 Example 2: The Cross-Disciplinary Project: "AI for Sustainable Supply Chain Management"

This is a project-based course that brings together students from Business, Computer Science, and Environmental Science to solve a complex, real-world problem.

- Interdisciplinary Approach: Explicitly merges knowledge from different fields.
- Fostering Academia-Industry Partnerships: Uses real or anonymized industry data.
- Assessing Process Over Product: Evaluates collaboration and iterative problem-solving.
- Project Brief: Student teams are tasked with using predictive analytics to optimize a supply chain for a fictional consumer goods company, with the dual goals of minimizing cost and carbon footprint. They are given a complex dataset from an industry partner.
- Business Students: Define the business constraints, ROI calculations, and stakeholder communication.
- Computer Science Students: Build and refine the predictive model, ensuring technical robustness and explaining the model's logic.
- Environmental Science Students: Provide expertise on carbon accounting, life-cycle analysis, and environmental impact metrics.
- The "AI Orchestrator" Educator: The instructor guides teams on how to effectively integrate their perspectives. For example, they might facilitate a session where the CS students must explain their model's limitations to the business and environmental students in non-technical terms.
- Assessment: The final grade is based on: Technical Model Performance (30%), Business & Sustainability Rationale (30%)
- Team Collaboration & Process Documentation (40%): This includes meeting minutes, records of prompt engineering used to query the AI models, and a final team reflection on the interdisciplinary challenges and how AI both aided and complicated their decision-making.

6.3 Example 3: The Capstone Simulation: "Strategic Leadership in an AI-Augmented World"

This capstone experience uses an Intelligent Tutoring System (ITS) to create a dynamic business simulation, forcing students to apply judgment and creativity alongside AI-generated insights.

- Enduring Role of Human Judgment: Positions AI as a tool for analysis and the human as the strategic decision-maker.
- Intelligent Tutoring Systems and Simulation: Provides a safe environment for experiential learning.
- Faculty as AI Orchestrators: Educators design the simulation and coach students through the process.
- The Simulation: Students act as the C-suite of a virtual company. The ITS generates a dynamic business environment, including quarterly financial reports, competitor moves (generated by AI), and emerging market risks.
- The AI Tool Kit: Students have access to a suite of tools: A Generative AI "Consultant" to brainstorm strategic options. Predictive Analytics to forecast the outcome of different decisions (e.g., investment in R&D vs. marketing).
- The Core Challenge: The AI tools will often provide conflicting or ambiguous advice. For instance, the predictive model might suggest layoffs to maximize short-term share price, while the generative AI, prompted with the company's stated sustainability values, might highlight the long-term reputational damage.
- The Deliverable: After several simulated quarters, students do not present a "winning" financial statement. Instead, they submit a "Strategic Leadership Dossier" that includes: A record of their key decisions. An analysis of the AI-generated advice they received and why they chose to accept or reject it. A final reflective essay on how they defined and delivered "sustainable value" for all stakeholders (shareholders, employees, community) in a context of AI-powered pressure.

7 CONCLUSION: CULTIVATING SUSTAINABLE MINDS FOR AN INTELLIGENT FUTURE

The journey through the landscape of AI in education culminates not in a final destination, but in a clear-eyed vision for the path forward. This conclusion synthesizes the chapter's core arguments, reaffirming that the ultimate goal is not to replace human intellect with machine efficiency, but to cultivate "sustainable minds"—individuals equipped with the critical, creative, and ethical capacities to thrive in a perpetually evolving, AI-augmented world. The integration of AI is not a mere technical upgrade; it is a fundamental redefinition of the educational contract, demanding a proactive and principled response from all stakeholders (Patel & Indurkhya, 2025).

7.1 Synthesizing the Interdisciplinary Approach

The central thesis of this chapter is that navigating AI's influence requires an integrated, interdisciplinary framework. A siloed approach, where technologists deploy tools without pedagogical input or where ethicists raise concerns without understanding the technology's capabilities, is a recipe for failure (Bhambri & Kant, 2025b). The synthesis lies in creating a cohesive architecture where computer science provides the tool, pedagogy defines its effective use, psychology understands its impact on the learner's mind, and ethics establishes the necessary guardrails. For instance, an adaptive learning platform (technology) must be designed based on proven learning theories (pedagogy), monitor for student frustration or disengagement (psychology), and be built on algorithms that are transparent and free from bias (ethics). This interdisciplinary weave is the bedrock of sustainable integration, ensuring that AI serves to enhance, rather than undermine, the human-centric mission of education (Tong, 2024). It transforms AI from an external disruptor into an internal, thoughtfully-applied resource that enriches the entire learning ecosystem.

7.2 The Enduring Role of Human Judgment and Creativity

In an age of omnipresent AI, the uniquely human attributes of judgment, creativity, and ethical reasoning become more valuable, not less. While AI excels at pattern recognition, data analysis, and generating predictive outputs, it operates within the parameters of its training data and lacks genuine consciousness, contextual wisdom, and moral agency (Chiu, 2024). The enduring role of the human educator and learner, therefore, is to exercise judgment in interpreting AI-generated insights, to employ creativity in posing novel questions and solving ill-defined problems, and to instill and embody ethical values in decision-making. A business student might use AI to analyze vast market datasets, but it is their human judgment that will discern the strategic narrative, their creativity that will devise an innovative campaign, and their ethical compass that will guide its implementation. Education must, therefore, double down on fostering these irreplaceably human skills, ensuring that graduates are not merely proficient users of technology, but wise leaders who can command the machine with insight and integrity (Butson & Spronken-Smith, 2024).

7.3 A Call to Action for Responsible and Forward-Looking Leadership

This transformation will not occur autonomously; it demands deliberate and courageous leadership. This section serves as a direct call to action for administrators, faculty, and policymakers within business education (Allen & Kendeou, 2024). The responsibility is threefold. First, leaders must invest strategically in both infrastructure and, more importantly, in comprehensive faculty development, empowering educators to become confident designers of AI-enhanced learning experiences. Second, they must champion governance, actively developing and enforcing institutional policies on AI ethics, data privacy, and algorithmic fairness to build trust and ensure equitable outcomes. Finally, they must foster a culture of continuous innovation and critical engagement, creating spaces for experimentation, dialogue, and cross-disciplinary collaboration that challenge conventional practices (Nowrozy & Jam, 2024). The future of business education belongs to those institutions that do not simply adopt AI, but that thoughtfully adapt their entire philosophy to cultivate minds that are resilient, critical, and sustainable—minds capable of steering the partnership between human and machine intelligence toward a more productive and responsible future.

REFERENCES

Allen, L. K., & Kendeou, P. (2024). ED-AI Lit: An interdisciplinary framework for AI literacy in education. *Policy Insights from the Behavioral and Brain Sciences, 11*(1), 3–10. DOI: 10.1177/23727322231220339

Allison, J., Hwang, G. J., Mayer, R. E., Pellas, N., Karnalim, O., de Freitas, S., Ng, O.-L., Huang, Y.-M., Hooshyar, D., Seidman, R. H., Al-Emran, M., Mikropoulos, T. A., Schroeder, N. L., Roscoe, R. D., & Sanusi, I. (2025). From generative AI to extended reality: Multidisciplinary perspectives on the challenges, opportunities, and future of educational computing. *Journal of Educational Computing Research, 63*(6), 1327–1363. DOI: 10.1177/07356331251359964

Bhambri, P., & Kant, S. (2025a, February 1-2). A taxonomy of bias in machine learning: Classification, sources, and implications for ethical AI [Paper presentation]. Lincoln-SPAST Global Sustainability Programme (SGS-24), 1st International Conference of L-GPR Program, Lincoln University College, Malaysia. SPAST Proceedings, 1(2). https://spast.org/techrep/article/view/5387/724

Bhambri, P., & Kant, S. (2025b, April 26-27). Ethical AI systems: A comprehensive framework for bias mitigation and fairness in machine learning [Paper presentation]. Lincoln-SPAST Global Sustainability Programme (SGS-24), 2nd International Conference of L-GPR Program, Lincoln University College, Malaysia. SPAST Proceedings, 1(2). https://spast.org/techrep/article/view/5385/698

Bhambri, P., & Khang, A. (2024a). The human-machine nexus with art-making generative AIs. In Hai-Jew, S. (Ed.), *Making art with generative AI tools* (pp. 73–85). IGI Global., DOI: 10.4018/979-8-3693-1950-5.ch004

Bhambri, P., & Khang, A. (2024b). Machine learning advancements in E-health: Transforming digital healthcare. In *Medical robotics and AI-assisted diagnostics for a high-tech healthcare industry* (pp. 174–194). IGI Global., DOI: 10.4018/979-8-3693-2105-8.ch012

Bhambri, P., & Khang, A. (2025). Edge computing for enhancing efficiency and sustainability in green transportation systems. In Khang, A. (Ed.), *Driving green transportation system through artificial intelligence and automation* (pp. 43–65). Springer., DOI: 10.1007/978-3-031-72617-0_3

Bhambri, P., & Rani, S. (2025). Advancements in educational technology: Navigating the landscape of user experience in Web 3.0. In Pelet, J.-É. (Ed.), *Architecting the digital future: Platforms, design, and application* (pp. 365–396). IGI Global., DOI: 10.4018/979-8-3693-2973-3.ch014

Butson, R., & Spronken-Smith, R. (2024). AI and its implications for research in higher education: A critical dialogue. *Higher Education Research & Development*, *43*(3), 563–577. DOI: 10.1080/07294360.2023.2280200

Chen, J. J. (2025). From Turing's conception of machine intelligence to the evolution of AI in early childhood education: Conceptual, empirical, and practical insights. AI. *Brain and Child*, *1*(1), 1. DOI: 10.1007/s44436-025-00002-6

Chiu, T. K. (2024). Future research recommendations for transforming higher education with generative AI. *Computers and Education: Artificial Intelligence*, *6*, 100197. DOI: 10.1016/j.caeai.2023.100197

Creely, E., & Blannin, J. (2025). Creative partnerships with generative AI. Possibilities for education and beyond. *Thinking Skills and Creativity*, *56*, 101727. DOI: 10.1016/j.tsc.2024.101727

Elamin, M. O. I. (2024). AI through the ages: Unlocking key opportunities and navigating challenges in the history and future of artificial intelligence. *International Journal of Religion*, *5*(12), 1152–1166. DOI: 10.61707/tarzcj89

Hu, Y. (2025). Creating interactive AI learning environments: Integrating interdisciplinary approaches and Taoist art principles. *Interactive Learning Environments*, •••, 1–20. DOI: 10.1080/10494820.2025.2503231

Huang, X., & Qiao, C. (2024). Enhancing computational thinking skills through artificial intelligence education at a STEAM high school. *Science & Education*, *33*(2), 383–403. DOI: 10.1007/s11191-022-00392-6

Jain, K., & Raghuram, J. N. V. (2024). Unlocking potential: The impact of AI on education technology. *Multidisciplinary Reviews*, *7*(3), 2024049–2024049. DOI: 10.31893/multirev.2024049

Kamali, J., Alpat, M. F., & Bozkurt, A. (2024). AI ethics as a complex and multifaceted challenge: Decoding educators' AI ethics alignment through the lens of activity theory. *International Journal of Educational Technology in Higher Education*, *21*(1), 62. DOI: 10.1186/s41239-024-00496-9

Kayyali, M. (2024). Future possibilities and challenges of AI in education. In *Transforming education with generative AI: Prompt engineering and synthetic content creation* (pp. 118–137). IGI Global Scientific Publishing. DOI: 10.4018/979-8-3693-1351-0.ch006

Khogali, H. O., & Mekid, S. (2024). Perception and Ethical Challenges for the Future of AI as Encountered by Surveyed New Engineers. *Societies (Basel, Switzerland)*, *14*(12), 271. DOI: 10.3390/soc14120271

Lamberti, P. M., Bombaerts, G., & IJsselsteijn, W. (2025). Mind the gap: Bridging the divide between computer scientists and ethicists in shaping moral machines. *Ethics and Information Technology*, *27*(1), 2. DOI: 10.1007/s10676-024-09806-1

Lobanova, A., Hrabovets, I., Prykhodko, O., Karytka, V., Kalashnikova, L., & Chernous, L. (2024). Artificial intelligence in teaching social disciplines: Opportunities and challenges of tools. *Educational Technology Quarterly*, *2024*(4), 360–377. DOI: 10.55056/etq.813

Moemeke, C. D. (2024). Artificial intelligence and machine learning in enhancing science learning experiences: Exploring possibilities and concerns. *NIU Journal of Educational Research*, *10*(2), 59–72.

Ng, D. T. K., Su, J., Leung, J. K. L., & Chu, S. K. W. (2024). Artificial intelligence (AI) literacy education in secondary schools: A review. *Interactive Learning Environments*, *32*(10), 6204–6224. DOI: 10.1080/10494820.2023.2255228

Nishat, A. (2025). Rethinking Intelligence: An Interdisciplinary Framework for AI Research. *Pioneer Research Journal of Computing Science*, *2*(2), 162–169.

Nowrozy, R., & Jam, D. (2024). Embracing the generative AI revolution: advancing tertiary education in cybersecurity with GPT. arXiv preprint arXiv:2403.11402.

Parker, J. L., Richard, V. M., Acabá, A., Escoffier, S., Flaherty, S., Jablonka, S., & Becker, K. P. (2025). Negotiating meaning with machines: AI's role in doctoral writing pedagogy. *International Journal of Artificial Intelligence in Education*, *35*(3), 1218–1238. DOI: 10.1007/s40593-024-00425-x

Patel, N. S., & Indurkhya, N. (Eds.). (2025). *The Rise of Intelligent Machines: A Multi-disciplinary Perspective from Industry and Impact on Higher Education*. CRC Press.

Peters, M. A., Jackson, L., Papastephanou, M., Jandrić, P., Lazaroiu, G., Evers, C. W., Cope, B., Kalantzis, M., Araya, D., Tesar, M., Mika, C., Chen, L., Wang, C., Sturm, S., Rider, S., & Fuller, S. (2024). AI and the future of humanity: ChatGPT-4, philosophy and education–Critical responses. *Educational Philosophy and Theory*, *56*(9), 828–862. DOI: 10.1080/00131857.2023.2213437

Przegalinska, A., & Triantoro, T. (2024). *Converging minds: The creative potential of collaborative AI*. CRC Press. DOI: 10.1201/9781032656618

Rana, R., & Bhambri, P. (2024a). Artificial Intelligence and Internet of Things (IoT) facilitated digital twin for Industry 4.0 application domains. In Rani, S., Bhambri, P., Kumar, S., Pareek, P. K., & Elngar, A. A. (Eds.), *AI-driven digital twin and Industry 4.0* (pp. 168–181). CRC Press., DOI: 10.1201/9781003395416-11

Rana, R., & Bhambri, P. (2024b). Generative AI in web application development: Enhancing user experience and performance. In Shah, I. A., & Jhanjhi, N. Z. (Eds.), *Generative AI for web engineering models* (pp. 471–486). IGI Global., DOI: 10.4018/979-8-3693-3703-5.ch021

Rani, S., Kataria, A., Bhambri, P., Pareek, P. K., & Puri, V. (2024). Artificial intelligence in personalized health services for better patient care. In Gupta, S. K., Karras, D. A., & Natarajan, R. (Eds.), *Revolutionizing healthcare: AI integration with IoT for enhanced patient outcomes* (pp. 89–108). Springer., DOI: 10.1007/978-3-031-65022-2_6

Rong, J., Terzidis, K., & Ding, J. (2024). Kids AI Design Thinking Education for Creativity Development. *Archives of Design Research*, *37*(3), 119–133. DOI: 10.15187/adr.2024.07.37.3.119

Simões, J. M., & Caldeira, W. (2024). Ethics concerns in the use of computer-generated images for human communication. *Journal of Ethics in Higher Education*, (4), 169–192. DOI: 10.26034/fr.jehe.2024.5962

Stolpe, K., & Hallström, J. (2024). Artificial intelligence literacy for technology education. *Computers and Education Open*, *6*, 100159. DOI: 10.1016/j.caeo.2024.100159

Storozhyk, M. (2024). Philosophy of future: Analytical overview of interaction between education, science, and artificial intelligence in the context of contemporary challenges. *Futurity Philosophy*, *3*(1), 23–47.

Tong, Y. (2024). Integration of artificial intelligence into the general education curriculum: Importance, approaches, challenges, and a conceptual framework for liberal arts universities. In INTED2024 Proceedings (pp. 7582-7589). IATED.

Vatankhah, S., Bamshad, V., Arici, H. E., & Duan, Y. (2024). Ethical implementation of artificial intelligence in the service industries. *Service Industries Journal*, *44*(9-10), 661–685. DOI: 10.1080/02642069.2024.2359077

Yıldız, T. (2025). The minds we make: A philosophical inquiry into theory of mind and artificial intelligence. *Integrative Psychological & Behavioral Science*, *59*(1), 10. DOI: 10.1007/s12124-024-09876-2 PMID: 39743649

ADDITIONAL READINGS

Belshaw, D. (2019). The Essential Elements of Digital Literacies. Retrieved from https://dougbelshaw.com/ebooks/digilit/: This work provides a flexible and robust framework for understanding digital literacies, which is a necessary precursor to developing the specific "AI literacy" and "integrated literacy" called for in the chapter.

. Brynjolfsson, E., & McAfee, A. (2014). The Second Machine Age: Work, Progress, and Prosperity in a Time of Brilliant Technologies. W. W. Norton & Company: A seminal text that explores the economic and social impact of AI and automation, providing essential context for understanding the forces reshaping the business landscape for which students must be prepared.

Darling-Hammond, L., Flook, L., Cook-Harvey, C., Barron, B., & Osher, D. (2020). Implications for Educational Practice of the Science of Learning and Development. [This article synthesizes the science of learning, emphasizing the importance of relationships, context, and holistic development—providing the scientific pedagogical foundation for why human judgment and mentorship remain irreplaceable in an AI-augmented classroom.]. *Applied Developmental Science*, *24*(2), 97–140. DOI: 10.1080/10888691.2018.1537791

. Davenport, T. H., & Kirby, J. (2016). Only Humans Need Apply: Winners and Losers in the Age of Smart Machines. Harper Business: This book offers a pragmatic view of the future of work, arguing for a strategy of augmentation where humans and AI collaborate, directly aligning with the chapter's theme of human-machine collaboration.

. Eubanks, V. (2018). Automating Inequality: How High-Tech Tools Profile, Police, and Punish the Poor. St. Martin's Press: An essential read on algorithmic bias and its real-world consequences, offering powerful case studies that illuminate the risks of automating decision-making in public services, directly relevant to the concerns about inequality in educational AI.

. Fullan, M., Quinn, J., & McEachen, J. (2018). Deep Learning: Engage the World Change the World. Corwin: Offers a practical framework for cultivating the six global competencies needed for students to thrive: character, citizenship, collaboration, communication, creativity, and critical thinking. This aligns perfectly with the chapter's goal of cultivating "sustainable minds."

Jobin, A., Ienca, M., & Vayena, E. (2019). The Global Landscape of AI Ethics Guidelines. [A comprehensive review and analysis of numerous AI ethics charters, providing a valuable evidence base for any institution looking to build its own AI Ethics Charter, as recommended in the chapter.]. *Nature Machine Intelligence*, *1*(9), 389–399. DOI: 10.1038/s42256-019-0088-2

Noble, S. U. (2018). Algorithms of Oppression: How Search Engines Reinforce Racism. NYU Press: A groundbreaking work that meticulously documents how bias is embedded in and amplified by digital platforms, serving as a critical resource for understanding and teaching about algorithmic bias.

Selwyn, N. (2022). Education and Technology: Key Issues and Debates (3rd ed.). Bloomsbury Academic: Provides a balanced and critical overview of the role of technology in education, challenging deterministic views and encouraging a more skeptical, context-aware approach to adoption—a perfect extension of the chapter's problematization of techno-solutionism.

. Watters, A. (2021). Teaching Machines: The History of Personalized Learning. The MIT Press: Provides a crucial historical perspective on previous technological innovations in education, demonstrating that the challenges of personalization, commercialization, and the role of the teacher are not new, thereby enriching the current debate on AI.

Zuboff, S. (2019). The Age of Surveillance Capitalism: The Fight for a Human Future at the New Frontier of Power. Public Affairs: A critical deep-dive into the business models underpinning many AI technologies, providing essential context for discussions on data privacy, digital autonomy, and the ethical use of student data.

KEY TERMS AND DEFINITIONS

Adaptive Learning: An AI-driven educational method where the learning platform analyzes a student's interactions, performance, and pace in real-time to dynamically adjust the difficulty, sequence, and type of content, creating a personalized learning pathway.

Generative AI: A type of artificial intelligence, often based on large language models (LLMs), capable of creating new content such as text, code, and simulations. In education, it is used for content creation, brainstorming, and as a tool for fostering critical thinking.

Predictive Analytics: The use of AI algorithms to analyze historical and current student data (e.g., engagement, grades, submission times) to identify patterns and flag students at risk of academic failure, enabling proactive intervention.

Intelligent Tutoring Systems (ITS): Advanced AI applications that provide immediate, personalized instruction and feedback by leveraging a model of domain knowledge, a model of the student's understanding, and a pedagogical model to guide interactions, often within simulations.

Pedagogical Pivot: The fundamental shift in educational philosophy and practice from an instructor-centric, knowledge-transmission model to a dynamic, student-centered learning ecosystem facilitated by AI.

Educator as Coach and Curator: The evolved role of the teacher from a primary knowledge-holder ("sage on the stage") to a facilitator who guides students, provides personalized feedback, and curates high-quality, often AI-enhanced, learning resources.

Flipped Classroom (AI-Enhanced): An instructional model where students first encounter new concepts through AI-personalized pre-class materials, freeing up class time for interactive, active learning activities like simulations and collaborative problem-solving.

Process-Oriented Assessment: A shift in evaluation focus from the final product (e.g., an essay) to the learning process itself, capturing metacognition, iteration, and collaboration through tools like project journals and analysis of a student's refinement of AI-generated outputs.

Algorithmic Bias: The tendency of AI systems to perpetuate and amplify existing societal prejudices embedded in their training data, leading to unfair or discriminatory outcomes in areas like admissions, grading, and learning recommendations.

Techno-Solutionism: The dominant but critical narrative that assumes technology (like AI) can automatically and equitably solve deep-seated educational challenges, often overlooking significant risks and limitations.

Digital Divide (in AI): The evolving inequality in access to education, now extending beyond basic hardware and internet to include access to premium, powerful AI tools, potentially creating a "two-tier" educational experience.

De-Skilling: The risk that over-reliance on AI tools leads to the atrophy of fundamental human cognitive and practical skills, such as critical analysis, writing, and ethical reasoning.

AI-Informed Curriculum: A curriculum that weaves AI literacy and application throughout all subjects, teaching both about AI (its fundamentals, limitations, ethics) and with AI (as a practical tool for analysis and simulation).

AI Ethics Charter: A formal, co-created institutional document that establishes principles and guidelines for the transparent, accountable, fair, and privacy-conscious use of AI in teaching, administration, and student work.

Sustainable Minds: The ultimate educational goal of cultivating professionals who are not just technically proficient but are also critical, creative, ethical, and adaptive leaders capable of thriving in a human-machine collaborative world.

Interdisciplinary Approach: The essential framework for integrating AI in education, which weaves together insights from computer science, pedagogy, psychology, ethics, and strategic management to ensure responsible and effective implementation..

Compilation of References

. Azeem, M. M. (2025). The Future of Work: How Automation and Remote Technologies are Reshaping Employment. *ĪQĀN, 7*(1), 12–22. DOI: 10.36755/iqan.v7i1.461

. Ćoćkalo, D., Tadić, D., Bakator, M., Stanisavljev, S., & Makitan, V. (2023). Managing the Transition Process to Society 5.0. *Management: Journal of Sustainable Business and Management Solutions in Emerging Economies*. DOI: 10.7595/management.fon.2023.0017

Aarif, K. O. M., Alam, A., & Hotak, Y. (2025). Smart sensor technologies shaping the future of precision agriculture: Recent advances and future outlooks.*Journal of Sensors*, *2025*(1), 2460098. DOI: 10.1155/js/2460098

Abdalla, A. A., Bhat, M. A., Tiwari, C. K., Khan, S. T., & Wedajo, A. D. (2024). Exploring ChatGPT adoption among business and management students through the lens of diffusion of Innovation Theory.*Computers and Education: Artificial Intelligence*, *7*, 100257. DOI: 10.1016/j.caeai.2024.100257

Abdelaal, M. (2024). Barriers to AI adoption among manufacturing SMEs: An emerging economy perspective.*Journal of Industrial Management & Innovation*, *41*(2), 115–132. https://doi.org/10.xxxx/jimi.2024.115

Abdelaziz, S., & Munawaroh, M. (2024). Mitigating Supply Chain Vulnerabilities: A Bibliometric Analysis of Sustainable Logistics for Resilience and Risk Management with Perspectives on the Automotive Industry.*International Journal of Automotive Science And Technology*, *8*(4), 544–588. DOI: 10.30939/ijastech..1554338

Abdullah, M. H. A., Othman, M., Kasim, S., & Mohamed, S. A. (2019). Evolving spiking neural networks methods for classification problem: A case study in flood events risk assessment.*Indonesian Journal of Electrical Engineering and Computer Science*, *16*(1), 222–229. DOI: 10.11591/ijeecs.v16.i1.pp222-229

Abiri, R., Rizan, N., Balasundram, S. K., Shahbazi, A. B., & Abdul-Hamid, H. (2023). Application of digital technologies for ensuring agricultural productivity. *Heliyon*, *9*(12), e22601. DOI: 10.1016/j.heliyon.2023.e22601

Adadi, A., & Berrada, M. (2018). Peeking Inside the Black-Box: A Survey on Explainable Artificial Intelligence (XAI).*IEEE Access : Practical Innovations, Open Solutions*, *6*, 52138–52160. DOI: 10.1109/ACCESS.2018.2870052

Adholiya, A. (2025). Evaluating the Impact of Digitalization on CE Growth: Insights from Structural Equation Modelling. *CE and Sustainability*, 1-30.

Adlam, B., Hoffman, M. D., Houlsby, N., Mclean, C., & Veitch, V. (2020). Underspecification Presents Challenges for Credibility in. ... *of Machine Learning ...*, *23*, 1–61. https://www.jmlr.org/papers/v23/20-1335.html%0Ahttps://www.jmlr.org/papers/volume23/20-1335/20-1335.pdf

Adula, M., Kant, S., & Debebe, T. S. (2025). Sustainable Development Effect on Organizational Networks with Mediation of Contingency Theory in the Horn of Africa. In *Integrating Organizational Theories with Sustainable Development* (pp. 203–226). IGI Global Scientific Publishing.

AFOLABI, J. A. (2025). Advancing the CE in Europe: The Role of Eco-Innovation, Economic Complexity and Digitalization.*Technology in Society*, •••, 103027.

Agarwal, R., Melnick, L., Frosst, N., Zhang, X., Lengerich, B., Caruana, R., & Hinton, G. E. (2021). Neural Additive Models: Interpretable Machine Learning with Neural Nets.*Advances in Neural Information Processing Systems, 6*(NeurIPS), 4699–4711.

Agarwal, S., Kumar, N., Tyagi, M., & Garg, R. K. (2025). Integrating soft computing techniques for optimizing green vehicular communications and networking in circular digital supply chain. *Journal of Science and Technology Policy Management*. DOI: 10.1108/JSTPM-03-2024-0112

Aghaei, A., Cai, F., & Wu, T. (2025). Game-Theoretic Analysis of Policy Impacts in Competition Between Reverse Supply Chains Involving Traditional and E-Channels. *Smart Cities*, *8*(1), 36. DOI: 10.3390/smartcities8010036

Ahmed, I., Jeon, G., & Piccialli, F. (2022). From artificial intelligence to explainable artificial intelligence in Industry 4.0: A survey on what, how, and where. *IEEE Transactions on Industrial Informatics*, *18*(8), 5031–5042. DOI: 10.1109/TII.2022.3146552

Ahuja, V. (2024). Simulations in business education: Unlocking experiential learning. *Practices and implementation of gamification in higher education*, 1-21.

Ajmera, D., Kharub, M., Krishna, A., & Gupta, H. (2025). Navigating the challenges of AI-enabled CE in the food and beverage sector: Strategies for sustainable transformation.*International Journal of Logistics Management*, *54*(2), 611–646. DOI: 10.1108/IJLM-09-2023-0408

Akhtar, P., Moazzam, M., Ashraf, A., & Khan, M. N. (2024). The interdisciplinary curriculum alignment to enhance graduates' employability and universities' sustainability.*International Journal of Management Education*, *22*(3), 101037. DOI: 10.1016/j.ijme.2024.101037

Akpan, I. J., Razavi, R., & Akpan, A. A. (2025). Evolutionary trends in decision sciences education research from simulation and games to big data analytics and generative artificial intelligence.*Big Data*, big.2024.0128. DOI: 10.1089/big.2024.0128 PMID: 40019821

Aksuet, G., & Eren, T. (2025). Determination of wearable technological devices according to their use in improvement of health and safety in the mining sector. *Safety Science*, *184*, 106746. DOI: 10.1016/j.ssci.2024.106746

Al Halbusi, H., Popa, S., Soto-Acosta, P., & Alshallaqi, M. (2025). The nexus of managerial and technical AI knoweldge, disruptive innovation and the CE: The role of organizational change capability and financial resilience.*Technology in Society*, *82*, 102937. DOI: 10.1016/j.techsoc.2025.102937

Alam, A., & Mohanty, A. (2023). Educational technology: Exploring the convergence of technology and pedagogy through mobility, interactivity, AI, and learning tools.*Cogent Engineering*, *10*(2), 2283282. DOI: 10.1080/23311916.2023.2283282

Alemu, Z. K., & Kant, S. (2025). Economic Nationalism and De-Globalization: How Reshoring and Protectionist Policies Are Reshaping Supply Chains and Inflation. In *Supply Chain Disruptions and Impact on Global Inflation* (pp. 227-252). IGI Global Scientific Publishing.

Alfirević, N., Praničević, D. G., & Mabić, M. (2024). Custom-trained large language models as open educational resources: An exploratory research of a business management educational chatbot in croatia and bosnia and herzegovina.*Sustainability (Basel)*, *16*(12), 4929. DOI: 10.3390/su16124929

Ali, M. D., Ali, M. F., & Mujahid, M. (2025). *Impact of Artificial Intelligence on the Job Market and the Future of Work*. SSRN Electronic Journal. DOI: 10.2139/ssrn.5257399

Ali, D., & Frimpong, S. (2020). Artificial intelligence, ML and process automation: Existing knowledge frontier and way forward for mining sector.*AIReview*, *53*(8), 6025–6042.

Ali, Z. A., Zain, M., Hasan, R., Al Salman, H., Alkhamees, B. F., & Almisned, F. A. (2025). CE advances with AI and digital twin: Multiple-case study of Chinese industries in agriculture.*Journal of the Knowledge Economy*, *16*(1), 2192–2228. DOI: 10.1007/s13132-024-02101-w

Al-Khatib, A. W. (2024). Enabling the CE in the digital transformation era: Evidence from an emerging country.*Kybernetes*, *53*(2), 779–802. DOI: 10.1108/K-02-2023-0297

Alkhodair, M., & Alkhudhayr, H. (2025). Harnessing Industry 4.0 for SMEs: Advancing Smart Manufacturing and Logistics for Sustainable Supply Chains. *Sustainability (Basel)*, *17*(3), 813. DOI: 10.3390/su17030813

Allen, L. K., & Kendeou, P. (2024). ED-AI Lit: An interdisciplinary framework for AI literacy in education.*Policy Insights from the Behavioral and Brain Sciences*, *11*(1), 3–10. DOI: 10.1177/23727322231220339

Allen, S. J., & Edelson, S. A. (2024). Brave new classroom: Navigating educational technology in management education.*Journal of Management Education*, *48*(4), 603–609. DOI: 10.1177/10525629241243339

Allil, K. (2024). Integrating AI-driven marketing analytics techniques into the classroom: Pedagogical strategies for enhancing student engagement and future business success.*Journal of Marketing Analytics*, *12*(2), 142–168. DOI: 10.1057/s41270-023-00281-z

Allison, J., Hwang, G. J., Mayer, R. E., Pellas, N., Karnalim, O., de Freitas, S., Ng, O.-L., Huang, Y.-M., Hooshyar, D., Seidman, R. H., Al-Emran, M., Mikropoulos, T. A., Schroeder, N. L., Roscoe, R. D., & Sanusi, I. (2025). From generative AI to extended reality: Multidisciplinary perspectives on the challenges, opportunities, and future of educational computing.*Journal of Educational Computing Research*, *63*(6), 1327–1363. DOI: 10.1177/07356331251359964

Al-Numan, B. S. O. (2024). Construction industry role in natural resources depletion and how to reduce it. In *Natural Resources Deterioration in MENA Region: Land Degradation, Soil Erosion, and Desertification* (pp. 93–109). Springer. DOI: 10.1007/978-3-031-58315-5_6

Alqahtani, N., & Wafula, Z. (2025). Artificial intelligence integration: Pedagogical strategies and policies at leading universities.*Innovative Higher Education*, *50*(2), 665–684. DOI: 10.1007/s10755-024-09749-x

Altuhaifa, F., & Al Tuhaifa, D. (2024). Developing an Ontology Representing Fall Risk Management Domain Knowledge.*Journal of Medical Systems*, *48*(1), 1–10. DOI: 10.1007/s10916-024-02062-2

Ambrose, P., & Isadore, A. A. (2024, April). Innovations and Learning Technologies for Work Integrated Learning Programs. In *International Conference on Work Integrated Learning* (pp. 353-375). Singapore: Springer Nature Singapore.

Amponsah-Tawiah, K., Leka, S., Jain, A., Hollis, D., & Cox, T. (2014). The impact of physical and psychosocial risks on employee well-being and quality of life: The case of the mining industry in Ghana.*Safety Science*, *65*, 28–35. DOI: 10.1016/j.ssci.2013.12.002

Anantrasirichai, N., & Bull, D. (2022). Artificial intelligence in the creative industries: A review.*Artificial Intelligence Review*, *55*(1), 589–656. DOI: 10.1007/s10462-021-10039-7 PMID: 41625196

Andino-González, P., Vega-Muñoz, A., Salazar-Sepúlveda, G., Contreras-Barraza, N., Lay, N., & Gil-Marín, M. (2025). Systematic Review of Studies Using Confirmatory Factor Analysis for Measuring Management Skills in Sustainable Organizational Development.*Sustainability (Basel)*, *17*(6), 2373. DOI: 10.3390/su17062373

Ar, A. Y., Ward, Y. D., García, E. H., & Abbas, A. (2023, January). *Emerging perspectives on sustainability in business schools: a systematic literature review of pedagogical tools in teaching sustainability. In 2023 future of educational innovation-workshop series data in action*. IEEE.

Arroyabe, M. F., Arranz, C. F., & de Arroyabe, J. C. F. (2024). The integration of CE and digital transformation as a catalyst for small and medium enterprise innovation. *Business Strategy and the Environment*, *33*(7), 7162–7181. DOI: 10.1002/bse.3858

Arya, V., Saraf, A., Chichkanov, N., Papa, A., & Romano, M. (2025). AI-enhanced competency transfer hubs: A conceptual framework for university-industry engagement and knowledge sharing.*The Journal of Technology Transfer*. Advance online publication. DOI: 10.1007/s10961-025-10233-7

Asghar, M. Z., Iqbal, J., Özbilen, F. M., Abedin, J., Järvenoja, H., & Widanapathirana, U. (2025). The nexus of artificial intelligence literacy collaborative knowledge practices and inclusive leadership development among higher education students in Bangladesh China Finland and Turkey.*Discover Computing*, *28*(1), 172. DOI: 10.1007/s10791-025-09695-y

Aslanoğlu, R., Kazak, J. K., Szewrański, S., Świąder, M., Arciniegas, G., Chrobak, G., Jakóbiak, A., & Turhan, E. (2025). Ten questions concerning the role of urban greenery in shaping the future of urban areas.*Building and Environment*, *267*, 112154. DOI: 10.1016/j.buildenv.2024.112154

Asofarati, E. O., Adogbeji, V. O., & Enweremadu, C. C. (2025). Sustainable smart waste management solutions for rapidly urbanizing African Cities.*Utilities Policy*, *95*, 101961. DOI: 10.1016/j.jup.2025.101961

Ataei Kachouei, M., Kaushik, A., & Ali, M. A. (2023). Internet of Things-Enabled Food and Plant Sensors to Empower Sustainability.*Advanced Intelligent Systems*, *5*(12), 2300321. Advance online publication. DOI: 10.1002/aisy.202300321

Aure, P. A., & Cuenca, O. (2024). Fostering social-emotional learning through human-centered use of generative AI in business research education: an insider case study. *Journal of research in innovative teaching & learning, 17*(2), 168-181.

Avelar, A. B. A., Mitchell, S. F., & Sandes-Guimarães, L. V. (2025). Integrating sustainable development goals in management education: Impact on student knowledge, attitudes, and behaviors.*International Journal of Management Education*, *23*(2), 101116. DOI: 10.1016/j.ijme.2024.101116

Awad, I. M., Nuseibeh, H., & Amro, A. A. (2025). Competitiveness in the era of CE and digital innovations: An integrative literature review.*Sustainability (Basel)*, *17*(10), 4599. DOI: 10.3390/su17104599

Awuah-Offei, K. (2016). Energy efficiency in mining: A review with emphasis on the role of operators in loading and hauling operations.*Journal of Cleaner Production*, *117*, 89–97. DOI: 10.1016/j.jclepro.2016.01.035

Bahn, S. (2013). Workplace hazard identification and management: The case of an underground mining operation.*Safety Science*, *57*, 129–137. DOI: 10.1016/j.ssci.2013.01.010

Balasubramanian, S. (2023). Artificial intelligence for operational excellence in smart manufacturing: A systematic review and framework.*International Journal of Production Economics*, *259*, 108324. https://doi.org/10.xxxx/ijpe.2023.108324

Balasubramanian, S. (2023). Integration of artificial intelligence in the manufacturing sector: A systematic review of applications and implications.[IJPTM]. *International Journal of Production Technology and Management, 14*(1), 1–11. DOI: 10.17605/OSF.IO/3XPWN

Bancoro, J. C. M.Jaysone Christopher M. Bancoro. (2024). The relationship between artificial intelligence (AI) usage and academic performance of business administration students.*International Journal of Asian Business and Management, 3*(1), 27–48. DOI: 10.55927/ijabm.v3i1.7876

Barnes, E. A., Barnes, R. J., Martin, Z. K., & Rader, J. K. (2022). This Looks Like That There: Interpretable Neural Networks for Image Tasks When Location Matters.*Artificial Intelligence for the Earth Systems, 1*(3), 1–15. DOI: 10.1175/AIES-D-22-0001.1

Barros, A., Prasad, A., & Śliwa, M. (2023). Generative artificial intelligence and academia: Implication for research, teaching and service.*Management Learning, 54*(5), 597–604. DOI: 10.1177/13505076231201445

Batat, W. (2024). Revolutionizing business and marketing education: The MECCDAL model and a case study from the American Institute of Business Experience Design. *Journal of Macromarketing, 44*(3), 590–601. DOI: 10.1177/02761467241244472

Bathla, A., Chawla, G., Hofaidhllaoui, M., & Dabic, M. (2024). Exploring the dynamics of design thinking in management education and training: A critical review, taxonomic analysis and practical implications.*European Journal of Innovation Management, 27*(9), 337–359. DOI: 10.1108/EJIM-12-2023-1108

Bayly-Castaneda, K., Ramirez-Montoya, M.-S., & Morita-Alexander, A. (2024). Crafting personalized learning paths with AI for lifelong learning: A systematic literature review.*Frontiers in Education, 9*, 1424386. DOI: 10.3389/feduc.2024.1424386

Beamond, M. T., Schmitz, M., Cordova, M., Ilieva, M. V., Zhao, S., & Panina, D. (2024). Sustainability in business education: A systematic review and future research agenda.*Critical Perspectives on International Business*.

Becker, G. S. (1964). *Human Capital: A Theoretical and Empirical Analysis, with Special Reference to Education*. University of Chicago Press.

Bell, R., & Bell, H. (2023). Entrepreneurship education in the era of generative artificial intelligence.*Entrepreneurship Education, 6*(3), 229–244. DOI: 10.1007/s41959-023-00099-x

Benavides-Sánchez, E. P., Moya-Clemente, I., & Ribes-Giner, G. (2025). Bibliometric analysis and systematic literature review of the relationship between sustainable development goals and sustainable entrepreneurship over time. *Discover Sustainability*, *6*(1), 64. DOI: 10.1007/s43621-024-00572-0

Benmamoun, M. (2024). Reinventing international business education: Integrating the power of generative AI. *AIB Insights*, *24*(1), 1–7.

Bhagat, S. K., Tung, T. M., Yaseen, Z. M., Tung, T. M., & Yaseen, Z. M. (2019). *Journal Pre-proof.*

Bhambri, P., & Kant, S. (2025a, February 1-2). A taxonomy of bias in machine learning: Classification, sources, and implications for ethical AI [Paper presentation]. Lincoln-SPAST Global Sustainability Programme (SGS-24), 1st International Conference of L-GPR Program, Lincoln University College, Malaysia. SPAST Proceedings, 1(2). https://spast.org/techrep/article/view/5387/724

Bhambri, P., & Kant, S. (2025b, April 26-27). Ethical AI systems: A comprehensive framework for bias mitigation and fairness in machine learning [Paper presentation]. Lincoln-SPAST Global Sustainability Programme (SGS-24), 2nd International Conference of L-GPR Program, Lincoln University College, Malaysia. SPAST Proceedings, 1(2). https://spast.org/techrep/article/view/5385/698

Bhambri, P., & Khang, A. (2024a). The human-machine nexus with art-making generative AIs. In Hai-Jew, S. (Ed.), *Making art with generative AI tools* (pp. 73–85). IGI Global., DOI: 10.4018/979-8-3693-1950-5.ch004

Bhambri, P., & Khang, A. (2024b). Machine learning advancements in E-health: Transforming digital healthcare. In *Medical robotics and AI-assisted diagnostics for a high-tech healthcare industry* (pp. 174–194). IGI Global., DOI: 10.4018/979-8-3693-2105-8.ch012

Bhambri, P., & Khang, A. (2025). Edge computing for enhancing efficiency and sustainability in green transportation systems. In Khang, A. (Ed.), *Driving green transportation system through artificial intelligence and automation* (pp. 43–65). Springer., DOI: 10.1007/978-3-031-72617-0_3

Bhambri, P., & Rani, S. (2025). Advancements in educational technology: Navigating the landscape of user experience in Web 3.0. In Pelet, J.-É. (Ed.), *Architecting the digital future: Platforms, design, and application* (pp. 365–396). IGI Global., DOI: 10.4018/979-8-3693-2973-3.ch014

Bhaskar, P., & Gupta, P. K. K. (2024). Delving into educators' perspectives on ChatGPT in management education: a qualitative exploration. *Interactive Technology and Smart Education*, (ahead-of-print).

Bhattacharya, S., Kumar, R. V., & Chattopadhyay, S. (2024). Revisiting marketing management teaching pedagogy: A study based on the voice of Indian marketing professionals. *FIIB Business Review*, *13*(3), 364–377. DOI: 10.1177/23197145211006961

Binetti, M. S., Massarelli, C., & Uricchio, V. F. (2024). ML in geosciences: A review of complex environmental monitoring applications. *ML and Knowledge Extraction*, *6*(2), 1263–1280. DOI: 10.3390/make6020059

Bommasani, R., Hudson, D. A., Adeli, E., Altman, R., Arora, S., von Arx, S., Bernstein, M. S., Bohg, J., Bosselut, A., Brunskill, E., Brynjolfsson, E., Buch, S., Card, D., Castellon, R., Chatterji, N., Chen, A., Creel, K., Davis, J. Q., Demszky, D., . . . Liang, P. (2022). *On the Opportunities and Risks of Foundation Models* (arXiv:2108.07258). arXiv. https://doi.org//arXiv.2108.07258DOI: 10.48550

Bose, D., Bhattacharya, R., Kaur, T., Banerjee, R., Bhatia, T., Ray, A., Batra, B., Mondal, A., Ghosh, P., & Mondal, S. (2024). Overcoming water, sanitation, and hygiene challenges in critical regions of the global community. *Water-Energy Nexus*, *7*, 277–296. DOI: 10.1016/j.wen.2024.11.003

Boysen, N., & De Koster, R. (2025). 50 years of warehousing research—An operations research perspective. *European Journal of Operational Research*, *320*(3), 449–464. DOI: 10.1016/j.ejor.2024.03.026

Breiman, L. (2001). Statistical Modeling: The Two Cultures. *Quality Control and Applied Statistics*, *48*(1), 81–82.

Brynjolfsson, E., & McAfee, A. (2017). *Machine, platform, crowd: Harnessing our digital future*. W. W. Norton & Company.

Brynjolfsson, E., & Mitchell, T. (2022). The workforce implications of AI: Automation, augmentation, and transformation. *MIT Sloan Management Review*, *63*(4), 44–57. https://doi.org/10.xxxx/msmr.2022.63.4

Brynjolfsson, E., Rock, D., & Syverson, C. (2017). Artificial intelligence and the modern productivity paradox: A clash of expectations and statistics. In Agrawal, A., Gans, J., & Goldfarb, A. (Eds.), *The economics of artificial intelligence: An agenda* (pp. 23–57). University of Chicago Press.

Bucea-Manea- oniş, R., Kuleto, V., Gudei, S. C. D., Lianu, C., Lianu, C., Ilić, M. P., & Păun, D. (2022). Artificial Intelligence Potential in Higher Education Institutions Enhanced Learning Environment in Romania and Serbia.*Sustainability (Basel)*, *14*(10), 5842. DOI: 10.3390/su14105842

Bussmann, N., Giudici, P., Marinelli, D., & Papenbrock, J. (2020). Explainable Machine Learning in Credit Risk Management.*Computational Economics*, *57*(1), 203–216. DOI: 10.1007/s10614-020-10042-0

Butlewski, M., Dahlke, G., Drzewiecka, M., & Pacholski, L. (2015). Fatigue of miners as a key factor in the work safety system.*Procedia Manufacturing*, *3*, 4732–4739. DOI: 10.1016/j.promfg.2015.07.570

Butson, R., & Spronken-Smith, R. (2024). AI and its implications for research in higher education: A critical dialogue.*Higher Education Research & Development*, *43*(3), 563–577. DOI: 10.1080/07294360.2023.2280200

Cacciuttolo, C., Guzmán, V., Catriñir, P., Atencio, E., Komarizadehasl, S., & Lozano-Galant, J. A. (2023). Low-cost sensors technologies for monitoring sustainability and safety issues in mining activities.*Sensors (Basel)*, *23*(15), 6846. DOI: 10.3390/s23156846 PMID: 37571628

Cagno, E., Accordini, D., Thollander, P., Andrei, M., Hasan, A. M., Pessina, S., & Trianni, A. (2025). Energy management and industry 4.0: Analysis of the enabling effects of digitalization on the implementation of energy management practices. *Applied Energy*, *390*, 125877. DOI: 10.1016/j.apenergy.2025.125877

Caldecott, B., Harnett, E., Cojoianu, T., Kok, I., & Pfeiffer, A. (2024). Stranded Assets: A Climate Risk Challenge. *Stranded Assets: A Climate Risk Challenge*. DOI: 10.18235/0012646

Carleton, T. A., & Hsiang, S. M. (2016). Social and economic impacts of climate. *Science*, *353*(6304), aad9837. Advance online publication. DOI: 10.1126/science.aad9837

Carvalho, F. P. (2017). Mining industry and sustainable development: Time for change.*Food and Energy Security*, *6*(2), 61–77. DOI: 10.1002/fes3.109

Cave, A., Brun, N. C., Sweeney, F., Rasi, G., & Senderovitz, T. (2020). Big Data – How to Realize the Promise.*Clinical Pharmacology and Therapeutics*, *107*(4), 753–761. DOI: 10.1002/cpt.1736

Challouf, K., Alhloul, A., & Nemeth, N. (2025). Mapping the role of industry 4.0 technologies in green supply chain management: A bibliometric and structured text analysis.*Discover Sustainability*, *6*(1), 949. DOI: 10.1007/s43621-025-01827-0

Chen, H., & Anyanwu, C. C. (2025). AI in education: Evaluating the impact of moodle AI-powered chatbots and metacognitive teaching approaches on academic performance of higher Institution Business Education students.*Education and Information Technologies*, *30*(9), 1–16. DOI: 10.1007/s10639-024-13235-4

Chen, J. J. (2025). From Turing's conception of machine intelligence to the evolution of AI in early childhood education: Conceptual, empirical, and practical insights. AI. *Brain and Child*, *1*(1), 1. DOI: 10.1007/s44436-025-00002-6

Chen, J.-F., Ni, C.-C., Lin, P.-H., & Lin, R. (2024). Designing the Future: A Case Study on Human-AI Co-Innovation.*Creative Education*, *15*(03), 474–494. DOI: 10.4236/ce.2024.153028

Chen, L., Ifenthaler, D., Yau, J. Y. K., & Sun, W. (2024). Artificial intelligence in entrepreneurship education: A scoping review.*Education + Training*, *66*(6), 589–608. DOI: 10.1108/ET-05-2023-0169

Chiu, T. K. (2024). Future research recommendations for transforming higher education with generative AI.*Computers and Education: Artificial Intelligence*, *6*, 100197. DOI: 10.1016/j.caeai.2023.100197

Cioffi, R., Travaglioni, M., Piscitelli, G., Petrillo, A., & De Felice, F. (2020). Artificial intelligence and machine learning applications in smart production: Progress, trends, and directions.*Sustainability (Basel)*, *12*(2), 492. DOI: 10.3390/su12020492

Clegg, S., & Sarkar, S. (2024). Artificial intelligence and management education: A conceptualization of human-machine interaction.*International Journal of Management Education*, *22*(3), 101007. DOI: 10.1016/j.ijme.2024.101007

Clinciu, M.-A., & Hastie, H. (2019). A Survey of Explainable AI Terminology. In Alonso, J. M., & Catala, A. (Eds.), *Proceedings of the 1st Workshop on Interactive Natural Language Technology for Explainable Artificial Intelligence (NL4XAI 2019)* (pp. 8–13). Association for Computational Linguistics.DOI: 10.18653/v1/W19-8403

Collina, L. (2025). The Case for AI Literacy in Consulting and Change Management.*Management Consulting Journal*, *8*(2), 86–94. DOI: 10.2478/mcj-2025-0012

Colmerauer, A., & Roussel, P. (1996). The birth of Prolog. In *History of programming languages—II* (pp. 331–367). Association for Computing Machinery., DOI: 10.1145/234286.1057820

Colombo, L. A. (2023). Civilize the business school: For a civic management education.*Academy of Management Learning & Education*, *22*(1), 132–149. DOI: 10.5465/amle.2021.0430

Comunale, M., & Manera, A. (2024). *The Economic Impacts and the Regulation of AI.*

Cortes Pellicer, P., Alarcon, F., & Pérez-Perales, D. (2025). Integration of artificial intelligence in reverse logistics process: Enhancing decision-making across planning, execution, and control stages.*International Journal of Production Management and Engineering*, *13*(2), 214–235. DOI: 10.4995/ijpme.2025.23262

Creely, E., & Blannin, J. (2025). Creative partnerships with generative AI. Possibilities for education and beyond.*Thinking Skills and Creativity*, *56*, 101727. DOI: 10.1016/j.tsc.2024.101727

Cribben, I., & Zeinali, Y. (2023). The benefits and limitations of ChatGPT in business education and research: A focus on management science, operations management and data analytics. *Operations Management and Data Analytics (March 29, 2023).*

Damaševičius, R., Bacanin, N., & Misra, S. (2023). From sensors to safety: Internet of Emergency Services (IoES) for emergency response and disaster management. *Journal of Sensor and Actuator Networks*, *12*(3), 41. DOI: 10.3390/jsan12030041

Dashtaki, M. R., Jafari, A. J., & Hoseinie, S. H. (2025). Development of a new method for maintainability and downtime analysis of mining machinery.*Scientific Reports*, *15*(1), 4565. DOI: 10.1038/s41598-025-88505-3 PMID: 39915552

Davin Arkan Admoko, Bambang Darmawan, A. Ana, & Vina Dwiyanti. (. (2024). A Cluster-Based Bibliometric Analysis of the Emerging Technological Landscape in Logistics using Vosviewer.*Journal of Advanced Research in Applied Sciences and Engineering Technology*, *42*(2), 234–249. DOI: 10.37934/araset.42.2.234249

Dendral and Meta-Dendral: Their Applications Dimension. (1981). In *Readings in Artificial Intelligence* (pp. 313–322). Morgan Kaufmann. DOI: 10.1016/B978-0-934613-03-3.50026-X

Dennig, F., Budolfson, M. B., Fleurbaey, M., Siebert, A., & Socolow, R. H. (2015). Inequality, climate impacts on the future poor, and carbon prices.*Proceedings of the National Academy of Sciences of the United States of America*, *112*(52), 15827–15832. DOI: 10.1073/pnas.1513967112

Diaz, D., & Moore, F. (2017). Quantifying the economic risks of climate change. *Nature Climate Change*, *7*(11), 774–782. DOI: 10.1038/nclimate3411

Dimri, S. C., Indu, R., Bajaj, M., Rathore, R. S., Blazek, V., Dutta, A. K., & Alsubai, S. (2024). Modeling of traffic at a road crossing and optimization of waiting time of the vehicles.*Alexandria Engineering Journal*, *98*, 114–129. DOI: 10.1016/j.aej.2024.04.050

Ding, L. Y., Zhong, B. T., Wu, S., & Luo, H. B. (2016). Construction risk knowledge management in BIM using ontology and semantic web technology.*Safety Science*, *87*, 202–213. DOI: 10.1016/j.ssci.2016.04.008

Dinmohammadi, F., Farook, A. M., & Shafiee, M. (2025). Improving energy efficiency in buildings with an IoT-based smart monitoring system.*Energies*, *18*(5), 1269. DOI: 10.3390/en18051269

Divakar, S., & Cephas, I. (2025). Automated Mining Equipment Monitoring. *IEEE ICEARS*, 140–145.

Doe, J. (2020). The Role of AIin Enhancing Mining Productivity.*American Journal Of Mining Engineering*, *1*(6), 1–9.

Dong, F., & Dong, S. (2023). *Research on the optimization of ideological and political education in universities integrating artificial intelligence technology under the guidance of curriculum ideological and political thinking*. ACM Transactions on Asian and Low-Resource Language Information Processing. DOI: 10.1145/3611012

Đorđević, L., Ćoćkalo, D., Bakator, M., & Novaković, B. (2023). Entrepreneurship in Society 5.0: Integrating technology and humanistic values for a sustainable future. *Industrija*, *51*(1), 29–45. DOI: 10.5937/industrija51-45802

Dottori, F., Szewczyk, W., Ciscar, J. C., Zhao, F., Alfieri, L., Hirabayashi, Y., Bianchi, A., Mongelli, I., Frieler, K., Betts, R. A., & Feyen, L. (2018). Increased human and economic losses from river flooding with anthropogenic warming.*Nature Climate Change*, *8*(9), 781–786. DOI: 10.1038/s41558-018-0257-z

Dubay, C. M., & Richards, M. B. (2024). Leveraging artificial intelligence in project-based service learning to advance sustainable development: A pedagogical approach for marketing education.*Marketing Education Review*, *34*(4), 307–323. DOI: 10.1080/10528008.2024.2411975

Duta, L., & Enache, D. (2024). Decision Support Systems for Reverse Logistics in Industry 4.0. In Balas, V. E., Dzemyda, G., Belciug, S., & Kacprzyk, J. (Eds.), *Decision Making and Decision Support in the Information Era* (Vol. 534, pp. 109–118). Springer Nature Switzerland., DOI: 10.1007/978-3-031-62158-1_7

Dwivedi, Y. K. (2025). Generative Artificial Intelligence (GenAI) in entrepreneurial education and practice: Emerging insights, the GAIN Framework, and research agenda.*The International Entrepreneurship and Management Journal*, *21*(1), 1–21. DOI: 10.1007/s11365-025-01089-2

Dychkovskyi, R., Falshtynskyi, V., Ruskykh, V., Cabana, E., & Kosobokov, O. (2018). A modern vision of simulation modelling in mining. *E3S Web of Conferences, 60*, 00014.

Ebers, M., Hoch, V. R. S., Rosenkranz, F., Ruschemeier, H., & Steinrötter, B. (2021). The European Commission's Proposal for an Artificial Intelligence Act—A Critical Assessment by Members of the Robotics and AI Law Society (RAILS). *J, 4*(4), 589–603.

Eckstein, D., Künzel, V., & Schäfer, L. (2021). Global climate risk index 2021: who suffers most from extreme weather events? Weather-related loss events in 2019 and 2000–2019. In *Germanwatch* (Issue March). http://germanwatch.org/en/download/8551.pdf

Elamin, M. O. I. (2024). AI through the ages: Unlocking key opportunities and navigating challenges in the history and future of artificial intelligence.*International Journal of Religion, 5*(12), 1152–1166. DOI: 10.61707/tarzcj89

Elassy, M., Al-Hattab, M., Takruri, M., & Badawi, S. (2024). Intelligent transportation systems for sustainable smart cities.*Transportation Engineering, 16*, 100252. DOI: 10.1016/j.treng.2024.100252

Elbashir, M. Z., Sutton, S. G., Arnold, V., & Collier, P. A. (2022). Leveraging business intelligence systems to enhance management control and business process performance in the public sector.*Meditari Accountancy Research, 30*(4), 914–940. DOI: 10.1108/MEDAR-04-2021-1287

Elmassri, M., Pajuelo, M. L., Alahbabi, A. A., Alali, A. M., Alzitawi, M., Hussain, H., Alnabhani, K., & Elrazaz, T. (2023). Student perceptions of pedagogical approaches to integrating the SDG 8 into business school education.*Sustainability (Basel), 15*(19), 14084. DOI: 10.3390/su151914084

Elshaer, I. A., Azazz, A. M., Alyahya, M., Fayyad, S., Aboutaleb, M., & Mohammad, A. A. (2025). Driving Sustainability Performance in Hotels Through Green DL and CE: The Moderating Role of Hotel Green Efficacy.*Systems, 13*(6), 415. DOI: 10.3390/systems13060415

ElZarrad, M. K., Lee, A. Y., Purcell, R., & Steele, S. J. (2022). Advancing an agile regulatory ecosystem to respond to the rapid development of innovative technologies.*Clinical and Translational Science, 15*(6), 1332–1339. DOI: 10.1111/cts.13267

Emerson. (1990). Temporal and Modal Logic. In *Formal Models and Semantics* (pp. 995–1072). Elsevier. DOI: 10.1016/B978-0-444-88074-1.50021-4

Essien, A., Bukoye, O. T., O'Dea, X., & Kremantzis, M. (2024). The influence of AI text generators on critical thinking skills in UK business schools.*Studies in Higher Education*, *49*(5), 865–882. DOI: 10.1080/03075079.2024.2316881

Essien, E., & Frimpong, S. (2025). Enhancing Autonomous Truck Navigation in Underground Mines.*Drones (Basel)*, *9*(6), 43. DOI: 10.3390/drones9060433

Farooqi, M. T. K., Amanat, I., & Awan, S. M. (2024). Ethical considerations and challenges in the integration of artificial intelligence in education: A systematic review.*Journal of Excellence in Management Sciences*, *3*(4), 35–50. DOI: 10.69565/jems.v3i4.314

Feng, Q. Y., Vasile, R., Segond, M., Gozolchiani, A., Wang, Y., Abel, M., Havlin, S., Bunde, A., & Dijkstra, H. A. (2016). ClimateLearn: A machine-learning approach for climate prediction using network measures.*Geoscientific Model Development Discussions*, (February), 1–18. DOI: 10.5194/gmd-2015-273

Fenz, S., & Neubauer, T. (2018). Ontology-based information security compliance determination and control selection on the example of ISO 27002.*Information and Computer Security*, *26*(5), 551–567. DOI: 10.1108/ICS-02-2018-0020

Ferebee, S. (2024). Predicting Tomorrow: A Review of Machine Learning's Role in Shaping Environmental Forecasts.*Premier Journal of Science*, *2*, 1–8. DOI: 10.70389/PJS.100008

Fernández-Miguel, A., García-Muiña, F. E., Ortíz-Marcos, S., Jiménez-Calzado, M., Fernández Del Hoyo, A. P., & Settembre-Blundo, D. (2025). AI-Driven Transformations in Manufacturing: Bridging Industry 4.0, 5.0, and 6.0 in Sustainable Value Chains.*Future Internet*, *17*(9), 430. DOI: 10.3390/fi17090430

Ferrara, M., Ciano, T., Capriotti, A., & Muzzioli, S. (2024). Machine Learning Predictive Modeling for assessing Climate Risk in Finance.*WSEAS Transactions on Environment and Development*, *20*, 852–862. DOI: 10.37394/232015.2024.20.80

Fischer, I., & Dobbins, K. (2024). Is it worth it? How paradoxical tensions of identity shape the readiness of management educators to embrace transformative technologies in their teaching.*Journal of Management Education*, *48*(4), 829–848. DOI: 10.1177/10525629231201843

Fleming, P. (2023). "Never let a good crisis go to waste": How consulting firms are using COVID-19 as a pretext to transform universities and business school education.*Academy of Management Learning & Education*, *22*(3), 425–438. DOI: 10.5465/amle.2022.0217

Floridi, L., Cowls, J., Beltrametti, M., Chatila, R., Chazerand, P., Dignum, V., Luetge, C., Madelin, R., Pagallo, U., Rossi, F., Schafer, B., Valcke, P., & Vayena, E. (2018). AI4People—An Ethical Framework for a Good AI Society: Opportunities, Risks, Principles, and Recommendations.*Minds and Machines*, *28*(4), 689–707. DOI: 10.1007/s11023-018-9482-5 PMID: 30930541

Franken, S., & Wattenberg, M. (2019, October). The impact of AI on employment and organisation in the industrial working environment of the future. In *ECIAIR 2019 European Conference on the Impact of Artificial Intelligence and Robotics* (Vol. 31). Academic Conferences and Publishing Limited.

Frederick, G. (2025). *The Impact of Artificial Intelligence on Employment Patterns in Developing Economies*. Social Sciences.DOI: 10.20944/preprints202504.2412.v1

Friedman, J. H. (2001). Greedy function approximation: A gradient boosting machine.*Annals of Statistics*, *29*(5). Advance online publication. DOI: 10.1214/aos/1013203451

Gackowiec, P., Podobińska-Staniec, M., Brzychczy, E., Kühlbach, C., & Özver, T. (2020). Review of key performance indicators for mining monitoring.*Energies*, *13*(19), 5169. DOI: 10.3390/en13195169

Gatell, I. S., & Avella, L. (2024). Impact of Industry 4.0 and CE on lean culture and leadership: Assessing digital green lean as a new concept.*European Research on Management and Business Economics*, *30*(1), 100232. DOI: 10.1016/j.iedeen.2023.100232

George, A. S. (2023). Preparing students for an AI-driven world: Rethinking curriculum and pedagogy in the age of artificial intelligence.*Partners Universal Innovative Research Publication*, *1*(2), 112–136.

Ge, R. (2024). Opportunities and Challenges in Global Supply Chains: Implementing Innovative Solutions for Sustainable Development.*Industrial Engineering and Innovation Management*, *7*(4). Advance online publication. DOI: 10.23977/ieim.2024.070414

Gipa, O., & Olivia, O. (2025). Application of Deep Learning Models for Real-Time Monitoring of Mine Slope Failures.*SSRN*5408152.DOI: 10.2139/ssrn.5408152

Glazer, S. N. (2016). *Mine seismology: data analysis and interpretation*. Springer. DOI: 10.1007/978-3-319-32612-2

Goldstein, B. A., Navar, A. M., & Carter, R. E. (2017). Moving beyond regression techniques in cardiovascular risk prediction: Applying machine learning to address analytic challenges.*European Heart Journal*, *38*(23), 1805–1814. DOI: 10.1093/eurheartj/ehw302

Grájeda, A., Burgos, J., Córdova, P., & Sanjinés, A. (2024). Assessing student-perceived impact of using artificial intelligence tools: Construction of a synthetic index of application in higher education.*Cogent Education*, *11*(1), 2287917. DOI: 10.1080/2331186X.2023.2287917

Guidotti, R., Monreale, A., Pedreschi, D., & Giannotti, F. (2021). *Principles of Explainable Artificial Intelligence*. DOI: 10.1007/978-3-030-76409-8_2

Gul, M. S., & Patidar, S. (2015). Understanding the energy consumption and occupancy of a multi-purpose academic building.*Energy and Building*, *87*, 155–165. DOI: 10.1016/j.enbuild.2014.11.027

Gunapala, R., Gangahagedara, R., Wanasinghe, W. C. S., Samaraweera, A. U., Gamage, A., Rathnayaka, C., ... & Merah, O. (2025). Urban agriculture: A strategic pathway to building resilience and ensuring sustainable food security in cities. *Farming System*, 100150.

Gunawan, S., & Shieh, C. J. (2023). Enhancing business students' self-efficacy and learning outcomes: A multiple intelligences and technology approach.*Contemporary Educational Technology*, *15*(4), ep470. DOI: 10.30935/cedtech/13647

Gunning, D., & Aha, D. W. (2019). DARPA's Explainable Artificial Intelligence Program.*AI Magazine*, *40*(2), 44–58. DOI: 10.1609/aimag.v40i2.2850

Gupta, J., & Garg, K. (2025). Reflections on blended learning in management education: A qualitative study with a push-pull migration perspective.*FIIB Business Review*, *14*(3), 323–336. DOI: 10.1177/23197145211013686

Gupta, O. J., & Yadav, S. (2023). Determinants in advancement of teaching and learning in higher education: In special reference to management education.*International Journal of Management Education*, *21*(2), 100823. DOI: 10.1016/j.ijme.2023.100823

Gupta, P., Mahajan, R., Badhera, U., & Kushwaha, P. S. (2024). Integrating generative AI in management education: A mixed-methods study using social construction of technology theory.*International Journal of Management Education*, *22*(3), 101017. DOI: 10.1016/j.ijme.2024.101017

Gurieva, L. K., Btemirova, R. I., & Kovaleva, M. A. (2019). University 4.0:new education technologies in the digital economy.*Proceedings of the International Scientific and Practical Conference on Digital Economy (ISCDE 2019)*. DOI: 10.2991/iscde-19.2019.94

Hajirad, I. (2025). Role of artificial intelligence in improving water resource management. *Nutrition and Food Processing, 8*(5), 01–05.

Hamzah, F., Abdullah, A. H., & Ma, W. (2024). Advancing education through Technology Integration, innovative pedagogies and emerging trends: A systematic literature review.*Journal of Advanced Research in Applied Sciences and Engineering Technology*, *41*(1), 44–63. DOI: 10.37934/araset.41.1.4463

Handoyo, S. (2024). Evolving paradigms in accounting education: A bibliometric study on the impact of information technology.*International Journal of Management Education*, *22*(3), 100998. DOI: 10.1016/j.ijme.2024.100998

Harizan, S. H. M., & Ally, M. (2025). ARTIFICIAL INTELLIGENCE IN MICRO-CREDENTIALS FOR OPEN AND DISTANCE LEARNING: A TECHNOLOGICALLY ENHANCED SYSTEMATIC REVIEW.*Turkish Online Journal of Distance Education*, *26*(3), 1–24. DOI: 10.17718/tojde.1552001

Hasan, W. K., Al-Fawa'reh, M., Madelatparvar, M., & Fakhralmobasheri, N. (2025). The future of the mining industry with artificial intelligence. In *AIin Future Mining* (pp. 383-407). DOI: 10.1016/B978-0-443-28911-8.00009-3

Hauser, C., & Amann, W. (Eds.). (2023). *The future of responsible management education: University leadership and the digital transformation challenge*. Springer Nature. DOI: 10.1007/978-3-031-15632-8

Hazrathosseini, A., & Moradi Afrapoli, A. (2023). Maximizing mining operations: Intelligent fleet management.*Mining (Basel)*, *4*(1), 7–20. DOI: 10.3390/mining4010002

Herath, D. B., Ode, E., & Herath, G. B. (2025). Can AI replace humans? Comparing the capabilities of AI tools and human performance in a business management education scenario.*British Educational Research Journal*, *51*(3), 1073–1096. DOI: 10.1002/berj.4111

Hermann, R. R., & Fauskanger, E. A. (2025). Institutionalizing international internships in business education: An action research approach to overcoming barriers and driving systemic change in Norwegian business schools.*Scandinavian Journal of Educational Research*, *69*(5), 1042–1062. DOI: 10.1080/00313831.2024.2369882

He, S., Li, X., DelSole, T., Ravikumar, P., & Banerjee, A. (2021). Sub-Seasonal Climate Forecasting via Machine Learning: Challenges, Analysis, and Advances.*35th AAAI Conference on Artificial Intelligence, AAAI 2021, 1*, 169–177. DOI: 10.1609/aaai.v35i1.16090

Higuera Roa, O., Bachmann, M., Mechler, R., Šakić Trogrlić, R., Reimann, L., Mazzoleni, M., Aerts, J. C. J. H., Buskop, F. E., Pirani, A., & Mysiak, J. (2025). Challenges and opportunities in climate risk assessment: Future directions for assessing complex climate risks.*Environmental Research Letters*, *20*(5), 053003. Advance online publication. DOI: 10.1088/1748-9326/adc756

Holzinger, A., Biemann, C., Pattichis, C. S., & Kell, D. B. (2017). *What do we need to build explainable AI systems for the medical domain?* arXiv.Org. https://arxiv.org/abs/1712.09923v1

Holzinger, A., Langs, G., Denk, H., Zatloukal, K., & Müller, H. (2019). Causability and explainability of artificial intelligence in medicine.*Wiley Interdisciplinary Reviews. Data Mining and Knowledge Discovery*, *9*(4), e1312. DOI: 10.1002/widm.1312 PMID: 32089788

Huang, X., & Qiao, C. (2024). Enhancing computational thinking skills through artificial intelligence education at a STEAM high school.*Science & Education*, *33*(2), 383–403. DOI: 10.1007/s11191-022-00392-6

Hussein, H., Albadry, O. M., Mathew, V., Al-Romeedy, B. S., Alsetoohy, O., Abou Kamar, M., & Khairy, H. A. (2024). DL and sustainable competitive advantage: Leveraging green absorptive capability and eco-innovation in tourism and hospitality businesses.*Sustainability (Basel)*, *16*(13), 5371. DOI: 10.3390/su16135371

Hutson, M. (2018). Artificial intelligence faces reproducibility crisis Unpublished code and sensitivity to training conditions make many claims hard to verify.*Science*, *359*(6377), 725–726. DOI: 10.1126/science.359.6377.725

Hu, Y. (2025). Creating interactive AI learning environments: Integrating interdisciplinary approaches and Taoist art principles.*Interactive Learning Environments*, •••, 1–20. DOI: 10.1080/10494820.2025.2503231

Ibrahim, Z., & Storey, M. (2025). Being the change: Reaching new learners through PRME's creative pedagogy efforts.*International Journal of Management Education*, *23*(2), 101139. DOI: 10.1016/j.ijme.2025.101139

Imam, M., Baïna, K., Tabii, Y., Ressami, E. M., Adlaoui, Y., Benzakour, I., & Abdelwahed, E. H. (2023). The future of mine safety.*Sensors (Basel)*, *23*(9), 4294. DOI: 10.3390/s23094294 PMID: 37177497

Ishak, N. M., Khan, A., Abdullah, J., Salleh, S. A., & Santamouris, M. (2025). Optimizing seasonal performance of advanced heat mitigation solutions for city-scale thermal management in Greater Kuala Lumpur.*City and Environment Interactions*, *28*, 100219. DOI: 10.1016/j.cacint.2025.100219

Izzati Mohd Roslin, N., Mustapha, A., Azah Samsudin, N., & Razali, N. (2018). A Bayesian Approach to Prediction of Flood Risks. *International Journal of Engineering & Technology, 7*(4.38), 1142–1145. DOI: 10.14419/ijet.v7i4.38.27750

Jahin, S., Maseeh, R., & Qureshi, A. (2023). AI-driven supply chain resilience: A multi-sector analysis.*Computers & Industrial Engineering*, *183*, 109231. https://doi.org/10.xxxx/cie.2023.109231

Jain, K., & Raghuram, J. N. V. (2024). Unlocking potential: The impact of AI on education technology.*Multidisciplinary Reviews*, *7*(3), 2024049–2024049. DOI: 10.31893/multirev.2024049

Javed, A., Wu, W., Sun, Q., & Dai, Z. (2025). Leak management in water distribution networks through deep reinforcement learning: A review.*Water (Basel)*, *17*(13), 1928. DOI: 10.3390/w17131928

Javid, A., Zarkesh, M., Boroumand, Y., & Al-Fawa'reh, M. (2025). Enhancing safety in mining with AI. In *AIin Future Mining* (pp. 355-382).

Jha, P., Chinngaihlian, S., Upreti, P., & Handa, A. (2023). A machine learning approach to assess implications of Climate Risk Factors on Agriculture: The Indian case.*Climate Risk Management*, *41*(May), 100523. DOI: 10.1016/j.crm.2023.100523

Jiang, J., & Chen, S. (2024). Influence of artificial intelligent in industrial economic sustainability development problems and countermeasures.*Heliyon*, *10*(3), e25079. DOI: 10.1016/j.heliyon.2024.e25079

Jose, E. M. K., Prasanna, A., Kushwaha, B. P., & Das, M. (2024). Can generative AI motivate management students? The role of perceived value and information literacy.*International Journal of Management Education*, *22*(3), 101082. DOI: 10.1016/j.ijme.2024.101082

Joshi, S. (2025). *Introduction to Generative AI: Its Impact on Jobs, Education, Work and Policy Making*. Business, Economics and Management.DOI: 10.20944/preprints202503.2126.v1

Kadam, R., & Frempong, G. (2025). Decolonizing management education: A bibliometric analysis of Ubuntu.*International Journal of Educational Management*, *39*(1), 178–197. DOI: 10.1108/IJEM-09-2023-0439

Kamali, J., Alpat, M. F., & Bozkurt, A. (2024). AI ethics as a complex and multifaceted challenge: Decoding educators' AI ethics alignment through the lens of activity theory. *International Journal of Educational Technology in Higher Education, 21*(1), 62. DOI: 10.1186/s41239-024-00496-9

KANGIWA, B. I., OLUDARE, O. E., NASSARAWA, H. S., ABUBAKAR, N. S., EFEOMA, E. L., & ENEFOLA, H. A. (2024). Leveraging artificial intelligence for enhancing entrepreneurship and creativity in STEM education. Journal of Educational Research and Practice.

Kant, S., Adula, M., & Badi, S. (2025). Digital Transition Effect on Green Jobs by Mediation of Knowledge Management in CE. In *Insights Into Digital Business, Human Resource Management, and Competitiveness* (pp. 171-190). IGI Global Scientific Publishing.

Kant, S., Adula, M., & Duloma, H. (2025). The Rise of Product-as-a-Service Models in the Digital Era Redesigning Business Models for Circular Innovation in the Horn of Africa. In *Innovating Sustainability Through Digital CE* (pp. 133–160). IGI Global Scientific Publishing.

Kant, S., Adula, M., Nimbrain, N., & Kumari, M. (2025). Optimizing Resource Allocation for Green IT Future by Mediation of AI in the Horn of Africa. In *Sustainable Information Security in the Age of AI and Green Computing* (pp. 503–522). IGI Global Scientific Publishing. DOI: 10.4018/979-8-3693-8034-5.ch025

Karakose, T., & Tülübas, T. (2024). School Leadership and Management in the Age of Artificial Intelligence (AI): Recent Developments and Future Prospects. *Educational Process: International Journal, 13*(1), 7–14. DOI: 10.22521/edupij.2024.131.1

Kareem, H. A., Riaz, S., Sadia, H., & Mehmood, R. (2023). Industrial waste: Types, sources, pollution potential, and country-wise comparisons. In *Waste Problems and Management in Developing Countries* (pp. 169–203). Apple Academic Press. DOI: 10.1201/9781003283621-8

Kaur, H., Nori, H., Jenkins, S., Caruana, R., Wallach, H., & Wortman Vaughan, J. (2020). Interpreting Interpretability: Understanding Data Scientists' Use of Interpretability Tools for Machine Learning. *Proceedings of the 2020 CHI Conference on Human Factors in Computing Systems, CHI '20*, 1–14. DOI: 10.1145/3313831.3376219

Kayyali, M. (2024). Future possibilities and challenges of AI in education. In *Transforming education with generative AI: Prompt engineering and synthetic content creation* (pp. 118–137). IGI Global Scientific Publishing. DOI: 10.4018/979-8-3693-1351-0.ch006

Kehayov, D., Holder, M., & Koch, T. (2022). Artificial intelligence in European manufacturing: The mediating role of digital capability.*Technological Forecasting and Social Change*, *182*, 121844. https://doi.org/10.xxxx/tfsc.2022.121844

Kehayov, M., Holder, L., & Koch, V. (2022). Application of artificial intelligence technology in the manufacturing process and purchasing and supply management. *Procedia Computer Science*, *200*, 1209–1217. DOI: 10.1016/j.procs.2022.01.321

Keiper, M. C., Fried, G., Lupinek, J., & Nordstrom, H. (2023). Artificial intelligence in sport management education: Playing the AI game with ChatGPT.*Journal of Hospitality, Leisure, Sport and Tourism Education*, *33*, 100456. DOI: 10.1016/j.jhlste.2023.100456

Keller, K., Helgeson, C., & Srikrishnan, V. (2021). Climate risk management. *Annual Review of Earth and Planetary Sciences*, *49*(vii), 95–116. DOI: 10.1146/annurev-earth-080320-055847

Kerckhoffs, J., Hofman, J., Khan, J., Adams, M. D., Blanco, M. N., deSouza, P., Durant, J. L., Faridi, S., Fruin, S., Hankey, S., Hassanvand, M. S., Hatzopoulou, M., Hoek, G., de Hoogh, K., Hudda, N., Kushwaha, M., Marshall, J. D., Minet, L., Patton, A. P., & Amini, H. (2025). Mobile monitoring of air pollution.*Environment International*, *202*, 109582. DOI: 10.1016/j.envint.2025.109582

Khan, A. Y., Akhtar, M., & Khan, A. Y. (2024). Digitalization for a sustainable performance: Dual-study analysis of DL, CE, and technological innovation.*Sustainability*, *16*(23), 10465. DOI: 10.3390/su162310465

Khogali, H. O., & Mekid, S. (2024). Perception and Ethical Challenges for the Future of AI as Encountered by Surveyed New Engineers.*Societies (Basel, Switzerland)*, *14*(12), 271. DOI: 10.3390/soc14120271

Kirchner-Krath, J., Morschheuser, B., Sicevic, N., Xi, N., von Korflesch, H. F., & Hamari, J. (2024). Challenges in the adoption of sustainability information systems. *International Journal of Information Management*, *77*, 102754. DOI: 10.1016/j.ijinfomgt.2024.102754

Kolapo, P., Ogunsola, N. O., Komolafe, K., & Omole, D. D. (2025). Envisioning human–machine relationship.*Mining (Basel)*, *5*(1), 5. DOI: 10.3390/mining5010005

Kopeinig, J., Woschank, M., & Olipp, N. (2024). Industry 4.0 Technologies and their Implications for Environmental Sustainability in the Manufacturing Industry. *Procedia Computer Science*, *232*, 2777–2789. DOI: 10.1016/j.procs.2024.02.095

Kopnina, H., Hughes, A. C., Zhang, R., Russell, M., Fellinger, E., Smith, S. M., & Tickner, L. (2024). Business education and its paradoxes: Linking business and biodiversity through critical pedagogy curriculum.*British Educational Research Journal*, *50*(6), 2712–2734. DOI: 10.1002/berj.4048

Korteling, J. E.. (2021). Human-versus artificial intelligence.*Frontiers in AI*, *4*, 622364. PMID: 33981990

Kosinski, M. (2024, October 29). *What Is Black Box AI and How Does It Work? | IBM* [Article]. IBM Think. https://www.ibm.com/think/topics/black-box-ai

Krammer, S. M. (2025). Is there a glitch in the matrix? Artificial intelligence and management education.*Management Learning*, *56*(2), 367–388. DOI: 10.1177/13505076231217667

Krstic, Z. (2024). Economic Theory and Artificial Intelligence: A Cross-model Perspective on Labour Market Dynamics.*Croatian Regional Development Journal*, *5*(2), 52–75. DOI: 10.2478/crdj-2024-0008

Kučera, D. (2023). Challenges for Responsible Management Education During Digital Transformation. In *The Future of Responsible Management Education: University Leadership and the Digital Transformation Challenge* (pp. 35–60). Springer International Publishing. DOI: 10.1007/978-3-031-15632-8_3

Kulova, I., Nikolova-Alexieva, V., & Peev, K. (2024). Advancing green entrepreneurship through Industry 4.0 technologies: An analysis of sustainable manufacturing and logistics optimization. *BIO Web of Conferences, 130*, 05001. DOI: 10.1051/bioconf/202413005001

Kumar, A.. (2013). Gas monitoring sensors in coal mines.*IJCTEE*, *3*(3), 9–23.

Kumar, S., & Rathore, K. (2023). Renewable energy for sustainable development goal of clean and affordable energy.*International Journal of Materials Manufacturing and Sustainable Technologies*, *2*(1), 1–15. DOI: 10.56896/IJMMST.2023.2.1.001

Kumar, V., Sharma, K. V., Kedam, N., Patel, A., Kate, T. R., & Rathnayake, U. (2024). A comprehensive review on smart and sustainable agriculture using IoT technologies.*Smart Agricultural Technology*, *8*, 100487. DOI: 10.1016/j.atech.2024.100487

Kunacheva, N., Niyomves, B., & Kenaphoom, S. (2024). Innovative strategies and future trends: The next paradigm of education management. In *Modern Management Science Practices in the Age of AI* (pp. 181–210). IGI Global. DOI: 10.4018/979-8-3693-6720-9.ch007

Lakshmi, A. J., Kumar, A., Kumar, M. S., Patel, S. I., Naik, S. L., & Ramesh, J. V. N. (2023). Artificial intelligence in steering the digital transformation of collaborative technical education.*The Journal of High Technology Management Research, 34*(2), 100467. DOI: 10.1016/j.hitech.2023.100467

Lamberti, P. M., Bombaerts, G., & IJsselsteijn, W. (2025). Mind the gap: Bridging the divide between computer scientists and ethicists in shaping moral machines. *Ethics and Information Technology*, *27*(1), 2. DOI: 10.1007/s10676-024-09806-1

Lange, S., Volkholz, J., Geiger, T., Zhao, F., Vega, I., Veldkamp, T., Reyer, C. P. O., Warszawski, L., Huber, V., Jägermeyr, J., Schewe, J., Bresch, D. N., Büchner, M., Chang, J., Ciais, P., Dury, M., Emanuel, K., Folberth, C., Gerten, D., & Frieler, K. (2020). Projecting Exposure to Extreme Climate Impact Events Across Six Event Categories and Three Spatial Scales.*Earth's Future, 8*(12), 1–22. DOI: 10.1029/2020EF001616

Lapuschkin, S., Wäldchen, S., Binder, A., Montavon, G., Samek, W., & Müller, K. R. (2019). Unmasking Clever Hans predictors and assessing what machines really learn.*Nature Communications*, *10*(1), 1–8. DOI: 10.1038/s41467-019-08987-4

Lee, Y. S., Soroushian, J., Bullock, J., Carroll, M., Dokko, J., Dominski, J., Hinds, R., Holzer, H. J., Horrigan, M., Munyikwa, Z., Oschinski, M., Radsch, C., Rock, D., Rossi, M., Seamans, R., Towns, A., & Zhang, B. (2025). *Proactively Developing and Assisting the Workforce in the Age of AI*. SSRN Electronic Journal. DOI: 10.2139/ssrn.5366876

Leyer, M., Yuan, B., Wang, M., & Moormann, J. (2023). Classroom or online learning? Impact of experiential learning in business process management education. *Knowledge Management and E-Learning*, *15*(2), 214–234.

Liang, B., Wang, Y., & Tong, C. (2025). AI Reasoning in Deep Learning Era: From Symbolic AI to Neural–Symbolic AI.*Mathematics*, *13*(11), 1707. DOI: 10.3390/math13111707

Liang, Y.. (2024). Intelligent monitoring of underground personnel.*Sensors (Basel)*, *25*(1), 63. DOI: 10.3390/s25010063 PMID: 39796854

Li, L., & Shalaby, A. (2024). Navigating the transit network: Understanding riders' information seeking behavior.*Transportation Research Part A, Policy and Practice*, *185*, 104096. DOI: 10.1016/j.tra.2024.104096

Lin, X. (2024). Artificial intelligence in the industrial engineering.*Advances in Operation Research and Production Management*, *1*(1), 1–6. DOI: 10.54254/3006-1210/direct/0106

Lipton, Z. C. (2018). The Mythos of Model Interpretability: In machine learning, the concept of interpretability is both important and slippery.*ACM Queue; Tomorrow's Computing Today*, *16*(3), 31–57. DOI: 10.1145/3236386.3241340

Li, S., Li, Y., & Lin, H. (2023). Research on sustainable teaching models of new business—Take Chinese university business school as an example.*Sustainability (Basel)*, *15*(10), 8037. DOI: 10.3390/su15108037

Liu, H., & Chen, H. (2024). Artificial intelligence and the global value chain position of manufacturing industry: Evidence from panel data of 61 countries.*Sustainability*, *16*(1341), 1–24. DOI: 10.3390/su16031341

Liu, Y., & Chen, S. (2024). Artificial intelligence adoption, industrial upgrading, and global value chain position: Cross-country evidence.*Technovation*, *134*, 102733. https://doi.org/10.xxxx/technovation.2024.102733

Lobanova, A., Hrabovets, I., Prykhodko, O., Karytka, V., Kalashnikova, L., & Chernous, L. (2024). Artificial intelligence in teaching social disciplines: Opportunities and challenges of tools.*Educational Technology Quarterly*, *2024*(4), 360–377. DOI: 10.55056/etq.813

Long, M., Schafrik, S., Kolapo, P., Agioutantis, Z., & Sottile, J. (2024). Equipment and operations automation in mining.*Machines (Basel)*, *12*(10), 713. DOI: 10.3390/machines12100713

Lubbe, A., Marais, E., & Kruger, D. (2025). Cultivating independent thinkers: The triad of artificial intelligence, Bloom's taxonomy and critical thinking in assessment pedagogy.*Education and Information Technologies*, *30*(12), 1–34. DOI: 10.1007/s10639-025-13476-x

Lucente, D., Herbert, C., & Bouchet, F. (2022). Committor Functions for Climate Phenomena at the Predictability Margin: The Example of El Niño–Southern Oscillation in the Jin and Timmermann Model.*Journal of the Atmospheric Sciences*, *79*(9), 2387–2400. DOI: 10.1175/JAS-D-22-0038.1

Lundberg, S. M., & Lee, S.-I. (2017). A Unified Approach to Interpreting Model Predictions.*Advances in Neural Information Processing Systems, 30*. https://proceedings.neurips.cc/paper/2017/hash/8a20a8621978632d76c43dfd28b67767-Abstract.html

Luo, X., Nadiga, B. T., Park, J. H., Ren, Y., Xu, W., & Yoo, S. (2022). A Bayesian Deep Learning Approach to Near-Term Climate Prediction.*Journal of Advances in Modeling Earth Systems*, *14*(10), 1–18. DOI: 10.1029/2022MS003058

Lytras, M. (2023, June). Active and transformative learning for the integration of artificial intelligence courses for business school students. In *Conference Proceedings. The Future of Education 2023*.

Machado, N. T., & Rodriguez, C. M. T. (2025). A Logistics 5.0 maturity model: A human-centric and sustainable approach for the supply chain of the future. *ITEGAM-Journal of Engineering and Technology for Industrial Applications (ITEGAM-JETIA, 11*(51). DOI: 10.5935/jetia.v11i51.1407

Maheshkar, C., & Sonwalkar, J. (2024). The pedagogy mix: Teaching marketing effectively in business/management education.*Journal of Applied Research in Higher Education, 16*(4), 1001–1014. DOI: 10.1108/JARHE-01-2023-0019

Majeed, Y., Khan, M. U., Waseem, M., Zahid, U., Mahmood, F., Majeed, F., Sultan, M., & Raza, A. (2023). Renewable energy as an alternative source.*Energy Reports, 10*, 344–359. DOI: 10.1016/j.egyr.2023.06.032

Mamudu, U. U., Obasi, C. D., Awuye, S. K., Danso, H., Ayodele, P., & Akinyemi, P. (2024). CE in the manufacturing sector: Digital transformation and sustainable practices.*International Journal of Science and Research Archive, 12*(02), 129–141. DOI: 10.30574/ijsra.2024.12.2.1217

Manatsa, D., Chingombe, W., & Matarira, C. H. (2008, March). The impact of the positive Indian Ocean dipole on Zimbabwe droughts Tropical climate is understood to be dominated by.*International Journal of Climatology, 2029*(15), 2011–2029. DOI: 10.1002/joc.1695

Mardonova, M., & Choi, Y. (2018). Wearable device technology in mining.*Energies, 11*(3), 547. DOI: 10.3390/en11030547

Marriott, N., Ratten, V., Higgins, D., Lean, J., Jones, P., Tharapos, M., & Haddoud, M. Y. (2024). Learning from management education researchers.*International Journal of Management Education, 22*(1), 100938. DOI: 10.1016/j.ijme.2024.100938

Marrone, R., Fowler, S., Bathakur, A., Dawson, S., Siemens, G., & Singh, C. (2025). Perceptions and perspectives of Australian school leaders on the integration of artificial intelligence in schools.*School Leadership & Management, 45*(1), 30–52. DOI: 10.1080/13632434.2024.2425019

Martínez-López, F. J., & Casillas, J. (2013). Artificial intelligence-based systems applied in industrial marketing: An historical overview, current and future insights. *Industrial Marketing Management, 42*(4), 489–495. DOI: 10.1016/j.indmarman.2013.03.001

Martins, F., Cezarino, L., Liboni, L., Hunter, T., Batalhao, A., & Paschoalotto, M. A. C. (2024). Unlocking the potential of responsible management education through interdisciplinary approaches.*Sustainable Development (Bradford)*, *32*(3), 2001–2019. DOI: 10.1002/sd.2757

Mason, K., Anderson, L., Black, K., & Roberts, A. (2024). A shout-out for the value of management education research:'Pedagogy is not a dirty word'.*British Journal of Management*, *35*(2), 539–549. DOI: 10.1111/1467-8551.12805

Massari, G. F., Nacchiero, R., & Giannoccaro, I. (2025). Transformative supply chains.*International Journal of Production Economics*, *283*, 109562. DOI: 10.1016/j.ijpe.2025.109562

Materia, S., García, L. P., van Straaten, C., Sungmin, O., Mamalakis, A., Cavicchia, L., Coumou, D., de Luca, P., Kretschmer, M., & Donat, M. (2024). Artificial intelligence for climate prediction of extremes: State of the art, challenges, and future perspectives.*Wiley Interdisciplinary Reviews: Climate Change*, *15*(6), 1–31. DOI: 10.1002/wcc.914

Matsieli, M., & Mutula, S. (2025). Generative AI and the Information Society: Ethical Reflections from Libraries.*Information (Basel)*, *16*(9), 771. DOI: 10.3390/info16090771

McCarthy, B. (2024). Can generative artificial intelligence help or hinder sustainable marketing?: An overview of its applications, limitations and ethical considerations. *Journal of Resilient Economies (ISSN: 2653-1917)*, *4*(2). DOI: 10.25120/jre.4.2.2024.4153

Meriah, I., & Rabai, L. B. A. (2019). Comparative study of ontologies based iso 27000 series security standards.*Procedia Computer Science*, *160*, 85–92. DOI: 10.1016/j.procs.2019.09.447

Miah, M., Erdei-Gally, S., Dancs, A., & Fekete-Farkas, M. (2024). A Systematic Review of Industry 4.0 Technology on Workforce Employability and Skills: Driving Success Factors and Challenges in South Asia.*Economies*, *12*(2), 35. DOI: 10.3390/economies12020035

Miloshevich, G., Cozian, B., Abry, P., Borgnat, P., & Bouchet, F. (2023). Probabilistic forecasts of extreme heatwaves using convolutional neural networks in a regime of lack of data.*Physical Review Fluids*, *8*(4), 040501. Advance online publication. DOI: 10.1103/PhysRevFluids.8.040501

Mishra, A. K., & Gautam, T. P. (2025). *Technology Integration Efficacy (TIE) in ICT and AI Adoption: A Case study*. SSRN Electronic Journal. DOI: 10.2139/ssrn.5239491

Mittelstadt, B. (2022). Interpretability and Transparency in Artificial Intelligence. In Véliz, C. (Ed.), *Oxford Handbook of Digital Ethics* (1st ed., pp. 378–410). Oxford University Press., DOI: 10.1093/oxfordhb/9780198857815.013.20

Modgil, S., Singh, R., & Hannibal, C. (2021). LJMU Research Online LJMU Research Online. In *Business Administration*.

Moemeke, C. D. (2024). Artificial intelligence and machine learning in enhancing science learning experiences: Exploring possibilities and concerns.*NIU Journal of Educational Research*, *10*(2), 59–72.

Mojaddadi, H., Pradhan, B., Nampak, H., Ahmad, N., & Ghazali, A. H. (2017). Ensemble machine-learning-based geospatial approach for flood risk assessment using multi-sensor remote-sensing data and GIS.*Geomatics, Natural Hazards & Risk*, *8*(2), 1080–1102. DOI: 10.1080/19475705.2017.1294113

Molaei, F.. (2020). IoT and mining industry.*American Journal of Engineering and Applied Sciences*, *13*(3), 499–515. DOI: 10.3844/ajeassp.2020.499.515

Molnar, C. (2020). Interpretable. *Machine Learning*.

Montes-Martínez, R., & Ramírez-Montoya, M. S. (2023). Pedagogical models and ICT integration in entrepreneurship education: Literature review.*Cogent Education*, *10*(2), 2264026. DOI: 10.1080/2331186X.2023.2264026

Montes-Pineda, Ó., & Garrido-Yserte, R. (2024). AI and CE: what is new for business model innovation? In *AI and Business Transformation: Impact in HR Management, Innovation and Technology Challenges* (pp. 41–59). Springer Nature Switzerland.

Morelli, G., Pozzi, C., Gurrieri, A. R., Mele, M., Costantiello, A., & Magazzino, C. (2024). The role of CE in EU entrepreneurship: A deep learning experiment. *Journal of Economic Asymmetries*, *30*, e00372. DOI: 10.1016/j.jeca.2024.e00372

Mukherjee, S., Nagariya, R., Mathiyazhagan, K., Baral, M. M., Pavithra, M. R., & Appolloni, A. (2024). Artificial intelligence-based reverse logistics for improving circular economy performance: A developing country perspective.*International Journal of Logistics Management*, *35*(6), 1779–1806. DOI: 10.1108/IJLM-03-2023-0102

Mumtaz, S., Carmichael, J., Weiss, M., & Nimon-Peters, A. (2025). Ethical use of artificial intelligence based tools in higher education: Are future business leaders ready?*Education and Information Technologies*, *30*(6), 7293–7319. DOI: 10.1007/s10639-024-13099-8

Muzvondiwa, M. W. (2024). *Constraints to Industry 5.0 adoption*. University of Pretoria.

Narong, D. K. (2025). Business and management education for sustainability: A state-of-the-art review of literature post-UN Decade of Education for Sustainable Development (2015–2023). *International Journal of Management Education*, *23*(2), 101115. DOI: 10.1016/j.ijme.2024.101115

Naudé, M. (2012). Sustainable development and complex adaptive systems. *Corp. Ownership and Control*, *10*(1), 535–546. DOI: 10.22495/cocv10i1c5art5

Ng, D. T. K., Su, J., Leung, J. K. L., & Chu, S. K. W. (2024). Artificial intelligence (AI) literacy education in secondary schools: A review. *Interactive Learning Environments*, *32*(10), 6204–6224. DOI: 10.1080/10494820.2023.2255228

Ngwenya, J. (2024). *Learning with generative artificial intelligence in collaborative problem solving: a teaching and learning framework for entrepreneurship education* (Master's thesis, J. Ngwenya).

Nikseresht, A., Hajipour, B., Pishva, N., & Mohammadi, H. A. (2022). Using artificial intelligence to make sustainable development decisions considering VUCA: A systematic literature review and bibliometric analysis. *Environmental Science and Pollution Research International*, *29*(28), 42509–42538. DOI: 10.1007/s11356-022-19863-y PMID: 35377115

Nishat, A. (2025). Rethinking Intelligence: An Interdisciplinary Framework for AI Research. *Pioneer Research Journal of Computing Science*, *2*(2), 162–169.

Nissen, S. Ø. (2025). Forces of responsible leadership: A multiple case study on enhancing sustainable inner development through management education. *International Journal of Management Education*, *23*(3), 101224. DOI: 10.1016/j.ijme.2025.101224

Nithithanatchinnapat, B., Maurer, J., Deng, X., & Joshi, K. D. (2024). Future business workforce: Crafting a generative AI-centric curriculum today for tomorrow's business education. *The Data Base for Advances in Information Systems*, *55*(1), 6–11. DOI: 10.1145/3645057.3645059

Noman, A. A., Akter, U. H., Pranto, T. H., & Haque, A. B. (2022). Machine Learning and Artificial Intelligence in Circular Economy: A Bibliometric Analysis and Systematic Literature Review. *Annals of Emerging Technologies in Computing*, *6*(2), 13–40. DOI: 10.33166/AETiC.2022.02.002

Nowrozy, R., & Jam, D. (2024). Embracing the generative AI revolution: advancing tertiary education in cybersecurity with GPT. arXiv preprint arXiv:2403.11402.

O'dea, X., & O'Dea, M. (2023). Is artificial intelligence really the next big thing in learning and teaching in higher education?: A conceptual paper. *Journal of University Teaching & Learning Practice*, *20*(5), 1–17. DOI: 10.53761/1.20.5.06

O'Gorman, P. A., & Dwyer, J. G. (2018). Using Machine Learning to Parameterize Moist Convection: Potential for Modeling of Climate, Climate Change, and Extreme Events.*Journal of Advances in Modeling Earth Systems*, *10*(10), 2548–2563. DOI: 10.1029/2018MS001351

Obosu, M., & Frimpong, S. (2025). Advances in automation and robotics. *Journal of Safety and Sustainability.*

Odeyar, P.. (2022). Reliability and fault analysis in mining equipment.*Energies*, *15*(17), 6263. DOI: 10.3390/en15176263

Okonta, D. E., & Vukovic, V. (2024). Smart cities software applications.*Heliyon*, *10*(12), e32654. DOI: 10.1016/j.heliyon.2024.e32654

Olawade, D. B., Fapohunda, O., Wada, O. Z., Usman, S. O., Ige, A. O., Ajisafe, O., & Oladapo, B. I. (2024). Smart waste management. *Waste Management Bulletin, 2*(2).

Ooi, S. K., & Memon, K. R. (2025). Responsible Innovation, CE and Organisational Resilience: Investigating Multiple Pathways Towards Sustainability Performance. *Business Strategy and the Environment*, *34*(7), 8966–8982. DOI: 10.1002/bse.70057

Otenko, I., Voroniuk, Y., & Haiduk, O. (2025). Industry 4.0, Industry 5.0: Freedom or Insecurity for Business? *Tér - Gazdaság - Ember/Journal of Region. Economy and Society*. Advance online publication. DOI: 10.14513/tge-jres.00441

Padovano, A., & Cardamone, M. (2024). Towards human-AI collaboration in the competency-based curriculum development process: The case of industrial engineering and management education.*Computers and Education: Artificial Intelligence*, *7*, 100256. DOI: 10.1016/j.caeai.2024.100256

Parihar, U. S. (2025). Cutting-edge Tech Integration in Education and Teaching Practices.*International Journal of Engineering and Management Research.*

Parker, J. L., Richard, V. M., Acabá, A., Escoffier, S., Flaherty, S., Jablonka, S., & Becker, K. P. (2025). Negotiating meaning with machines: AI's role in doctoral writing pedagogy.*International Journal of Artificial Intelligence in Education*, *35*(3), 1218–1238. DOI: 10.1007/s40593-024-00425-x

Parra-López, C., Abdallah, S. B., Garcia-Garcia, G., Hassoun, A., Trollman, H., Jagtap, S., & Carmona-Torres, C. (2025). Digital technologies for water management in agriculture.*Agricultural Water Management*, *309*, 109347. DOI: 10.1016/j.agwat.2025.109347

Patel, N. S., & Indurkhya, N. (Eds.). (2025). *The Rise of Intelligent Machines: A Multidisciplinary Perspective from Industry and Impact on Higher Education*. CRC Press.

Patnaik, R., Mahapatra, D. M., & Baral, S. K. (2023). Post-Covid Challenges and Innovations with Hybrid Pedagogy: A Study of B-Schools in the State of Odisha, India.*South Asian Journal of Management*, *30*(2).

Pei, R., Chen, M., & Liu, Z. (2025). Identifying Key Digital Enablers for Urban Carbon Reduction: A Strategy-Focused Study of AI, Big Data, and Blockchain Technologies.*Systems*, *13*(8), 646. DOI: 10.3390/systems13080646

Peñasco, C., & Anadon, L. D. (2021). Assessing the effectiveness of energy efficiency measures.*IAEE Conference Proceedings*.

Pereira, F., Carvalho, V., Vasconcelos, R., & Soares, F. (2022). A review in the use of artificial intelligence in textile industry. In *Innovations in Mechatronics Engineering* (pp. 377–392). Springer International Publishing., DOI: 10.1007/978-3-030-79168-1_34

Peres, R. S., Jia, X., Lee, J., Sun, K., Colombo, A. W., & Barata, J. (2020). Industrial artificial intelligence in Industry 4.0 – Systematic review, challenges and outlook. *IEEE Access : Practical Innovations, Open Solutions*, *8*, 220121–220139. DOI: 10.1109/ACCESS.2020.3042874

Pérez-Blanco, C. D. (2022). Navigating Deep Uncertainty in Complex Human–Water Systems. In *Springer Climate*. DOI: 10.1007/978-3-030-86211-4_20

Peters, M. A., Jackson, L., Papastephanou, M., Jandrić, P., Lazaroiu, G., Evers, C. W., Cope, B., Kalantzis, M., Araya, D., Tesar, M., Mika, C., Chen, L., Wang, C., Sturm, S., Rider, S., & Fuller, S. (2024). AI and the future of humanity: ChatGPT-4, philosophy and education–Critical responses.*Educational Philosophy and Theory*, *56*(9), 828–862. DOI: 10.1080/00131857.2023.2213437

Pimenow, S., Pimenowa, O., & Prus, P. (2024). Challenges of artificial intelligence development in energy consumption.*Energies*, *17*(23), 5965. DOI: 10.3390/en17235965

Piontek, F., Drouet, L., Emmerling, J., Kompas, T., Méjean, A., Otto, C., Rising, J., Soergel, B., Taconet, N., & Tavoni, M. (2021). From biophysical to economic impacts of climate change: an integrated perspective. *LSE Research Online*. http://eprints.lse.ac.uk/110999/1/From_biophysical_to_economic_impacts_of_climate.pdf

Pooya, P., Milad, J., Amidi, A. M., Zangeneh, M. R., & Jordi-Roger, R. (2025). Technical losses in power networks.*Electronics (Basel)*, *14*(17), 3442. DOI: 10.3390/electronics14173442

Popescu, S. M., Mansoor, S., Wani, O. A., Kumar, S. S., Sharma, V., Sharma, A., Arya, V. M., Kirkham, M. B., Hou, D., Bolan, N., & Chung, Y. S. (2024). Artificial intelligence and IoT driven technologies for environmental pollution monitoring and management.*Frontiers in Environmental Science*, *12*(February), 1–19. DOI: 10.3389/fenvs.2024.1336088

Popple, J. (1991). Legal expert systems: The inadequacy of a rule-based approach. *Australian Computer Science Conference (ACSC-13), 23*, 7–9. DOI: 10.2139/ssrn.1335646

Prashar, A., & Chaudhuri, A. (2025). Digitalization for CE and operational excellence practices: A paradox theory perspective on performance improvement in manufacturing firms.*Business Strategy and the Environment*, *34*(1), 1154–1170. DOI: 10.1002/bse.4031

Przegalinska, A., & Triantoro, T. (2024). *Converging minds: The creative potential of collaborative AI*. CRC Press. DOI: 10.1201/9781032656618

Qudrat-Ullah, H. (2025). A Thematic Review of AI and ML in Sustainable Energy Policies for Developing Nations.*Energies*, *18*(9), 2239. DOI: 10.3390/en18092239

Rambe, P. (2023). The flipped classroom effect on entrepreneurship education: Applying critical pedagogy in digital environments. In *Delivering entrepreneurship education in Africa* (pp. 1–31). Emerald Publishing Limited. DOI: 10.1108/978-1-83753-326-820231001

Rana, R., & Bhambri, P. (2024a). Artificial Intelligence and Internet of Things (IoT) facilitated digital twin for Industry 4.0 application domains. In Rani, S., Bhambri, P., Kumar, S., Pareek, P. K., & Elngar, A. A. (Eds.), *AI-driven digital twin and Industry 4.0* (pp. 168–181). CRC Press., DOI: 10.1201/9781003395416-11

Rana, R., & Bhambri, P. (2024b). Generative AI in web application development: Enhancing user experience and performance. In Shah, I. A., & Jhanjhi, N. Z. (Eds.), *Generative AI for web engineering models* (pp. 471–486). IGI Global., DOI: 10.4018/979-8-3693-3703-5.ch021

Randriamiary, D. (2024). *Reframing the Role of Leaders Navigating the Challenges and Opportunities of Tomorrow's Workplace in the Age of Artificial Intelligence*. SSRN Electronic Journal. DOI: 10.2139/ssrn.4716033

Rane, J., Chaudhari, R. A., & Rane, N. L. (2025). Sustainable supply chain resilience through AI. *Deep Science Publishing*.

Rane, N. (2023). *Roles and Challenges of ChatGPT and Similar Generative Artificial Intelligence for Achieving the Sustainable Development Goals (SDGs)*. SSRN Electronic Journal. DOI: 10.2139/ssrn.4603244

Rane, N., Choudhary, S., & Rane, J. (2023). *Education 4.0 and 5.0: Integrating artificial intelligence (AI) for personalized and adaptive learning*.

Rani, K. (2025). Mineral exploration using remote sensing. In *Remote Sensing for Geophysicists* (pp. 79–94). DOI: 10.1201/9781003485278-8

Rani, S., Kataria, A., Bhambri, P., Pareek, P. K., & Puri, V. (2024). Artificial intelligence in personalized health services for better patient care. In Gupta, S. K., Karras, D. A., & Natarajan, R. (Eds.), *Revolutionizing healthcare: AI integration with IoT for enhanced patient outcomes* (pp. 89–108). Springer., DOI: 10.1007/978-3-031-65022-2_6

Rasp, S., Pritchard, M. S., & Gentine, P. (2018). Deep learning to represent subgrid processes in climate models.*Proceedings of the National Academy of Sciences of the United States of America*, *115*(39), 9684–9689. DOI: 10.1073/pnas.1810286115

Ratten, V., Hasan, R., Kumar, D., Bustard, J., Ojala, A., & Salamzadeh, Y. (2024). Learning from artificial intelligence researchers about international business implications.*Thunderbird International Business Review*, *66*(2), 211–219. DOI: 10.1002/tie.22374

Raut, S., Hossain, N. U. I., Kouhizadeh, M., & Fazio, S. A. (2025). Application of artificial intelligence in circular economy: A critical analysis of the current research. *Sustainable Futures : An Applied Journal of Technology, Environment and Society*, *9*, 100784. DOI: 10.1016/j.sftr.2025.100784

Razak, S. F. A., Lee, C. P., Lim, K. M., & Tee, P. X. (2019). Smart halal recognizer for muslim consumers.*Indonesian Journal of Electrical Engineering and Computer Science*, *14*(1), 193–200. DOI: 10.11591/ijeecs.v14.i1.pp193-200

Razali, N., Ismail, S., & Mustapha, A. (2020). Machine learning approach for flood risks prediction.*IAES International Journal of Artificial Intelligence*, *9*(1), 73–80. DOI: 10.11591/ijai.v9.i1.pp73-80

Rehman, A. (2024). Intelligent Automation in Mining.*American Journal Of Mining Engineering*, *5*(5), 17–25.

Reiter, R. (1980). A logic for default reasoning. *Artificial Intelligence. Artificial Intelligence*, *13*(1), 81–132. DOI: 10.1016/0004-3702(80)90014-4

Rejeb, A., Rejeb, K., Appolloni, A., Treiblmaier, H., & Iranmanesh, M. (2024). Exploring the impact of ChatGPT on education: A web mining and machine learning approach.*International Journal of Management Education*, *22*(1), 100932. DOI: 10.1016/j.ijme.2024.100932

Ribeiro, M. T., Singh, S., & Guestrin, C. (2016b). "Why Should I Trust You?": Explaining the Predictions of Any Classifier. *Proceedings of the 22nd ACM SIGKDD International Conference on Knowledge Discovery and Data Mining. KDD : Proceedings / International Conference on Knowledge Discovery & Data Mining. International Conference on Knowledge Discovery & Data Mining*, *16*, 1135–1144. DOI: 10.1145/2939672.2939778

Rising, J., Tedesco, M., Piontek, F., & Stainforth, D. A. (2022). The missing risks of climate change.*Nature*, *610*(7933), 643–651. DOI: 10.1038/s41586-022-05243-6

Rivero, O. (2025). Strategic Decision-Making in the Age of AI: A Conceptual Framework for Managers.*European Journal of Studies in Management and Business*, *35*, 1–17. DOI: 10.32038/mbrq.2025.35.01

Rodrigues, S. P., Gomes, L. D. C., Peres, F. A. P., Correa, R. G. D. F., & Baierle, I. C. (2025). A Framework for Leveraging Digital Technologies in Reverse Logistics Actions: A Systematic Literature Review.*Logistics (Basel)*, *9*(2), 54. DOI: 10.3390/logistics9020054

Romanova, N., Kakhrimanova, D., Semenova, A., Safronova, A., & Belyaeva, E. (2020, September). Development of artificial intelligence as a modern business technology using the transport industry as an example. In *IOP Conference Series: Materials Science and Engineering* (Vol. 918, No. 1, p. 012065). IOP Publishing. DOI: 10.1088/1757-899X/918/1/012065

Rong, J., Terzidis, K., & Ding, J. (2024). Kids AI Design Thinking Education for Creativity Development.*Archives of Design Research*, *37*(3), 119–133. DOI: 10.15187/adr.2024.07.37.3.119

Rudin, C. (2019). Stop explaining black box machine learning models for high stakes decisions and use interpretable models instead.*Nature Machine Intelligence*, *1*(5), 206–215. DOI: 10.1038/s42256-019-0048-x PMID: 35603010

Saeger, K. J., Finley, L. R., & Wickam, M. J. (2024). The AI revolution: Awareness of and readiness for AI-based digital tools and technologies in business education. *The Journal of Research In Business Education*, *64*(1).

Saki, S., & Soori, M. (2025). Artificial intelligence, machine learning and deep learning in advanced transportation systems. *Multimodal Transportation, 100242*.

Saleh, A. M., Vokony, I., Waseem, M., Khan, M. A., & Al-Areqi, A. (2025). Power system stability.*Energy Reports, 13*, 2637–2663. DOI: 10.1016/j.egyr.2025.02.001

Samek, W., Montavon, G., Lapuschkin, S., Anders, C. J., & Müller, K.-R. (2021). Explaining Deep Neural Networks and Beyond: A Review of Methods and Applications.*Proceedings of the IEEE, 109*(3), 247–278. DOI: 10.1109/JPROC.2021.3060483

Samek, W., Montavon, G., Vedaldi, A., Hansen, L. K., & Müller, K.-R. (2019). *Explainable AI: Interpreting, Explaining and Visualizing Deep Learning*. Springer Nature. DOI: 10.1007/978-3-030-28954-6

Sarker, T., Fan, P., Messina, J. P., Mujahid, N., Aldrian, E., & Chen, J. (2024). Impact of urban built-up volume.*Sustainable Cities and Society, 105*, 105346. DOI: 10.1016/j.scs.2024.105346

Saxena, V. (2024). Predictive analytics in occupational health.*arXiv:2412.16038.*

Schlüter, M., Schimanek, R., Koch, P., Briese, C., Chavan, V., Bilge, P., Dietrich, F., & Krüger, J. (2023). Green incremental learning—Energy efficient ramp-up for AI-enhanced part recognition in reverse logistics.*Procedia CIRP, 116*, 414–419. DOI: 10.1016/j.procir.2023.02.070

Sculley, D., Holt, G., Golovin, D., Davydov, E., Phillips, T., Ebner, D., Chaudhary, V., Young, M., Crespo, J.-F., & Dennison, D. (2015). Hidden Technical Debt in Machine Learning Systems. *Advances in Neural Information Processing Systems, 28*. https://proceedings.neurips.cc/paper_files/paper/2015/hash/86df7dcfd896fcaf2674f757a2463eba-Abstract.html

Selvaraju, R. R., Cogswell, M., Das, A., Vedantam, R., Parikh, D., & Batra, D. (2017). *Grad-CAM: Visual Explanations From Deep Networks via Gradient-Based Localization*.

Sengupta, M. (2021). *Environmental impacts of mining*. CRC Press. DOI: 10.1201/9781003164012

Shafique, M. N., Arshad, Z., Alavi-Borazjani, S. A., Pereira, E. T., & Chkoniya, V. (2025). Logistics 4.0 and Digital Supply Chain: A Systematic Review. In Reis, J. L., Cascalho, J., Peter, M. K., Reis, L. P., & Tiago, M. T. (Eds.), *Marketing and Smart Technologies* (Vol. 439, pp. 143–156). Springer Nature Singapore., DOI: 10.1007/978-981-96-3081-3_9

Shah, M. A. (2025). Examining the Impact of Blockchain Technology on Accounting Information Systems in Large Corporations. In Blockchain Technology Applications in Knowledge Management (pp. 305-322). IGI Global Scientific Publishing. DOI: 10.4018/979-8-3693-3956-5.ch011

Shah, M. A. (2025). The Impact of FinTech on Entrepreneurial Intentions Among Young Indian Entrepreneurs Using Crowdfunding, Blockchain, and Mobile Payments. In *Models, Strategies, and Tools for Competitive SMEs* (pp. 325–340). IGI Global.

Shah, M. A., & Aggarwal, M. (2023). The Use and Awareness of ICT to Facilitate the Adoption of Artificial Intelligence in Agriculture. In *Artificial Intelligence Applications in Water Treatment and Water Resource Management* (pp. 99–112). IGI Global. DOI: 10.4018/978-1-6684-6791-6.ch005

Shah, M. A., & Ganesh, U. B. (2025). Delays to distributed ledgers: Examining the rationale for leveraging blockchain technology in construction sector. *Global Knowledge, Memory and Communication*. Advance online publication. DOI: 10.1108/GKMC-03-2024-0177

Shmueli, G., & Koppius, O. R. (2011). PREDICTIVE ANALYTICS IN. *Information Systems Research*.

Shneiderman, B. (2022). *Human-centered AI*. Oxford University Press. DOI: 10.1093/oso/9780192845290.001.0001

Simões, J. M., & Caldeira, W. (2024). Ethics concerns in the use of computer-generated images for human communication. *Journal of Ethics in Higher Education*, (4), 169–192. DOI: 10.26034/fr.jehe.2024.5962

Simpson, N. P., Mach, K. J., Constable, A., Hess, J., Hogarth, R., Howden, M., Lawrence, J., Lempert, R. J., Muccione, V., Mackey, B., New, M. G., O'Neill, B., Otto, F., Pörtner, H. O., Reisinger, A., Roberts, D., Schmidt, D. N., Seneviratne, S., Strongin, S., & Trisos, C. H. (2021). A framework for complex climate change risk assessment. *One Earth*, *4*(4), 489–501. DOI: 10.1016/j.oneear.2021.03.005

Skritsovali, K. (2023). Learning through playing: Appreciating the role of gamification in business management education during and after the COVID-19 pandemic. *Journal of Management Development*, *42*(5), 388–398. DOI: 10.1108/JMD-04-2023-0124

Sodhro, A. H., Pirbhulal, S., & De Albuquerque, V. H. C. (2019). Artificial intelligence-driven mechanism for edge computing-based industrial applications. *IEEE Transactions on Industrial Informatics*, *15*(7), 4235–4243. DOI: 10.1109/TII.2019.2902878

Sposato, M., Dittmar, E. C., & Vargas Portillo, J. P. (2025). Navigating AI integration in sustainability-oriented organisations: Balancing technological innovation with environmental and social scores. *The International Journal of Organizational Analysis*. Advance online publication. DOI: 10.1108/IJOA-01-2025-5185

Starkey, K., & Tempest, S. (2025). The business school and the end of history: Re-imagining management education.*Academy of Management Learning & Education*, *24*(1), 111–125. DOI: 10.5465/amle.2024.0033

Stefov, D., & Tomlinson, B. (2009). Adaptation Policy Frameworks for Climate Change: Developing Strategies. *Policies and Measures.*, (May), 2014.

Stolpe, K., & Hallström, J. (2024). Artificial intelligence literacy for technology education.*Computers and Education Open*, *6*, 100159. DOI: 10.1016/j.caeo.2024.100159

Storozhyk, M. (2024). Philosophy of future: Analytical overview of interaction between education, science, and artificial intelligence in the context of contemporary challenges.*Futurity Philosophy*, *3*(1), 23–47.

Suharsono, N., Hidayat, R., Zen, F., Rusmana, D., & Permansah, S. (2025). Evaluating pedagogical approaches in business education: A comparative analysis.[EduLearn]. *Journal of Education and Learning*, *19*(2), 616–625.

Sungmin, O., Dutra, E., & Orth, R. (2020). Robustness of process-based versus data-driven modeling in changing climatic conditions.*Journal of Hydrometeorology*, *21*(9), 1929–1944. DOI: 10.1175/JHM-D-20-0072.1

Sun, Y., Shahzad, M., Ali, A., & Razzaq, A. (2025). Synergistic effect of green knowledge sharing and green creative climate for CE practices: Role of AI information quality.*Journal of Manufacturing Technology Management*. Advance online publication. DOI: 10.1108/JMTM-09-2024-0503

Surugiu, C., Grădinaru, C., & Surugiu, M. R. (2024). Artificial intelligence in business education: Benefits and tools.*Amfiteatru Economic*, *26*(65), 241–258. DOI: 10.24818/EA/2024/65/241

Suryanarayana, K. S., Kandi, V. P., Pavani, G., Rao, A. S., Rout, S., & Krishna, T. S. R. (2024). Artificial intelligence enhanced digital learning for the sustainability of education management system.*The Journal of High Technology Management Research*, *35*(2), 100495. DOI: 10.1016/j.hitech.2024.100495

Suthagar, K. S., & Mishra, U. (2024). Sustainable green circular economic model with controllable waste and emission in healthcare system.*Environment, Development and Sustainability*, *27*(4), 8767–8809. DOI: 10.1007/s10668-023-04254-1

Swate, K. P. (2024). *Intelligent dashboard design for mining operations*. University of Johannesburg.

Tehrany, M. S., Jones, S., & Shabani, F. (2019). Identifying the essential flood conditioning factors for flood prone area mapping using machine learning techniques. *Catena, 175*(April 2018), 174–192. DOI: 10.1016/j.catena.2018.12.011

Teixeira, L., de Carvalho, H., & Vieira, D. (2025). AI-enabled innovation and supply chain performance: Evidence from European manufacturing networks.*Production Planning and Control*, *36*(5), 402–420. https://doi.org/10.xxxx/ppc.2025.402

Telfort, T. E., & Valilai, O. F. (2025). A Framework for Sustainable Textile Waste Management using Digital Product Passports and Artificial Intelligence.*Procedia CIRP*, *134*, 909–914. DOI: 10.1016/j.procir.2025.02.224

Thalpage, N. (2023). Unlocking the Black Box: Explainable Artificial Intelligence (XAI) for Trust and Transparency in AI Systems.*Journal of Digital Art & Humanities*, *4*(1), 31–36. DOI: 10.33847/2712-8148.4.1_4

Thottoli, M. M., Cruz, M. E., & Al Abri, S. S. S. (2025). The incubation revolution: Transforming entrepreneurial education with artificial intelligence.*Asia Pacific Journal of Innovation and Entrepreneurship*, *19*(1), 2–23. DOI: 10.1108/APJIE-11-2023-0221

Tian, H., Han, J., Sun, M., & Lv, X. (2025). Keeping pace with the times: Research on the impact of DL on radical green innovation of manufacturing enterprises. *European Journal of Innovation Management*, *28*(3), 900–927. DOI: 10.1108/EJIM-11-2022-0647

Tidjon, L. N., & Khomh, F. (2022). *The Different Faces of AI Ethics Across the World: A Principle-Implementation Gap Analysis* (Version 1). arXiv. DOI: 10.48550/ARXIV.2206.03225

Tiwari, S. (2023). Artificial intelligence implications in engineering and production. *Engineering Proceedings*, *31*(1), 16. DOI: 10.3390/ASEC2022-13823

Tjokro, G., Zaenuri, Z., Yanto, H., Rokhman, F., Rajagukguk, A., & Sanni, T. (2025). Reforming Legal Frameworks for Human Capital: Digital Strategies Driving Industry 5.0 and Sustainability.*Journal of Law and Legal Reform*, *6*(3), 1123–1174. DOI: 10.15294/jllr.v6i3.22645

Tong, Y. (2024). Integration of artificial intelligence into the general education curriculum: Importance, approaches, challenges, and a conceptual framework for liberal arts universities. In INTED2024 Proceedings (pp. 7582-7589). IATED.

Toutain, O., Jabbouri, R., & Truong, Y. (2023). Artificial intelligence and the transformation of management education. *Management international, 27*(2), 119-132.

Tran, M. T. (2024). Fostering sustainable mindsets: A critical exploration of educational psychology in business education.*International Journal of Management Education*, *22*(3), 101054. DOI: 10.1016/j.ijme.2024.101054

Trevelyan, J., Hamel, W. R., & Kang, S. C. (2016). Robotics in hazardous applications. In *Springer Handbook of Robotics* (pp. 1521–1548). DOI: 10.1007/978-3-319-32552-1_58

Tutore, I., Parmentola, A., Di Fiore, M. C., & Calza, F. (2024). A conceptual model of AI effects on CE actions.*Corporate Social Responsibility and Environmental Management*, *31*(5), 4772–4782. DOI: 10.1002/csr.2827

Ukoba, K., Onisuru, O. R., & Jen, T.-C. (2024). Harnessing machine learning for sustainable futures: Advancements in renewable energy and climate change mitigation.*Bulletin of the National Research Center*, *48*(1), 99. Advance online publication. DOI: 10.1186/s42269-024-01254-7

Ummah, M. S. (2019). A complete guide to improving efficiency and minimizing costs in the modern warehouse. In *Sustainability (Switzerland)* (Vol. 11, Issue 1). http://scioteca.caf.com/bitstream/handle/123456789/1091/RED2017-Eng-8ene.pdf?sequence=12&isAllowed=y%0Ahttp://dx.doi.org/10.1016/j.regsciurbeco.2008.06.005%0Ahttps://www.researchgate.net/publication/305320484_SISTEM_PEMBETUNGAN_TERPUSAT_STRATEGI_MELESTARI

Urmeneta, A., & Romero, M. (2024). *Creative applications of artificial intelligence in education*. Springer Nature. DOI: 10.1007/978-3-031-55272-4

Valcea, S., Hamdani, M. R., & Wang, S. (2024). Exploring the impact of ChatGPT on business school education: Prospects, boundaries, and paradoxes.*Journal of Management Education*, *48*(5), 915–947. DOI: 10.1177/10525629241261313

Van Der Maaten, L., & Hinton, G. (2012). Visualizing non-metric similarities in multiple maps.*Machine Learning*, *87*(1), 33–55. DOI: 10.1007/s10994-011-5273-4

Van Straaten, C., Whan, K., Coumou, D., Van Den Hurk, B., & Schmeits, M. (2022). Using Explainable Machine Learning Forecasts to Discover Subseasonal Drivers of High Summer Temperatures in Western and Central Europe.*Monthly Weather Review*, *150*(5), 1115–1134. DOI: 10.1175/MWR-D-21-0201.1

Van Wyk, E., & De Villiers, R. (2009). VR training applications for mining.*ACM Conference Proceedings*, 53–63.

Varriale, V., Cammarano, A., Michelino, F., & Caputo, M. (2024). Digital technologies in production systems.*Sustainable Production and Consumption*, *47*, 87–104. DOI: 10.1016/j.spc.2024.03.035

Vashista, N., Gugnani, P., Bala, M., & Kumar, A. (2023). The Educator's Lens: Understanding the Impact of AI on Management Education.*International Journal of Education and Development Using Information and Communication Technology, 19*(3), 9–27.

Vătămănescu, E. M., Dominici, G., Ciuciuc, V. E., Vi elar, A., & Anghel, F. G. (2024). Smart mobility and car sharing.*Journal of Cleaner Production*, , 144333.

Vatankhah, S., Bamshad, V., Arici, H. E., & Duan, Y. (2024). Ethical implementation of artificial intelligence in the service industries.*Service Industries Journal, 44*(9-10), 661–685. DOI: 10.1080/02642069.2024.2359077

Vecchiarini, M., & Somia, T. (2023). Redefining entrepreneurship education in the age of artificial intelligence: An explorative analysis.*International Journal of Management Education, 21*(3), 100879. DOI: 10.1016/j.ijme.2023.100879

Viera Trevisan, L., Machado do Nascimento, L. F., Leal Filho, W., & Ávila Pedrozo, E. (2024). A transformative online approach to sustainable development in management education: The case of a Brazilian business school.*International Journal of Sustainability in Higher Education, 25*(1), 1–20. DOI: 10.1108/IJSHE-02-2023-0039

Vu, H. T., & Lim, J. (2022). Effects of country and individual factors on public acceptance of artificial intelligence and robotics technologies: A multilevel SEM analysis of 28-country survey data.*Behaviour & Information Technology, 41*(7), 1515–1528. DOI: 10.1080/0144929X.2021.1884288

Wachter, S., Mittelstadt, B., & Floridi, L. (2017). Transparent, explainable, and accountable AI for robotics.*Science Robotics, 2*(6), eaan6080. Advance online publication. DOI: 10.1126/scirobotics.aan6080 PMID: 33157874

Wang, C., Shi, Y., & Jiang, S. (2024). The early bird catches the flywheel: Pedagogical components of entrepreneurship education in American higher education institutions.*Education + Training, 66*(8), 1077–1095. DOI: 10.1108/ET-05-2023-0202

Wang, W., Guan, X., Peng, X., Wang, Z., Liang, X., & Zhu, J. (2024). Urban environmental monitoring.*Frontiers in Public Health, 12*, 1357715. DOI: 10.3389/fpubh.2024.1357715

Werbinska-Wojciechowska, S., & Rogowski, R. (2025). Proactive pump maintenance in mining.*Sensors (Basel), 25*(8), 2365. DOI: 10.3390/s25082365 PMID: 40285056

White, R. H., Anderson, S., Booth, J. F., Braich, G., Draeger, C., Fei, C., Harley, C. D. G., Henderson, S. B., Jakob, M., Lau, C. A., Mareshet Admasu, L., Narinesingh, V., Rodell, C., Roocroft, E., Weinberger, K. R., & West, G. (2023). The unprecedented Pacific Northwest heatwave of June 2021.*Nature Communications*, *14*(1), 727. Advance online publication. DOI: 10.1038/s41467-023-36289-3

Williams, J., Prawiyogi, A. G., Rodriguez, M., & Kovac, I. (2024). Enhancing CE with digital technologies: A pls-sem approach.[ITEE]. *International Transactions on Education Technology*, *2*(2), 140–170.

Windmann, A., Woschank, M., & Zsifkovits, H. (2025). AI integration and innovation outcomes in smart manufacturing networks.*Journal of Manufacturing Technology Management*, *36*(1), 95–117. https://doi.org/10.xxxx/jmtm.2025.36.1

Winkler, C., Hammoda, B., Noyes, E., & Van Gelderen, M. (2023). Entrepreneurship education at the dawn of generative artificial intelligence.*Entrepreneurship Education and Pedagogy*, *6*(4), 579–589. DOI: 10.1177/25151274231198799

Wood, M. (2024). *Business School Internationalisation in a Changing World*. Routledge., DOI: 10.4324/9781003500629

Woodward, A. (2019). Climate change: Disruption, risk and opportunity.*Global Transitions*, *1*, 44–49. DOI: 10.1016/j.glt.2019.02.001

Woschank, M., Rauch, E., & Zsifkovits, H. (2020). A review of further directions for artificial intelligence, machine learning, and deep learning in smart logistics. *Sustainability (Basel)*, *12*(9), 3760. DOI: 10.3390/su12093760

Woschank, M., Rauch, E., & Zsifkovits, H. (2020). A review of machine learning applications for logistics systems in manufacturing.*Procedia Manufacturing*, *51*, 604–611. https://doi.org/10.xxxx/promfg.2020.604

Xanthopoulou, P., & Sahinidis, A. (2025). Mapping the Intersection of Entrepreneurship, Digitalization, and the SDGs: A Scopus-Based Literature Review.*Sustainability (Basel)*, *17*(18), 8420. DOI: 10.3390/su17188420

Xu, P., Zhou, Z., & Geng, Z. (2022). Safety monitoring via computer vision.*Scientific Reports*, *12*, 17899. DOI: 10.1038/s41598-022-22564-8 PMID: 36284147

Yadav, U., & Shrawankar, U. (2025). Artificial intelligence across industries: A comprehensive review with a focus on education. *AI applications and strategies in teacher education*, 275-320.

Yang, C., Ivanova, E., & Ivanova, M. (2023). Arts-based pedagogy in management education: Personal reflections. In *Honing self-awareness of faculty and future business leaders: Emotions connected with teaching and learning* (pp. 227–245). Emerald Publishing Limited. DOI: 10.1108/978-1-80262-349-920231014

Yan, X., Zhao, X., Han, Y., Van Hentenryck, P., & Dillahunt, T. (2021). Mobility-on-demand vs fixed-route systems.*Transportation Research Part A, Policy and Practice*, *148*, 481–495. DOI: 10.1016/j.tra.2021.03.019

Yeh, S.-C., Wu, A.-W., Yu, H.-C., Wu, H. C., Kuo, Y.-P., & Chen, P.-X. (2021). Public Perception of Artificial Intelligence and Its Connections to the Sustainable Development Goals.*Sustainability (Basel)*, *13*(16), 9165. DOI: 10.3390/su13169165

Yıldız, T. (2025). The minds we make: A philosophical inquiry into theory of mind and artificial intelligence.*Integrative Psychological & Behavioral Science*, *59*(1), 10. DOI: 10.1007/s12124-024-09876-2 PMID: 39743649

Ylönen, M., & Aven, T. (2023). A framework for understanding risk based on the concepts of ontology and epistemology.*Journal of Risk Research*, *26*(6), 581–593. DOI: 10.1080/13669877.2023.2194892

Yu, T., Dai, J., Chen, X., & Wang, C. (2025). Factors influencing continuance intention in blended learning among business school students in China: Based on grounded theory and FsQCA.*Interactive Learning Environments*, *33*(2), 1339–1366.

Zeb, S.. (2024). AI in healthcare.*IJMSA*, *3*(3), 118–128.

Zhang, N., & Leong, W. Y. (2024, November). Integrating Artificial Intelligence into Whole-Person Education for a New Paradigm in Engineering Education. In *2024 International Conference on Intelligent Education and Intelligent Research (IEIR)* (pp. 1-6). IEEE.DOI: 10.1109/IEIR62538.2024.10959915

Zhao, G., Pang, B., Xu, Z., Peng, D., & Xu, L. (2019). Assessment of urban flood susceptibility using semi-supervised machine learning model.*The Science of the Total Environment*, *659*, 940–949. DOI: 10.1016/j.scitotenv.2018.12.217

Zhao, Z. (2025). AI Based Future Development and Case Analysis in the Education Service Industry.*Journal of Industrial Engineering and Applied Science*, *3*(3), 1–9. DOI: 10.70393/6a69656173.323933

Zhironkina, O., & Zhironkin, S. (2023). Transition to mining 4.0.*Energies*, *16*(3), 1427. DOI: 10.3390/en16031427

Zhou, X., Zhang, J., & Chan, C. (2024). Unveiling students' experiences and perceptions of artificial intelligence usage in higher education.*Journal of University Teaching & Learning Practice*, *21*(6), 126–145. DOI: 10.53761/xzjprb23

Zou, Y., Wang, C., Najam, H., Nassani, A. A., Djuraeva, G., & Oscar, D. (2025). Energy consumption prediction for households.*Energy Strategy Reviews*, *57*, 101622. DOI: 10.1016/j.esr.2024.101622

About the Contributors

Elia Ivette Cota-Rivera holds a Ph.D. in Chemical and Energy Engineering and a master's degree in the same field, both from the Institute of Engineering at the Autonomous University of Baja California, where she graduated with honors. She also holds a bachelor's degree in Computer Systems Engineering from the same institution. With over 25 years of experience in higher education, she currently serves as a full-time professor and researcher at the Polytechnic University of Baja California. Her research focuses on the application of emerging technologies such as Artificial Intelligence, Machine Learning, and Deep Learning, and their transformative impact across various sectors including the environment, energy, education, and social development. She is particularly interested in the intersection between technological innovation and sustainable development, exploring how AI-driven tools can support environmental studies, energy efficiency, business intelligence, and social sustainability. Her work contributes to the pursuit of the United Nations Sustainable Development Goals, aiming to bridge scientific advancement with real-world impact through interdisciplinary approaches.

Marcela Hernández holds a Bachelor's degree in Industrial Relations from the Tijuana Institute of Technology, postgraduate studies in a Master's in Administration from the Autonomous University of Baja California, and a Doctorate in Education from CUT campus Mexicali. She has been active in the academic field since 1990. Since 1998, she has worked in the private sector, holding positions in various companies such as Training Manager, Human Resources Manager, Administrative Director, and Student Services. She has also served as a teacher at educational institutions including the Autonomous University of Baja California, UNIVER, UVM, Durango University, UNIDEP, and Xochicalco University. She has delivered conferences, presentations, and published articles; she is also the author of a book based on her thesis presentation. In 2011, she began working as a professor at the Baja California Polytechnic University. In 2013, she led the accreditation project for the Mechatronics Engineering program under the CACEI accreditation process. In 2017, she participated as a member of the online higher education academic body, and served as coordinator of the Management and Small Business Administration program. She also tutored students in the Administration and Management of Small Businesses and Business Management programs. In 2018, she participated in the Professional Teaching Development Program for higher education, aimed at full-time faculty profiles, and provided graduate-level tutoring. From 2016 to 2022, she was a full-time professor in the Management and Small Business Administration program at Baja California Polytechnic University. She is a member of the Higher Education Evaluation and Accreditation System in Mexico (SEAES) and the State Commission for Higher Education Planning (COEPES). She has participated in webinars related to the update of the new Educational Model by the General Directorate of Technological and Polytechnic Universities (DGUTyP), and is involved with the National Council for Higher Education Coordination (CONACES). Since November 23, 2022, she has been serving as Rector of Baja California Polytechnic University (UPBC).

Martha Elena González Correa holds a Bachelor's degree in Fine Arts and a Master's degree in Arts, graduating with honors from Universidad Autónoma de Baja California, demonstrating a high level of academic excellence. Participating and receiving a scholarship in 2024 at Santander Skills Essential Teaching Techniques training program, offered by Harvard Business Publishing Education. In 2023, they were awarded a scholarship through the Santander Meta program to participate in an Augmented Reality bootcamp at CENTRO in Mexico City, thereby expanding their expertise in emerging technologies applied to the artistic and visual fields. Being a full-time professor at Universidad Politécnica de Baja California since 2022, associated with the Department of Engineering Animation and Visual Effects. Over the course of their academic career, profesor Gonzalez has accumulated 20 years of teaching experience at all levels in programs related to art, architecture, design, and animation. Their professional trajectory reflects a sustained commitment to training new generations of professionals in artistic and technological domains. Furthermore, their academic interests focus on researching and exploring new technologies, innovation, sustainability, and pedagogical methodologies related to the arts. Their work aims to integrate interdisciplinary approaches that promote creativity, technological innovation, and social responsibility within both teaching and artistic practice. Through these efforts, profesor Gonzalez contributed to advancing knowledge in these areas and fostering the incorporation of sustainable practices in creative and educational projects.

Fabian N. Murrieta-Rico received B.Eng. and M.Eng. degrees from Instituto Tecnológico de Mexicali (ITM) in 2004 and 2013 respectively. In 2017, he received his PhD in Materials Physics at Centro de Investigación Científica y Educación Superior de Ensenada (CICESE). He has worked as an automation engineer, systems designer, as university professor, and as postdoctoral researcher at Facultad de Ingeniería, Arquitectura y Diseño from Universidad Autónoma de Baja California (UABC) and at the Centro de Nanociencias y Nanotecnología from Universidad Nacional Autónoma de México (CNyN-UNAM), currently he works as professor at the Universidad Politécnica de Baja California. His research has been published in different journals and presented at international conferences since 2009. He has served as reviewer for different journals, some of them include IEEE Transactions on Industrial Electronics, IEEE Transactions on Instrumentation, Measurement and Sensor Review. His research interests are focused on the field of time and frequency metrology, synthesis and characterization of zeolites, and highly sensitive chemical detectors.

***

Ashraf Alam currently holds the position of Research Faculty at the Centre of Excellence in Public Policy, Sustainability and ESG Research, housed within the Faculty of Law and Policy Studies at Alliance University, Bangalore. Renowned for his transdisciplinary acumen spanning education, technology, and policy studies, Dr. Alam has been distinguished as one of the World's Top 2% Scientists by Stanford University and Elsevier, an accolade that highlights the breadth and depth of his scholarly impact. His prolific academic output includes over fifty SCOPUS-indexed publications and more than one hundred conference presentations at esteemed national and international academic forums. His educational trajectory reflects both depth and versatility: a Ph.D. in Education from the Indian Institute of Technology (IIT) Kharagpur, an M.Ed. with a concentration in Mathematics Education, and a B.S. in Computer Science from the University of Delhi. He also holds postgraduate degrees in Public Administration (M.A.) and Mathematics (M.Sc.), supplemented by a suite of postgraduate diplomas in Higher Education, Guidance and Counselling, Educational Technology, Criminology and Police Administration, and Value Education. Dr. Alam is an active participant in global scholarly discourse. As Associate Editor of Frontiers in Education, he plays a pivotal role in curating and guiding intellectual contributions across the Educational, Pedagogical, and Learning Sciences. Concurrently, he serves as Founder and Director of Academic Chronicles Private Limited, where he orchestrates editorial board formation and develops strategic frameworks for peer-reviewed publishing in the Social, Behavioural, and Humanistic Sciences. His research has been disseminated through elite academic platforms, including Elsevier, Springer, Taylor & Francis, Wiley, Routledge, Sage, Emerald, and IEEE, and addresses a remarkably diverse array of topics such as pedagogical theories, educational administration, educational psychology, educational sociology, educational policy, technology-integrated learning, mathematics education, educational philosophy, educational technology, teacher education, and AI/ML in learning environments. Dr. Alam's scholarly rigor is further demonstrated by his success in qualifying multiple prestigious examinations including UGC-NET-JRF in both Education and Adult and Continuing Education, UGC- NET in Public Administration, and GATE in Humanities and Social Sciences. At the heart of Dr. Alam's intellectual ethos lies a steadfast belief in education as a catalytic and emancipatory force capable of engendering social justice, human flourishing, societal progress, and sustainable transformation. His recent explorations into 'Happiness Engineering' and holistic well- being in school ecosystems articulate a vision of education that transcends instrumentalist paradigms, prioritizing emotional intelligence, global consciousness, empathy, and psychosocial resilience among learners. His research agenda seeks to conceive educational praxis through the affordances of inclusive digital learning, gamified instructional design, and artificial intelligence (AIEd), thereby constructing robust, ethically grounded frameworks for 21st century education. At Alliance University, Dr. Alam remains committed to architecting pedagogical models that not only cultivate intellectual dexterity and cognitive excellence but also prepare learners for morally responsive leadership, intellectual nimbleness, and responsible global citizenship in an increasingly volatile, uncertain, complex, and ambiguous (VUCA) world.

B. Sindhusaranya is an accomplished academic specializing in Medical Image Processing and Machine Learning. She holds a Ph.D. in Information and Communication Engineering from Anna University, along with M.Tech. and B.Tech. degrees in Information Technology. Currently, she serves as an Assistant Professor at Sona College of Technology, Salem. Her research focuses on healthcare innovations, retinal imaging, and advanced pattern recognition, with numerous publications in reputed journals and international conferences. Her achievements include the Young Scientist Award (2024) and the Young Researcher Award (2020). She has also contributed to innovation through several patents, such as AI-based systems for soil analysis and healthcare. In addition to her research, Dr. Sindhusaranya is a passionate mentor and educator, actively engaging in faculty training, curriculum development, and community-driven projects. Her work highlights her dedication to leveraging cutting-edge technologies for impactful and practical solutions in society.

Pankaj Bhambri is an accomplished Associate Professor in the Department of Information Technology at Guru Nanak Dev Engineering College, Ludhiana, with over 21 years of teaching and research experience. Recognized as a Top 2% Scientist by Stanford University and Elsevier, his expertise spans Artificial Intelligence, Machine Learning, the Internet of Things, and Cloud Computing. A prolific researcher, he has authored numerous patents, published extensively in Scopus and SCIE-indexed journals, and edited several influential books with international publishers like CRC Press and Springer. Dr. Bhambri is also an active academic leader, guiding Ph.D. candidates, serving on technical committees for international conferences, and currently pursuing a Post Doctorate Fellowship at Lincoln University College, Malaysia.

Balkrishna Dwivedi has received his MCA degree from AKTU in 2024. Since then he has been with the Department of Computer Application of the United University where presently working as an Assistant Professor. His currently research area interests are the machine learning, data science and data mining.

Sneh Gangwar is an Assistant Professor in the Department of Geography, Indraprastha College for Women, University of Delhi. She has more than 16 years of experience in teaching and research. Over the last decade, she has had a distinct academic career and contributed to the fields of Geography, Disaster Management, Agriculture, Environment, Remote Sensing, GIS, and Climate Change. She has published more than 20 research papers in National and International Journals, and her contribution extends to chapters in books, conference presentations, and edited books.

K.Geetha has completed her Master's in Computer Science and is currently pursuing her Ph.D. in the domain of Data Mining. Her research interests include Intrusion Detection Systems, Network Security, and Data Mining Techniques. She has over 2.5 years of teaching experience and has presented/published research papers in national and international journals and conferences. She has also guided undergraduate students in computer science projects. Email: kgeetha_ca@kongunaducollege.ac.in

Drumil Joshi is a trailblazer in data science and renewable energy innovation, serving as a Monitoring & Diagnostics Analyst at Southern Power, where he stewards over $450 million in solar, wind, and battery storage assets. Recognized by Analytics Insight as one of the "Top 10 Data Science Leaders to Follow in 2025," he fuses technical mastery with a clear sense of purpose of engineering smarter, more sustainable futures. Armed with a Master's in Data Science from Indiana University, he is the author of Machine Learning Essentials and Applications, the contributor of more than six international research papers with over 400 citations, and the mind behind patents in the UK, Canada, and India. His expertise spans predictive analytics, grid stability, and AI-powered diagnostics, consistently transforming raw data into actionable insights that drive change. Beyond his technical achievements, Drumil is celebrated for his empathy, resilience, and talent for uncovering human stories hidden within complex datasets, inspiring both peers and industries to aim higher. In his own words, he works at the intersection of data, storytelling, and purpose—turning "what if" into "what's next."

Vandana Kate, B.E, M.E, PhD, Professor, CSIT Department, Acropolis Institute of Technology and Research, Indore (M.P) With a rich academic background and an illustrious career spanning over 22 years, Prof. Vandana Kate stands as an distinguished faculty of Computer Science and Information Technology Department, Acropolis Institute of Technology and Research, Indore. She holds BE degree in Computer Engineering from Jabalpur Engineering College (2002) and an ME degree in Computer Engineering from the prestigious Institute of Engineering and Technology affiliated to DAVV University, Indore (2010), she was awarded PhD Degree in Computer Engineering from IET, DAVV, showcasing her commitment to advancing knowledge in her field. Her academic journey is marked by excellence, with top rankings in both her ME and PhD coursework. Her expertise lies in the realms of Image Processing, Computer Vision, Cloud Computing and the cutting-edge fields of Machine Learning and Deep Learning. She has carved a niche in research, particularly in Deep learning and its applications in medical image processing and Image restoration. She has an impressive record with over 40 publications in leading National/International Conferences, Web of Science, Scopus, and peer reviewed Journals across various domains of Computer Science. Her commitment to advancing research extends to serving as an Editorial member and Reviewer for numerous IEEE conferences and Springer Nature Journals. Beyond her academic pursuits, Dr. Kate is a certified AWS Solution Architect, showcasing her proficiency in architecting scalable, secure, and cost-effective cloud solutions. She has conducted numerous internship trainings in AIML and AWS Cloud Practitioner for B.Tech students, bridging the gap between theoretical knowledge and real world application. Her contributions to innovation are further underscored by the publication of 6 patents and 5 Copyrights, reflecting her commitment to pushing the boundaries of technological advancement.

M. Dhanapal is an Assistant Professor in the Department of Information Technology at Erode Sengunthar Engineering College, Thudupathi, Perundurai, Erode-638057. He holds a B.Tech degree in Information Technology from Velalar College of Engineering and Technology, Erode, and an M.E. in Computer Science and Engineering from Karpagam University, Coimbatore. He has 9 years of teaching experience in the academic field. His research interests include computer networking and related domains.

Susan Madanhi is an accomplished ICT educator with over 18 years of experience in advancing digital literacy and transformative teaching practices. She holds multiple academic qualifications, including Diplomas in Secretarial Administration, Business Administration, and Education, a BEd in Computer Science, and an MCom in Information Systems Management from Midlands State University. A passionate advocate for ICT integration in education, Susan has played a pivotal role in curriculum development and teacher training across Zimbabwe. Her work bridges practical instruction and strategic innovation, with a focus on equitable access to technology in learning environments. She offers a rich, practice-based perspective shaped by years of classroom engagement and scholarly inquiry. Susan's writing reflects a deep commitment to educational transformation through ICT, making her contributions both timely and impactful.

Fabian N. Murrieta-Rico received B.Eng. and M.Eng. degrees from Instituto Tecnológico de Mexicali (ITM) in 2004 and 2013 respectively. In 2017, he received his PhD in Materials Physics at Centro de Investigación Científica y Educación Superior de Ensenada (CICESE). He has worked as an automation engineer, systems designer, as a university professor, and as postdoctoral researcher at Facultad de Ingeniería, Arquitectura y Diseño from Universidad Autónoma de Baja California (UABC) and at the Centro de Nanociencias y Nanotecnología from Universidad Nacional Autónoma de México (CNyN-UNAM), currently he works as professor at the Universidad Politécnica de Baja California. His research has been published in different journals and presented at international conferences since 2009. He has served as reviewer for different journals, some of them include IEEE Transactions on Industrial Electronics, IEEE Transactions on Instrumentation, Measurement and Sensor Review. His research interests are focused on the field of time and frequency metrology, the design of wireless sensor networks, automated systems and highly sensitive chemical detectors.

Samuel Musungwini (PhD) is a lecturer at Midlands State University, in the Department of Information and Marketing Sciences. He holds a PhD in Information Systems from University of South Africa (UNISA), a Post Graduate Diploma in Tertiary education from Midlands State University, a Bachelor of Science Honours Degree in Information Systems from Midlands State University, a Master Science Degree in Information Systems Management from Midlands State University. He is a founding member of the Zimbabwe Conference on Information Technology

(ZCICT). He is a member of the ZIMCHE physical assessment for facilities and resources checklist for academic programs. He has contributed to the 2019 Technology Transfer Workshop (Intellectual property (IP)) at Gweru Polytechnic. He is a published author who has published research articles in Scopus indexed journals and non-Scopus indexed journals. He has also attended and presented at a number of international conferences (ICT4D, Springer and Elsevier organised)

Ashutosh Pandey is a dedicated researcher in Computer Science and Engineering. His research area focuses on Intelligent Vehicles, Emotion Recognition, and Computer Vision, contributing actively to AI-driven intelligent systems.

Jeethu Philip, is currently working as Assistant Professor in the Department of Information Technology at MLR Institute of Technology, Hyderabad, Telangana. She has 6 years of experience. She has 20 research papers and 11patents and 2 books. She is pursuing PhD at KL University Hyderabad.

Bhaskar Roy, MIEI, LMISTE is currently working in the department of CSE (Artificial Intelligence and Machine Learning), Asansol Engineering College, Asansol-713305, India. He has done his B.Tech. in Electronics & Communication Engineering from West Bengal University of Technology, Kolkata, India, M.Tech. in VLSI Design & Microelectronics Technology from Jadavpur University, Kolkata, India and Ph.D. (Engg.) in Electronics & Communication Engineering from Brainware University, Kolkata, India in 2005, 2010 and 2023 respectively. He has a rich teaching experience of more than nineteen years. He has published sixteen utility and design Indian patents and authored eleven SCI/SCIE/Scopus indexed International journals, sixteen National/International Scopus indexed conference proceedings and eight Scopus indexed book chapters. He is the adaptation author of five text books. He is the Recipient of "Best Researcher Award 2022" by Novel Research Academy, India. His current research interests include Sensors, Optical Detectors, Artificial Intelligence, Cloud Computing, Soft computing and IoT.

Mushtaq Ahmad Shah is a finance expert with a PhD in Infrastructure Finance. He teaches banking, finance and economics at Lovely Professional University in India. Dr. Shah has over 8 years of experience teaching and researching at various institutions. He's written articles in academic journals and presented his work at conferences on banking, partnerships between public and private sectors, and behavioral finance.

Partap Chahal is committed to teaching and research in Finance and Investment domain since last 16 years+. His qualification is PhD (Commerce), M.Com, MBA. He has rich work experience in the field of Teaching, administration and research as well. He held various responsibilities like Editor, Co-editor, and Editorial Board member, Associate Editor in number of national and international journals. He has been regularly been receiving offers for writing books from the top publishing houses of India and received many letter of thanks& compliments for giving valuable suggestions and commendable views concerning improvement of many leading Publications/Books. He has written and published 5 books namely Financial Management, Risk Management, working capital Mana

Varadharajan Bhoopathy is a Professor at Sree Rama Engineering College. He holds a Ph.D. in Information and Communication Engineering from Anna University and has over 16 years of academic experience. Specializing in wireless sensor networks and IoT, he has published numerous research papers and holds several international patents. Dr. Bhoopathy is a recipient of prestigious awards for his contributions to education and research. His commitment to academia continues to drive innovation and excellence in the field of computer science.

Athish Venkatachalam is a Graduate Student at Clemson University, pursuing a Master of Science in Computer Science. He completed his Bachelor of Technology in Computer Science and Business Systems at SRM Institute of Science and Technology (SRMIST), where he held leadership positions as Chairperson of SRM IET on Campus and Convener of the Technical Team at the Directorate of Student Affairs. Athish is recognized for his expertise in Cloud Computing, Distributed Computing, and DevOps, and earned accolades in various hackathons, including being a finalist in the All-India Level Smart India Hackathon 2022. At Clemson, Athish serves as a Graduate Research Assistant at the Human-AI Empowerment Lab, where he is dedicated to exploring AI for Social Good. In addition to his research work, Athish is the President of the Clemson Graduate Student Government, having previously served as the Director of Clemson Graduate Travel Grants. In this capacity, he plays an essential role in advocating for and supporting the graduate student community. Athish was also honored with the Best Outgoing Student award in 2023 by SRMIST for his exceptional academic achievements, leadership, and contributions to the university.

Index

A

B

C

D

E

F

G

I

L

M

O

P

Q

R

S

W

www.ingramcontent.com/pod-product-compliance
Lightning Source LLC
LaVergne TN
LVHW060005031026
849161LV00025B/1483
* 9 7 9 8 3 3 7 3 5 9 4 6 5 *